HERSCHELL GORDON LEWIS

on the Art of Writing Copy

HERSCHELL GORDON LEWIS

on the Art of Writing Copy

PRENTICE HALL
Englewood Cliffs, New Jersey 07632

Prentice-Hall International (UK) Limited, *London*
Prentice-Hall of Australia Pty. Limited, *Sydney*
Prentice-Hall Canada Inc., *Toronto*
Prentice-Hall Hispanoamericana, S.A., *Mexico*
Prentice-Hall of India Private Ltd., *New Delhi*
Prentice-Hall of Japan, Inc., *Tokyo*
Simon & Schuster Asia Pte. Ltd., *Singapore*
Editora Prentice-Hall do Brasil Ltda., *Rio de Janeiro*

© 1988 by

PRENTICE-HALL, INC.

Englewood Cliffs, N.J.

Printed in the United States of America
10 9 8 7 6 5 4 3 2
10 9 8 7 6 5 4 3 2   PBK

Library of Congress Cataloging-in-Publication Data

Lewis, Herschell Gordon, date
   Herschell Gordon Lewis on the art of writing copy.

   Includes index.
   1. Advertising copy. I. Title.
HF5825.L44 1987   659.13′22   87-11489

ISBN 0-13-387309-9

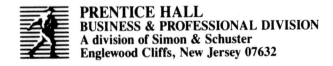
PRENTICE HALL
BUSINESS & PROFESSIONAL DIVISION
A division of Simon & Schuster
Englewood Cliffs, New Jersey 07632

Preface

Is writing a chore for you? A delight? A tedious way to spend an afternoon? A challenge you meet with lance at the ready or with sweaty palms?

Depending on how you approach writing, you will or won't be thrilled to see some hard rules in print. The notion of superimposing principles on an "art form" may gall you because it's unseemly to replace—or even modify—talent with mechanical principles. But isn't it time, in a computerized, word-processed era, to figure out why some word sequences sell and some don't?

Have you ever sold shoes in a department store on a commission basis? Then you know a peculiar truth:

One salesperson, week after week, outsells all others. That person may be male or female; he or she isn't the best looking, doesn't have the best vocabulary, isn't the best dresser, doesn't have the best knowledge of stock on hand, and—most frustrating to the other salespeople—doesn't fight to confront a new customer wandering into the department. Yet, when sales are toted up, that same nondescript salesperson invariably has the highest sales total.

Book after book tries to explain why. Most books on salesmanship deal in perseverance or personality or deliberate psychological matchup with the customer. Great. I agree. The winning salesperson has all these, plus an implicit knowledge of how to communicate on the *prospect's* level of understanding.

What has puzzled me, right up to the publication date of this book, is that nobody has adapted rules of salesmanship to media advertising. Yes, we have books on mass communications, and I've even written some of them. But how about some *rules?* How about some codified, organized techniques to transform the guesswork of everyone-can-write-it copy to I'm-beating-the-odds copy?

I'm a copywriter-chauvinist, and I'm quick to defend my profession when critics claim (even though they're often justified) we don't know what we're doing. "You guys put words on paper, and somebody reads, sees, or hears them," our critics chide. "You don't know *why* your words sell, if they do. You're still in the Stone Age."

Not so. I, for one, am firmly convinced that we're starting to forge some iron spears. At last we're bringing into organized focus a handful of the rules for force-communication that hover elusively in the Copywriter's Heaven above us.

A professional copywriter may know the answers implicitly, but now we begin to recognize them *explicitly*. The difference isn't one of content; it's one of organization.

A bright-eyed student, copywriter-to-be, enrolls in a college course. The student typically wants to write clever copy; the instructor encourages or discourages, based on an individual prejudice which in turn is based on an experiential background that may or may not be valid.

The instructor transmits and superimposes a set of copywriting fiats without regard (or, often, knowledge) of universal truths. Hard rules for selling a "what" to a "who" are buried in the folds of a huggy blanket: "This is how *I* learned to do it, so it's how I'll teach *you* to do it."

A mathematics instructor who taught, "Two plus two are seven—because I like it that way," would be laughed out of class within the first two minutes. The geography teacher who taught, "The Monongahela River is the longest river in the world; it's the only river I've navigated, and it's *long*," would last only until a student became forever cynical by learning that the teacher is substituting his own limited sphere of knowledge for incontrovertible, tested, proved fact.

Why can't the budding copywriter have the benefit of rules? Why can't an experienced copywriter, shifting from consumer to business copy, know which gears to engage? Why can't a nonwriter doggedly apply rules and write as well as someone who labels himself or herself a professional? Well, one reason is: The people we're trying to influence don't run on tracks. Or do they? You'll have to decide, after plowing through whichever sections of this book interest you.

If you say to me: "In three words, tell me how to write effective copy," I'll answer: "Sure. The three words are *clarity*, *benefit*, and *verisimilitude*. Combine those three and your copy can't miss."

You may wonder, if it's that easy, why I've turned my brains to mashed potatoes, isolating, culling, and refining solid rules. Why do we need hundreds of rules when we can get by with the three-word formula?

You know the answer, of course. Knowing the three magic words is like spotting intelligent life in another galaxy through a powerful telescope. You know they're out there, but to get to them you first have to invent faster-than-light drive. The rules in this book are just the beginning. They'll tell you how to hold the screwdriver to open the crate of parts.

To my successor, a hundred years down the road, who picks up the torch, who adapts the rules of force communication as a changing society changes buyer attitudes, who might be kind enough to cancel my mistakes, and who is born into a copywriting climate made a shade more hospitable by this uncertain beginning, I say—as Columbus might have said to Rand McNally—Greetings! I may have had only the vaguest notion of where I was going, and I may not have known where I was when I got there, and I may have thought west was east—but I got there first!

Herschell Gordon Lewis

Acknowledgments

Two lovely young ladies, both named Nelson, helped immeasurably in the preparation of this book. Peggy Nelson organized and typed many of my notes. Carol Nelson, the California copywriter-whiz, was my source for much of the information and examples relating to electronic media copywriting.

My perspicacious son, Robert Lewis, who can spot an oxymoron, a cliché, or an overused superlative at 60 paces, supplied many examples of these curios.

My favorite proofreader, Ruth Moffett, once again kept me from a severe case of foot-in-mouth disease.

As usual, the expert team at Prentice Hall made typographic sense of the huge pile of words and an endless stack of exhibits. I'm grateful to my editor, Bette Schwartzberg, who kept pushing until I finally sent the manuscript and then pushed again until I organized it properly. And the most difficult job of all, production-editing, has been handled with ultra-professionalism by Catherine Johnson.

But anyone who knows how I work and live also knows who should get credit for these words appearing at all: my wife and business partner, Margo. Not only is she the world's number one sounding board for ideas, but she's the world's number one originator of ideas. How lucky I am!

My thanks to all—and to you, for reading the result.

What This Book Will Do for You

Should you write "3" or "three"? "30 Minutes" or "Half an Hour"?

These questions are typical of the mini-problems besetting the copywriter in the last decade of the twentieth century. Every word counts ... so which one should you use?

Yes, the answer is in this book. And deciding logically and deliberately whether to use "3" or "three" can be the beginning of a transformation from copywriting-as-art to copywriting-as-science.

We sit at our keyboards. We sift through the layers of experience and intellectual scar tissue. We make decisions, some of them automatic and some of them tortured. Are we right or are we wrong when we change "Can you ..." to "Will you ..."?

If you picked up this book and are reading the preface, you're serious about copywriting. You want your words to be dipped in the magic bucket of power.

Should you write "This is the information you requested" or "This is the information you asked for"?

When should you avoid using asterisks?*

How many ways are there to write a guarantee? What should you promise and what should you avoid?

What's a better word to replace the word "should," which appears so often in these first paragraphs?

Do you write "A historic ..." or "An historic ..."?

Should (do) you write "One mile"? "5,280 feet?" Or (and what's the difference?) do you leave out the comma and write "5280 feet"?

What's a simple test you can give a writer who wants to work for you?

What's wrong with this seemingly harmless line of copy: "The manufacturer has told us the quantity we are to receive will be small"?

What changes in spelling and word construction do you make when you want your copy to appear "British"?

---

*All the time.

vi

What's wrong with using the word "disbelieves" in a radio spot?

If you're inventing a brand name, what's the difference between an "ush" syllable and an "usk" syllable?

Do you know the three "can't miss" tips for writing news releases?

What's wrong with paragraphs starting with the word "As"?

These are only a handful of the tips, rules, laws, and commandments, covering just about every commercial-writing circumstance and medium I can think of, in this book. As far as I know, this is the first time anyone (or should it be "anybody"?) has stuck his head in the lion's mouth, attempting to codify rules of copywriting. Even if the book doesn't help you, it has a certain historical value!

Depending on how you approach writing, you will or won't be thrilled to see some hard rules in print. If you welcome the notion that at last it's possible to check your copy against a statutory base, anticipate the marketplace in the year 2001: By then, I hope, someone will have put together a computer program incorporating these rules. Make a mistake and a red flag will go up.

But if you think reducing the creative process to a series of rules is a serious offense—breaking and entering the writer's hallowed seat-of-the-pants domain, a sacred land violated only by nonthreatening (because they're uncreative) researchers—then you'll find the whole concept repulsive, and I guess we aren't going to convince each other of anything.

I think I'm safe. Why? Because if you pooh-pooh the concept behind this book—that writing deliberately and confidently is better than writing haphazardly and fearfully—you wouldn't buy a book whose whole premise, cover-to-cover, fights your own philosophy.

Okay, if you're ready let's plow ahead. Welcome to the shining new world of thoughtful, dynamic copy.

H.G.L.

Contents

HERSCHELL GORDON LEWIS

on the Art of Writing Copy

1

Form or Substance: Which Makes for More Effective Copy?

> The overriding determinant of word choice is
> THE CLARITY COMMANDMENT:
>
> When choosing words and phrases, clarity
> is paramount. Let no other component of the
> message-mix interfere with it.

WHY RULES MEAN BETTER COPY

This book is jampacked with rules, laws, commandments, concepts, precepts, principles, and savage opinions.

Why, after all these years, does the copywriter need some rules, laws, and all the rest of it? I'll tell you why: Organized society is becoming more and more dependent on communicators.

We've moved from the safe, shallow waters of an industrial society to the roiling seas of a communications society. It's unthinkable that an event, an individual, or an invention could achieve significance without media attention.

So . . . isn't it high time for us to begin codifying rules of the road?

Psychology and communications push upward through the crust of human activity, like twin giant volcanoes changing the landscape.

During the maturation process over the last 200 years or so, psychologists and communicators alike have ignored the bond they need to dominate twenty-first century thought: Psychologists aren't good communicators and communicators are at best seat-of-the-pants psychologists.

Microchips and Microthinking

This first chapter begins what I hope will be an ongoing welding of psychology to communications . . . plus the formalizing of rules good copywriters sense but haven't had available to them in organized form.

We're late with this. One reason is that the puppet strings of mass communications have been pulled and tugged by individuals who recognize and are comfortable with the *technique* of communication, but who don't give equal status to semantics or phonetics. They're uneasy with linguistics and philology, the study of the words.

Glorification, especially in art-directed communications, has been of *medium*, not *message*. That's how a writer or an artist builds a portfolio, leading to a better-paying job—that's where the cycle of "creating" good-looking ads continues.

Did the ads pull? Who cares? They look good, don't they?

THREE KEY RULES FOR WORDSMITHS

For the foreseeable future, I plead that those who go into battle carrying the title *Wordsmith* observe three key rules:

1. The Form Worship Maxim (coming right up)
2. Roget's Complaint (which is: with all the specific descriptive words available, the writer who regards neutral, non-impact words such as *needs*, *quality*, *features*, and *value* as creative should agree to work for no pay)
3. The Clarity Commandment (which began this chapter)

To the Clarity Commandment we might append a subrule, the Say What You Mean Mandate:

The reader invariably will apply a negative interpretation to statements which violate the Clarity Commandment.

Want proof that copywriting is approaching the wonderful intersection beyond which logical rules can prevent mistakes? There it is! Observing those three rules (and any beginner can put them to use during the first five minutes at the keyboard) will result in usable copy.

But I Don't Mean . . .

We can't overlook the one big difference between copywriting as a science and some of the more natural sciences:

If you screw up a chemical formula, your compound won't work. Not at all. Zero. But if you screw up a copy formula, your ad still may bring in some business. It won't pull as well as it would have if you'd written it according to the rules, but it probably won't draw a total blank.

This is because the enormous distribution of most advertising messages puts the odds against zero-pull in the writer's favor. Your miscreated formula reaches thousands, even millions of people. Some, like the hardiest Mediterranean fruit flies in a cloud of lethal insecticide, will penetrate to the message core.

The point? "The ad didn't draw a blank" is no reason to discard these fragile rules.

Form or Substance

Is copywriting an art or a science? I say it's about one-third of the way across the bridge from art to science. What makes the current position uncomfortable is the absence of professional standards . . . and until we have professional standards, anyone can hang out a shingle and claim to be a copywriter.

Poseurs have no difficulty aping the *form* of an ad or a mailing piece someone else created; their difficulty lies in paralleling *substance*. What, for example, is the message transmitted in Figure 1–1? For those who believe mechanical tricks can cover or replace imaginative sterility, I propose the Form Worship Maxim:

The writer who puts *form* ahead of *substance* implicitly admits a creative deficiency. Communications infected with this deficiency call attention to format rather than to what they say. Invariably the writer has a way to transmit the message more effective than the one he used.

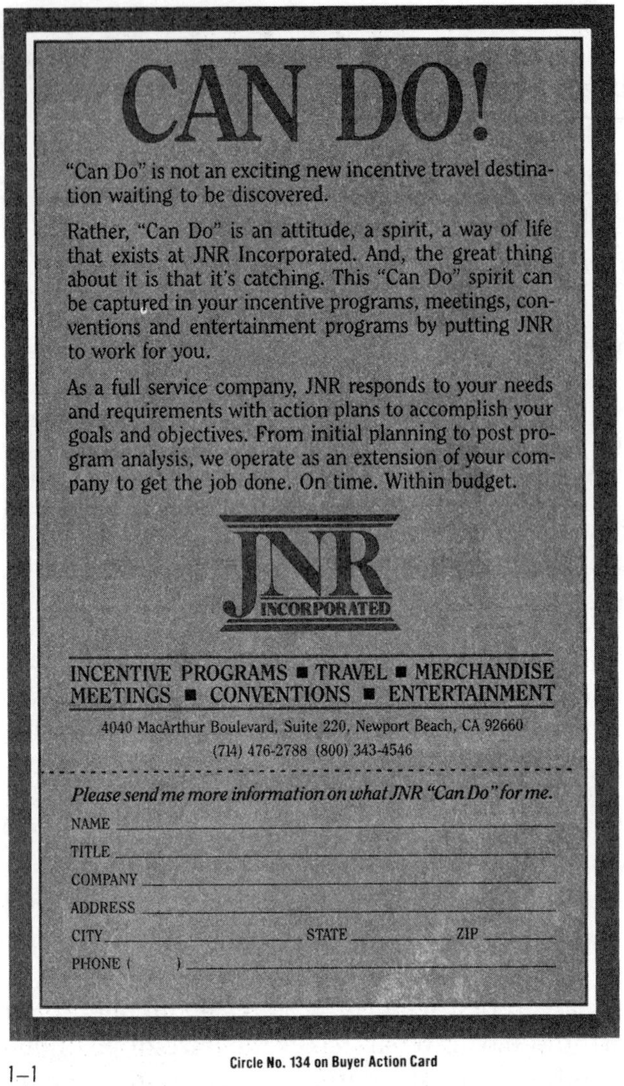

FIGURE 1–1

Circle No. 134 on Buyer Action Card

This three-color ad is inspirational, the way a Knute Rockne halftime speech is inspirational. But inspiration isn't even half the mix. What are they selling? Lack of clarity damages *any* message.

THE FOUR (FIVE?) GREAT MOTIVATORS

In the Age of Skepticism, we recognize four great motivators.

Remember when primitive classes in advertising taught that food, clothing, and shelter were motivators? Remember when instructors talked about "primary needs" and "secondary needs"? No more. We're in the Age of Skepticism, and anyone who might be moved by food, clothing, or shelter isn't worth your promotional dollars. *Gourmet* food? Yes. *Designer* clothing? Yes. *Status-laden* shelter?

Yes. But it's the qualifier words that give us the motivators, not the bald requirements of life.

If you want your message to work, you can't consider "primary needs" and "secondary needs." First, the word "needs" is a generalization that won't connect solidly when it comes up against a specific appeal. Second, you're way, way off the center of the target if you even consider "secondary" sales arguments. It's a competitive marketplace, and you have to whang them right between the eyes.

So you lean on one of the four great motivators:

1. Fear
2. Exclusivity
3. Guilt
4. Greed

If you write clearly, within the reader's experiential background, and present benefits based on an appeal to one of these motivators, you can't miss!

As the mass communications juggernaut rumbles toward 1990, a fifth motivator separates its components from their position within the other four:

5. Ego gratification

It's increasingly safe to build a sales appeal around the periphery of fear, exclusivity, guilt, and greed. That periphery, like cosmic dust hardening into a planet, becomes the fifth motivator on its own.

Ego gratification isn't new, but *as a valid motivator* it's the natural child of the "I deserve everything" attitude which seems to infect all strata of society.

Ego gratification gathers to itself these ingredients:

▶ praise from others
▶ being in style
▶ emulating and being recognized by those we admire
▶ attracting an admirer or lover of our own
▶ having our lifestyle become congruent with lifestyles we regard as superior

You can see the evolution: Each of these could be sandwiched into one of the four great motivators. Together, they form a new one—ego gratification.

And How About Envy?

How about *envy?* Unquestionably, copy with a "Don't you wish you could be like . . . " theme has substance, although I'm not enamored of headlines beginning with "Don't. . . . "

In the motion picture *Close Encounters of the Third Kind,* François Truffaut (playing a distinguished scientist) says to Richard Dreyfuss (playing a clodlike anti-hero), "I envy you." The effect on the viewer is electric; it's the denouement of the movie.

FIGURE 1–2

The photograph is unimaginative but the message is clear and direct, an appeal to greed. Body copy doesn't follow up on the emotional inroad the headline has plowed; imagine how powerful the ad might have been if body copy had kept the pistons pumping.

6

1 in 1,020,914

TOJAN: *the American exotic*

There are over 159,178,720 registered motor vehicles in the United States. 829,036 Mercedes. 461,286 BMWs. 415,611 Corvettes. 236,257 Porsches. 113,182 Jaguars. 9,720 Ferraris.¹

And fewer than 155 Tojans.

Hand built one at a time by skilled American craftsmen, powered by the proven technology of a high performance 5.0 liter fuel injected V-8 and serviceable at over 2900 dealerships nationwide. Under **$30,000.**²

Literally. One in a million.

for more information call: **(800) 824-2222, ext. 142**

WINKEL PONTIAC	**EXECUTIVE AUTO**	**FAEBER MASERATI**	**VICKY THOMAS PONTIAC**
RENO, NV	SCOTTSDALE, AZ	VAN NUYS, CA	LOS ANGELES, CA
(702) 329-0831	(602) 949-8227	(518) 785-7111	(213) 629-4000
BILL LANG PONTIAC	**AUTO TRENDS, INC.**	**VOLVO OF RIVERSIDE**	**TOJAN WEST, INC.**
VALLEJO, CA	N. HOLLYWOOD, CA	RIVERSIDE, CA	PALO ALTO, CA
(707) 552-5555	(818) 985-9002	(714) 687-0304	(415) 494-7474

¹Estimates by R. L. Polk & Co. Used by permission.   ²Mfr's suggested retail price. Actual prices may vary. Destn. charges, taxes, dealer prep., optional equip. and license fees are extra.

FIGURE 1–3
Exclusivity is the easiest of the four motivators to write. This ad suffers from production problems—some layout genius decided to run black type over a 70 percent black background—but the energy survives. Only 155 "Tojans" exist, says the copy. "One in a million." (A million what isn't clarified.)

Dear Cardmember,

I have an apology to make . . . I hope you will understand. The protection offered here is not available to everyone.

. First -- you must be an American Express Cardmember.

. Second -- you must be under age 70.

. Third -- you must be in good health to qualify.

Fireman's Fund American Life wants to give those Cardmembers who are "preferred risks" a break on their premiums . . . high cash benefits . . . at a low group rate.

SHOULD YOU APPLY?

Of course . . . it doesn't cost you a penny to apply, there is no risk, no obligation. If you've had a medical condition in the past, you should apply anyway.

If you qualify, you will receive a letter that says you have been accepted in the American Express® Group Hospital Cash Plan for Preferred Risks, underwritten by Fireman's Fund American Life Insurance Company. It gives you meaningful daily cash benefits at economical, group rates.

Is it worth it to you? Check the hospital rates in your area and find out how much it

FIGURE 1–4
This weak appeal to exclusivity was mailed to American Express cardmembers. Ostensibly the mailer knows which of its cardholders are under 70, so the only qualifier is that the individual "be in good health." Still, a weak appeal is better than no appeal. Exclusivity, however overused, does work during the Age of Skepticism.

Years ago, when television was an expensive luxury, a radio commercial had a young child pleading plaintively, "I want a television Christmas . . . a world of magic all my own!" So dynamic was this message that various parent groups militated to have it banned.

But how often can we as writers mount an envy argument without betraying our own position of *greed*? We're handling live grenades, hot radium. Envy, like the prime mover *fear*, isn't for the beginner. It's for the maestro who knows the reader, listener, or viewer. It's for a trained or instinctive master psychologist. Safety lies in the four great motivators. With them, you can't miss; stray from them and your message—and you—can wind up in the wastebasket.

HOW MUCH DO YOU TELL THEM?

Transmitting their message, copywriters walk the tightwire between puffery and dullness. How much should you say about what you're selling? A safe rule is the Rule of Partial Disclosure:

> **Tell the target individual as much as you can about what your product or service can do for him or her. If you have space or time left over, don't move down to the next information level (facts unrelated to benefit); instead, restate or illustrate some of the benefits.**

The First Canon of Salesmanship wasn't created exclusively for writers, but its aptness applies to every force-communication message:

> **When the prospect says yes, quit selling.**

A False Sense of Integrity

Totality of facts—an encyclopedic recitation of every scrap of information about what you're selling—not only may bore people out of buying; the procedure also can unsell by including facts *you* don't think are negative . . . but *they* do. The frantic obsession with emptying the information bag mixes desperation with exhibitionism: Total disclosure is undressing in public.

Here is an example of copywriting without exercising the sense or discipline of discrimination. Copy for a Talking Telephone has these four "bullets":

► Can be taught to respond to one voice only
► Made to conform to U.S. govt. regulations
► Pulse/touchtone switchable
► 16-number memory

I hope your question is the same as mine: What is that second bullet doing there? The word *made* is considerably weaker than the word *manufactured*, but

EDITOR'S NOTES
by Robert Reed

Humble Musical Bank Becomes 20th-Century Antique

A STRIKING LIKENESS TO THE ORIGINAL MUSIC BOX BANK

Music box now goes to tune of 3Gs
by JOAN SHEPARD

Now you may get your National Shrine music box bank for a small sum of money. It is made of very fine white china, and is 13" high and 5" wide at the base. A gold freedom statue is atop, and a silk flag towers over the lower part of the building. The photos of all of the Presidents from Washington to Reagan, their names and the words of the national anthem are written on the bank. Under the dome is a color photo of President Kennedy.

The bank won an International Gold Medal and is a 20th-century antique. Complete article as antique enclosed with order. Also a forty-page book telling how the artist made the music box. The dome plays soft music of the Star Spangled Banner. Will be worth $3,000 in a few years, just as the original is now worth $3,000. A grand gift for a child, grandchild, or anybody that you care for.

To order, send $150 to: CN
    House of Great Creations
    210 Fifth Avenue
    New York, New York 10010.

    Please print. Send check or money order payable to the House of Great Creations.

Name:_____

Address:_____

City: _____

State/Zip:_____

FIGURE 1–5
This ad seems harmless, if disorganized (for example, two bylines—"Robert Reed" and "Joan Shepard"). But hold it; the body copy makes an impossible promise: *Will be worth $3,000 in a few years, just as the original is now worth $3,000.* Is it a lie or just a too-enthusiastic promise? What difference does it make if the reader doesn't believe it?

the biggest objection to this bullet is its reference to a point which (a) has no apparent benefit to the reader and (b) has negative overtones. The word *regulation* is deadly in selling copy, especially when any form of the word *approved* might be a substitute.

When a writer becomes Pandora, opening wide the box of evils locked in a corner of every business enterprise, often the opening has as its justification the "integrity" of the writer.

If you write copy like this and begin to feel that your dispassionate and enlightened viewpoint is superior to your employer's desire to sell something, quit before you're fired. You're in the wrong job.

What bothers me far more than an occasional misguided eruption of conscience is seeing or hearing the result of such an eruption in print or broadcast ads. Somebody had a noble idea and somebody else okayed it. Even more puzzling, a born-again advertiser thinks the public will applaud utter honesty which makes him look bad.

Yes, I know the fifteenth Way to Thwart the Age of Skepticism—*Admit an Achilles' heel*. (See "Skepticism" in Chapter 25 of this book for the other 14 ways.) But the admission is supposed to temper what otherwise is an incredible claim, not to become the linchpin selling argument.

We hear this radio commercial:

> Sheehan Leasing isn't the lowest-priced leasing company. But does cheap really fit your lifestyle? Isn't it worth a little more—not a lot more, a little more—to get Sheehan service? . . .

. . . and we quit listening. Sheehan has admitted an Achilles' heel, all right, but that's the only part of its physique the company has described. We're not tempering incredulity and thereby adding verisimilitude; we're blurting out a negative which overpowers the mildest of positives—"Sheehan service," an unexplained molecule of puffery.

Figures 1–6 and 1–8 typify the "negative information" ads we see too often. Why write ads which raise more questions than they answer?

A catalog description of "The Robot Zoids" has this copy:

> Each uses two C batteries and Terox also requires two AA batteries for lights (no batteries included).

Analyze those words: *no batteries included*. Can you think of a more negative way to transmit this information? Why not the standard *batteries not included*, which doesn't violate the Rule of Negative Transmission:

Unless you want the reader or viewer to think you're the originator or generator of the reason for negative information, don't put this information aggressively.

SPECIFICS SELL—NONSPECIFICS DON'T

The writer who substitutes generalities for specifics has a real problem: He's automatically selling less than he could. If the generalities stem from lack of information, the problem lies in the transmission of salesworthy fact; writer and source should attack the problem jointly. But if the generalities stem from the copywriter's own philosophy, the problem is far more severe, because the procedure suggests a deficiency in the writer's professional qualifications.

An example: What's wrong with this copy?

A sleeping bag or a bed?
Travasleep gives you the convenience of both.

Right! No specifics. The writer says to the reader, "You know more about this than I do, so you fill in the gaps." The reader logically says, "Forget it." Certainly the writer has enough information to replace the nonspecific puffery with what appears to be specific information:

A sleeping bag or a bed?
Travasleep gives you the convenience of a sleeping bag with the comfort of a soft, downy bed.

Since nonspecifics are a key "Don't Do That!" warning, let's add another example. Here's part of a letter selling a privately printed magazine:

We don't claim your magazine would be as good as *Modern Executive* but we do point out that . . .

You caught it, of course: "as good as" isn't as good as a specific might be. Replace it with specifics and the argument springs to life. Even knowing nothing about *Modern Executive*, we can replace *as good as* with a better "as" phrase. Pick one or invent your own:

▶ as professionally edited as . . .
▶ as beautifully printed as . . .
▶ as perfectly targeted to today's executive as . . .
▶ as big a bargain as . . .

Specificity Equals Felicity

Specific words generate a far greater emotional reaction than generalized words; the more specific the words, the more the writer controls emotions.

Example: a writer referred to a rock musician as "dirty." Yes, *dirty* is an emotion-loaded word, but overtones differ from intent. An editor, after discussion with the writer, changed *dirty* to *unwashed*—the description the writer actually meant. The editor asked and answered the question the writer should have asked and answered: What conclusion do I want the reader to draw?

You won't hear these "lines" from this agency.

Sundberg,
Mills &
Demougeot
*Advertising
and Marketing Communications*
402 Main St., Ridgefield, CT 06877
Telephone: (203) 438-2344

Reader Service #160

(Speech bubbles within image: "Sorry I haven't gotten back to you sooner." / "Sure, we can try another approach." / "It's high because. . . ." / "Well, it's tough to really measure industrial." / "It'll look a lot better when you see it in print." / "Media recommends the same schedule as last year." / "Trust me. It won't happen again. How about lunch?")

FIGURE 1–6

Specificity equals felicity. This ad by an advertising agency, of all people, tells the reader what "lines" we won't hear; what it doesn't tell us is what lines we *will* hear. Think of what the agency might have told us, to push us toward the phone to call. Why didn't they inject a single benefit into the copy?

13

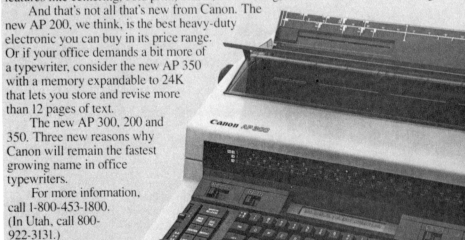
FIGURE 1–7

We *thought* this electronic typewriter printed in upper case *and* lower case; but what we see in the display window is upper case only. That's a mistake, because now we have a question we didn't have before. Illustration should clarify, not obfuscate.

14

15

FIGURE 1–8
Yes, in general I know what they mean, but so what? Phony stroking isn't a motivator except on the most primitive level. In no way is an ad like this competitive with an ad which spells out what the reader wants to see.

"Aw, They Know What I Mean"

Writing is conscious, not unconscious. You can ruminate to yourself almost unconsciously, because you have no trouble decoding what you mean. But copywriting is aimed at a target on the other end.

Suppose I write "The oldest group of members." What does it mean? Are these the members who are the oldest in age? Or are they the ones who have been members for the longest period of time? I've committed the hit-and-run tactic so many writers do, damaging the message the way static damages radio reception. The message-recipient hesitates because of possible misinterpretation, and *hesitation weakens impact.*

If we, casual readers, can replace nonspecifics with specifics, how much better a piece of copy the original writer might compose with even a little thought. After all, the writer has ammunition we don't—all the facts.

AND WE'RE OFF!

Even from this mild beginning you can see how copywriting has the seeds of logical analysis in its structure.

Logic, you say, which kills creativity? Heck, no. Don't fear it any more than you'd fear a newly discovered antitoxin for a noxious disease. It's parallel to a spelling-checker, not to a creativity suppressor.

Is seat-of-the-pants copywriting on the way out? I hope so. It would be good for advertising if its practitioners could replace "This copy worked" with "This copy worked *because.* . . ."

2

You, Me, and What Makes Us Respond

Unless the reader regards himself as the target of your message, benefit can't exist. Benefit demands a "We/You" relationship.

What, then, is wrong with this opening?

The person whose name appears on the label is entitled to . . .

Right! The writer is Pygmalion. His dispassionate copy generates a dispassionate reader. Uninvolved, the reader remains an observer, not a participant. Emotion is sapped out of the decision-making process (see "Put Emotion to Work for You," later in this chapter, and the Emotion/Intellect Rules, Chapter 25). When the vendor is uninvolved, the buyer is uninvolved. And when the buyer is uninvolved, the vendor loses.

So we change the approach just a hair:

If you're the individual whose name appears on the label, you're entitled to . . .

"I Am the Greatest" copy generates a ho-hum reaction at best. On "down" days, when our brains are out of gear but deadlines loom, any of us may have written an advertising headline such as the following:

Your expectations rate a Renaissance.

When you rate excellence
above ostentation, your expectations
rate a Ramada Renaissance hotel. The intelligent
choice for travelers who believe that
premier service needn't cost a
premium price. RAMADA
RENAISSANCE.
INTERNATIONAL HOTELS

No other fine hotel offers more. For less.

Next Time, Ramada Renaissance. 1-800-228-9898. In the U.S.: Atlanta, Atlantic City/Tropicana, Buffalo, Jackson, Mississippi, Las Vegas/Tropicana, Long Beach, Richmond, San Francisco, Saratoga Springs, Springfield, Illinois, Walnut Creek, California, Washington, D.C., City and Dulles Airport. And 21 other locations around the world.

A.

FIGURES 2–1A, 2–1B, and 2–1C
These three ads ran in the same issue of an inflight magazine. The obvious competitive purpose of all three: to convince travelers to stay at *this* hotel. The Ramada ad has no specifics and seems to equate expensive production with communication. The Viscount ad states a benefit but neither describes nor illustrates it. The Marriott ad is loaded with specific benefits for the business traveler. After seeing all three ads, where would you decide to stay?

19

> There is a difference in
> quality and service, and the
> difference is ALPHA OMEGA

Suppose we're bright enough to replace those deadly words *quality* and *service*. Have we helped the ad enough to make it professional? In my opinion, no. There's still a zero "YOU factor" in this headline.

Putting YOU into the mix doesn't just mean inserting the word *you* into self-aggrandizing copy. Don't make your copy a megalomaniacal mirror. Go *through* the looking glass. That's the tactical difference between Figure 2–1C, which bubbles with benefits, and Figures 2–1A and 2–1B, which strut and preen.

This strutting-preening attitude results in advertising copy such as the following:

> *We're Moving!*
> Our new building and expanded facilities
> will enable us to serve you better!

They will, huh? How? Will you speed up *my* order, and if so, by how much? Will you carry a bigger inventory of what *I* order? I'm the skeptical ad receiver of the late 1980s and 1990s. I don't care about you, I care about me. Unless you show me benefits, I regard your "new building" ad as another piece of puffery. If you want me to react to your move, give me some specifics, aimed at me. Don't give me empty self-flattery such as Figures 2–2 and 2–3.

The "You First" Rule can be a moneymaker for you:

Tell the reader, listener, or viewer what's in it for him, not for you.

Everybody knows this, you say? Not the writer of this communication, mailed to "Resident":

I AM YOUR COLDWELL BANKER KLOCK COMPANY REPRESENTATIVE

1. I AM A FULL-TIME PROFESSIONAL, enjoy my work, and am determined that you will receive the finest real estate service possible!

2. I have available the FINEST REAL ESTATE SALES TRAINING PROGRAM IN THE NATION!

3. I am supported by a DYNAMIC, FULL-TIME MANAGEMENT TEAM who have the time to help me help you! . . .

This exercise in consummate modesty has ten statements in all. Nine begin with the word "I" and the tenth, for variety, begins with "Our." Its egocentricity parallels the bore who, after talking about himself for half an hour, says, "Enough about me. Let's talk about you. What do *you* think of me?"

FIGURE 2–2

Leaving *you* out of a selling argument is a sure way to generate a ho-hum reaction. This ad pats itself on the back with unspecific self-flattery. Why on earth would an advertiser think a reader would respond to a nonsense argument such as:

"We make creative products, designed by professionals to meet the specific needs of our clients."

HOW TO MAKE EMOTION
A POWERFUL ADVERTISING WEAPON

An article in *Advertising Age* was headed, "Emotion a powerful tool for advertisers."*

As an example, the writer used a MasterCard campaign whose theme was "So worldly, so welcome." That's about as emotion-laden as a volume of nineteenth-century legal statutes. Think for a moment: What emotional satisfaction can MasterCard bring you? You might argue it makes you feel *worldly*; in turn, the emotional side of you argues the relative emotionalism of *worldly*. *Welcome?* This word is too generalized to have any emotional impact.

Another example described in this article was a campaign by Minolta: "Only from the Mind of Minolta." Referring to an automatic-focusing camera called the Maxxum, the writer commented, "To anyone who has missed a shot while fiddling with a focusing ring, the fact of auto-focus is emotional enough."

Seems to me this commentator missed a shot. Product *per se* isn't emotional. "Only from the Mind of Minolta" is a crowing self-encomium which leaves the reader out.

The Minolta Maxxum was an innovative and superior product; that's why it sold well, *despite* the nondescript theme lauded by the article in *Advertising Age*. True emotionalism is the reverse-face of intellectualism. Here's proof that "Only from the Mind of Minolta" doesn't qualify: The word *mind* is an intellectual word; *brain* is more emotional. Whatever stimulators the creator of that theme may have intended to apply, emotion wasn't one of them.

The Rule of Emotional Mandate

Active voice, not passive, is a major component of emotional copy. A help-wanted ad in an advertising publication, recruiting a director for a university's graduate program in corporate communications/public relations, had these qualifiers:

> Evidence of scholarly capabilities through publishing and research is required. Previous classroom teaching experience mandatory. Practical industry experience is highly desirable. Proven administrative abilities are necessary as the candidate will be responsible for curriculum development . . .

Let's say you qualify for this job. Unless you were desperate for food, would you, as a professional in communications and public relations, feel comfortable answering this ad? The standoffish tone, icy words such as *mandatory* and *required*, Kafkaesque avoidance of "we" as the source, reference to you as a

---

*Issue of July 8, 1985, page 28.

OXFORD

Structured Mortgage Securities Programs

For

Financial Institutions

Expect the Best

Oxford Mortgage Securities Corporation
4550 Montgomery Avenue, Suite 300
Bethesda, MD 20814   (301) 469-3230

FIGURE 2–3
This full-page ad doesn't bring a shred of emotional response to its selling argument. What *is* the selling argument? What convincers overcome our skepticism? What, in fact, relates uniquely to the advertiser? "Expect the Best" could mean fish or tennis shoes. It's nonwriting.

candidate—these will bring in the bureaucrats, not the creatives. Result? The gap between academia and the real world gets a little wider.

Classified help-wanted ads aren't exempt from human reaction; in fact, they should be more aware of it. The Rule of Emotional Mandate is a handy one to keep in your hip pocket:

Unless you want to avoid reader involvement in your message, always write in the active voice.

Let technicians write for one another's uninvolved nonreactions. To sell, you need reader involvement . . . and that means looking for a reaction, not giving a recitation.

Emotion in Fund Raising—A MUST

In fund raising copy it's suicidal to start reciting statistics, leaving the reader's emotions safely locked in his head without a single clamor to get out and participate. This copy leaves the reader uninvolved:

These girls must live—and study—in wooden huts.

I've pointed this out elsewhere: If you can't think of any other way to involve your target, ask a question:

What's it to you if these girls have to live—and study—in wooden huts?

While we were putting air in the tires we fixed the transmission too: We changed *must* to *have to*. We didn't mess with the word *study*, which can get in the way of fund raising by suggesting they can't be *in extremis* if they have the time and facilities for organized education.

HOW TO PUT PSYCHOLOGY TO WORK FOR YOU

Some of the easiest rules of communication are rules of psychology (Psychology + Communication = Salesmanship). We stumble upon these rules by asking ourselves, "Why did I react that way?" and then chipping away personal prejudice and other impurities. What's left is a shining, valuable rule which benefits communicators by letting us play virtuoso cadenzas on the psychological strings of our targets.

While writing a direct mail offer, I decided to strengthen the money-back guarantee by changing the risk-free inspection period from 30 days to one month.

FIGURE 2–4
What emotion is this two-page ad supposed to fire up? Does the reader admire or want to emulate the indolent model who stole the sample bottle? Opinion: The ad was designed to draw attention to itself as an ad, not to breed an emotional reaction to the product.

Then, like Archimedes in the bathtub, I yelled "Eureka!" as the reason for the change hit me:

The generic determines reaction more than the number.

And what, you ask, does that mean? You can feel relief when you see how what appears to be a pedantic rule is instead a holster for one of the easiest weapons in your argumentative arsenal.

One month is a longer time than 30 days. Oh, not really; it's *perceived time*—and perception is the psychological key that can unlock the previously locked door of buyer receptivity. What the rule means is that a generic (in this case, *month* and *day*) exercises greater control over human reaction than the number associated with it (in this case, one and 30).

Does it work? You bet. Half an hour is a longer time than 30 minutes. The generics are *hours* and *minutes*. The numbers are *one* and *thirty*. One half-hour ... thirty minutes. The rule says generics determine reaction more than numbers. That being true, minutes are less than hours. Sixty minutes seems to be less time than one hour.

Similarly, seconds are less than minutes; hours are less than days. Sixty seconds is a shorter span of time than one minute. Twenty-four hours is a shorter span of time than one day. Attention is to the *generic unit*—seconds, minutes, hours, or days—not to the number, sixty, twenty-four, or one.

This piece of information is *not* trivial. You can control the reader's reaction without changing the facts.

If you want to suggest you process claims in a shorter time, you write "48 hours"; if you want the time to seem longer, you write "two days." Shorter distance: "Five thousand, two hundred and eighty feet"; longer distance: "one mile." But five thousand, two hundred and eighty feet is a longer distance than fifty-two hundred and eighty feet, because hundreds are smaller than thousands.

Smaller quantity: "one pint"; larger quantity: "half a quart." Less weight: "eight ounces"; more weight: "half a pound."

Let's move up to the second level: Which of these seems to be a longer period of time?

Established 1967

or

More Than 20 Years at This Location

Let's expand the Generic Determination Rule to cover this second-level concept:

Does the experiential background of your primary targets include a date within their adult experience? Then numbers of years, months, or days are apparently longer.

Using the expanded rule we can widen our generic determinations in both directions. If it's supposed to be recent, it didn't happen three months ago; it happened last April ("back in April" artificially pumps up the time gap). "I haven't seen you for ten years" is a considerably longer gap than "I haven't seen you since 1978."

In the other direction, "You've only had it since 1988" is less time, in 1990, than "You've only had it two years."

The Psychology of Tense Selection

Present tense: "This sells elsewhere for $100."

Past tense: "This sold elsewhere for $100."

What's the difference? Plenty. Present tense has the power, because *right now* somebody else is selling this for $100. Past tense loses strength because it's history, not current events.

What do you do if you can't claim a current competitive marketplace at $100? Simple—you split the difference by moving into the *present perfect* tense: "This has sold elsewhere for $100."

Present perfect links the immediacy of the present with the factual comfort of the past. Don't worry about terminology or the forgotten sentence-parsing of Miss Norwalk's third-grade class. Keep repeating, as I do: Copywriters are communicators, not grammarians. What matters isn't your knowledge of which tense is which; it's your knowledge of how to transform the lead of drab fact into the gold of lustrous attraction.

One exception: Use *sold*, not *has sold* or *have sold*, when suggesting a break with the past, especially in headline copy:

Thousands Sold at $100!

Why is "*This* has sold . . ." usually better copy than "*These* have sold . . ."? Two reasons:

1. *Exclusivity* is one of the four great motivators. Singularity suggests exclusivity; pluralizing makes both what you're selling and those to whom you sell it anonymous.

2. The singular implicitly suggests quantity limitation. It's the same impulse-building syndrome that brings crowds to the door half an hour before a store opens—"Only 11 at This Price!"

(The reason for the word *usually* in the explanation: When quantity *is* small, pluralizing emphasizes fewness.)

When writing "accomplishment" copy, past perfect creates an immediacy you can't achieve with past tense. Example: A piece of copy about miniaturized firearms read:

Sr. Alberti created a perfect working replica . . .

which lost the selling hook by turning Sr. Alberti's accomplishment into a historical incident. The work becomes a current event with a single word change:

> Sr. Alberti has created a perfect working replica . . .

Check your copy for lost timing. You can lose the reader's or listener's interest by wandering through history, and you can yank that interest string back into the present by a tense change. Instead of

> The work had a profound effect . . .

which doesn't have a profound effect, since it seems to have come and gone before your target individual came onto the scene, you can write:

> The work has had a profound effect . . .

The profundity seems to have continued right up to the moment your words hit the paper. "Has had" can be even more dynamic than "is having," because present tense can have a subtle overtone of incompleteness or a changeable circumstance.

MAXIMIZING IMAGE

What's wrong with this copy?

> Joseph's SuperValue Warehouse is located on Cambridge Highway, on the corner of Central—Suite 902.

The mixed message destroys the size impression we want. How can a warehouse be in Suite 902? For advertising purposes, leave that suite number out. It makes the enterprise seem to be a one-room company (which it may be, but why advertise a negative?).

Procter & Gamble can use a post office box; most medium-sized companies look better and bigger if, instead of having as an address *P.O. Box 897* they use either *Box 297* or *Lock Box 297*. It's the same information, but the image is stronger.

Does your post office have a name? You can adopt it and gain luster: *Box 297, Grand Central Post Office* (or—and check with the local postmaster first to get approval, which you'll probably get because post offices have their own ZIP codes—*Box 297, Grand Central*).

If you've won a meaningless award, either glorify it or convert it to a generic. Example: You've won the North Belle Vernon, PA "Best Grocer Award." To glorify it, add a descriptive word: "Winner of the coveted North Belle Vernon Best Grocer Award"; or convert it to a generic: "The award-winning store." Careful—if you claim "Winner of the coveted Best Grocer Award," be sure it's in context. Never let puffery overexpand to lying.

FIGURE 2–5
Okidata uses the "touchstone" technique of image enhancement in this ad. The Okidata printer is shown about 1/50 the size of the Rolls-Royce grill. Copy calls Okidata "the Rolls-Royce of printers," attempting to transfer the top-of-the-market image, for which the motorcar is famous, to the printer. Opinion: The connection isn't clarified because the illustration makes no tie between the Rolls-Royce and the printer.

30

FIGURE 2–6
Maximizing image means stifling the urge to say too much. In this case, did the
advertiser say enough? What look are we supposed to capture? Does the typical
reader know what "Lancaster" is? (No, it isn't supposed to be the city in Pennsylvania.)

So daring is the entrepreneurial spirit,
it cannot survive rigid thinking.

There is at Dominion a flexibility uncommon to other large banks. Which
allows us to go beyond conventional thinking to assist business opportunities.
Such was the case when we were presented with a challenging plan to
restore the 1950's ocean liner S. S. United States to service as a luxury cruise
ship. We responded quickly with interim financing for the purchase and
feasibility study. We do not take lightly our responsibility to analyze risks.
But we're also committed to creating new ways to nurture business growth.
Let us show you how accommodating a good bank can be.

DOMINION
BANK

Member Dominion Bankshares Corporation. $5 billion resources.
182 offices. All across Virginia. Member FDIC.

FIGURE 2–7
I challenge anyone, including the CIA's Cryptography Section, to decode this headline.
If you really want to be confused, take two more steps: (1) Try to relate the illustration
to the subject, and (2) try to relate the body copy to the headline.

"If you ask me Thompson, these new CCI Officepower work stations from STC are just a little too user friendly."

32

FIGURE 2–8
Cartoon humor damages both image and message beyond repair. "User-friendly" is an uncomfortable concept, and this ad enhances discomfort. (The missing comma before "Thompson" doesn't help.) Reading the copy, one wonders: Does the copy under the heading WHY IS IT SO FRIENDLY? explain why it's friendly? Does the copy under the heading WHAT'S SO DIFFERENT ABOUT THIS SYSTEM? tell us what's different? Nope. And except for the first half-sentence, the illustration might as well have been (and should have been) forgotten.

You Don't Have to Be a Poet

One advantage you as copywriter will have from knowing a few rules is that you won't have to wait for inspiration to hit you. If you think using logic instead of waiting for inspiration isn't a healthy notion because you abandon your "creative genius" mantle, you've never had a deadline.

For those of us who can't stall, praying that our feeble creative fires will start to burn brightly, knowing logical rules is the sign of professionalism.

3

The Lean Machine: How to Use Words

GOOD WRITING IS LEAN WRITING

You've heard it many times before: Good writing is lean.

Don't mistake leanness for anorexia. You want to get rid of fat, not muscle. Most first drafts are heavily insulated with fat, and exercising your editing muscle will break down and flush away those greasy globules without cutting into the meat.

Here's a quick test: This is one of five "bullets" describing a portable radio:

▶ Has a stereo/mono switch that helps you pull in weak or distant stations

You have to leave the meat alone. So *stereo/mono switch* has to remain intact. How can you tighten and strengthen this line?

▶ Stereo/mono switch helps you to pull in weak or distant stations

Notice anything else? What's the word *to* doing there? It's part of the fat, not the meat; so you slice it out and you have:

▶ Stereo/mono switch helps you pull in weak or distant stations

The Slasher would go even farther:

▶ Stereo/mono switch gets weak/distant stations

I don't agree. This turns leanness into anorexia. Instead of taut copy the overcondensed bullet seems frantic. There's a rule for this, The Tightness Rule:

Keep copy tight enough so it fits the reader's skimming without forcing a comprehension stop.

Live or Dead Words

The copywriter's job is to bring an image to life. Did a copywriter have anything to do with this line of copy?

This toothpaste is specially made to prevent cavities.

Even a beginner should be able to spot the weakness in the word *made*. One doesn't need five years of post-graduate copywriting training to recognize how much more power lies in words such as *compounded* or *formulated*. Why? Because by using *compounded* or *formulated* the writer bestows accomplishment on the toothpaste. Anyone can *make* something.

From an automobile manufacturer came this limp line:

Mazda trucks provide a new standard of quietness.

Can't you see the word *provide* draining strength out of the truck? *Provide* is an accountant's or an economist's term. In the dynamic and competitive world of salesmanship you write copy in color, not black-and-white.

The dictionary does list the word *quietness*, but the word is altogether too peaceful for truck copy, even compared with *quiet*.

"I wish to . . ." has a limp-sponge impact; "I want to . . ." indicates character and position.

A billboard for a restaurant has this line of copy:

All baking done on premises.

Did a lawyer write that? A copywriter would have written:

We do all our own baking.

If the writer knew the restaurant business, the copy would have a little more specificity:

We bake our own rolls, bread, cakes, and pies.

A manufacturer's camera *magalog* (magalog = catalog set up in magazine format) has this line:

The Professional MAXXUM is the fastest operating camera available today.

That word *available* is the leech in this sentence. Like *quality* and *service*, *available* is a neutral word, marking time. Take out the word; isn't the sentence stronger without it?

If your copy is consistently flat, don't go mad with a riot of color; add pastel tints with an occasional flare.

Exotic words can be land mines. What good is a word if the reader or listener doesn't know it? *Goodbye* is colorless, but does your target individual know what *auf Wiedersehen* means? If you're sure, use it. If you're not sure, *farewell* is a word everyone knows, and it has hue.

Don't strain for it, but when you're word picking, think of a bin of corn at the supermarket: Every ear costs the same, so why not pick the biggest, juiciest ones in the bin?

HOW TO USE WORDS AS AMMUNITION AND HOW TO AVOID FIRING BLANKS

You and I both know writers who have favorite words and phrases. They're comfortable with those terms and take a proprietary view of them. One writer's copy has become recognizable because of overuse of the word *captured*—"In a single painting he has captured . . ."; "This book captures the spirit of . . ."; "She captured the flavor of. . . ." *Captured* is a perfectly acceptable word, but it isn't worth a love affair.

Another writer just has to use *What's more* in every piece of copy. It's like a trademark, and that's what's wrong: A professional copywriter shouldn't have a trademark. Words should fit what you're selling, and when you try to fit what you're selling to your favorite words, you have inferior copy. That's the reason for the Rule of Word Matching:

> **Use words that match the image you're trying to build. An out-of-key word changes the image.**

Word matching picks up steam when some of your key words not only fit the subject but have *color*. Look for colorful words to tint your copy with imagery to fire the reader's imagination.

To Coin a Cliché . . .

A not-so-gentle warning to those who write news releases, broadcast copy, and direct mail, with an all-media alert: Comb your copy for clichés.

A cliché bleaches the color out of writing. What a paradox! Consider how many writers, fishing around for colorful phraseology, give up and pepper their copy with the blandest of seasonings—clichés. Awareness is the key to cliché elimination. If you're cliché-prone, start life-extending treatment for your copy by using these words less than you used to:

A breed apart.

Add years to your life and life to your years.

As far as (WHATEVER) is concerned . . .

Ask us about our . . .

FIGURE 3–1
This ad screams a cliché:
YOU'VE TRIED THE REST
• NOW TRY THE BEST •
What are they advertising? A golf course. What possessed the writer to let copy collapse atop this weak, trite phrase? A selling point is at hand—the course has been rated one of the ten best in the county. Why not build a copy platform around the specific? A cliché is *never* the best way to sell, even when used as satire.

. . . as we possibly can.

At this point in time

The best in . . .

Bright-eyed and bushy-tailed.

Due to the fact that . . .

Each and every . . .

Enclosed please find . . .

[AND or DESPITE] the fact that . . .

FIGURE 3–2
Here we go again with the same tired cliché. "You've seen the rest. Here's your chance to buy the best." The best what? And *how* is it best? One test of a headline is its singularity—its pertinence to what's being sold and *only* to what's being sold. A "boiler-plate" headline is a meaningless nonargument. The ad shown in Figure 3–1 was the 13,985th time an unwitting advertiser used the "You've seen the rest . . ." line. Now, why did this advertiser have to become the 13,986th? (Suggestion: Don't let your ad become number 13,987.)

The finest in [WHATEVER].

First-class quality, first-class service.

Great (especially "Feels great" or "Tastes great") . . .

Heartwarming . . .

Hustle and bustle.

I couldn't care less

If you can find a better [WHATEVER], buy it.

. . . in any way, shape, or form.

In other words . . .

In view of the fact that . . .

Let's face it.

[WHATEVER] means business.

New and improved . . .

No customer too big or too small.

Prioritize.

Quite simply, . . .

Regardless of race, color, or creed.

Revolutionary . . .

Sit up and take notice.

State of the art.

You've tried the rest. Now try the best.

. . . very . . .

Watch for it.

We hear you.

When you think of [WHATEVER], think of [WHATEVER].

When you want the best.

Why settle for [WHATEVER] when you can have [WHATEVER]?

World class . . .

Colors are much abused by cliché users. A short spectrum: red tape, rosy future, tickled pink, purple passion, blue funk, green with envy, silver lining, white as snow. They put us in a black mood, white with anger, because they're permanent—usually dyed-in-the-wool.

No copywriter can have an unblemished career. Clichés creep into our writing like weevils into flour when our thoughts wander. An occasional cliché may actually bring relief to a torrent of tortured rhetoric. But when a writer looks at his copy sheet, sees "If you can find a better automobile, buy it!" or "Our computers mean business," and doesn't do something about it—it's time to cover the keyboard. (You may attribute this to a personal prejudice, but my 'Enry 'Iggins ear has

FIGURE 3–3
As long as we're paying for space, why not write an ad that sells something? "... the finest in selection, service and value" is the type of cliché that says, "The writer gives up. Your turn."

convinced me that people who have a verbal "You know" and "I mean" habit are the most cliché ridden among us.)

As the saying goes, "When clichés become thick as fleas, it's time to avoid them like the plague." (With that in mind, inspect cliché-ridden Figures 3–1, 3–2, and 3–3.)

Schlock Words

Schlock words aren't onomatopoeic (see Chapter 4). They aren't clichés. They're lowbrow. Only about 5 percent of the schlock words we see in ads have the strength of the same description properly presented. You should know them, though, because of the 5 percent. Here are some schlock words:

brite

kleen

lite

nite

thru

xtra

Having seen these samples, can you tell when the 5 percent applies? Right: when you're writing for bottom-end buyers.

FIGURE 3–4

This ad is an exact lift from one of the two most famous ads of all time: John Caples's "They Laughed When I Sat Down at the Piano" (the other, which ran for 45 years: "Do You Make These Mistakes in English?" for the Sherwin Cody School). It's a winner with those who remember the Caples ad; but is this group, most of whom are beyond their working years, a good prospect for Courseware? I was delighted to see this ad again, complete with vintage display type and illustration. Whether the reader considers it a stupid cliché or not depends on the reader's own background. Opinion: a dangerous crap-game.

FIGURE 3–5
"Improve Your Odds," and the picture is a pair of dice, get it? It's surprising to see a company of Nielsen's stature running four-color hucksterish ads. Did the company have a better way of selling consumer sales information? Unquestionably.

43

FIGURE 3–6
This is a trade show air-freight company. Suppose you're planning a trade show and *need* an air-freight company: Would this mess sell you on the company?

Words You Should Never Use in Copywriting

access (as a verb)
at this point in time
define
despite the fact that
due to (instead of *because of*)
etc.
[the] fact is
for (instead of *because*)
frankly
has got, have got
however
I could care less
I mean (followed by a comma)
impact (as a verb)
importantly
indeed (as first word of a sentence)
in terms of
meaningful
muchly
needs
prioritize
remember (imperative followed by a comma)
thusly
utilize (instead of *use*)
what's more
-wise (as a suffix—"price-wise," "wisdom-wise")
you know (as a substitute for *uuuuh*)

Weak Words You Sometimes Have to Use

available
(the) fact that; (in) fact
feature
one of the most
quality
receive
value

CCi / Communication Channels, Inc.
6255 Barfield Road • Atlanta, Georgia 30328 • (404) 256-9800
Telex 4611075 COMCHANI

Please reply to: 18601 LBJ Freeway, Suite 240 • Mesquite (Dallas), Texas 75150 • (214) 270-6651

May

Dear Marketing Director:

Communication Channels, Inc. is proud to introduce our newest Direct Response Postcard Deck -- EXECUTIVE MARKET OPPORTUNITIES.

Communication Channels, Inc. has developed an extremely unique formula for selecting the 250,000 names that make up the mailing list for EXECUTIVE MARKET OPPORTUNITIES. These responsive business leaders are a known quantity ... high level senior management of top companies with the power to buy. These buyers are taken from Communication Channels, Inc.'s trade magazines circulation lists audited by Business Publication Audits, an independent auditing service. Because our magazines are audited, we know what these names represent in terms of industry and title.

As you know, card deck advertising is one of the most cost-effective ways for you to promote via direct response. A card in EXECUTIVE MARKET OPPORTUNITIES costs only $3,195. You might ask yourself, why is the CPM so low? It's simple; our overhead is low. We own our lists where many of our competitors rent their lists, even from us. So, why not advertise from the source where we pass the savings on to our advertisers?

Because of your interest in reaching an affluent, financially astute audience, I am confident you will agree that EXECUTIVE MARKET OPPORTUNITIES will develop fresh, fast and high quality sales for your company at a nominal cost, and yet with the prestige of the nation's most foremost trade publications.

We are now accepting space reservations for our September 1986 deck. The closing date for insertion orders and materials is August 10th. To reserve space in EXECUTIVE MARKET OPPORTUNITIES' premier issue, just return the enclosed insertion order, or if you have any questions, please feel free to call. Don't delay! Early space reservations assure good positioning.

Very truly yours,

Mike DeLatte

Mike DeLatte
Director of Advertising
EXECUTIVE MARKET OPPORTUNITIES

bw

Publishers of Adhesives Age / Air Cargo World / Airline Executive/ American City & County / Art Material Trade News / Atlanta Magazine / Better Nutrition / Buildings Design Journal
Business Atlanta / Commuter Air / Container News / Design Graphics World / Elastomerics / Fence Industry-Access Control / Health Foods Retailing / Midwest Real Estate News
Modern Paint and Coatings / National Real Estate Investor / Pension World / Robotics World / Selling Direct / Shopping Center World / Southeast Real Estate News / Southwest Real Estate News
Swimming Pool Age & SPA Merchandiser / The Management of World Wastes / Today's Living / Trusts & Estates

FIGURE 3–7
In the second sentence this mailer uses the phrase *extremely unique*. The word "extremely" damages the copy, not only because it has a pejorative overtone but because *any* qualifier for "unique" is a mistake. Can you see how the reader is suddenly aware—"I'm being pitched?" The weak first paragraph starts the letter off with a limp; this wound becomes mortal.

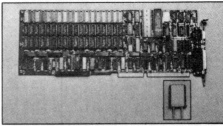

FIGURE 3–8
This ad is full of specifics. The headline is full of something else. In 30 seconds, can't you think of a more effective headline for this ad, even if you know absolutely nothing about Turbo? Look at the body copy: Powerful headlines are buried there.

Redundancies

Some redundancies, such as *free gift*, help credibility, a benefit which transcends the usual weakness of repetition. For example, "100% aspirin free" is a redundancy Anacin used successfully for years. (If it's aspirin free, it *has* to be 100% aspirin free. But like *free gift*, this redundancy adds emphasis.)

The Redundancy Control Rule tells you when to repeat and when to strip out the extra words:

Use redundancies only when you want the reader to know you've repeated or doubled words to show emphasis.

Redundancy Control suggests you question constructions which seem to be inadvertent padding:

- actual fact
- advance planning
- another alternative
- beginning of a new era
- consensus of opinion
- depreciate in value
- 8 A.M. in the morning
- final expiration date
- foreign import
- last year's recent achievements
- little babies
- necessary requirement
- new innovation
- new breakthrough
- old adage
- postpone until later
- reasonable and fair
- safe haven
- uniformly consistent
- young child

Compare the weakness of those redundancies with the power of the next examples. The reader recognizes your intention to emphasize, and reader recognition is your justification:

- genuine leather
- I myself

▶ last and final opportunity
▶ my personal attention
▶ satisfaction 100% guaranteed

We stumble inadvertently into redundancies as we fight for stronger emphasis. It doesn't work that way. Adding words is adding *bulk*, not power.
An example:

My company has never done business that way, and we aren't about to change now.

The weakness might be hard to spot if we weren't concentrating on redundancy. The word *now* is a classic power adder, but not when it's a redundancy. "We aren't about to change" is stronger than "We aren't about to change now" because the redundancy becomes a qualifier.
For some readers, this line of copy causes confusion:

Heinz Veuhoff is an in-house staff designer for Olympic Litho Corporation of Brooklyn, New York.

An *in-house staff* designer? We won't ask whether the parallel might be an out-house staff designer. Instead, we ask: What does *staff* add to *in-house*? The two words are the same to the reader; but because this company is named Olympic, somehow we get the impression Mr. Veuhoff designs staffs. Why add bulk without adding information?
The definitive word about redundancies: They're copy weakeners.

4

How to Write Motivational Copy

HOW TO TELL THE READER WHAT TO DO

The Fourth Great Law of mass communications is *Tell the reader what to do.* It's the easiest law to follow, which may be why it's so often ignored. (For all four Great Laws, see Chapter 25.)

The beginner who takes my word for it and writes with slavish obedience to this law might be surprised at how effective copy becomes. If the writer of Figures 4–1, 4–2, 4–3, 4–4 and 4–5 had considered this law, their messages might have had some impact.

Three principal reasons are interlocking rules which tie the law to grammar. If you stay away from *would* or *could* words you'll have more octane in your word mix.

Here are the three rules. I've given each one a high-sounding name:

1. **The Conditional Declension Syndrome—**
   The more conditional the statement, the weaker it is.

2. **The Comparative Conditional Declension Syndrome—**
   The conditional isn't as impelling as the imminent.

3. **The Subjunctive Avoidance Commandment—**
   Avoid the subjunctive. It denies actuality.

How to Change Weak Conditional Statements

Obviously if conditional statements are feeble, they're implicitly weaker than imminent statements. Let's take a look at how changing a conditional statement to an imminent statement pumps power into what you say:

We'll squeeze every nickel and stretch every dollar, but we're desperately close to running out of money. If we did, we'd have to cut back on programs that might have been the only act of friendship for helpless children.

The rules tell us to change a couple of words, closing the loophole the first draft gave the reader. Can you see how much stronger a suggestion of imminent problems is than a conditional statement?

We squeeze every nickel and stretch every dollar, but we're desperately close to running out of money. If we do, we'll have to cut back on programs that might be the only act of friendship for helpless children.

This same principle underlies the difference between *can* and *will*. Which word would you use?

You've helped us before. (Can) (Will) you, again?

Right! *Can* is conditional; it gives the donor an out. *Will* puts the act right where it belongs—within the donor's control.

In this same category are "As . . ." phrases. I *don't* include the invaluable *As you know* in any pejorative reference; "As . . ." limpness pertains to *as*-refer-backs—the likes of "As previously stated" or "As mentioned above." At best, this phraseology is a holding action; at worst, it's a strength sapper.

Even in the active tense, an *as* phrase probably is weaker than the same phrase without it:

As I told you, we'll . . .

has far less impact than

I told you we'll . . .

Solving a Predicament Means Writing Winning Copy

If your copy leads the reader into visualizing himself in a predicament and then leads him out, you're writing a winner.

"Predicament" copy is one of the most venerable forms of professional copywriting. Two of the best-known ads of all time use a predicament as their setting—John Caples's masterpiece, "They Laughed When I Sat Down at the Piano," and the Sherwin Cody School's classic which ran for 45 years, "Do You Make These Mistakes in English?"

Most professional writers have a loose knowledge of the value of predicaments. Where so many fall flat is in failing to know or care about the difference between a *credible* predicament and an *incredible* predicament.

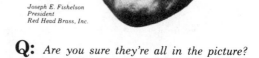
FIGURE 4–1

This infuriating ad admits in its first lines of body copy: The headline has nothing to do with what the company sells. Ads like this often ignore the Fourth Great Law as they merrily violate the Second Great Law. Information is here; somebody told the advertiser the magic word *sex* would induce the readers of this magazine to read his ad. But what are they supposed to do as the result of reading it? The company's image isn't helped, and only partial information is transmitted.

Imagine what they could have done
if they'd had the Sony incentive program.

When it comes to building sales and excitement, the Sony incentive program just might be the eighth wonder of the world.

To find out what the Sony incentive program can do for you, contact: Sandy Evans, 9 West 57th Street, New York, New York 10019. Or call (212) 418-9431.

SONY®
THE ONE AND ONLY™

FIGURES 4–2 and 4–3

This ongoing campaign has a problem: Because it violates the Fourth Great Law, we don't know what Sony is selling. The full-page ads, in color, were expensive. What was in the writer's mind? Sony manufactures electronic instruments, so it can't be that their incentive program will send us to India or Greece. An advantage of the Fourth Law: It enhances clarity; without clarity no message has been transmitted.

If it's in The Courant, it's on their minds.

The Hartford Courant, making you memorable.

FIGURE 4–4
This full page in an advertising trade publication has two problems: First, the cutline
has no relationship with the picture; second, the ad violates the Fourth Great Law. The
payoff line, "The Hartford Courant, making you memorable," is one of the least-
memorable lines of advertising we've read. Copywriters who think of the Fourth Great
Law as they write can't turn out messages as insignificant as this one.

FIGURE 4–5
Teaser ads implicitly violate the Fourth Great Law. What about this ad justifies the
space cost? If the "Square" is taking on a new shape, why does the ad show the old
shape? Opinion: a total waste of money.

So we have this predicament set up by a television writer:

"The most important conference of my life . . . and you switch deodorant
soaps!"

How much more powerful is the predicament in which the viewer can visualize himself. One example: A group enters a conference room. One, obviously
the boss, points at an attractive woman, sniffs, and nudges his assistant—

"I don't want to sit next to her."

Writing predicament copy is easy. A single rule covers it, The Predicament
Method Principle:

**Establishing a predicament as a sales argument has these five sequential com-
ponents:**

1. **Create a predicament the reader, viewer, or listener finds credible.**
2. **Put your target individual into that predicament, either by unmistakable association or by hard use of the word** *you.*
3. **Demonstrate whatever you're selling as the solution to the predicament.**
4. **Restate the circumstance with a happy conclusion.**
5. **Have the central character in the predicament state satisfaction.**

The Predicament Method Principle is one of the most mechanical rules, which makes this procedure a can't-miss cushion on those days when nothing coherent seems to flow out of your keyboard.

Hucksterism

Right after World War II a man named Frederick Wakeman wrote a book about advertising called *The Hucksters.* Rightly, the book ridiculed some of the creative techniques springing up during that period. The term *hucksterism* has stayed with us over the years. It describes the obnoxious procedure of coattail riding behind a phrase, a saying, or a slogan which has no relationship to what's being sold. An example is a loose deck card (see Chapter 21) with this headline:

SCORE BIG!
Direct Press Gives You the Scoring Point
That Will Keep You Ahead of the Game!

The illustration is a football referee, raising his hands to indicate a touchdown. What's being offered for sale? Printing. We have a pure case of hucksterism on both levels:

1. The headline can refer to any type of business.
2. The graphics relate to the nonrelevant headline, not to whatever the advertiser is selling.

Elsewhere in this text is a group of Unassailable Loser Statutes. Statute III declares:

Illustration should agree with what we're selling, not with headline copy.

On this basis alone, hucksterism fails. But it fails on a far more serious level: It has no motivators. A distressing aspect of hucksterism is the business classification which seems to use it most: companies in the world of mass communications. Broadcast stations, print media, and suppliers to the trade gravitate toward this annoying approach like flies gathering around a lump of dung.

You've already guessed my opinion: Don't write huckster-ads. All you have to do is ask, "Why should somebody buy what I have to sell?" and put the answer to that question into your copy. There's no way you'll end up with hucksterism.

FIGURE 4–6

Ghastly! It's warehouse space and we deal in square feet, get it? So let's show some square feet. The illustration transforms the ad from a harmless announcement to hucksterism at its worst. Suppose you're looking for office space. What's your instant opinion of this advertiser?

FIGURE 4–7

Whoever told the writer of this ad, "What a clever person you are!" better steer clear of I.Q. tests. It doesn't even show what it's supposed to, because Russian Roulette would have the woman pointing the gun at her own head, not recoiling as her stylist, "Mr. Big Al," tells her she didn't leave a big enough tip. Hucksterism at its worst!

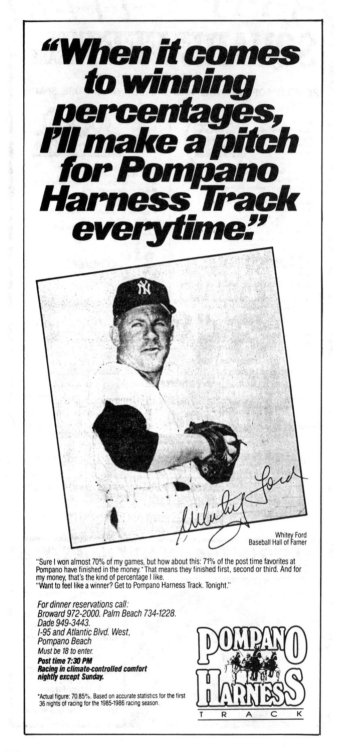

FIGURE 4–8
Classic Hucksterism! Whitey Ford was a pitcher, so his endorsement says, "I'll make a *pitch* for Pompano Harness Track." Opinion: The ad strikes out, as most huckster-ads do.

Take Your Best Shot at a Mortgage With the Morsemere Mortgage Team

The Morsemere Mortgage Team is a group of highly skilled professionals, trained to help you select the right mortgage suitable for your lifestyle and your budget.

As a mortgage banker, Morsemere offers more flexibility in their lending programs than other lenders in addition to the standard conventional programs, they offer graduated payment mortgages, adjustable rate programs and government financing for FHA and VA mortgages. As a subsidiary of Morsemere Federal Savings & Loan, they provide the financial strength and stability you want when selecting your mortgage.

Serving Dade, Broward, Palm Beach and Martin Counties, Morsemere's team of representatives will visit with you in the privacy of your own home, or if you prefer, in their conveniently located national headquarters at Glades Road and

the I-95 interchange.

So whether you're buying a first or second home, re-financing or investing, talk with a Morsemere Mortgage Corp. professional first. With competitive rates, a wide range of mortgage programs to choose from and an eager and friendly staff, why would you want to go anywhere else for something as important as your mortgage?

MORSEMERE MORTGAGE CORP.

Call today for information on our most current programs. Boca Raton (305) 392-5002, Broward (305) 462-4633, North Palm Beach County (305) 832-0707.

Morsemere Mortgage Corp.
1900 Glades Road,
Suite 250, Boca Raton,
FL 33431.

FIGURE 4–9

We see ads like this every day. Matching the illustration to the headline instead of to what we're selling results in hucksterism instead of communication. An easy test: Take the company name out of the headline and try to guess what kind of product or service the company sells. (The last sentence in the ad: "With competitive rates, a wide range of mortgage programs to choose from and an eager and friendly staff, why would you want to go anywhere else for something as important as your mortgage?" Reply: With this nonspecific buffoon approach, why would we want to go to you?)

Choosing the right shipyard to place a ship when it's in need of repairs may be puzzling for some shipowners. Particularly so, since everyone claims to be the best, most economical, fastest or most modern — a perplexing state and certainly a matter of opinion.

We at Todd, being no exception, like to believe we are the best. We strive to be cost effective through increased productivity at our upgraded facilities which, in turn, allows us to offer speedier service.

Another factor in Todd's favor is experience. We've had 70 well-rounded years worth and continue to seek new challenges to bolster our expertise.

Todd's management and labor force are at the disposal of prospective clients around-the-clock at all of our modern and complete shipyards.

Executive Offices - (212) 668-4700
Galveston Division - (409) 744-4581   **San Francisco Division (415) 621-8633**
Los Angeles Division - (213) 832-3361   **Seattle Division - (206) 623-1635**

Todd Shipyards Corporation
One State Street Plaza, New York, NY 10004

Get More Facts, Circle **34**

60

FIGURE 4–10
Borderline hucksterism here. The advertiser, a shipyard, does show drydocks; the word "Puzzled?" isn't all that bad. But superimposing the jigsaw-puzzle effect hurts clarity. What's the selling argument? What competitive advantage does this shipyard offer? Let's exploit it.

FIGURE 4–11
Ready for some ridiculous hucksterism? Compare the size of the huckster illustration with the inset pictures of the company's products. "Instrumental" is the key word here, and look what it leads to—an expensive, noncommunicative ad. The tiny line, "Superset telephones are manufactured for use with the complete MITEL PBX product line," isn't explained: What's a "superset" telephone? Why should we buy it? If the phones are for use *only* with the complete MITEL PBX product line, we need some ammunition both ways.

FIGURE 4–12
The hucksterism here is laughable. If the McCulloch 610 is a "real animal," what kind of animal is it? A tiger? A wolf? A bull? Nope, it's a little rodent. Maybe it's a woodchuck. Or is it a beaver cub? However much power "60cc's" might be, it looks to be barely enough to gnaw through the electric cord. If you were writing this ad, what would you have suggested for copy platform and illustration?

63

FIGURE 4–13
If you aren't a fan of the old TV show "M*A*S*H," this probably makes no more sense
to you than "Tippecanoe and Tyler Too." The actor played the part of a character
named Klinger; these stick-on notes are called "Clingers." Clever, eh? And the way he
uses them as eyeshades is even more clever, eh? What? You don't think so? That
shows how much you know about show-biz.

64

FIGURE 4–14
If you ask what Country Home has to do with rough-carved wooden fish, join the club. The relationship between this illustration and what they're selling—"Matched Schedule Discounts"—is a puzzlement.

FIGURE 4–15
Every ten years or so, an advertiser unearths the old World War I recruitment poster. Hucksterism often sacrifices specifics on the altar of attention getting, and that's what this ad does. In its defense: A typical Saturday metropolitan newspaper is loaded with real estate ads, indistinguishable from one another. Getting attention isn't easy. But then, once you have their attention, what do you do with it? The selling proposition here is that you can buy this house for $840 down and $465 per month. What house, you ask? That's the problem with this ad, which asks us to drive out to the site but doesn't tell us what we'll see there.

SOUTHERN CALIFORNIA'S BEST MARKET IS ITS WORST KEPT SECRET

Orange County, Southern California's most affluent market with a median household income 29% higher than Los Angeles, is now a national advertising target. In 1985, its leading newspaper — The Orange County Register — carried more full-run daily advertising than any other newspaper…in the nation.

Source: Media Records, Inc., 1985

THE ORANGE COUNTY
Register
METROGROUP
The *only* way to influence
Southern California's best market.

Represented Nationally by Cresmer, Woodward, O'Mara & Ormsbee, Inc.

66

FIGURE 4–16
Southern California's worst-kept secret may be masked by one of its worst-conceived ads. The concept here is both hucksterish and muddy, an impossible combination. Lots of good, chewable information in the body copy, but we may never get that far.

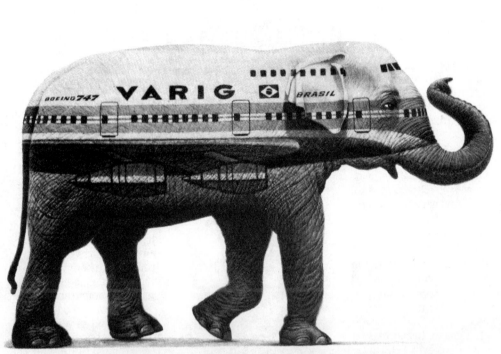

FIGURE 4–17
Want to ride an elephant? We do get the idea, especially since the 747 is the "Jumbo
Jet." But somehow we don't want to ride an elephant. It's uncomfortable, jouncy,
smelly, and slow. The writer shouldn't have settled for the first idea to cross his brain.

FIGURE 4–18

See how easy it is to match up the elements? The ad talks about zippers—and shows a zipper, dramatically enough to catch our eye. What if the writer had succumbed to hucksterism and written, "We'll *zip* your order off to you?" Instead of this clean, clear ad we'd have had another sample of what not to do. Read the copy, because this is a good ad!

The biggest barrier to computer integrated manufacturing sales is the information barrier. And that barrier just got broken. With the publication of MANAGING AUTOMATION, the first magazine designed to reach all key decision makers involved in the complex, step-by-step process of automating a manufacturing facility.

MANAGING AUTOMATION is a new kind of publication. For today's new needs of management. Cutting across all disciplines, it addresses every aspect of factory automation: organizational, financial and technological. With it, you can reach everyone from CEO, CFO and Factory Information Systems Director to the operating managers of production, engineering, marketing and purchasing. All with verified responsibility in planning and implementing automation. Without it, you'd need to advertise in at least ten different publications.

To survive, American industry must automate. But to do so, it must have the kind of practical yet technologically-sophisticated information provided each month in MANAGING AUTOMATION. The Editorial Board and staff are without peer. And so is the editorial environment.

Some of America's leading advertisers have already signed up for major schedules in MANAGING AUTOMATION.

Shouldn't you join them?

THE BIGGEST BARRIER TO COMPUTER INTEGRATED MANUFACTURING SALES JUST GOT BROKEN.

Call Peter Aldo at (212) 868-5661

69

FIGURE 4–19
Obviously the biggest barrier to computer-integrated manufacturing sales is the building next door. That's the only excuse for showing a wrecking ball when we're selling advertising space in a magazine. Media are principal users of hucksterish ads, which may be why outsiders call us hucksters. With ads like this, we deserve the name.

FIGURE 4–20
Time for a little contest: The first adperson who can figure out what the illustration has to do with whatever this company is selling wins the advertising account. If "Edgar Watkins design" is such a potent selling point, why don't they show us some designs? If we're interested in plastic drinkware, will this ad have us running to the phone? We can't; the company left its number out of the ad.

HOW TO MOVE THEM OFF DEAD-CENTER

Implicit in the Fourth Great Law, "Tell the reader what to do," is the recognition that the writer has to know what the reader is supposed to do. A writer is only as effective as the information source. I can't tell you what to do if I don't know what I want you to do. But copywriters can't abandon responsibility by wailing, "Nobody told me what I'm supposed to say."

Unless legal restrictions forbid absolutes, use strong, recognizable words. If you tell the reader what to do, you've done a big hunk of the job and you've moved your seat away from the amateur bullpen and into the big leaguers' dugout.

USING COLORFUL WORDS IN COPY

Within the active vocabularies of most individuals and all successful copywriters are words touched with spice. Use them as you'd use spice in a recipe—to enhance flavor without drowning or desensitizing the palate. (Figure 4–21 is a good example of colorful word use.)

When you have a flavorful word, consider all forms of it. For example, *triumph* is a noun or verb, with *triumphant* the adjectival form. Most of the words I've tabulated in the preliminary list are adjectives, but please don't look for adjectives only. Nouns have the power and verbs have the action. Many adjectives also have a noun variation.

Here are a few samples of colorful words you can start using today:

adventure	glow	provocative	sultry
bagatelle	graceful	pulse-pounding	sumptuous
bazaar	haughty	radiant	sunny
bewitching	innocent	regal	thrilling
bizarre	jaunty	rogue	thundering
buccaneer	luminous	saucy	torrid
danger	lusty	savage	tranquil
devilish	lyrical	scorching	transform
enchanting	majesty	scramble	urbane
executive	marvel	sensuous	valor, valiant
explosive	mellow	serene	vibrant
ferocious	meteoric	smoky	vigor
fierce	naughty	spicy	vital
fiery	nimble	splendor	wicked
flaming	opulent	startle	wild
frivolous	preposterous		

JACQUES-YVES COUSTEAU

Dear Citizen of the Water Planet,

A shipwrecked sailor was struggling in the water. The shore was near, but his strength was almost spent.

Then suddenly there was a friendly presence in the water, a strong, sleek body that buoyed him up, escorted him to shallow water, saved his life.

This story, or something akin to it, has been told countless times about dolphins and porpoises. When I take it, together with what we have learned about these marvelous creatures in the past forty years, I have to give credence to at least some of these tales.

In fact, dolphins, porpoises and their larger cousins, the great toothed whales, do have a formidable intelligence. We hope some day to understand the subtleties of their brains, which rely heavily on an acoustical perception of the world around them. But the stories of rescued swimmers may find their explanation in a simpler trait, a trait that dolphins share with a majority of us animals, a trait which may be more important than any amount of brain power.

When a dolphin mother gives birth, her baby is expelled underwater. The first act following birth is critical: to lift the freshly born youngster up to the surface for its first breath. So powerful is this motherly instinct that other struggling animals have been pushed to the surface instinctively by female dolphins.

How marvelous and beautiful! The instinct to protect the next generation drives some automatic motor response in the dolphin and in many other species. To me this is marvelous because the successful replication of life is what makes our Oasis in Space such a rich biomass, fecund and prolific, forever generating and nurturing new organisms.

Surely this blessed miracle of life is the greatest treasure on earth. Yet do we earthlings cherish and guard it? On the contrary. Each month we now pour millions of tons of poisonous waste into the global water system. Many of our lakes, rivers, and coastal waters have received their mortal wound. The water is undrinkable. The fish and shellfish, if they exist at all, are contaminated.

I do not say this lightly. During the past forty

(over, please)

The Cousteau Society   930 West 21st Street   Norfolk, Virginia 23517

72

FIGURE 4–21
This letter, from the Cousteau Society, is six pages long. Will people read a six-page letter? Yes, if the language is colorful and exciting, as it is here.

These are words inside the vocabularies of most adults. To unlock their spice use them obliquely. For example, "a wicked person" is too straightforward to be spicy; "a wicked tennis serve" has spice, and "a delightfully wicked evening dress" is spice saturated.

Don't use colorful words as an artifice to show off your vocabulary. The Concept of Reader Dominance should temper the very human desire to show the reader the size of your vocabulary. The Concept:

The writer's knowledge of the colorful words in a piece of copy is inconsequential. What matters is whether or not the reader knows them.

Words like *fustian* and *bombast* and *diffident* can kill you instead of your target, because using words your message recipient doesn't understand violates the paramount Clarity Commandment. A college sophomore, trying to bolster a knowledgeable image, might put it this way: Eschew obfuscatory adages. We say simply: For the sake of your professionalism, obey The Clarity Commandment.

Steely or Spongy Words

We've long known that *tiger* is a more powerful word than *lion*. It's time we began to formalize the reasons why. We know that *William* is wearing his necktie today, that *Bill* is out bowling, that *Will* is a lawyer, that *Willie* likes to make harmless practical jokes, and that *Billy* is from the Southwest.

Aw, of course that's nonsense. And of course, too, it's the instant image that leaps to mind *until* we know that William, Bill, Will, Willie, and Billy are the same guy.

This is what we call the *Humphrey Bogart Syndrome*. The name *Humphrey* suggests bookishness—a person who fondles his violin instead of a Saturday Night Special. But in one piece, Humphrey Bogart conjures up an entirely different image. We *know* who he is.

But we don't know the fellow in the beer commercial. We're safer calling him Bill than we would be if he were William or Willie. That's the point. We might as well benefit from another of the human realities that help us form rules of copywriting.

We know that *Mike* is a tough guy and *Michael* is a poet and Mickey is easygoing.

We know that *rock* is harder than *stone*.

We know that a *stag* may be dangerous but an *antelope* isn't.

We know that *beef* is tastier as a fast food than *meat*.

We know that *farewell* is more dramatic than *goodbye*.

We know that *artificial* isn't good for us but *man-made* is.

We know that *half a pound* is a greater quantity than *1/2 pound*.

We know that an *engine* seems more complicated (ergo, worth more money) than a *motor*.

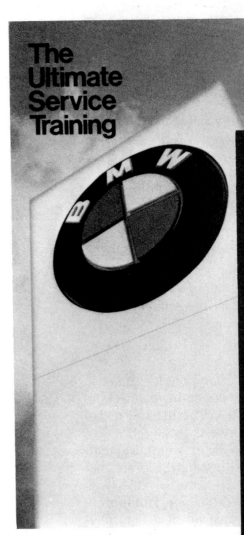

FIGURES 4–22 and 4–23
Copywriters have discovered the word "ultimate," and it has become one of our most overused and abused adjectives. What a shame! A perfectly good word now has all the impact of a sponge.

We know that *slim* looks good and *thin* looks unhealthy.

We know that a *trip* is a shorter journey than a *voyage*.

We know that *naked* is more sensual than *nude* and that kissing someone on the *mouth* is sexier than kissing that same person on the *lips*. For that matter, we somehow know the sexiness of the word *wet*, the result of a language "feel" outside the help any dictionary or thesaurus can give us.

TRICKS WITH WORDS

Oxymorons

Oxymorons are skyrocketing in popularity. The only explanation I can offer is the equivalent skyrocketing of the "That-which-is-different = That-which-is-better" cult.

An oxymoron combines two contradicting words into a single phrase: "Wise fool" is not only an oxymoron; it explains the word itself, *oxys* being ancient Greek for *sharp* and *moron* meaning just what it means today.

Tongue-in-cheekers say that word combinations such as *legal ethics* or *government efficiency* or *military intelligence* are oxymorons, because in each instance the two words are an impossible combination. Maybe so, but we're ad people and our job is to make words work for us. What we learn from those examples is (1) creating oxymorons can be fun, and (2) the two words don't have to be exact opposites, although most advertising use does pick opposites (see Figures 4–24, 4–25, 4–26, and 4–27).

Years ago Revlon shook up the world of cosmetics with a product line called "Fire and Ice"—an oxymoron. The arthritis rub "Icy Hot" is a current oxymoron. "Where Business Is a Pleasure" is a mild oxymoron, as is "The Birth of a Legend."

Less convincing is "A New Family Heirloom," too tortured and contrived to be effective. "Old New Mexico" has a peculiar ring to it.

Constructing an oxymoron is one of the simplest of all mechanical grammatical tricks. Just pick a word and look up its antonym. String the two words together with "and" or use one as an adjective to modify the other. "Young Senior Citizen" is obvious because *young* is the antonym of *old*. "Tiny Monster" or "Giant Midget" or "Dawn at Sunset" are oxymorons, and all are nonsense because they draw no word image at all.

"Poor Little Rich Girl" and "benevolent despot" are popular oxymorons; "Dumb genius" is another we understand—someone is bright but lacks common sense. "He is regarded as an unknown" appeared in print; it's nonsense because if he's regarded as anything, he can't be unknown.

A wonderful oxymoron is this overline on a full-page ad for a beauty product (Figure 4–26):

Famous Hollywood Secret Revealed . . .

If it's famous, how can it be a secret? The writer was carried away by a desire to excite the reader.

FIGURE 4–24
"The Birth of a Legend" is an oxymoron because *birth* and *legend* are at opposite ends of the temporal line. Copy has an additional hyperbole: ". . . the majestic Monterey Plaza has become the most talked about hotel in the world." Oh, yeah? When was the last time *you* heard anybody talking about it?

FOUR COLLECTIONS
IN ONE COMMEMORATIVE PROGRAM

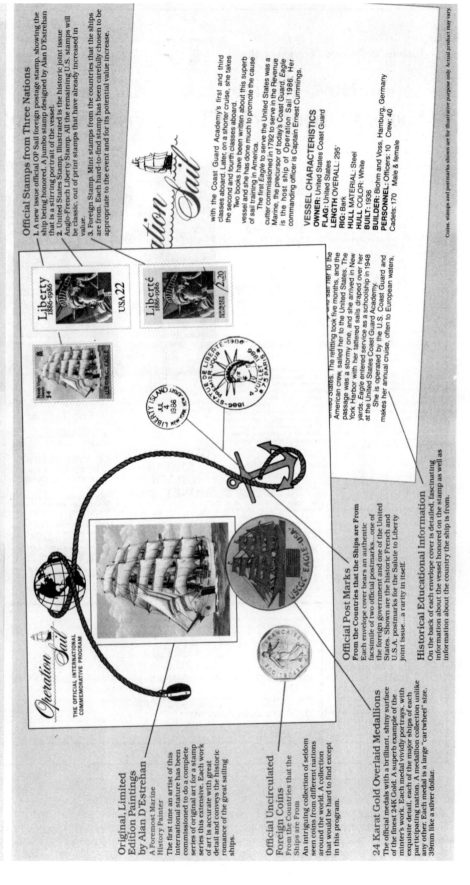

Original, Limited Edition Paintings by Alan D'Estrehan
A Foremost Marine History Painter

The first time an artist of this international stature has been commissioned to do a complete series of original art for a stamp series this extensive. Each work of art is accurate with great detail and conveys the historic romance of the great sailing ships.

Official Uncirculated Foreign Coins
From the Countries that the Ships are From

An intriguing collection of seldom seen coins from different nations around the world. A collection that would be hard to find except in this program.

24 Karat Gold Overlaid Medallions

The official medals with a brilliant, shiny surface of the finest 24K Gold. A superb example of the minter's work. Each medal vividly portrays, with exquisite detail, each of the major ships of each participating nation. A medallion collection unlike any other. Each medal is a large "cartwheel" size, 39mm like a silver dollar.

Official Post Marks

From the Countries that the Ships are From Each envelope cover bears an authentic facsimile of two official postmarks...one of the foreign government and one of the United States. Shown are the historic French and U.S.A. postmarks for the Salute to Liberty joint issue...a rarity in itself.

Historical Educational Information
On the back of each envelope cover is detailed, fascinating information about the vessel honored on the stamp as well as information about the country the ship is from.

Official Stamps from Three Nations

1. A new issue official OP Sail foreign postage stamp, showing the ship being honored. A jumbo stamp designed by Alan D'Estrehan that is a stirring portrait of the vessel.
2. United States Stamp. Illustrated is the historic joint issue Anglo-French Liberty Stamp. All the remaining U.S. stamps will be classic, out of print stamps that have already increased in value.
3. Foreign Stamp. Mint stamps from the countries that the ships are from. Each hard-to-find stamp has been carefully chosen to be appropriate to the event and for its potential value increase.

with the Coast Guard Academy's first and third classes aboard. Later, on a shorter cruise, she takes the second and fourth classes aboard.

Two books have been written about this superb vessel and she has done much to promote the cause of sail training in America.

The first *Eagle* to serve the United States was a cutter commissioned in 1792 to serve in the Revenue Marine, the precursor of today's Coast Guard. *Eagle* is the host ship of Operation Sail 1986. Her commanding officer is Captain Ernest Cummings.

VESSEL CHARACTERISTICS
OWNER: United States Coast Guard
FLAG: United States
LENGTH OVERALL: 295'
RIG: Bark
HULL MATERIAL: Steel
HULL COLOR: White
BUILT: 1936
BUILDER: Blohm and Voss, Hamburg, Germany
PERSONNEL: Officers: 10   Crew: 40
Cadets: 170   Male & female

...United States. The refitting took five months, and the American crew, sailed her to the United States. The passage was a stormy one, and she arrived in New York Harbor with her tattered sails draped over her yards. *Eagle* entered service as a schoolship in 1948 at the United States Coast Guard Academy.
She is operated by the U.S. Coast Guard and makes her annual cruise, often to European waters.

FIGURE 4–25
Copy under "Official Post Marks" reads: "From the Countries that the Ships are From" [two "froms"—ugh!] and continues, "Each envelope cover bears an authentic facsimile of two official postmarks ..." *Authentic facsimile* is an authentic oxymoron, because a facsimile can't be authentic. A parallel: "Genuine imitation leatherette."

78

FIGURE 4–26

The overline: "Famous Hollywood Secret Revealed"; the subhead: "An Amazing Scientific Discovery from Paris." You've heard, of course, we've shipped Hollywood to France. In a mad desire to stuff buzzwords into the copy, the writer credited both Hollywood and Paris as the source. Copy would have worked if, recognizing the discrepancy, the writer had tied the two together—a mission that isn't at all impossible.

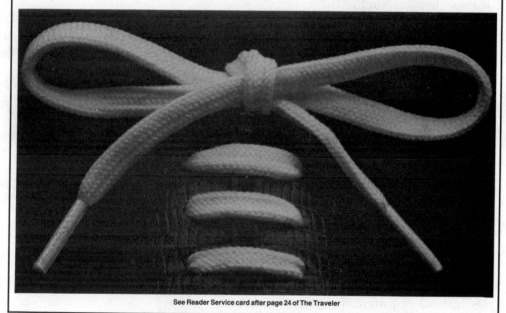

FIGURE 4–27
"Bring your high-heeled sneakers" is a deliberate, and moderately charming, oxymoron.
We don't object because the writer *meant* to pull us up short with a deliberate
mismatch. Oxymorons work if the reader understands they're supposed to stimulate the
pairing of opposites.

Officials from the city of Philadelphia ran an image ad with this headline (Fig. 4–27):

Bring Your High-Heeled Sneakers

It's a true oxymoron—sneakers can't have high heels. We might or might not understand this headline; we *think* we do, but our interpretation could differ from the writer's. That's the problem with it and with most oxymorons: We're never quite sure we understand what the message is supposed to be. Think about the "High-Heeled Sneakers" headline; can't you, in a few seconds, come up with a clearer, more dynamic one?

For product or company names an oxymoron might be a catchy answer— "The Red Greenhouse." Or if you're in a trap for a slogan or a headline, with deadline at hand, an oxymoron can bail you out. But except for the rare inspired combination, an oxymoron is at best a chewing gum patch in the copy radiator.

"Continental" Variations:
Writing for British Publications

The obvious note: When writing for United States readers, make only those changes the typical reader can accept comfortably. The issue you as copywriter face isn't whether your words are proper "Britishisms" but whether the reader will accept them as such.

Although in Great Britain you might write "I shall be there directly" instead of "I'll be there soon," most Americans don't recognize *directly* as a parallel to *soon* . . . so don't use this construction. In any type of writing, clarity should be paramount.

- ▶ Instead of *aluminum*, write *aluminium*
- ▶ Instead of *the committee is* . . . write *the committee are* . . .
- ▶ Instead of *defense*, write *defence*
- ▶ Instead of *elevator*, write *lift*
- ▶ Instead of *in the hospital*, write *in hospital*; but even though *in future* is correct, American readers are uncomfortable with it; use *in the future* as you normally do.
- ▶ Instead of *jewelry*, write *jewellery*.
- ▶ Instead of *or* for nouns, write *our* (colour, favour, glamour)
- ▶ Instead of *pharmacist*, write *chemist*
- ▶ Instead of *program*, write *programme*
- ▶ Instead of *right away*, write *straightaway*
- ▶ Instead of *skepticism*, write *scepticism*
- ▶ Instead of *subway*, write *underground* (*subway* is a walkway)

FIGURE 4–28
American spelling is *Encyclopedia*; British spelling is *Encyclopaedia*. We accept the British spelling for two reasons: First, to be consistent with the second word, *Britannica*, the first word should carry the traditional extra "a"; second, this encyclopedia was here long before we began tinkering with the language. Most readers don't notice the difference.

▶ Instead of *tire*, write *tyre*

▶ Instead of *traveler's check*, write *traveller's cheque*

▶ Instead of *truck*, write *lorry*

▶ Instead of z or soft c in some words, write s (organisation, practise)

▶ Put the period outside quotation marks for titles (The book was "Gone with the Wind".)

Be Careful with These Words

Some words have too much power for most advertising copy. When they appear in a headline or copy-block they taint the whole message. Sex used to be one of these words, although *sexy* had no negative implications. Sex no longer is a word that needs a more acceptable substitution, but the writer still should use *sexual* with care.

Use these words with care. You'll look for them and their fellows when your emphasis is negative or when you want to shake up the reader or listener.

bitch	mess
bleed	ooze
damn	rot
decay	scum
decompose	slimy
filth	snake
garbage	soil
grisly	suck
hell	vomit
labor	worm
leprosy	

Within your own field, compellingly negative words come to mind. Add them to this list, labeling them: "For Emergency Use Only."

THEOREMS OF WORD CONSTRUCTION

We know many words that sound like what they are.

As a start, as the first shovel in a ground-breaking that ultimately will result in a multistory structure with interlocking cubicles, we have The First Theorem of Word Construction, which should surprise nobody:

When naming or describing product or company, matching word sounds to the intended effect will heighten that effect until repetition blurs it.

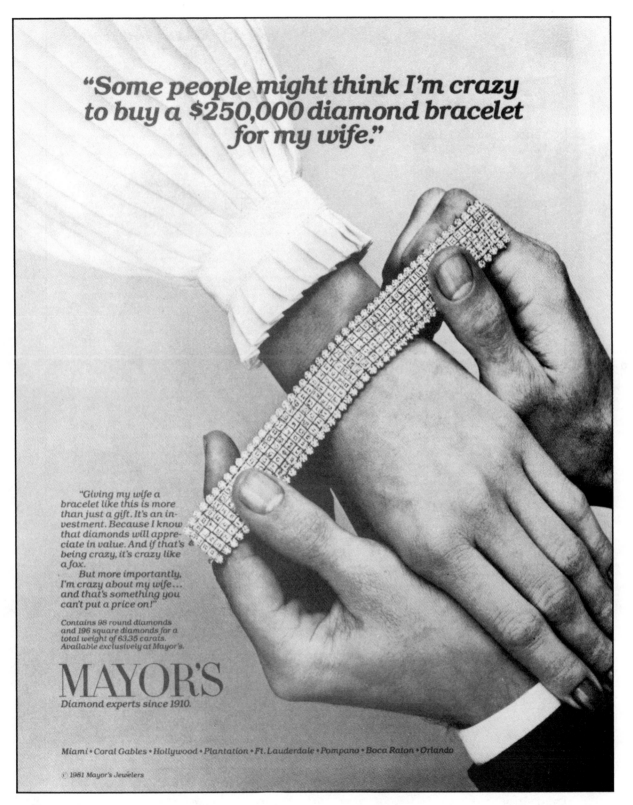

FIGURE 4–29

Use the word *crazy* carefully or you'll turn away buyers. No one wants the suggestion of craziness for buying a diamond bracelet. So many *positive* ways to present this same sales argument are apparent that one wonders what was in the copywriter's mind. Can you imagine a store clerk saying to a customer, "Some people might think you're crazy to buy a $250,000 diamond bracelet for your wife?"

The Atari 520 ST is a serious challenge to the Apple Macintosh and will open up a major fight in the personal computer market.

FIGURE 4–30

Didn't you recoil a bit from the word *explodes*? The word certainly is an eye-catcher, and that's why the writer used it. Many writers would have written a longer headline. The second sentence of body copy, for example:

> If I could offer you a Macintosh computer—
> a computer that sells for over $2000—
> for one-third the price, you might wonder.

Short of a split-run test, we never know whether short or long, startling or benefit-suggesting, works best.

PAID ADVERTISEMENT

BARBADOS ADVOCATE, Wednesday, December 11, 1985 Page 15

NOTICE

It has come to our attention that at a
POLITICAL MEETING HELD UNDER THE AUSPICES OF THE

DEMOCRATIC LABOUR PARTY

on

SUNDAY DECEMBER 8, 1985.

It was announced that

HILL MILLING CO., LTD.

closed its RICE MILL as a result of an objection to its operation made by this company to the Ministry of Trade.

THIS IS A DOWNRIGHT LIE

This company wishes to assure the public that it has never ever (repeat)...never ever made an objection to the operation of a RICE MILL by HILL MILLING CO., LTD. to the Ministry of Trade, any Government Ministry, any Minister of Government, any Parliamentarian - DLP or BLP, any Civil Servant or any other person in Barbados or elsewhere and challenges the Democratic Labour Party to produce evidence to the contrary.

Further we take this opportunity to remind the public of the laws of SLANDER OF TITLE AND LIBEL.

David Seale

David Seale
Managing Director
R. L. SEALE & CO., LTD.

FIGURE 4–31
This ad, in the Barbados Advocate, gains power from its straightforward projection of outrage. No pussyfooting here:

THIS IS A DOWNRIGHT LIE

In most countries, not only would the word "lie" give way to a weaker, less dynamic term; newspapers probably would refuse to run the ad for fear of involvement in a lawsuit.

The Second Theorem of Word Construction:

One-syllable words are harder, tougher, and stronger than their softer, more reasonable multisyllabic equivalents.

(The Second Theorem may be of value when writing about foods and transportation.)

The Third Theorem of Word Construction:

Flat vowels are crisper and are spoken faster than long vowels, so the words they represent seem crisper and faster.

The bag has been opened; it will pour hundreds of its more obvious rules onto these pages. The less obvious rules, the evolutionary rules, the rules requiring a specialist's laying on of hands—these surely will come between now and the year 2001.

A New Road, Not Yet Fully Paved

The road down whose mysterious length we walk has never been trod before . . . except by gremlins laying land mines. How brave, how rash we are to take even the first step.

So a plea: Our goal shouldn't be the search for words whose meanings are at variance with the suggested implicit syllable psychology. Don't look at *ama*, which in this list suggests "display," and exclaim, "Aha! What about Alabama and pajama?" Assail the notion if you like, but not because of exceptions.

Here we go! (An obvious note: We don't need a book on writing copy to tell us that the prefix *ante* means before and *post* means after, that *tri* means three and *quad* means four. These are venerable procedures of word construction, and it would be sophomoric and presumptuous to relist them here. This list is a distant cousin to such components. It looks into the "feel" of words and is a loose yardstick of how the writer can get word-feel to help create a flavor.)

ag = unsettled

agon (as suffix) = exotic

ama (as suffix) = display

bl = breaking loose

bla + soft consonant = weak, helpless

cag = tough, in motion

com = total, electronic

cr = rough, harsh, dynamic

eal = weak, unwholesome

eep = low and slow

esh = mushy

ette (as suffix) = miniature, feminine

fic = childish, harmless, primitive

ga = open, wide, stretched

gr + vowel + hard consonant = rough

har = trim, sharp, strident

iam = weakly foreign

imp = weak or stupid

ish = weak, nonthreatening

j = nonthreatening

j + (vowel) + (soft consonant) = happy beginning

k = (as replacement for *c* or *ck*) unsophisticated emphasis

ka = odd

kh = exotic, Mongolian

lot = neatly sorted

ock = hard

oke = agricultural, bucolic

oin = mushy, meaty

onic = smartly contemporary

oon = funny

oor = weak, feeble

orc or *ork* = bizarre, meaty

org = bloated, electronic

poo = harmless

qui + soft consonant = peaceful, dependable

ram = hard, powerful

rce (as ending) = action

shl, shm, shn = messy, inferior

shr = disconnecting, loosely raucous

sk = hardness (*sch* does not have this overtone)

sl = skewed, wetness

sn (as prefix) = unpleasant, underhanded

spl = bursting out

squ = messy

str = incorruptible, organized, power

thr = action

tor = unhappy

tr + (vowel) + (soft consonant) = bright, happy, neat

u (short) = slightly nasty

urk = evil, grotesque, abnormal

ush = wet, soft

usk = rough, exotic, animal-like

v = action

xton (as ending) = contemporary, smartly done

z + (short vowel) + (hard consonant) = controlled fast action

zz = bizarrely awry

ONOMATOPOEIC VALUE FOR THE COPYWRITER

Onomatopoeia is a tongue-twister word whose definition is simpler than its pronunciation: a word whose sound when spoken parallels what the word is describing.

One of the most famous onomatopoeic inventions is the word *chortle*, coined by Charles Dodgson (Lewis Carroll) in the poem "Jabberwocky." *Chortle* sounds like what it is, and people who never heard of "Jabberwocky" know the word.

For the copywriter, finding an onomatopoeic word is a bonus which pays off in a doubled emotional impact. Many are one-syllable words with implicit emotional power.

True Onomatopoeia

A starter kit of onomatopoeic words:

boom	poof
burst	pop
buzz	power
crash	rock
fizz	rumble
gristle	scratch
growl	shriek
hiss	smack
luminous	smash
melt	spurt
muck	zipper

Manufactured Words

Some words are "manufactured" to represent an effect. These aren't onomatopoeic in the true sense, but we're copywriters, not philologists. Some of these manufactured words:

aargh	phooey
bam	slop
bash	slurp
blooper	smog
gack	ugh
glarp	whack
glop	wham
goof	yuck
gunk	zap
oof	

And Tomorrow We'll Have . . .

This is an elastic—and iconoclastic—chapter. Language evolves; today's innovations become tomorrow's clichés, and some of these concepts will flare like novas and then shrink into obsolescence.

As other rules for copywriting become accepted principles, the value of word-use knowledge will move out of the icy innards of the computer (which produced winners such as *Exxon*, losers such as *Citgo*, hopeless cases such as *Unisys* and *Allegis*, and puzzlers such as *Navistar*) and into the happy daylight of creative writing, as a standard space-age weapon.

This chapter is only a beginning, a minor foundation on which you'll build your own lists. Practice with words even when nobody is paying you to do it. That's the way to become a virtuoso of the keyboard.

5

How to Use "If," "Can," "Will," and Other Pitfalls

Which is more persuasive copy?

Why not see for yourself?

or

See for yourself.

How about these?

Shouldn't you cut down on your smoking, starting today?

or

Cut down on your smoking—starting today.

The answer may not please you: It depends.

Use a statement when you, the message source, take an expert or authoritarian position. The statement itself emphasizes: You know more than your message recipient. To accept a controverting opinion weakens your Olympian posture.

Use a question when you want to suggest the buyer has a choice. If you have great guts, drop all persuasion from the question.

When to Use Which Type of Question

The persuasion-dropping decision makes less message difference when you use conditional questions. Instead of "Why don't you . . ." the persuasion-dropper might phase through "Wouldn't you . . .," ending with "Would you. . . ."

In the hands of the writer playing Russian Roulette, "Shouldn't you . . .," "Won't you . . .," or "Can't you . . ." become "Should you . . .," "Will you . . .," or "Can you."

In my opinion, drop the negative inclusion ("n't") only when you're issuing a challenge or a dare. The danger lies in the reader asking a question of his own: "Who are you to confront me?"

"Can you do it?" unquestionably has power you'll never find in "Can't you do it?" Unquestionably, too, hurling down the gauntlet isn't a writing job for beginners. *Don't* do it when you want the reader to be a partner: "Wouldn't you really rather have a Buick?" works; "Would you really rather have a Buick?" suggests the opposite of the original intention.

In headlines and in "confrontational" broadcast commercials, don't ask questions to which the reader or viewer can answer, "No," unless you want a "No" (see Figure 5–2).

Questions have an implicit advantage: Their construction alone involves the target individual.

The "If" Peril

An "If . . ." situation is always precarious for the copywriter. Sometimes you'll want the conditional "Wouldn't you . . ." and sometimes the circumstance demands the direct challenge of "Would you. . . ." For example:

> If you were on a desert island and could have only one book as your companion, (wouldn't) (would) you want the book to be *The Bedside Companion*?

Automatic indicators point to *wouldn't*. But the super pro sees possibilities in *would*. Apply two rules of question asking:

1. **Don't ask a question which risks rejection by your best potential buyers.**
2. **Don't be afraid to shake up borderline prospective buyers by challenging them to make up their minds.**

The "If" peril extends beyond questions and *should/would*. Conditional statements are even more difficult to control than conditional questions. Some of the best uses I've seen lately are references to unpleasant situations over which the reader has no control: "If you're going to smoke, try Carltons"; "If you have to take a red-eye flight, make the best of it."

Would that last one be better as a question? "If you have to take a red-eye flight, why not make the best of it?"

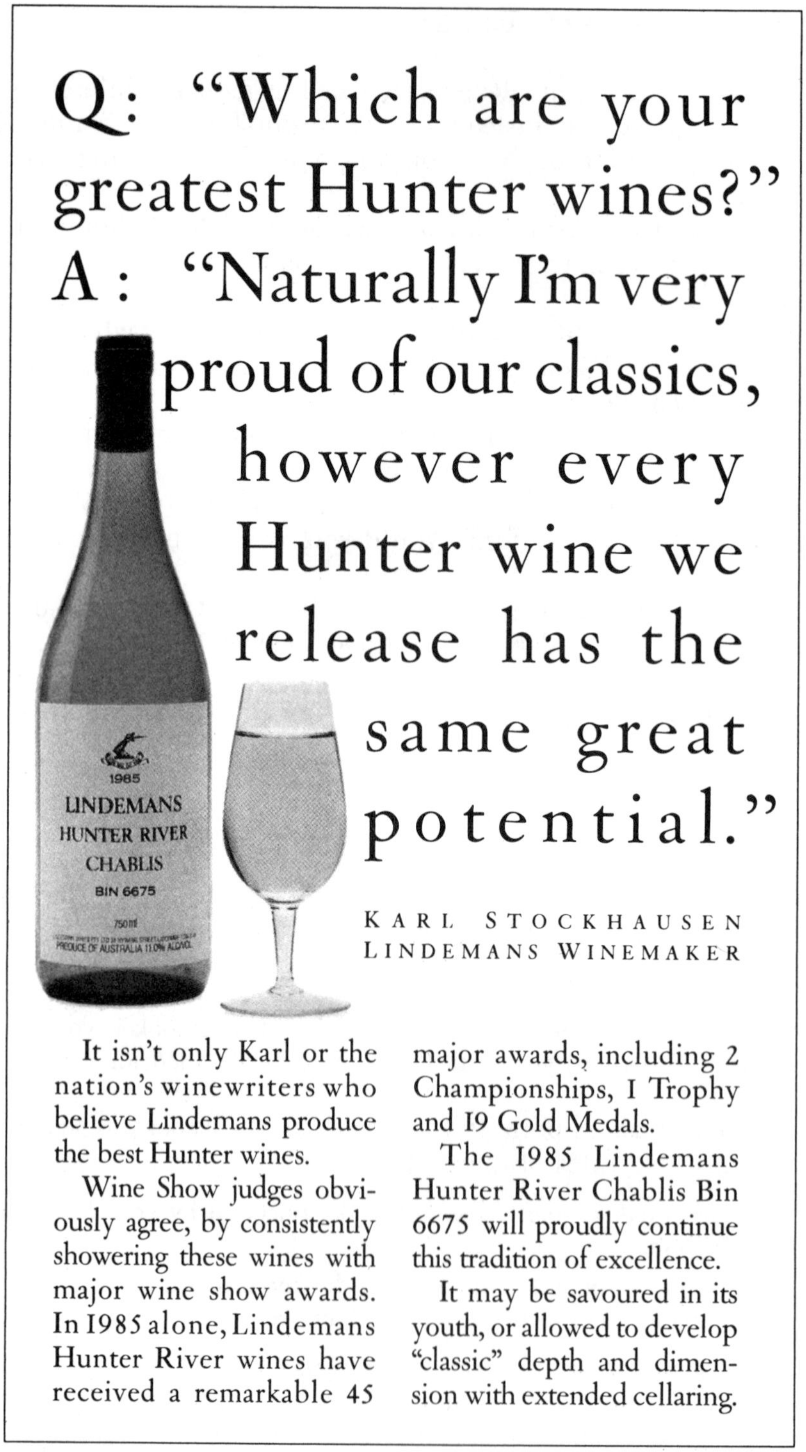
Q: "Which are your greatest Hunter wines?"
A: "Naturally I'm very proud of our classics, however every Hunter wine we release has the same great potential."
KARL STOCKHAUSEN
LINDEMANS WINEMAKER
1985
LINDEMANS
HUNTER RIVER
CHABLIS
BIN 6675
750ml
PRODUCE OF AUSTRALIA 11.0% ALCVOL
It isn't only Karl or the nation's winewriters who believe Lindemans produce the best Hunter wines.
Wine Show judges obviously agree, by consistently showering these wines with major wine show awards. In 1985 alone, Lindemans Hunter River wines have received a remarkable 45 major awards, including 2 Championships, 1 Trophy and 19 Gold Medals.
The 1985 Lindemans Hunter River Chablis Bin 6675 will proudly continue this tradition of excellence.
It may be savoured in its youth, or allowed to develop "classic" depth and dimension with extended cellaring.

FIGURE 5–1
Even a weak question such as this one spurs readership. Imagine how strong the ad would be if the question had some reader-interest.

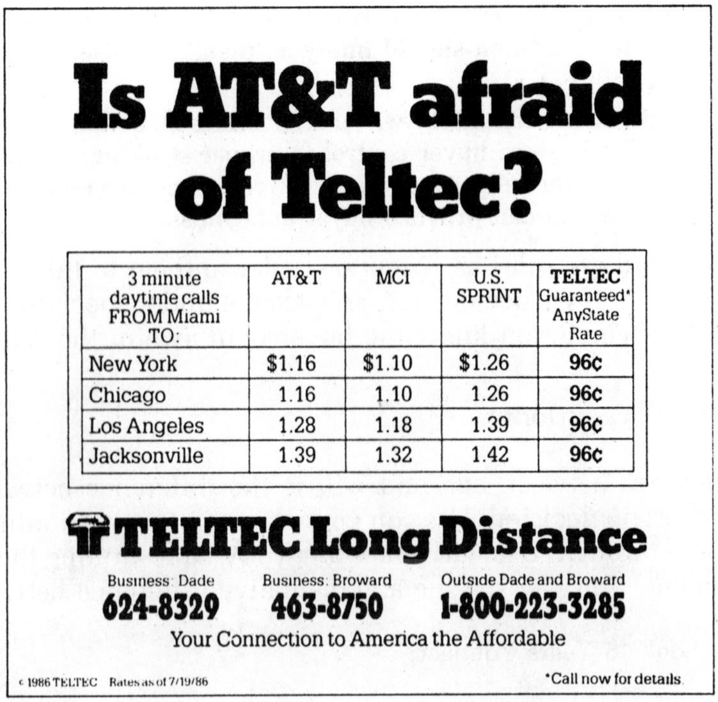

Is AT&T afraid of Teltec?

3 minute daytime calls FROM Miami TO:	AT&T	MCI	U.S. SPRINT	TELTEC Guaranteed* AnyState Rate
New York	$1.16	$1.10	$1.26	**96¢**
Chicago	1.16	1.10	1.26	**96¢**
Los Angeles	1.28	1.18	1.39	**96¢**
Jacksonville	1.39	1.32	1.42	**96¢**

☎ TELTEC Long Distance

Business: Dade	Business: Broward	Outside Dade and Broward
624-8329	**463-8750**	**1-800-223-3285**

Your Connection to America the Affordable

© 1986 TELTEC Rates as of 7/19/86   *Call now for details.

FIGURE 5–2
The question is ridiculous and doesn't mirror what the ad is about—comparative rates (see Chapter 9 on comparative advertising). MCI and U.S. Sprint also are compared in the chart, whose numbers clearly favor Teltec. Wouldn't a question referring to comparative rates have been more apt and less likely to breed a negative reader-reaction?

It's a toss-up; the question adds a little energy and the *why not* saps out a little energy.

This use of *if* in a headline damaged the impact:

If Mom Is Someone Special,
Give Her Something Special

Adding a condition to Mom's special place in our hearts adds a negative condition. Maybe she isn't so special. The writer has planted a doubt—almost subliminal, but why do it? The headline has better success without the *If*:

Mom Is Someone Special . . .
So Give Her Something Special

Dampening impact by using *if* phrases in or out of a question frame is a common writer mistake, even among professionals. We can apply two rules to make the *ifs* work for us.

   1. **The Principle of "If" Control:**
      An "If" condition should imply a "then" promise.
   2. **The "If" Subdecree:**
      Logic stands behind the writer who makes an action conditional for the buyer, since buyer control is proper stroking; but to give this control to the seller through an "If" reference suggests seller superiority, which can provoke buyer antagonism.

   If you regard these rules as obscure, condense them to this: "If you decide . . ." is permissible; "If we decide . . ." isn't, except under specialized "Key Club" circumstances in which you know the buyer is in awe of the seller.

"Can" and "Will" Questions

   The difference between *can* and *will* is the difference between uncertain ability and uncertain decision. Use *can you* when you're questioning the reader's ability to follow through. Use *will you* when you're questioning the reader's voluntary agreement. You can see the argumentative difference between

   Can You Look 15 Years Younger?

and

   Will You Look 15 Years Younger?

   When your copy refers to whatever you're selling, *will* is the better word. When your reference is to the prospective buyer, *can* might be the better word. Notice the qualifier—*might be*—which suggests you're usually safer with *will*.

Turning Statement Into Question

   The copywriter can turn any statement into a question. The question about this question-making technique: Why would you want to?
   Some writers claim they see greater strength in statement-turned-into-question than in straight question. The question

   Won't you try this new taste-experience?

becomes, as a statement-turned-into-question

   You'll try this new taste-experience—won't you?

   The argument in favor of statement-turned-into-question is obvious: The writer has the benefit of the imperative without risking target antagonisms. The sales message is dynamic, but the reader still has a sense of control.

My own reservation is the danger of pomposity. Statement-turned-into-question has an overtone of superciliousness, the superimposition of the writer's conclusion on the reader's conclusion.

If you can avoid statement/questions that carry these seeds of unease, then sure, go ahead. It's an advanced procedure, though, and I suggest mastering basic question asking before running the rapids of statement/questions.

THE WRITER AS MANIPULATOR

A question is a challenge. That's the blessing in it . . . and that's the danger in it. Do you want your reader, listener, or viewer to be challenged? Part of the answer to this question is implicit in the form I just used to make an argumentative point. I wrote, "Do we want our reader . . ." Why didn't I write "We want our reader . . ."?

Playing the game? You may have glossed over the last couple of questions because you now accept the challenge. If you *did* recognize what I was doing—involving you not in one question but in a series of questions I admit are a series of challenges—you probably aren't a good prospect for this kind of advertising.

But a lot of people are.

To the writer who's stumped for a copy approach, being able to ask a question can be as beneficial as a hip replacement. A mechanical technique that not only is respectable but has force in its very format is superior to almost any crutch.

So practice question asking. It's a technique you should know. After all, asking questions worked for Socrates. There's no reason it won't work for you—is there?

6

The Pros and Cons
of Comparative Copy

UNEXPLAINED COMPARATIVES:
DON'T USE THEM

The complete copy for a television commercial:

Brown's Fried Chicken. It tastes better.

Give that writer a C-minus. Brown's Fried Chicken tastes better than what? Other fried chicken? In that case, *which* other fried chicken? The thinness of this copy becomes apparent when (as an exercise) you complete the unexplained comparative:

Brown's Fried Chicken. It tastes better than Kentucky Fried.

With this second version the writer now gives us "desperation" copy, an unproved comparison showing neither imagination nor salesmanship. *How* does Brown's taste better than Kentucky Fried? Do research findings support taster preference? If Kentucky Fried sues us, what evidence can we bring to court?

Still, the specific comparison with Kentucky Fried is better than "It tastes better," a line of copy of which no copywriter should be proud. If accompanied by evidence (a chart, a taste-test report, photographs or videotapes of people tasting the two and saying, "This one!") within the ad, the comparison gets some muscles on its bony frame.

A detergent advertises itself with limp-wristed self-puffery:

It gets clothes whiter.

You rate higher at SFB.

With personal attention and south Florida's best interest rates on our Money Builder money market account.

7.30% RATE

7.57% ANNUAL YIELD

$2500 minimum deposit required.

Here's the account that tops them all: the SFB Money Builder. Which consistently pays Florida's highest interest rates.

The SFB Money Builder offers you total liquidity. Plus insured safety. All for a low minimum balance of just $2500.

So stop by the SFB branch office nearest you. And make your move to the top money market account in Florida.

All accounts insured to $100,000 by FSLIC. Rates are subject to change without notice.

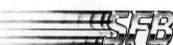

Southern Floridabanc Savings Association

Moving people and banking closer together.

RIVIERA BEACH:
1217 East Blue Heron Boulevard, 845-1000
BOCA RATON:
160 West Camino Real, 368-0905
TAMARAC:
5100 West Commercial Boulevard, Sabal Palm Plaza, 733-2100

PALM BEACH GARDENS:
1963 PGA Boulevard (West of U.S. 1), 627-2500
LEHIGH ACRES:
1177-1179 Homestead Road (Sunshine Shopping Center), 369-6137
SARASOTA:
240 Southgate Shopping Center, 952-0530
DELRAY BEACH:
4965 West Atlantic Avenue, Delray Square, 496-0500

VENICE:
2077 South Tamiami Trail, Galleria Plaza (U.S. 41 in South Venice), 493-1866
BRADENTON:
5717 A Manatee Avenue West, Palma Sola Plaza (At 59th Street), 792-6703
DEERFIELD BEACH:
1880 (A) West Hillsboro Boulevard, 428-8200

97

FIGURE 6–1

The comparative headline says, "You rate higher at SFB." Higher than what? The unexplained comparative is punchless and without substance. (While we're at it, the illustration is nonsensical too.) Buried in the copy are seeds for a logical comparative headline.

If you don't have a Hercules Graphics Card, you could end up looking like this:

"I know, because one day it happened to me...

"I was running some routine tests on a non-Hercules monochrome graphics card when I was struck by a severe case of *low resolutionitis*. I'm the president of Hercules and that's me exhibiting the symptoms of the disease in its advanced stages. Not a pretty sight, is it?

"What causes *low resolutionitis?* Experts point to ordinary monochrome graphics cards with coarse, hard-to-read graphics. A bad case of eyestrain may develop if action is not taken immediately.

"Fortunately for me, a Hercules Graphics Card was nearby. A quick change brought soothing 720 x 348 graphics. That's twice the resolution of ordinary 640 x 200 graphics cards.

"Which means better graphics for Lotus™ 1-2-3™ Symphony™ Framework™ pfs:Graph; Microsoft® Chart and Word, SuperCalc3; AutoCad™ and dozens of other programs.

"Including Microsoft Flight Simulator, now Hercules compatible!

"Oh, and don't forget that a parallel printer port is standard on the Hercules Graphics Card, not an extra cost option.

"Now, if you're worried about buying a new product that hasn't had all the bugs worked out, relax. Hercules has sold more monochrome graphics cards for the IBM® PC,XT™ and AT™ than anyone else in the world.

"So...you're convinced that you should buy a Hercules Graphics Card. Now, steer clear of cheap imitations. You may save a few bucks, but you won't get all of these five essential features which only Hercules has:

"1) A safety switch that helps prevent damage to your monitor, 2) the ability to keep an IBM or Hercules Color Card in your system, 3) the ability to use the PC's BASIC to do graphics, 4) a Hercules designed chip that eliminates 30% of the parts that can go wrong, and 5) a two year warranty, because we think reliability is something you should deliver and not just talk about."

Call **1-800-532-0600 Ext 401** for the name of the Hercules dealer nearest you and we'll rush you our free info kit.

Hercules.
We're strong on graphics.

Address: 2550 Ninth St., Berkeley, CA 94710 Ph: 540-6000 Telex: 754063   **Trademark/Owners:** Hercules/Hercules Computer Tech; IBM,XT,AT/IBM; Lotus 1-2-3, Symphony/Lotus Development; Framework/Ashton-Tate; Microsoft/Microsoft; pfs:Graph/Software Publishing; SuperCalc 3/Sorcim-IUS; AutoCad/AutoDesk.

Circle 77 on reader service card

Why the Hercules Color Card is better for your XT than IBM's.

Did you know that there's a color graphics card specially designed for the XT™? It's called the Hercules™ Color Card. We think that it's better for your XT than the IBM® Color Graphics Adapter. Here's why.

The XT comes with an empty short slot. IBM's card is too long to fit in it, so you're forced to sacrifice a valuable long slot, while your XT's short slot goes unused.

The Hercules Color Card is designed to fit in this short slot. It's the smartest way to maximize the usable slots in an XT and provide for your future expansion needs.

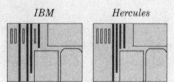

IBM   *Hercules*

Notice how much more efficiently Hercules makes use of the XT's slots.

Our efficient use of an XT's slots is not the only reason to buy a Hercules Color Card instead of IBM's. We give you a parallel printer port at no extra cost. (IBM charges extra and takes up another slot.)

A lot of people wonder how Hercules can do everything that IBM can in a card less than half the size. We do it by designing our own graphics microchips. Just one of our chips packs the punch of dozens of IBM's, reducing by more than 50% the number of components that can fail.

And we'll do just about anything to make our products the most reliable you can buy.

Hercules   *IBM*

Of course, you *will* have to give up something when you buy a Hercules Color Card. You'll have to give up software incompatibility. With Hercules, there is none. Every program that runs on the IBM color card will run on the Hercules Color Card.

You'll have to give up IBM's ninety day warranty. Ours is two years.

	Compare warranties
IBM	▬ 3 months
Hercules	▬▬▬▬▬▬▬ 2 years

And you'll have to give up a dollar. The Hercules Color Card is $245—IBM's is $244.

Look into the Hercules Color Card for the XT, PC or AT™ Find out why the readers of *PC World* voted the Hercules Color Card 1985's best color graphics card—ahead of IBM's. Call **1 800 532-0600 Ext. 421** for the name of the dealer nearest you and we'll rush you our free info kit.

Hercules.
We're strong on graphics.

FIGURES 6–2 and 6–3
Here are two ads by Hercules. The first ad is a "negative comparison," one of the weakest crutches in advertising. The second ad is a hard-hitting comparative attack on IBM. Which ad is (a) the most inviting to read? (b) the ad you think will give you the most information? (c) the ad most likely to stimulate orders?

Years ago one competitor in Detergent Murderers' Row advertised itself as getting clothes "whiter than white," which, however nonsensical the claim, still drew a word image. But "gets clothes whiter" draws none. Whiter than what? Whiter than green? If it's whiter than the white this same product used to get clothes, say so. It's a sales point. If it's whiter than specific competitors, say so. It's an even better sales point, but be prepared to back up your claim with evidence.

THE POWER OF COMPARATIVE ADVERTISING

Comparative advertising can bring a weak advertising campaign to life. It can make one of the pack an instant contender.

The Comparative Imperative

A challenger can leap to the attack; the leader, by joining the battle, acknowledges the challenge—and in doing so tarnishes his leadership.

We formulate the Comparative Imperative:

Good marketing strategy calls for Brand No. 2 to shout superiority over Brand No. 1; good marketing strategy calls for Brand No. 1 to shout superiority over all others without singling out any one of them.

The best demonstration of the Comparative Imperative is politics. Usually the incumbent is favored; a head-to-head debate has to help the other candidate through increased visibility and—by the very nature of a one-on-one debate—*admission by the incumbent that another candidate exists.*

Avis can attack Hertz, but Hertz, from its Olympian number one position, is better off ignoring the gauntlet thrown at its feet. It made sense for Toyota to join the competitive attack on Volkswagen when VW was the leading import car, but once Toyota ascended the throne the brickbats by competitors, now including Volkswagen, were reaimed at the new leader. It makes sense for a challenging politician to attack the incumbent and militate for a debate, but the incumbent seldom can benefit from entering the debate arena.

How to Attack with This Mighty Weapon

Comparative advertising, like eye makeup and lipstick, is a concept once considered obscene, then an indication of being not-quite-nice, then a novelty, then an accepted practice, then essential.

Effective comparative advertising, like most effective advertising, is specific. Raw claims of superiority not only have little impact; they're what the consumer expects an advertiser to say in the Age of Skepticism.

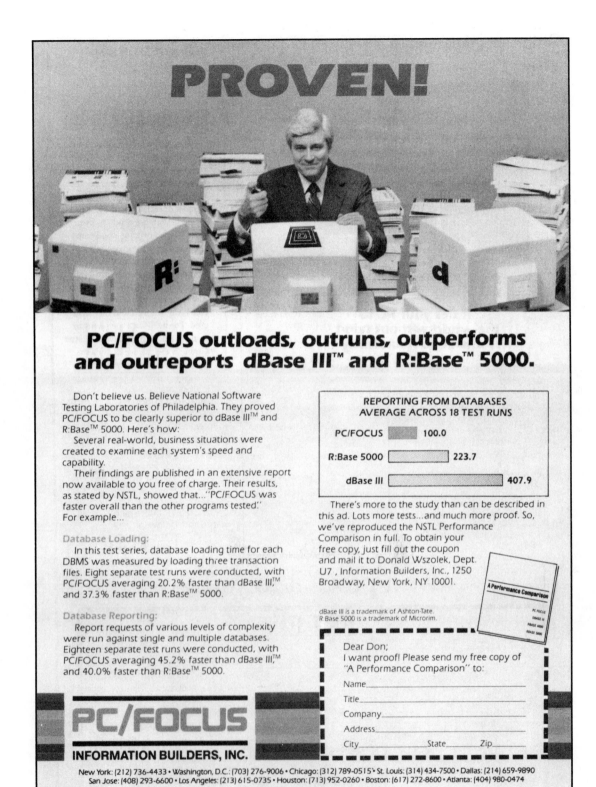
FIGURE 6–4
The word "Proven" is soft, but the sales argument is hard. The bar chart seems to be a convincing piece of comparative evidence, even if its numbers aren't explained (they should have been). As examples in this section will show, comparative advertising is a popular and effective technique among computer and computer-allied manufacturers.

WARNING:

Buying a CD for retirement could be a very costly mistake!

It's true! If you are saving for retirement in a certificate of deposit or a money market account . . . you may actually be *losing* money! That's because you must pay taxes on the interest you earn . . . as you receive it . . . year after year.

But there *is* a money-saving solution.

It's Sun Life's no-load annuity. It allows for a greater cash accumulation because your interest is *tax-deferred* and it provides you with valuable options for lifetime income.

To prove our point, we'd like to send you a *free* personalized Financial Comparison Illustration. It will show you why our no-load, tax-deferred Certificate of Annuity offers you important advantages for your future in comparison to a Certificate of Deposit.

Get these valuable guarantees from Sun Life:

- $ 10% current interest* guaranteed for 10 years.
- $ Your choice of 3 . . . 5 . . . or 10 year guaranteed interest periods.

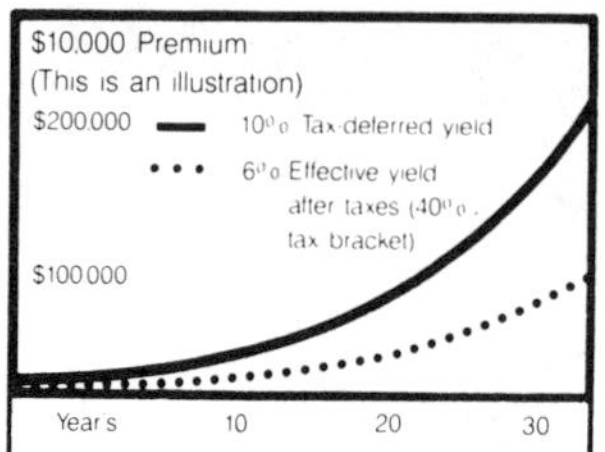

Tax-deferred interest means *more* for you!

If you currently own a 10% taxable certificate of deposit, you may have *thought* you were earning a full 10% interest. But, remember, if you're in a 40% tax bracket 10% actually pays you only 6% net! This illustration shows a major advantage of a deferred annuity. You accumulate more money because your taxes are deferred until payments are made to you. This larger cash accumulation is the source of more retirement benefits for you. Note that even if the entire balance were withdrawn from the annuity at the end of 30 years, you would have $92,247 after taxes (assuming a 50% tax bracket), so you would still have an advantage of $34,812. This is a hypothetical illustration only. Sun Life guarantees 4% for the life of the contract. Current interest rates for initial periods are higher.

- $ Your choice of pay-out options — including a tax-favored guaranteed income *you can never outlive.*
- $ You can get started for as little as $2,500.
- $ *No taxes* until payments are made to you.
- $ Security and safety guaranteed by Sun Life.
- $ NO-LOAD — No commissions or fees of any kind are deducted. *All* your money works for you.

Act now for FREE information!

Get all the facts right now by mailing the coupon below. Or, for fastest action, call toll-free **1-800-841-8000**. We'll send you your specially-prepared Financial Comparison Illustration and free information on our no-load Certificate of Annuity!

So why buy a CD when you can have the advantages of a Certificate of Annuity? Act today!

For FREE information, mail coupon below or call:

TOLL-FREE
1-800-841-8000
ANYTIME!

*As of 1/1/86

We'll prove it to you...

FREE!

☐ **YES!** Show me the advantages of your tax-deferred annuity vs. Certificates of Deposit!

Please prepare a personalized Financial Comparison Illustration based on the information I have specified below. I understand that there is no cost or obligation for this information.

Comparison Amount:

☐ $ 2,500 ☐ $10,000
☐ $25,000 ☐ Other $ ________

Currently available rates for Initial Guaranteed Interest Periods:

☐ 3 years at 9% ☐ 5 years at 9.5% ☐ 10 years at 10%

Not available in all states. Rates subject to change.

Name ____________________
First Middle Initial Last

Street ____________________

City __________ State _____ Zip _____

Date of Birth ____________________
Month Day Year

Phone (   ) ____________________
Area Code

Mail to: Sun Financial Services Division
343 Willowbrook Lane
West Chester, PA 19382

Sun Life Insurance Company of America

MD

FIGURE 6–5
This comparative ad damns generic competition in its headline, then waits until the reader, curiosity piqued, plows into the body copy to make its point. Although the ad is visually unattractive and hard to read, the technique is logical: Copy is aimed at those considering a CD. When the target is so specific, a "warning" approach has merit.

STYLE.

STYLE AND SUBSTANCE.

The differences between the Citibank Preferred® Visa card and the other card that happens to be pictured here are, in a word, substantial.

To start, we offer a credit line of $5,000 to $50,000.* Their minimum is $2,000.** And our card is accepted in about 4 times as many places as theirs. From restaurants to resorts, on business trips or pleasure trips, it's always the right card in the right place.

What's more, the Citibank Preferred Visa card gives you immediate access to twice as many cash machines. At bank branches, shopping centers, and major airports.

You also have the advantage of Citibank's 24-hour, toll-free Customer Service. And, if you need additional cards, you can get them at substantial savings. Free. American Express Gold charges you an extra $30 for each additional card.

Also, every time you use our card for purchases, you'll earn CitiDollar$® Bonuses good for valuable discounts on brand-name merchandise, from the truly extravagant to the downright practical.

No other card gives you as much. Not some other bank's premium card. Not American Express® Gold, despite their fancy annual fee.

If your household income is at least $35,000, fill in the application and mail it today.

Everyone can use a touch of style. But there's no substitute for substance.

CITIBANK⊕®
A CITICORP COMPANY

THE CARD TO END ALL CARDS.

FIGURE 6–6
Here we have an elegant and commanding comparative ad. Piling all the body copy under the Citibank VISA card is a master stroke; and the copy itself is specific and vigorous. The asterisks weren't necessary, and the negative reaction they create could have been avoided easily, by integrating the qualifiers into the text (see Chapter 23). Altogether, though, a stunning comparative ad.

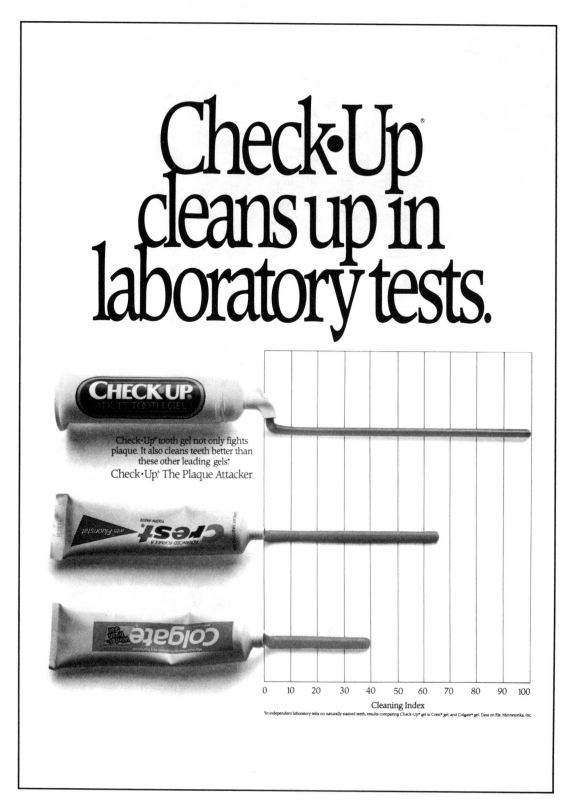

FIGURE 6–7
Whatever the "Cleaning Index" is, this ad presents the evidence effectively and
forcefully. Using the toothpaste dispensers themselves for the comparatives is an
inspired and memorable idea.

Why Specifics Outpull Generalities

Comparative advertising, to be effective, has to be based on *fact*. Fact can come from research, from product testing, or—and this is one source the creative thinker can explore without technical help—from opinions of others who, originally undecided, bought what you're selling.

Opinion becomes fact if it appears to be epidemic. A good copywriter can make it so.

Is it better to name the competitor or to cavil with "The Number One Brand" ("Zilch Beer has 20 percent fewer calories than the best-selling beer")?

In my opinion—excluding another weakness in this example, using percentage instead of actual numbers—it's no ball game. Attacking a generalization doesn't have any wallop; instead, the ad becomes a public admission that another beer is more popular, a better seller. No! "Zilch Beer has 20 percent fewer calories than Belch Beer!" If you really want to put steam into the argument, specify the number of calories.

HOW TO KILL THE COMPETITION
WHEN YOU DON'T HAVE SUPPORTING FACTS

Let's approach the marketing problem through the eyes of a copywriter who doesn't have implicit ammunition. Zilch Beer *doesn't* have 20 percent fewer calories. Obviously it doesn't sell as well as Belch. What can the writer do?

Easy. He moves to Position "B" and creates a comparative ad in which opinion becomes fact because it seems to be epidemic:

Does Zilch Beer taste better than Belch Beer?
These beer drinkers think so!

—"I used to drink Belch but no more. Not since I tasted Zilch, the New Brew!" (Larry Smith, Pottstown)

—"I've tried them both and I choose Zilch!" (Harry Jones, Springfield)

—"Zilch or Belch? My friends drink Zilch!" (Mary Brown, Center City)

If the ad has a dozen more of these, its space is crammed with endorsements of Zilch. In a broadcast campaign it's just as uncomplicated.

ANNOUNCER: Here's praise for Zilch Beer number six-hundred-and-sixty-two.

SMITH: I'm Larry Smith from Pottstown. I used to drink Belch Beer, but no more. Not since I tasted Zilch, the New Brew.

Caution: You'd better have an actual Larry Smith and have his signature verifying that he used to drink Belch. Fiction doesn't enhance the noble cause of advertising. (Fortunately, romance does.)

Want ultimate power? Whack the better-known competitor over the head with its own market position: "The Grunge power-press became a best-seller, and it only has two ball bearings; Sludge has four. Which one should *you* buy?"

HOW TO MAKE OUR CAR STEREO AS GOOD AS A PIONEER.

Over the years, Pioneer has built a reputation for building quality car stereos. So what does it take to make the Sparkomatic SR-315 car stereo every bit as good as Pioneer's top-of-the-line, KE-A880?

First, you have to cut Sparkomatic's power from 30 watts down to Pioneer's 20 watts.* And in the process cut Sparkomatic's full, rich sound by one-third.

Then, you have to remove our highly intelligent brain. This microprocessor does a lot of the work you used to do. So you can keep your mind where it belongs. On the road.

Next, remove our Tape Scan, Blank Skip and Repeat. Three features that let you spend less time playing with your car stereo and more time listening to your music.

You'll also take out our Dolby C and our Dynamic Noise Reduction System. Those two systems help eliminate unwanted noise. So all you're left with is clean, clear music.

The choice is yours. Pay more‡ for Pioneer's top-of-the-line car stereo and get many of the features you'd like.

Or pay less for Sparkomatic's SR-315 and get all of them.

For a free brochure and the name of your nearest Sparkomatic dealer, write to Sparkomatic Corporation, Milford, PA 18337. Or call 1-800-233-8837 (in PA, 1-800-592-8891).

SPARKOMATIC.®
THE MOST MUSIC YOU CAN FIT IN A CAR.™

*Pioneer is a registered trademark. Ad hoc power ratings are through 2 speakers into 4 ohms at 5% THD. All Pioneer data from Pioneer 1985 catalog. ‡Based on manufacturers' suggested retail price. Dolby is a registered trade-mark of Dolby Laboratories, Inc. Dynamic Noise Reduction (DNR) is a registered trademark of National Semiconductor Corporation. Sparkomatic Corp. Milford, PA. 18337

106

FIGURE 6–8

Sparkomatic's attack on Pioneer is innovative and breathtakingly dangerous. If the casual skimmer thinks Sparkomatic is a half-finished mess of wires and parts, the ad fails. If, though, the reader gets the idea—that the way to make this car stereo parallel to Pioneer is to take half the guts out of it—the ad is a striking success. Opinion: Placed in media whose readership regards car stereos with reverence, this ad should be a winner.

SAME DAY DELIVERY. VS. THE SAME OLD STORY.

"It'll be there today."

"Absolutely, positively ...uh...tomorrow morning."

Fresh Air Courier

FEDERAL EXPRESS

INTRODUCING FRESH AIR DELIVERY.™ SAME-DAY SERVICE VIA THE EASTERN AIR-SHUTTLE® FOR SMALL PACKAGES.

When you're shipping small packages, some companies will promise you the world.

But they can't promise it today, like Fresh Air Delivery™ can.

It's a new service for packages weighing from two pounds up to 70 pounds. And it operates on the schedule of the Eastern Air-Shuttle®

That means you get same-day delivery—door-to-door, when you're shipping a package between New York, Boston and Washington, DC.

What's more, Fresh Air

not only takes your packages places, it takes you places. And that's because every time you ship with us, you'll earn Free Fare Bucks (FFB's). Save up enough FFB's and you can swing a free round-trip ticket to practically any place Eastern Airlines flies.

For details or a pickup, call Fresh Air at 1-800-AIR-2-DAY. In New York, (212) 397-9009. Because now you have a choice. Same-day delivery from Fresh Air.

Or the same old story from *them*.

Fresh Air Courier

FIGURE 6–9

As an introductory ad, this has two deficiencies:
First, the company name is curiously underplayed. That's the easy one. But second, in its attack on Federal Express, the ad buried deep in its body copy a point any shipper would anticipate: The service exists only between New York, Boston, and Washington. Should the advertiser have used such a direct attack? Or would an overline with the words "Between New York, Boston, and Washington . . ." have strengthened and clarified the factual core mandatory for every comparative attack? I vote for the change, which wouldn't have some readers muttering, "I thought so," when they hit the qualifier in the body copy.

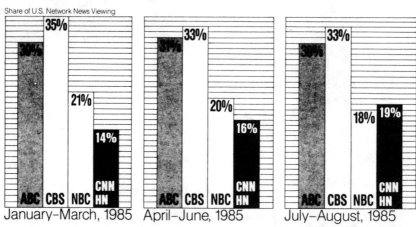

108

FIGURE 6–10
This ad ran in advertising publications a few years ago. Notice that although CNN and Headline News is still far from dominant, the share of news viewing constantly moves up, while the other three are static or dropping. Body copy doesn't rest on the statistics but adds comments such as, "What's more, the CNN/Headline News audience is more upscale and influential . . ."—unsupported by evidence but acceptable to the reader because the claims appear adjacent to verified ratings reports.

WHO EVER HEARD OF A FORBES 500s COMPANY?

Or a Business Week Corporate Scoreboard company? The only companies people talk about are FORTUNE 500 companies—both in the industrial and service sectors of the economy. If you want people to talk about your company, avoid pale imitations. Advertise in the one magazine that offers its readers original ideas.

FORTUNE
REQUIRED READING FOR THE BUSINESS CLASS.

FIGURE 6–11
Fortune attacks Forbes with an unusually readable ad. The ad offers no statistical base, nor should it. The "Fortune 500" is so thoroughly established that choosing it for the comparative attack is unassailable, regardless of any surveys, readership studies, or circulation figures other publications might bring to the arena.

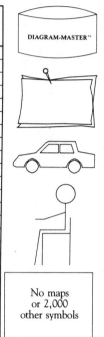
FIGURE 6–12

One problem with this comparative ad: In its direct attack on Diagram-Master (in the best tradition of comparative advertising), Diagraph doesn't play up its own name enough. The ad should have been signed something like this:

DIAGRAPH
the high-resolution, multisymbol program from
Computer Support Corporation
[ADDRESS]

This becomes more imperative when the reader sees that after an unbroken list of "Yes" answers, the price is higher than the competition.

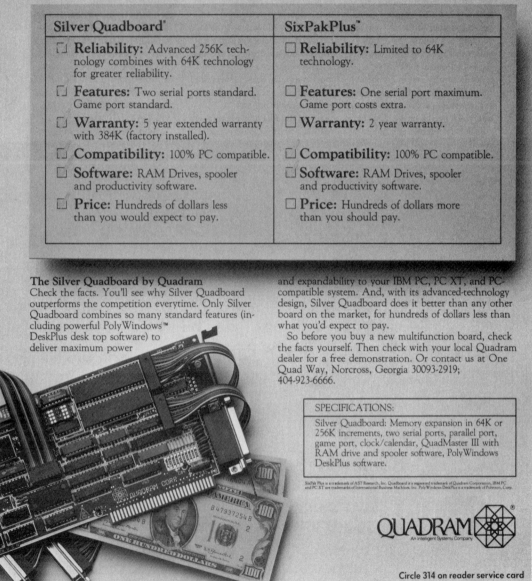

111

FIGURE 6–13
Quadram compares itself in the headline with AST; but the actual comparison is between Silver Quadboard and SixPakPlus. Why didn't this advertiser either add "Quadram" and "AST" to the various sides of the text comparison, or change the headline to product rather than company? No comparison can be completely effective if it ignores the Clarity Commandment.

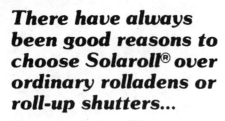
112

FIGURE 6–14
This comparative ad tells us it has the facts, but it doesn't bother to give us even one. Rather, it asks us to call for a catalog. Instead of cheating the reader, this advertiser should share some of his comparative advantages if he wants the reader to get excited enough to call.

The View from Olympus—Call in the Engineers

Often you do have technical ammunition you can aim at not only one competitor but many, or even all. The gap between technicians and marketers often bears the blame for not using this ammunition, or even knowing where it's buried.

In a casual conversation with a technician working for the same company, a writer may hear, "I don't know why we can't bury them in the marketplace. Our computer makes every other AT clone, including the AT itself, seem like a snail." It's the first time the writer has even heard that his company's computer is the fastest. When he pursues the point, the technician drags some test results out of his desk, surprised that anyone is even interested in the specifics of the claim.

In major industries, availability of comparative statistical evidence is not only common; it's doggedly pursued. In a smaller or more local situation, somebody has to prime the comparative pump, as the advertiser in Figure 6–15 has done.

HOW TO REPLACE BLANKS WITH CANNONBALLS

Are you the copywriter whose gun seems to be loaded with blanks? If so, pushing for an answer to the question, "Why is what we're selling better than any competitor's?" can make you a hero. Example: An ad for a word processing program has this unimaginative, pedestrian heading:

volkswriter <u>3</u>
the word processing program
you won't outgrow

The text of the ad isn't powerful; competitive references are casual and unspecific:

Lifetree believes you shouldn't have to sacrifice important features for simplicity's sake. Because sooner or later you'll wish your program could keep pace with your needs. And when that happens you'll wish you had purchased the new <u>Volkswriter 3</u>.

Boxed, in the middle of the ad, is a direct comparison which justifies the otherwise limp rhetoric (including the partial sentence, that ghastly word *needs*, and the use of *purchase* instead of *buy*):

	Volkswriter 3	*PfsiWrite*	*Easy*
Spells and hyphenates	Yes	No	No
Mini-spreadsheet	Yes	No	No
Style sheets	Yes	No	No
Sorts	Yes	No	No
Personalized mailings	Yes	No	No

FIGURE 6–15
This ad, comparing Bondstrand with a generic—steel—is full of specifics, as it must be to convince the reader. Instead of crowing, "We're better," the ad explains, calmly and specifically, the weight and strength benefits of this pipe.

Notice two techniques of effective comparative advertising.

1. The advertiser picks the elements he wants to compare. It's his ad, and even though the other word processing programs may have dominance in other areas, he theorizes, quite rightly, "I'm paying for this ad; if they want to tout their benefits let them do it in their own ads" (See Figure 6–16.)

Not all comparative ads are so absolute. An absolute claim can breed reader hostility and skepticism, so (especially in a list longer than this one) the advertiser feels safe as long as he has more "Yeses" in his list than any competitor does. Showing an occasional Achilles' heel, in a feature no buyer would regard as important, helps overcome skepticism because it enhances verisimilitude . . . all without danger to salesmanship.

2. The advertiser picks the competitors with whom he wants to make a comparison. Do WordPerfect or Xywrite compete on better terms? Maybe, but once again the company paying for the ad can make any comparisons it wants to.

Damning *all* the competition doesn't require copywriting talent. Damning all the competition *effectively* does.

An ad in an inflight magazine tries this approach:

We Apologize to Everyone
On This Plane Who Just Bought
A New Garment Bag.

Body copy begins:

Because your new bag just became obsolete. Now introducing the System 4 Valet Garment Bag. . . .

I'd have preferred a more energetic approach, just as effortless to write:

To Anyone On This Plane
Who Just Bought a New Garment Bag:
Too Bad.

My body copy would have put the sales argument in a more direct line with the ad's intention. As written, the copy loses impact because it says the other new bag *just* became obsolete. My replacement:

If you'd waited until you read this magazine, you wouldn't have bought a garment bag that was obsolete the moment you bought it . . .

Comparative advertising can rescue a flat or unconvincing ad. In capable hands, it can be a grenade, not only shattering or at least damaging a competitor but, more to the point, gathering benefit from the damage.

HOW DO YOU FIGHT BACK
IF YOU'RE NUMBER ONE?

What can the top dog, under constant attack, do to counterattack? Easy. The most powerful battering ram in the communications universe is lying at his feet, ready for use when he feels statesmanship has run its course.

Ridicule.

If you use this potent club, don't swing it wildly at individual competitors; that drops you onto the dusty floor of the comparative arena, where you don't belong. Instead, ridicule competitors as a group. If you run a "Comparative Features" ad, the comparison should be with as many parallel products as you can cram into the space.

Singling out a single competitor is a "You're another" tactic, an admission you've been stung. Even if it's only one company whose sniping is eroding your share of total market, don't abandon your superior position to scrabble around in the dust. Your ridicule should remain generic, and this is one of the few aspects of advertising in which specificity—at least, the specificity of your target—may not be the best course.

The Burger Wars:
Comparative Advertising at Its Most Shrill

McDonald's is the traditional number one marketer in fast foods, so it's natural for this sophisticated advertiser to bypass comparative advertising.

Burger King and Wendy's are contenders, so it's natural for their advertising to be aggressively comparative.

McDonald's president Michael Quinlan was quoted in *Advertising Age* in 1986, attacking "those people in our industry who have espoused comparative advertising that takes a denigrating tone."

As might be expected from the front-runner, Mr. Quinlan said, "If the best my marketing department could do is tear down [a competitor] I'd get a new marketing department." Mr. Quinlan concluded, "It's not good for the industry as a whole."

The obvious reference was to a current $30 million Burger King campaign promoting the company's Chicken Tenders as superior to "chicken nuggets." Burger King president Jay Darling replied as a pugnacious competitor should: "Our Chicken Tenders ads say they're real chicken cooked in vegetable shortening. I don't think that damages the industry, just as I don't think our 'broiling versus frying' advertising damaged the industry."

The two comments underscore an unlikely, but possible, danger in comparative advertising: If the arguments become shrill, suggesting an intramural squabble, the public has every right to say, "A plague on both your houses."

If you write comparative ads, stick to the subject—the superiority of what you're selling—not the inferiority of your competitor. (One exception is exemplified in Figure 6–18.)

117

FIGURE 6–16
Accepting no competitors as equals, this ad looks down on all of them—an implicit claim to being number 1. A factual reason validates the claim.

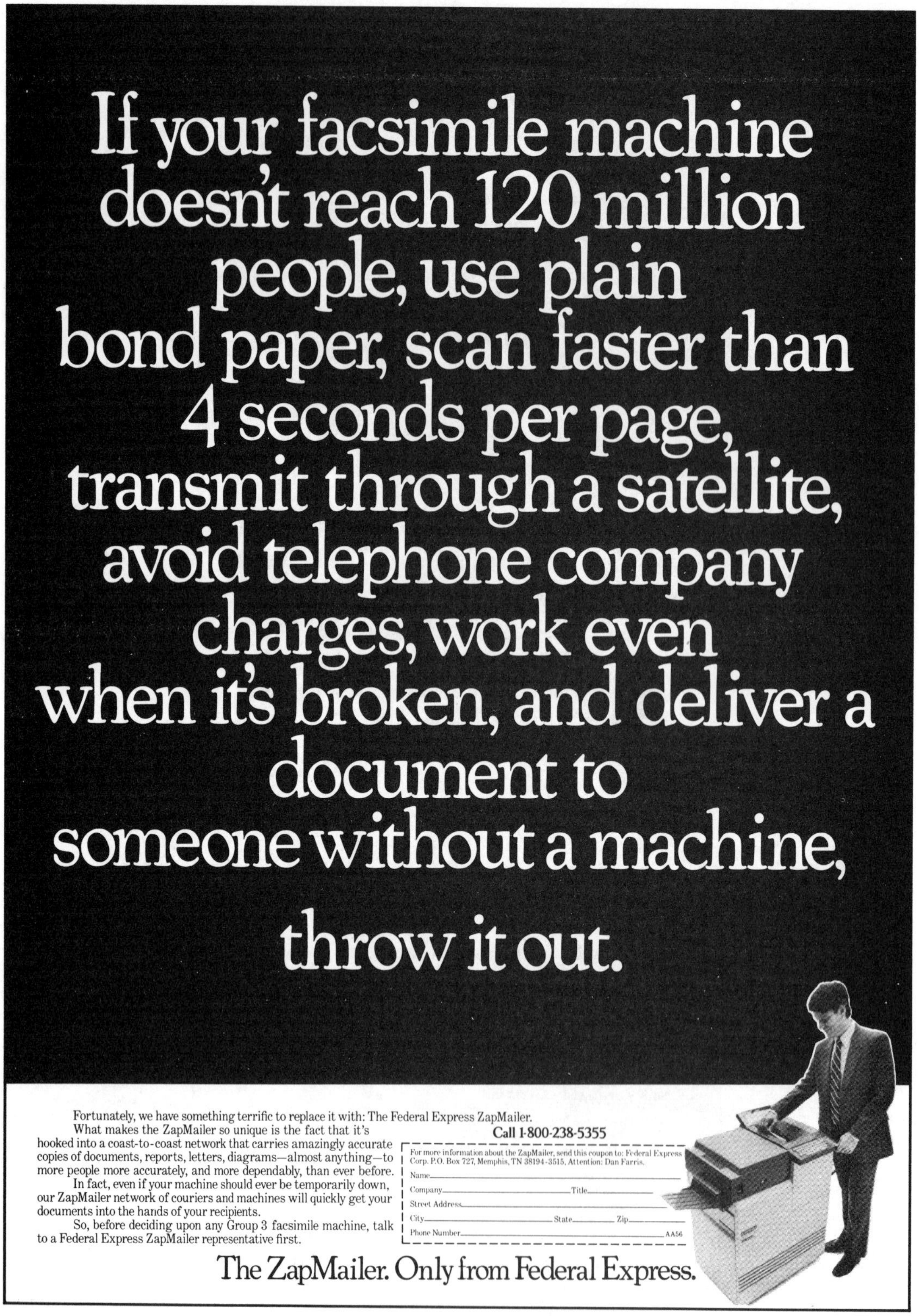

FIGURE 6–17
Federal Express eliminates every type of competition with this ad for its ZapMailer. Whoever wrote this might have written a straight claim of superiority or listed the benefits of a ZapMailer. And maybe that's what the writer should have done for a service whose purpose few potential users understood. ZapMail never caught on, and the company dropped the idea after losing many millions of dollars.

119

FIGURE 6–18
Atari comes out swinging with an ad that doesn't just claim price advantage; it claims its three biggest competitors have overpriced their computers. Shrill? Yes. Potent? Yes. Dignified? When you're fighting for your life, does dignity matter?

HOW TO WRITE "PARITY" ADVERTISING

Parity advertising is copy which seems to claim superiority but actually states only parity—"We're as good as they are."

The hopeless cliché, "If you can find a better [WHATEVER], buy it," is *inverted* parity advertising, challenging a competitor to prove superiority but claiming only equivalence. True parity advertising usually begins with the word "No":

No bank pays higher interest.
No other cereal has more vitamin C.
No detergent, dry or liquid, gets clothes whiter.

Analyze these claims. Each one claims equivalence, not superiority. A knowledgeable copywriter won't strut and preen over parity advertising, but the technique is serviceable when you're advertising against competitors whose offers vary only fractionally from yours.

Lumping a group of parities results in a realistic image of superiority:

No other bank pays higher interest. No other bank gives you more free services, such as traveler's checks and free foreign currency exchange. No bank is open longer hours. Ask yourself: Shouldn't *I* bank at the First National?

Add in *even one* genuine claim of superiority, however minor, and the whole message becomes an unrivaled claim:

No other bank pays higher interest. No other bank gives you more free services, such as traveler's checks and free foreign currency exchange. No bank is open longer hours. And—get this—no other bank gives you an hour's free downtown parking every time you come in. Ask yourself: Shouldn't *I* bank at the First National?

In this type of mix, the benefit of putting the single absolute, unrivaled claim at the end is its reflection on the whole statement. Placing "free parking" first can trivialize the whole claim; placing it last reflects superiority back through the rest of the message.

What if your single absolute, unrivaled claim isn't "free parking" but a higher rate of interest?

Easy! Then you don't need parity advertising at all. You have a major competitive advantage to exploit, and instead of starting your claim with the parity revealing "No . . ." you'd begin with:

Where's the highest interest rate in Jonesville? Only *one* bank has it—the First National. Don't bother looking anywhere else.

If you've used up your parity, another approach might be a challenge:

Hey, First National Bank. What's your answer to this? The State Bank of Commerce challenges you to disprove this statement: No other bank in Jonesville pays higher interest than the State Bank of Commerce. Not one. Not the First National, not the Exchange Bank, not one. The State Bank of Commerce—that's where *your* money will grow and grow.

Parity advertising can be a bail-out on those days when you as copywriter stare at the keyboard, cursing the cruel fate that stuck you with a copywriting assignment for a company or product that doesn't seem to be worthy of any statement other than, "We're the same as all the rest."

If you decide to go the parity route, don't waver. An office products catalog has this line of copy:

Guaranteed to be the same quality as the more expensive brands.

Instead of this approach, which suggests inferiority even as it claims equality, why not present the information more dynamically:

Guaranteed identical to brands costing considerably more.

(You and I wouldn't have used the neutral-gear word *quality*, would we?)

HANDLING 2000-VOLT WIRES

Comparative advertising and its stepnephew, parity advertising, are hot wires with 2000 volts running through them. Handle these ads the way you'd handle a live wire. You don't mind if they knock unconscious somebody you're jabbing with the end of the wire, but you don't want the uninsulated end to touch *you*.

When writing comparative ads, keep them sane. Keep them logical, and for the love of heaven, keep them truthful. Since you're in command and can pick and choose from a grab bag of facts, pick the ones that help you. If what you've picked seems stupid and trivial, maybe comparatives aren't the way to go.

Or maybe you, as copywriter, have the professional job of making the stupid and trivial seem bright and significant.

7

How to Write
a Guarantee

A STAPLE IN THE WORD STORE

The guarantee has become a staple in our word store. Copy looks naked without it. Some publications won't take mail-order space ads unless they offer a buy-back guarantee.

Assuming your copy isn't written with the deliberate intention of grabbing some orders and then going out of business, both the wording of your guarantee and the intention behind it should be less casual than the "throwaway" guarantees used by many local advertisers who think they're safe from being nailed.

A Marketing Weapon

The legal difference between a guarantee and a warranty usually is the difference between a promise to take something back and a promise to fix or replace something. That's an oversimplification, but this book is for marketers, not lawyers, and for our purposes "Guarantee" is the umbrella word covering our covenant with the buyer.

The Magnuson-Moss Warranty Act is a "Lemon Law." It says if your product costs $15 or more your warranty has to be available for inspection before purchase. (This refers only to *written* warranties to *consumers*.)

If You Do It, Why Not Advertise It?

I was discussing guarantees with some veteran direct marketers, a group whose advertising claims always are under close scrutiny. One of them made a comment worthy of answer in print. "If a customer sends something back, we don't even ask a question. We issue a refund. There isn't any right or wrong. So why bother using space in an ad or a mailing, when we're going to honor a refund claim regardless?"

My answer was one I hope you'll share:

"Except for the last sentence, what you've just said is powerful copy. Why not use it?"

In my opinion, direct marketers have a far more statesmanlike attitude toward guarantees of satisfaction than do retailers. The vendor-by-mail doesn't put customers through "Adjustment Departments" and doesn't ask them to go to three different stations to get signatures. Someone sends something back or changes his or her mind; for most mailers and catalog houses the response is knee-jerk quick.

We've come a long way from the "Shifty Hedge" guarantee we used to see— "During the fifth year in which you own the complete collection, we'll buy it back for the full purchase price . . ."—which in a three-year continuity program meant the buyer had to wait eight years before he could enforce his guarantee. But don't rest too easily. I recently saw this guarantee:

> The (NAME OF COMPANY) pledges to redeem or repurchase your commemorative, upon demand, any time you desire within the next fifty years, for the full cash price you paid.

If you're still alive and that company is still in business fifty years from now, hobble over to the nearest window facing east so you can watch the star rise.

THE FOUR STANDARD GUARANTEES
AND HOW TO USE THEM

The loose "We Guarantee Your Satisfaction!" doesn't hack it any more, because it's unspecific. We live in the Age of Skepticism, remember? If someone tells us he guarantees our satisfaction, we ask him *how* he guarantees it.

I offer the First Rule of Guarantees:

Unless a guarantee specifically offers a refund, it probably is a cynically inspired sales gimmick, not a true guarantee.

I've identified four standard ways a copywriter can reach his target customer with a clear, easily understood guarantee. All four include a refund provision.

Guarantee No. 1:

> We Guarantee Your Satisfaction.
> If for any reason you aren't happy with your purchase, bring or send it back for a 100% refund.

Guarantee No. 2:

> We Guarantee the Quality of Everything We Sell.
> If you think something doesn't measure up to our description of it, bring or send it back for a 100% refund.

Guarantee No. 3:

> We Guarantee Lowest Prices.
> If within 30 days of your purchase you find the identical item advertised for less, bring or send us the ad and we'll refund the difference.

Guarantee No. 4:

> Unconditional 30-Day Guarantee.
> At any time within 30 days, if for any reason you decide you don't want to keep what you've bought, bring or send it back undamaged for a 100% refund.

Yes, it's possible to combine guarantees. Really, all the guarantees except number 3 make the same promise: if you don't like it, return it and we'll give your money back. (See Figures 7–1, 7–2, and 7–3.)

One of the best, seemingly honorable guarantees I've read lately is from a catalog by a company called Brookstone. It combines Standard Guarantees 1, 2, and 4:

> You must be delighted—or you get your money back. We sell only high-quality products, and we describe them truthfully. Each is carefully tested in actual use before acceptance for our catalog. We use these products ourselves.
>
> But you are always the final judge. If for any reason or no reason, you want to return an article to us, please do so. We will gladly exchange it or return your money promptly.

This guarantee not only has the ring of truth—verisimilitude gushing from every pore—but it also builds an aura of confidence among those who don't even know the company. What an accomplishment!

The third guarantee is a specialty. Not every company wants to have the lowball-price image. For those that do, this becomes an absolute, and the very wording of the guarantee inspires confidence.

Some Minor Refinements

I believe in maximizing benefit, so I prefer "one full month" to "30 days." I prefer "send it back" to "return it," because ownership seems less conditional. I prefer "we'll send you our check or charge card credit for every cent you paid" to "we'll issue a 100% refund," because the action seems more positive and dynamic.

Who Can Match the Famous Impact 2000 FOUR-WAY GUARANTEE?

We know our great success is based on customer satisfaction. So Impact 2000 wants everyone who is considering buying *anything* in these pages to know and understand our unique Guarantee, which actually *guarantees the Guarantee!*

1. We GUARANTEE your satisfaction.

If for any reason you aren't happy with your purchase send it back for a 100% refund.

2. We GUARANTEE the quality of everything we sell.

If you think something doesn't measure up to our description of it, send it back for a 100% refund.

3. We GUARANTEE lowest prices.

If within 30 days of your purchase you find the identical item in another catalog, we'll refund the difference.

4. We GUARANTEE unconditionally for a full month.

We don't just let you have a quick look before you have to decide whether or not you really want what you've bought. At any time within 30 days, return it undamaged for a 100% refund.

ONLY IMPACT 2000 GUARANTEES ITS GUARANTEE!

1

DAK
INDUSTRIES
INCORPORATED
8200 REMMET AVE., CANOGA PARK, CA 91304

DOUBLE RISK FREE OFFER

We want you to try anything in this catalog risk free. You'll find our product descriptions more complete than in any other catalog that we have seen. Our feeling is that the more you know about a product the more likely you are to like it when it comes.

And, that's important to us because when you do receive a product from us, you have a full **30** days to decide if 1) it's what we described, 2) it fits your needs, and 3) if you like it.

All you need to do to get your money back, is return the product to us prepaid and insured, in new unmarked condition with all its original parts, instructions, packing boxes and our original invoice (or a copy) within 30 days of when you receive it.

Price Protection. You can't lose. As part of our 30 day risk free trial, in the unlikely event that you find any product that you buy from this catalog selling for less than our catalog price, just send us a copy of any newspaper or magazine advertisement that appears during the 30 day period, and a copy of your invoice.

We will issue you an immediate merchandise credit for the difference in merchandise price. So, you'll have both a satisfaction guarantee plus price protection for 30 days from the time you get any DAK product purchased from this catalog. Of course you are also protected by the individual manufacturer's warranties on all the products we offer.

2

READ THIS FANTASTIC GUARANTEE
It Applies to **Everything** in This Catalog

Try it, use it, test it, enjoy it. Do anything you like except break it. Keep it for up to 30 days. If you decide not to keep it, return it undamaged for a 100% refund.

3

FIGURES 7–1, 7–2, and 7–3
These three guarantees are from mail-order catalogs. Figure 7–1 mirrors the four standard guarantees described in this chapter. A guarantee can reflect officialdom or it can be highly personal. The choice should match the copy style of the selling document.

NOTICE

We are notifying you of a number of points which the U.S. Government has made about our advertising of these Sea and Field binoculars: (1) ''Marine Surplus Depot'' does not sell surplus military equipment, and this firm has no connection with the U.S. Government. (2) Our advertising for the binoculars stated that they were ''all in original cases.'' The Binoculars come in hard plastic cases, soft plastic cases, cardboard boxes, or cloth draw string sacks. (3) According to inspection and tests on three pairs of our binoculars conducted by a Professor at the State College of Optometry on behalf of the United States Postal Service: The term ''7×50'' referred to in some of our advertising and imprinted on some of the binoculars indicates 7 times magnification. Tested samples of our binoculars were between 2.0 and 3.0 × magnification. (4) Our advertising said the lenses on our binoculars have no distortion or minimum distortion. The professor's report states that the tested lenses have ''significant'' distortion. (5) Some of our advertising described the binoculars as follows: ''Precision engineered with haze resistant lenses, these rugged light weight Sea and Field Binoculars withstand rough conditions—all sorts of weather.'' The binoculars are made out of plastic. The professor's report states that the housings are so imprecise as to induce double images when viewing with both eyes.

In all fairness, we believe the only way for you to judge the true value of these binoculars is to use them. We invite you to try them for 30 days. Take them to sporting events, to the beach, out in the forest, or any other place where you would enjoy a closer look at things. If after using them you are not fully satisfied please return them for a full purchase price refund plus return of your postage expenses.

Thank you.

SEE OTHER SIDE
FOR MONEY—SAVING ORDER FORM

126

FIGURE 7–4

The "guarantee" is the last sentence of what apparently is a disclaimer demanded by the U.S. Postal Service, enclosed with the order. After admitting that the magnification of the binoculars is only 2.0 to 3.0, not the 7.0 advertised; that the lenses have "significant" distortion; and that the housings are "so imprecise as to induce double images when viewing with both eyes," this company tacks on a refund offer—and a reorder suggestion! The effect blunts the admission of misrepresentation because the final reference is positive, not negative.

THE KEY QUESTION: DOES IT HELP SALES?

You may not prefer what I prefer, and these probably aren't major issues. If you sell by mail, three little words do become major issues if you decide to include them in your guarantee:

Even Including Postage.

If you offer this golden guarantee you have my admiration, because I've seen the confusion, harsh words, and threats from ne'er-do-well buyers who try to make a little profit from the transaction.

Some guarantees seem to be more truthful by seeming to be cold-blooded. This is a dangerous game, but if you know how to play it you can have what few marketers have: an instant image of integrity. Here's an example of a guarantee that can kill the desire to order:

We will exchange any factory defective furniture if you pay the freight both ways. Any freight-damaged item can be returned to us at the carrier's expense for repair or replacement.

Damage must be noted on bill of lading at time of delivery if carrier is to pay for the damage.

Some vendors offer 90-day guarantees because they think it appears to be three times better than a 30-day guarantee. (Once again, I'd change it to three months.) Are they right?

In my opinion, they're safe but they aren't right unless they add some seasoning to the stew. Safety comes from some recent testing which showed that regardless of guarantee length, returns usually come back within 30 days.

The extended guarantee becomes valuable *only when it's promoted*, on a comparative basis. A 90-day guarantee is just a word change unless the company makes a competitive issue of it. A lifetime guarantee, accompanied by the ring of truth, can boost an offer beyond the reach of a lower-priced competitor.

A catalog of data processing equipment has this headline on a page of computer disks:

BASF Qualimetric Disks are Certified 100%
Error-Free with a Lifetime Guarantee!

The descriptive copy repeats the "100% error-free" claim, but nowhere is the Lifetime Guarantee explained. So the reader, if he cares, has no answer to the questions: Do they mean it? Whose lifetime, mine or the computer's? Or is it a Catch-22 guarantee, referring to the disk's own lifetime? And, oh, yeah—what does the word "Qualimetric" refer to?

The hit-and-run guarantee shows up on another page of the same catalog, in which "IBM Diskettes are certified Error-Free." Certified by whom? What's my recourse? Does certification mean pretesting? Why leave us feeling you're just stroking us, not talking straight?

TOO GOOD TO BE TRUE?

A carefully tailored guarantee can make an offer credible. The reader says to himself, "This is just too good to be true." Then he reads the guarantee and is born again: "It's true, after all."

The Second Rule of Guarantees covers this contingency:

When the buyer feels he is in total command, the offer becomes true regardless of its incredible nature.

That's a deep one, and the best way of illustrating it is this guarantee from a full-page newspaper ad by one of the more innovative—and controversial—mail order companies:

Postdate Your Check for
30 Days—Free Inspection
In Your Home!

We are so certain that you'll be very pleased with a (NAME OF) Diamond that we will let you examine them in your home without risking a dollar. If for any reason you don't like the (NAME OF) Diamond, just mail it back to us within 30 days and we will return your postdated check uncashed.

Obviously the company takes a considerable risk, since these "diamonds" sell for as much as $60, and fake checks are epidemic in today's mail-order jungle. At least two of these four factors have to be dictating this marketing decision:

1. The company is extraordinarily courageous.
2. The company has an enormous markup and feels credit card sales will more than cover any losses from bad checks.
3. The company feels the powerful guarantee will increase total sales far beyond any possible individual losses.
4. The company depends on typical buyer indolence to prevent complaints and returns from those whose dissatisfaction is based on Buyer's Remorse rather than product deficiency.

The key is the *postdated* check. The company doesn't just offer to hold your check; they *can't* deposit it because you've postdated it. The buyer is in command, and the offer is true.

In the same ad is a product warranty:

The (NAME OF) Diamond will last many lifetimes without any worries. In fact, you will receive a lifetime warranty against any defects.

Clever, because any defects in a diamond, mined or synthetic, are apparent at once. Defects don't appear gradually, the way they would with a set of tires. Yes, it's a marketing ploy. Yes, unquestionably it helps sales volume. Ethical? I didn't order a diamond, so I haven't the foggiest notion.

But What If. . .?

But what if the buyer returns merchandise *not* in the original condition? What if a shirt or dress has sweatmarks under the sleeves? What if a toy is broken? What if the BASF Disk has a huge buyer-inflicted scratch on it?

That's a marketing problem, not a copy problem. But copy can set the right climate.

A product enclosure, properly worded, can head off arguments. For example: You sell consumer electronics. Into each box goes a neatly typed or printed piece of copy:

> If you send it back . . . send it *all* back.
> We'll gladly refund your money if you decide you don't want to keep this precision electronic instrument. But don't make it impossible for us to send it back to the factory. If we included batteries, then please—include batteries. Warranty, instructions, plugs, ear-jacks? We included them, so you include them. An incomplete return can cause a delay in your refund.

Depending on your company's attitude toward refunds, you can include an admonition against intentionally damaged or abused merchandise. You might even insist on an explanation of *why* the buyer is returning it. But good marketing strategy tells you not to include an automatic return form, encouraging the buyer to send the item back, *unless you've made a positive sales point of this in your original ad or literature.*

And this brings us to the Third and final Rule of Guarantees:

Deliver what you promise.

This is another marketing circumstance that bleeds over into copywriting. If you regard your guarantee as an absolute personal promise and ask only that customers return your pledge to do business with honor, your guarantee will be the Bird of Paradise, not the albatross around your corporate neck.

I guarantee it.

8

The Importance
of Saying "Important"

IF YOU CLAIM IT, PROVE IT

How long has it been since you were able to write copy introducing a product, projecting viewpoint, or trying to impale a buyer on the point of your message saber without using the word "Important"?

Overuse leads to abuse, and in my opinion "Important" is about to join "Quality" and "Service" in the Deadwood Gulch cemetery of killed-off words.

What's wrong is the thrust. The word has become a crutch copywriters use to prop up weak, staggering sales arguments. If you walk through a town and everyone you see uses crutches, you quit recruiting for your track and field team. (See Figs. 8–1 and 8–2.)

The First Rule of Implied Importance

Everyone uses the word, but few know and follow the First Rule of Implied Importance:

Importance should relate to the state of mind of the reader, not the writer.

It's a simple enough rule to understand: "Here's *why* this is important *to you*": It may not be so simple to execute, because a sudden attack of writer's cramp can strike when the bewildered writer, having word-painted the promise into a corner, struggles to get out of his own trap. (See Figure 8–3.)

FINANCIAL FEDERAL
SAVINGS & LOAN ASSOCIATION
7007 West Broward Blvd.
Plantation, Florida 33317
(305) 584-1584

MR. HERSCHELL G LEWIS
9748 CEDAR VILLAS BL
FT LAUDERDALE FL 33324

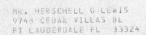

IMPORTANT INFORMATION

FINANCIAL FEDERAL
SAVINGS & LOAN ASSOCIATION
7007 West Broward Blvd.
Plantation, Florida 33317
(305) 584-1584

March 18, 1988

Hi there!

I am Doris Duane, the new branch manager at the Plantation Office of Financial Federal Savings and Loan in the Plantation Shopping Center. Financial Federal is over 53 years old, insured by the FSLIC, and $1.3 billion strong with 25 branches. We are a full service bank striving to meet all of your banking needs with a professional, but personal touch.

I would like to extend a personal invitation to you and introduce you to our latest PROMOTION offered at this office only:

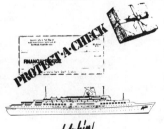

FREE GIFTS to the first 100 new accounts with a minimum of $100.

FREE CHECKING for one year. With direct deposit..... forever!

FREE DRAWING for a three night cruise on Dolphin Cruise Line sailing to the Bahamas - Nassau and Dolphin Cove. You'll enjoy the finest cuisine and complimentary wines with dinner. You will be pampered! One entry per family, trip is non-transferable.

And of course, last but not least, the personal attention you will receive from our experienced staff of skilled professional bankers backed by the strength and security of FINANCIAL FEDERAL will make you feel like a member of the family. We want your business and we are ready to earn it.

Looking forward to meeting you.

Doris Duane

Doris Duane
Branch Manager
Hours: Mon. – Thurs. 9 AM to 3:30 PM, Fri. 9 AM to 6 PM

131

FIGURES 8–1 and 8–2
The envelope makes the flat claim:
    IMPORTANT INFORMATION
    The letter violates the First Rule of Implied Importance. Important to whom?
Nothing in the text can lay even a 1 percent claim to the word "Important."

FIGURE 8–3

Copy is reasonably harmless here, except for peculiar phrases such as "one of the world's most legendary flowers" and the suggestion that nature lovers "wait anxiously" for the Iris to appear. But halfway down the left column the writer says this is "an important, new collection of limited edition sculptures created to honor legendary flowers." If you believe honoring legendary flowers (can anybody "honor" a flower?) is important, I can arrange to send some important dandelions to your front lawn.

THE RHETORICAL ASPIRIN

What called my attention to the rampant overuse of "Important" was the accidental overlap of three pieces of third class mail.

One, from an insurance company, was headed:

IMPORTANT NOTICE TO ALL
U.S. VETERANS

A second was a no-nonsense claim:

IMPORTANT NOTICE!

The third was in French, but the message was understandable on a universal level:

Communication importante—
OUVRIR IMMEDIATEMENT!

This last one was the catalyst. Struggling through the enclosures—all in French, from a Swiss company—I learned what was so important: The company wanted to sell me portfolios of tips and methods for speech making.

They'd had their way. I believed their assertion that this was an important communication; I obeyed their demand to open it immediately. And, recognizing the tragic flaw, I damned them and their followers with the double-whammy they themselves had generated:

1. You lied to me, so I reject your total sales argument.
2. You've added a little more cynicism to my rejection mix.

Sure, what the writer is selling is important *to him*. But so what? I'm just as entitled to my own set of values as he is.

The writer who misuses, overuses, and abuses the word "important" is dishing it out like aspirin: "Take this and call me in the morning." The word becomes the writer's instant solution to all marketing problems. Labeling the product or service *Important!* eliminates all the bother of having to organize a coherent, dynamic sales argument.

Aspirin reduces my fever, but, brother, you should be *building* my fever. Aspirin numbs my pain, but you should be sharpening my senses.

Important to Whom?

The "Important Notice to All U.S. Veterans" suffered because of my generic reaction, stimulated by the "Communication Importante" mailing. How many U.S. veterans are there? I wondered. Twenty million? Is this important to all of them?

134

FIGURE 8–4
Count the number of times the word *important* appears in the first three sentences. I count four. The hit-and-run use of *important* costs the word its importance.

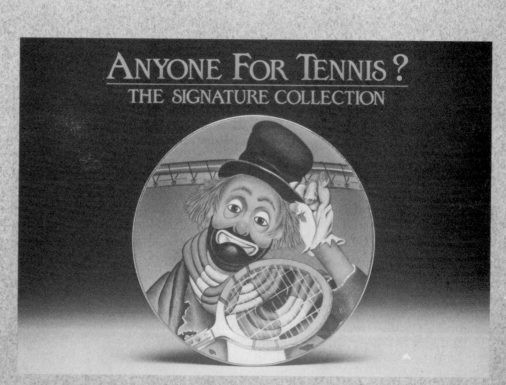

FIGURE 8–5
The main subhead says:
    AN IMPORTANT NEW FIRST EDITION BY RED SKELTON
Body copy carries through this odd theme:
    This new collection could be the most important plate introduction of the year!
    Why? Because Mr. Skelton has responded to the requests of his many fans.
    Oh, I see. I'm glad you explained why it's so important. Until you did, I wouldn't have attached cosmic overtones to a collector's plate with a clown motif.

Actually, it may have been. The offer, well written and cleverly couched, was for term insurance. The offer began:

> This is to inform you of a BENEFIT OFFER (No. MP818) approved for all qualified Honorably Discharged United States Veterans . . . up to $50,000.00 Term Life Insurance based on the group-buying principle of G.I. Insurance.

Clever, huh? Official, isn't it? "MP818" just has to be a government regulation, doesn't it? "Approved" means approved by the government, doesn't it? And the "group-buying principle of G.I. Insurance" *is* G.I. insurance, isn't it? By carrying through on the "official notification" level, which this piece does for a while (later, subheads carry exclamation points, which give away the game, but by then the reader may be hooked), the word *important* actually becomes important.

Not so with "Important Notice." The next three lines answered the question, "Important to whom?"

> CARPETS OF DISTINCTION WILL SELL
> ½ MILLION DOLLARS OF NAME BRAND CARPET
> TO YOU

Not since the demise of the St. Louis Browns has any news been so important.

The Second Rule of Implied Importance

The Second Rule of Implied Importance is the killer for those who pass out samples of their rhetorical aspirin:

> **If the copy message following the word "Important" is a letdown to the reader, copy is more likely to breed rejection or contempt than to initiate a buying urge.**

The curse isn't that dire. To avoid the penalty of this rule, all the writer has to do is tailor his message to *avoid* reader letdown. What an easy charge that is! If, writing a piece of copy, you can't redeem the word *Important!* with a follow-up that keeps the power at 440 volts, all you do is restructure the opening to get rid of the claim you can't prove.

A cry of importance from the magazine published by the nation's most august museum lost me with this violation of the Second Rule. After a computer-personalized overline telling me I'm "one of a small group . . . invited to become national associates," the cover letter has these first two paragraphs:

> I know you receive many "personal" (i.e., computer-printed) invitations but this is special.

> By accepting this particular invitation you will join a special group of Americans whose importance to our national culture I'll explain later.

The letter never does "explain later," but even if it did, I resent, on behalf of the letter readers of this land, being told "I'll explain later" by *anyone*. Why not explain *now*, which not only eliminates the waste of precious words used to hold us off and (if they'd done it) to reintroduce the subject later, but also keeps the power white-hot at the reader's critical go/no-go interest point?

Even if the point were explained later, words such as *special*, used twice, and *important* become nonmotivational clichés when, in the next paragraph, the writer lets his armor drop: it's a bald plea for a subscription.

Suppose, instead of this, the letter had opened:

Let me tell you why I'm writing specifically to *you* and why you're so special to us:

You're one of the few people who (STROKE, STROKE) . . .

WHY AM I IMPORTANT TO YOU?

A credit card company writes me:

Dear Gold Cardmember:

You will be receiving many communications from us in the coming months— but none, perhaps, as important as this one.

Okay, I'm an old weasel word expert, and I know what that word "perhaps" is doing there. It's the copywriter's acknowledgement that this "communication" isn't the most important I'll be "receiving" (a weak, passive word) after all. So the Card giveth and the Card taketh away, because as I read the letter and the accompanying brochure, I can't find any benefit of the Gold Card except over no card at all, of any color.

Probably the Gold Card does have a comparative benefit. But why make me fish for it? If this is, perhaps, the most important communication from the source, why don't they back up the claim of importance with some hard evidence of importance? This is their big chance, because from now on any claim of importance will "receive" a ho-hum.

WOLF, FIRE, AND IMPORTANT

"Important" is an attention-getting device.

So is crying, "Wolf!" So is yelling, "Fire!"

There's nothing wrong with crying, "Wolf!" if you show your readers, listeners, or viewers a wolf (see Tip No. 42, Chapter 13). There's nothing wrong with yelling, "Fire!" if you show them a fire. And there's nothing wrong with claiming, "Important!" if your claim really is important.

The mailing to those on social security is right on target when it says on the face of the envelope:

URGENT! IMPORTANT SOCIAL SECURITY
AND MEDICARE INFORMATION ENCLOSED

It's on target because the claim of importance relates to the recipient's own background. And the letter, to "Dear Concerned American," doesn't let the reader down.

As you consider how the word can be used effectively, consider how it already has been weakened by casual or desperate use. Then join me in chiding the writer of copy selling books. This writer chips away at the strength of the word with

And, importantly, these are books *fully bound in genuine, first-quality leather.*

I agree, the books are superior to paperbound or clothbound books. But why the hit-and-run use of the inapt word *importantly*? Instead of using the word as an unexplained label, why not explain the superiority in terms of exclusivity, one of the great motivators of the late twentieth century?

The brochure describing a limited edition plate cries "Wolf!" in a subhead:

The important back stamp in 24-karat gold

Why is *important* the wrong word here? Because it doesn't lead to the copy following it:

Each Inaugural Day Plate in this Signature Edition will bear artist Jeffrey Matthews' full signature in 24-karat gold.

Maybe artist Jeffrey Matthews' full signature in 24-karat gold is important, especially if you compare it to his partial signature in black paint. But *why* is it important? If you can't tell me, don't abuse the word. While you're at it, why not look for another word to replace *bear*?

That goes for you, too, cataloger of book remainders who heads a whole page of closeouts "Important Histories of W.W. II." And for you, vendor of the "authentic" (but unofficial) Statue of Liberty Double Eagle, who invites me "to participate in a historic event—perhaps the most important collector's opportunity of the century." And you, fund raiser, who tells me, "Your check is more important now than ever," knowing it's important to *you* and too terrified of language use to tell me straightforwardly, "Your check means more now than it ever did before."

So the next time you look at the screen or the paper and realize you've written, "It is important to remember that . . ." either add the words "Here's why" to the front or quietly hit the "delete" key. You'll do yourself, and the person who gets your message, a favor.

Remember that, will you? It's important.

9

How to Take Control
of the Seller/Sellee
Relationship

HOW TO UNDERSTAND AND USE THE RULES OF POSITIVISM

An old song lyric suggests that we "accentuate the positive." I'm not at all certain any song with inspirational lyrics, no matter how full of jargon it might be, could survive today. I *am* certain the message makes more sense for advertisers than it ever could to lyric historians.

Obviously, where we have a *positive* we have a *negative*. As copywriters, we consciously choose one or the other; if we're uncertain, we skip both and write "in between" copy. Ugh.

The pertinence of "accentuating the positive" is tied to a negative, a common advertising mistake—accepting *description* as *sell*.

Seller Meets Sellee:
Bambi Meets Godzilla?

The roles of the two parties in a marketing situation are neither parallel nor equal. We have the *seller*—who, usually uninvited, wants a transaction to occur. We have the *sellee*—whose skepticism has to metamorphose through three phases or the order form goes unheeded.

Phase One: I might benefit from this.

Phase Two: Yes, I'd benefit from this.

Phase Three: I'll get it and I'll benefit from this.

Note the evolution of sellee attitude. It moves in a dynamic line, *out of the* subjunctive and *into* the active. The embryo, "Might benefit," becomes a recognizable fetus, "Would benefit," and finally hatches as "Will benefit."

Some marketers (and many salespeople) are afraid of the confrontation that demands a decision from the sellee. They take comfort in *description* because it doesn't set up a circumstance in which the other guy can state an aggressive "No!" Instead, without leadership from the seller, the sellee makes up his own mind.

Isn't that the gentlemanly or ladylike way to sell? In my opinion it's the gentlemanly or ladylike way to make one of two catastrophic admissions: (a) Your selling argument is weak, or (b) you as a salesperson are weak.

That's why I suggest you examine copy which begins, "Can you imagine . . ." and exorcise the first two words. "Imagine," without the weakeners, leaves you in control with no possibility of generating the answer, "No, I can't."

More and more, as competition for attention *on any level* becomes murderously overpopulated, the vendor who displays his wares in the back row of the cosmic flea market dooms himself to the quiet disregard of those who, pushed a little, might buy something. Remember the Fourth Great Law?

Tell the reader what to do.

We conclude our selling argument—in person, in print, over the airwaves, or in the mail—by telling our target sellee what to do. The gentlemanly or ladylike facet doesn't enter into the mix. We didn't write the ad to impress Miss Manners; we wrote it to sell something.

The Two Rules of Positivism

Fighting for power in our messages, we struggle with the handles of our only weapon: the language. Power is there for us—right behind the filter, like gasoline behind a plugged line in our fuel injectors.

The First Rule of Positivism becomes an easy criterion for message strength:

Stay out of the subjunctive and replace *can* with *will*.

The difference between *can* and *will* isn't subtle at all. *Can* puts the ability to decide or perform in limbo; *will* puts it in the hands of the message recipient.

(Before examples, a caution: *We're talking about buyer attitude, not product capability.* If you're selling FDA-influenced products, your lawyer may advise using *can* instead of *will* for safety in product claims. Listen to him.)

Couching the same message in each of five levels of strength will illustrate the point. Level One:

Can you see the difference this would make in your life?

Level Two:

Can you see the difference this will make in your life?

Level Three:

You can see the difference this will make in your life.

Level Four:

You'll see the difference this will make in your life.

Level Five requires the Second Rule of Positivism, one which is such a sharp verbal sword you dare not swing it wildly:

After telling the reader you've presented a logical argument, take acceptance for granted.

So we have a Level Five sales argument:

What a difference this will make in your life!

Don't be misled. Contractions and exclamation points are parenthetical to what we're talking about. I stuck the exclamation point at the end of the Fifth Level argument because as we become more imperative, we become more exclamatory.

(In fund raising, "Can you help us?" is a weak plea combining an admission of weakness with the suggested possibility of reader weakness; "Will you help us?" tells the donor he has the capability; it's up to his sense of honor—guilt-creating copy with far greater strength.)

HOW TO USE THE CONNOTATION RULE

Sure, we all know the Connotation Rule:

Substitute words and phrases with a positive connotation for words and phrases with a neutral or negative connotation.

By now we know how easy it is to spot negatively connoting words and phrases. They're the constructions which usually have a "don't" or "can't" or "no" or "not" in them, unrelated to the central selling argument.

(If the negative *is* related to the central selling argument, such as "Won't stain your clothes," the rule doesn't apply.)

But knowing the rule doesn't mean you can recognize neutral words as painlessly as you recognize negative words. It's an exceptionally sticky wicket because a word which might have power in one circumstance becomes a weak sister in another.

That's why a beginning writer has no trouble replacing negatives but turns butcher by extending the scalpel to include the "good" negative words . . . while blithely bypassing neutral words.

Example? Here's a standard opening line:

I'm delighted to be able to send you this private notice.

Here's the same line, one word changed:

I'm delighted to be able to send you this private offer.

When Is "Notice" Stronger Than "Offer"?

The beginner leaps blindly into the fray, saying, "*Offer* is positive and *notice* is neutral, so *offer* is the better word."

Is it? Maybe. Maybe not. I made the change *from* "offer" *to* "notice" on a piece of copy I was writing for a public utility which didn't want to suggest it was "pitching" the reader. *Notice* becomes a more positive word than *offer* because we give the reader the impression that he or she is forming a positive reaction instead of our trying to sell something.

The picking of nits like this is what copy that *sells* is all about. Our targets are *individuals*, not *people*. They don't run on tracks, and as professionals we're supposed to tailor our message to the circumstance.

THE "INVERSION TECHNIQUE": A SHOPWORN GAUNTLET

In the 1930s and 1940s some advertisers thought it was cute to invert a sales message so it was negative instead of positive—"Don't Read This Ad . . ."; "Why You Shouldn't Buy at Smith's"; "A Dozen Reasons Why Shoppers Avoid Us." The idea was to startle us into reading the ad by fashioning what appeared to be an outrageous ad.

Hold it! We've come hurtling through future shock and have bounced twice at the far end. This type of ad is about as startling as "Why does a chicken cross the road?"

But we still see it. (See Figure 9–1.) A writer, slightly out of phase with to-day's seller–sellee relationships, uses the tired Inversion Technique. It's easy to write an inverted ad. All you have to do is, with whatever tongue-in-cheek talent you may have, suggest to the reader that he *not* buy from you.

The reader is supposed to say, "What a clever fellow that writer is."

You lose both ways. If the reader doesn't say it, your wit isn't as projectible as you thought it was. If he does say it, you've violated another Great Law:

In this Age of Skepticism, cleverness for the sake of cleverness may well be a liability, not an asset.

So when I saw a coupon ad with an inverted headline, I was neither startled nor titillated. Instead I was annoyed that the writer couldn't think of a less transparent gimmick. The headline:

Six reasons for *not* sending for *absolutely* Free details about the Home Business Directory

After a listing of six cliché-generated "reasons" ("We have so much money now, we never want for anything") the ad's body copy begins with my second least-favorite line:

Be honest!

(This line is ranked in obnoxiousness only by "Let's face it!")

I'm beating this approach about the head and shoulders not because of a blind prejudice against the Inversion Technique . . . not because it isn't ever possible to use a negative effectively . . . but because whoever wrote this ad cheated whoever hired him or her by delivering a less effective message than was so readily at hand.

The Difference Between Writers and "Word Stringers" Is . . .

Changing a negative to a positive can make a prosaic line exciting. Most readers wouldn't find fault with this line:

That's a marvelously low price, but it isn't all I have for you today.

No, it isn't bad; the line transmits information clearly and efficiently. But would it have taken any longer to squeeze off a little shot of excitement, a tiny barb added to the bullet?

That's a marvelously low price, but I have even better news for you today.

What's the difference in impact? 20 percent? 10 percent? 1 percent? I hope you see the point: However fractional it is, why not take advantage of it? That's why writers get paid.

HOW TO CONTROL THE PLAY

When copy lapses into *should* and *would* and *could*, the writer cedes control to the target individual. In my opinion, the target has no right to usurp control; we should fight like tigers to prevent it.

That's right, don't do it—until you know the whole story
and the difference between the HARRISBURG MSA (Metro) and the HARRISBURG ADI:

	Counties	Population	Effective Buying Power
Harrisburg MSA	4	487,600	$ 7,292,319,000
Harrisburg ADI	9	1,196,900	$16,395,314,000

Local Harrisburg radio stations are just that: local Harrisburg stations, having little or no effect in the York and Lancaster portions of the Harrisburg ADI.
…Something like buying a whole pizza and getting only 3 slices instead of 8!

So when you "Buy Harrisburg", use the Harrisburg ADI (Harrisburg-York-Lancaster-Lebanon), not just the MSA/city of Harrisburg.

The Harrisburg MSA is only part of the story; the Harrisburg ADI is The Whole Story—over $16 billion worth of buying power!

Buy the Harrisburg ADI—not Harrisburg Metro—for proper and maximum use of your clients' advertising dollars.

Harrisburg	(717) 234-9967
York	(717) 757-9402
Lancaster	(717) 392-1250

Proud to be the #1 most-listened-to radio station in the Harrisburg-York-Lancaster-Lebanon ADI!

In fact, with the exception of Philadelphia and Pittsburgh, Q106 WQXA-FM is the most-listened-to radio station in the state of Pennsylvania!

(Source: Arbitron, Spring 1986, Total Weekly Listeners, Mon-Sun 6AM-MID, Harrisburg-York-Lancaster-Lebanon ADI)

FIGURE 9–1
Sophomoric, isn't it? "Don't Buy Harrisburg Radio" is a weak way to present a competitive sales argument. If you're tempted to write this type of headline, ask yourself, "Why not?" The answer undoubtedly will be a stronger headline.

So how can we let the reins go slack? How can the pilot say to a passenger, "If you don't want to go to our scheduled destination we can go somewhere else"?

We risk a "No" when we ask our reader, "Couldn't you . . ." or "Wouldn't you . . ." or "Shouldn't you . . ." The reader's "No" may be crashing. It may be flat. It may be thoughtful. It may be subliminal. The result is the same: No sale.

I say, *control the play*. Move into the subjunctive as part of your selling pattern, offering a glimmering of relief to your reader . . . but sliding out of the subjunctive before any cataclysmic decision comes forth. Use *could* and *would* and *should* to lengthen the leash, creating an impression of reader independence; but never actually slip the leash off the reader's neck.

Is this procedure automatic, easy to do? Only on the crudest, most primitive level. A good ad, whether sales letter or space ad or commercial, flows smoothly, immersing the reader's attention in a pleasant or energetic sea of words. The writer who fears the reader will surely drown in his own sea.

Don't Let the Prospect Off the Hook

An "If . . ." clause makes an action conditional; a "When . . ." clause makes it unconditional. If you write nonprofit institutional copy this difference is etched on your forehead because conditional wording ("If you decide to contribute, we'll be able to . . .") usually won't bring in as many dollars as unconditional wording ("Your contribution makes it possible for us to . . .").

Fund raisers know how to close loopholes through which their targets might escape. Mightn't it be a good idea for those selling product or service to close the same loopholes?

Now, a key point: Did that last paragraph leave you feeling a tad unconvinced? I'm counting on it, because I slipped that word *mightn't* in there like a Mickey Finn to torpedo the power. You can raise the sentence to 92 octane with an easy change:

It's a good idea for those selling product or service to close the same loopholes.

Or, if you want jet fuel, take out all qualifiers:

Those selling product or service have the same loopholes. Close them.

Contraindications

Yes, we have contraindications for assuming the affirmative stance. Writing isn't yet an automated science; it's a learned art built atop a scientific base that's only gradually being excavated for professional examination. Sure, we know we have circumstances in which turning on the full force of our words can alienate half-sold readers.

Just what are those contracircumstances?

I can think of three:

1. A sales argument written with finesse can shift from gear to gear. A good writer can begin in a low-key conditional vein, shifting upward and upward with gathering speed until, wham! The reader is transported into Copywriters' Heaven, the state in which we lead and the reader follows like a captive dance partner.

If you can write accelerating copy, you're among the best and can disregard this admonition: Don't linger in low gear for one sentence longer than you have to. Readers will be peeling away.

2. When you want to project an I-don't-give-a-damn image, invert your forceful copy to mask the intent. Start with a dynamic statement of position; shift to a conditional statement of possible acceptance; then shift into a third stance—a difficult one for even the most accomplished wordsmith—supremely logical control, for the close.

This type of writing is tough to do well because the effectiveness of the third leg depends on the writer's ability to convince the reader: "You'll be lucky if we open the door and let you in."

3. For specific marketplaces—art, for example—poetry might be better than hard sell.

Qualifiers all over the place! Note the word *might*. A rule might be:

The more exclusive the offering, the more valid is withdrawal from vigorous copy.

I suggest testing, because schlock art often depends on the image of exclusivity to sell itself and really fine art can be sold nonchalantly to someone who feels accepted into the "In Group."

These variations don't skew the rule; they skew the classification of what belongs where, under the rule. If you write copy for fine art or "Let's pretend fine" art, you already know what approach forces your buyers through the maze; but if you're taking your first shot, test hard and soft copy against each other if you can.

SAY WHAT YOU MEAN

I'm looking at a space ad for a chain of banks. The illustration—four color, naturally—is a tropical fish. All the copy—naturally—is reversed out of black. This is the heading (See Figure 2-7, page 31.):

So daring is the entrepreneurial spirit,
it cannot survive rigid thinking.

Is this revelation true? Hard to tell, because in order to judge it you have to decode it. Go ahead, try: If the entrepreneurial spirit is daring, how can it be so fragile? So that isn't what the writer means.

If we were dinner companions, I've become enough of a curmudgeon that I'd ask flat out: "What are you trying to tell me?"

Whatever the answer to that question might be, it would be clearer and more to the point than the headline copy in the ad, an expensive but noncommunicating message.

Say Clearly to the Rats:
"Here's the Maze. And Here's the Way Through It."

If we're trying to train rats to go through a maze, we don't close the gate so they can't even get into the maze. *The Clarity Commandment*, the overriding determinant for word choice, is branded on our foreheads:

When choosing words and phrases, clarity is paramount. Let no other component of the message-mix interfere with it.

Might the commandment have suggested a less professorial tone for this next ad, which ran in an advertising publication? This was the promising headline:

HOW TO THINK CREATIVELY
ABOUT YOUR
BUSINESS PROBLEMS

Here's the entire text of the ad, except for name and address:

We've built a unique reputation as corporate growth and development consultants, with a track record of over $1 billion in incremental business for our consumer goods and industrial clients (not including acquisitions).
Our ability to develop innovative solutions to tough business problems is the result of:
• Structured Creativity principles and practices developed by the firm over the last twelve years, which are proprietary to [NAME OF COMPANY]
• performance-oriented professionals with individual track records in a broad array of disciplines including strategic growth planning, acquisition strategy, marketing, new product development, technology optimization and market research

The lack of punctuation at the end is advertiser's choice, not mine. (Again, the entire ad is a reverse. There has to be a relationship between reverse typeblocks and obfuscation. Maybe it's the desperate substitution of production techniques for communication.)
Okay, find *one* sentence—no, find one *phrase*—which keeps the promise of the headline. Chest-thumping ads aren't a novelty, but this one thumps with sterilized gloves.
A major financial institution has built an entire campaign around this theme:

The latest
get-rich-slow
scheme.

It's hard to believe that someone in management, if not in the creative department of the institution or its advertising agency, didn't ask, "Hey, guys, isn't the combination of *slow* and *scheme* pretty sleazy copy for what we're selling?"

Why didn't they say what they mean? Probably because, in love with their own cleverness or position, they thought they *were* saying what they meant. It's the contemporary equivalent of the old artist/poet "Public-be-damned" arrogance.

HURLING DOWN THE GAUNTLET

The disadvantage of picking a fight with a random stranger is that you might get your head blown off for no reason. Why do it?

Somebody, somewhere, suggested in a writing class: "Challenge the reader." The result has been copy which swerves from the direct-to-sale path of *challenge- + -reward* to the rutted trench of *I dare you, you coward*. We have enough natural enemies without having to find a stranger to insult.

This is the opening of a form letter that came to me:

Dear Mr. Lewis:

You consider yourself a hot shot direct-mail writer.
I consider myself the hottest investment writer in America.
I believe we can make big money together.

The letter has such neanderthal motivators as "I'm offering creative types like you the opportunity to profit from their own performance" and "If you believe in yourself, and if you can *really produce*, you'll get rich." The deal is for me to mount and mail a direct-mail campaign for this man's investment newsletter at my own expense, and—benevolent despot that he is—he'll let me keep 90 percent of the $125-a-year subscription fee.

The letter ends, appropriately, with this warm expression of friendship:

If you're ready to put your wallet where your mouth is, now is the time.

Put yourself in this man's position. You want to convince copywriters to spend X-thousands of dollars promoting your newsletter. Would you launch into a blind diatribe, with your message recipient wondering, "Whose benefit is this, anyway?" or would you try to tailor an appeal to the recipient's ego, based on one of the great motivators—fear, exclusivity, guilt, or greed?

Even if I were interested in working with someone whose whole approach is "I just don't think you can produce results," the opening—"You consider yourself a hot shot direct-mail writer"—has me reaching for my holster before I even know what the fight is all about.

My reaction symbolizes a universal reaction, and we as writers (hot shot or not) can formulate *The Say What You Mean Mandate*:

The reader inevitably will apply a negative interpretation to statements which violate the Clarity Commandment.

Too late to plead, "That isn't what I really meant," after your crumpled dispatch is lying dead in the wastebasket.

Compare the hottest investment writer's letter with this slick winner:

Dear Mr. Lewis:

You and prize winners Rita Eickhoff, Marjorie Solberg, and Bob Thomas all have something special in common. Each of you were invited to participate in one of our national consumer programs with an opportunity to own an expensive new car without having to buy it . . . plus collect up to $10,000.

This letter is crammed with incentives such as ". . . here's your opportunity to . . . ," ". . . you can collect up to . . . ," and ". . . you really can collect. . . ." Even though this writer uses the plural verb *were* after the singular subject *each*, I don't object because the writer strokes my dignity instead of shredding it.

A Not-So-Gentle Shove

Restrained terminology is a gentle shove, useful only in an *exclusivity* appeal that's genuinely exclusive. Neutral words take our hands off the semantic steering wheel: We might reach our destination or we might crash into a garbage can.

Copy selling limited edition books has this curious phrase:

The paper used for this superb edition . . .

Of course you spotted the neutral word, *used.* (Neutral here but heroic compared with *utilized.*) Why didn't the writer give us *selected,* in key with what's being sold? *Used,* relative to paper, has no class—and, in fact, has a scatological overtone. We *use* Scottissue, but we *select* the fine paper for this volume.

Fund raisers sometimes project their dedication onto the whole world. When they do, their copy goes flat because it assumes a common interest base which doesn't yet exist. Here's the entire sales argument a mailer offers:

Dear Friend,

The American Institute for Cancer Research (AICR) is now conducting its Annual Fund Drive.

During this time, tens of thousands of Americans will make their annual contribution to fight cancer through AICR.

In the next several weeks, I will be meeting with several members of the AICR Board of Directors to plan our coming year's budget. During these meetings, it would be a big help to know what programs we will be able to afford next year.

So, if you could please use the enclosed postage paid envelope to make your contribution to fight cancer, it would be greatly appreciated.

I want you to know that we look forward to counting you among our friends and supporters in the coming year.

Sincerely,
Dr. J. Dan Recer
President

P.S. If you make only one contribution to fight cancer every year, please use the enclosed postage paid envelope to make your gift now during our Annual Fund Drive.

Just as *fear* is the natural motivator for insurance, so is *guilt* the natural motivator for fund raisers. But this copy shifts into neutral, shoving us sideways.

The second paragraph eliminates any possible *exclusivity* or sense of urgency: If "tens of thousands of Americans" will contribute, my contribution is a bucket of water in the Atlantic Ocean.

The next paragraph uses sand as a seasoning. Not only don't I care that Dr. Recer is meeting with his board of directors, I'm turned off by the image of malefactors of great wealth lounging around, deciding what to do with my money. The word *programs* is especially ill-chosen.

A nonprofit group I usually admire stumbled, I felt, in a recent mailing which included an ersatz cable from the organization's office in Sudan. A paragraph begins with this sentence, highlighted in yellow:

AROUND 2.5 MILLION HUNGRY PEOPLE
IN THE TWO WESTERN REGIONS OF SUDAN
WILL SOON RUN OUT OF FOOD . . .

Why *around*? Why not *nearly* or *more than* or any word which doesn't seem vague and casual? *Around* lacks concern; it's an arm's length word, an uninvolved word, a loose guess.

The writer forgot one of the Rules of So-What Turnoff Control:

Using a "so what" statement as a major selling point adds confusion in direct ratio to the reader/viewer/listener's own interest/knowledge.

We also employ *Unassailable Loser Statute I*, not only for *around* but for the statistician-accountant term *2.5 million:*

When seller and buyer both are uninvolved, the seller loses.

Why do so many sales arguments lean on neutral or negative words? It might be because some writers have difficulty projecting themselves inside the hides of their readers.

How Can You Mesmerize Someone Who Doesn't Understand You?

What impresses a reader who never heard of you before? Will one of your in-terms grab him and shake him until he lifts his pen or the phone?

Maybe a hundred years ago a mailer could bully his target by suggesting the reader knew less than the writer. No more. We're in the Age of Skepticism, and term throwing is out of fashion.

A mailing from what seemed to be a print shop came to me. Glancing through it I saw sample prices for various quantities of printing. But the heading didn't match:

"TAKE CONTROL OF YOUR FUTURE FINANCIAL SUCCESS!"

I'm an old hand at unidentified quotations, so this imperative didn't bother me, although the thought itself is almost impenetrable: If I have future financial success, isn't control implicit? And if I'm successful without control, so what? I've beaten the system.

Anyway, the heading on this "Dear Friend" letter rated a "So what?" but the first paragraph dropped the reaction way down the scale, to a "Huh?"

> Valley Distributing Company has recently introduced a fantastic FINANCIAL SUCCESS PROGRAM. This program is a completely new and revolutionary WHOLESALE PRINTING MULTI-LEVEL MATRIX MARKETING PROGRAM . . .

I wonder how many recipients stopped right there. I didn't, sucker for puzzles that I am, and I was rewarded with this explanation:

> By limiting the number of distributors allowed on the first sales level of each member, and by paying sales commissions on each VDC CERTIFICATE purchased through seven complete sales levels, it is possible to build a very strong and profitable downline.

Downline? What's a downline? For that matter, what's a VDC Certificate? I had the same frustrated feeling I sometimes have with *Time*, thinking if I go back to the beginning of the story the initials will be explained.

All right. Let's suppose "VDC" stands for the company name, Valley Distributing Company. The company might have told me what it meant instead of saying, "Fish for it." It might have told me what the seven sales levels are and what they mean. Instead, the letter lapsed into "in-talk," and I'm left out.

Once again I invoke the Clarity Commandment:

When choosing words and phrases for forceful communication, clarity is paramount. Let no other component of the message mix interfere with it.

I'm not asking for oversimplification. I'm asking for adherence to a tenet of advertising copywriting which should be inviolable for anybody who wants to sell something: Write inside the reader's experiential background, not your own. That's one of the separators dividing professional writers from amateurs.

What Did He Say?

When a writer doesn't say what he or she means because of a grammatical lapse, justification usually comes swiftly: "Aw, they'll understand what I meant."

Maybe so, maybe no. How many sets of eyes saw this copy from a fine arts catalog before it hit the mailbags?

> *Aphrodite by Erté*
> At 92 years old, Erté's costume designs are as popular today as they were in the 1920s. Aphrodite's dress was originally created for a 1914 show with the same name . . .

Now we have to sort out the dates. If I take the message literally, Erté's costume designs are 92 years old; they're from the 1920s; this one was created in 1914. I say, "Huh?"

As an Erté fan, I know it's the *artist* who was 92 years old, not his costume designs. You and I would have clarified: "Erté is 92 years old, but his costume designs are as popular . . ." The writer has to hook onto, "Aw, they'll know what I meant."

Sorry, but we don't. Why bring in the 1920s if this design was executed in 1914? What kind of show was it? A musical? Or was it an art show? An art show named Aphrodite? We're asking even more questions because the writer was too cryptic.

How about this to begin a sales letter?

> Dear Executive:
>
> Besides a rare mix of economic factors, another main force behind the coming super-boom in real estate is a new kind of *"factual* consensus."
>
> For the facts from every quarter are all in agreement—consensus—that the American executive can make immensely more money in a single real estate deal than from decades of regular hard work.
>
> And the growing awareness of this compelling point gives a further boost to natural demand, hence to prices, for real estate of all kinds. Coupled with the unusually favorable economic factors . . .

Opinion: a brutally uninviting opening. If an American executive (why "executive" I don't know, unless it's just everyday phony stroking) can make more money in one real estate deal than in ten years of hard work, why not put some *you* into the opening, together with a promise of what this company will do?

The point is obfuscated as it is. The writer doesn't say *ten years*; he uses the standoffish *decades* and the qualifier *regular* before *hard work*.

Why use phraseology such as "factual consensus" and "decades"? Don't we want rapport with the reader?

Hara-Kiri and Other Keyboard Tricks

Stringing words together is easy. It becomes difficult when a writer wants to lead the reader by the hand, through the mystic maze of potential misinterpretation.

Suppose you're selling a new vitamin supplement. You're in a mine field sown by regulatory agencies and years of claim sameness. You can tinker with wording the way a racing-car mechanic tinkers with the engine, for maximum power:

1. WE MAKE NO CLAIMS AND MAKE NO PROMISES. BUT WE'LL TELL YOU WHAT OTHERS SAY . . .

2. WE CAN MAKE NO CLAIMS AND CAN MAKE NO PROMISES. ALL WE CAN DO IS TELL YOU WHAT OTHERS SAY . . .

3. WE WON'T MAKE ANY CLAIMS OR PROMISES. BUT READ WHAT OTHERS SAY . . .

4. THE LAWS WON'T LET US MAKE CLAIMS OR PROMISES. SO READ WHAT OTHERS SAY . . .

The differences aren't vast. But the sales arguments *aren't* identical. No two have parallel impact. Each positions the marketer differently. Each tries to establish a buyer attitude toward the company.

If you see how word choice affects reader reaction, you also see that casual slopping through rhetorical alternatives can betray your message. Saying what you mean is implicit in effective copywriting.

Take a look at whatever piece of copy is sitting on your desk, ready to go. Does it really say what you mean to say?

ALL OF WHICH MEANS WHAT?

The writer's *control* of the communication relationship can dwarf every other facet of copywriting. Taking charge—with the reader becoming your willing follower, then your captive—is a formidable talent.

To me, the reward is that the talent can be developed, honed, sharpened, and perfected—an impressive credential, irresistible when your copy goes head-to-head against that of someone who hasn't polished the talent because he or she doesn't know it exists.

10

How to Warm Up Your Copy

EXAMPLES? YES. STATISTICS? NO.

One reason I admire good fund-raising writers is their knowledge of something lousy fund-raising writers don't know—the Rule of Statistical Deficiency:

Readers respond less to cold-blooded statistics than they do to warm-blooded examples.

So instead of writing—

75% of the children affected might be saved

they'll write—

Of four afflicted children who died, we might have saved three of them.

Boy, that's easy. What isn't so easy is adding some *wham* to a journeyman line such as—

Save up to $81!

Nothing wrong, you say? You're right. It isn't *wrong*; it just isn't as exciting as it might be. Tinker with it for five seconds and you have—

Save as much as $81!

What's the difference? This: The hairline edge for excitement goes to "as much as," over "up to." Nitpicking does pay off in a business which measures effectiveness the right way—by fractions of a percent of response.

HIRING WRITERS? HOW TO SEPARATE WHEAT FROM CHAFF

I long have suggested an early-weeding procedure for employers and headhunters to separate the chaff from the real copywriters. Give the prospects—and they're all whizzes at writing resumés—an opportunity to write some descriptive selling copy while sitting at a keyboard right in front of you or your personnel manager. Lard the information sheet they're to use as background information with words such as *utilize, annual, requested,* and *commence.* While you're at it, use *for* when you mean *because.*

If the sample copy regurgitates those words back at you, pass. You have a writer to whom exciting the reader is secondary to projecting the writer's own image.

REMEMBER WHO YOUR READER IS

We're selling books or records or videotapes or memberships. Staring at our merciless screens, we see what we've written:

If you sign up for the program . . .

The writer who would have flunked the *utilize* test plows merrily ahead. What the heck—the reader will understand what she's supposed to.

That's exactly what's wrong. Signing up for a program can seem to be too profound a commitment when blared from the keyboard halfway through a pitch. Instead:

If you decide to go into the program . . .

Still too big a commitment? We have lots and lots of words to choose from:

If you decide to try out this program . . .

The writer might have written *participate* instead of *go into* or *try out.* It's a better description of the act we want them to perform—except for one aspect: *Participate* intellectualizes the sales argument, and we've known for years that emotion outsells intellect.

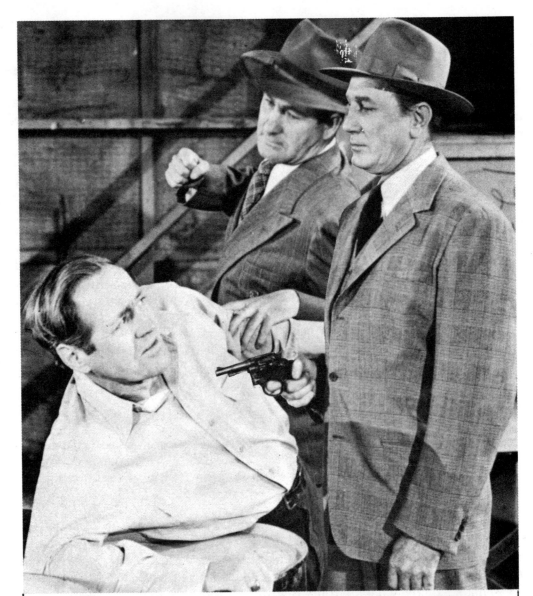

HOW MUCH PERSUASION DOES IT TAKE TO CONVINCE YOU THAT 7.75% INTEREST IN OUR MONEY MARKET BEATS 5.25% IN YOUR CHECKING ACCOUNT?

Take advantage of the hefty interest in a Commonwealth Money Market account. It comes with a free checkbook. Keep at least a $1,000 balance, and you can make withdrawals anytime simply by writing a check. With no penalty of interest whatsoever.**

Your money will also be insured up to $100,000 by the FSLIC—a U.S. Government agency—which makes it the safest investment in town.

So instead of settling for a low-interest checking account, call or

see us today. And check out our high-interest money market account.

Commonwealth
SAVINGS & LOAN

SUNRISE: 3401 Pine Island Road, Sunrise, FL 33321 **TAMARAC:** 7118 N. University Drive, Tamarac, FL 33321 **MARGATE:** 1200 N. State Road 7, Margate, FL 33063 **W. MARGATE:** 7388 W. Atlantic Blvd., Margate, FL 33063 **DEERFIELD BEACH:** 1862 W. Hillsboro Blvd., Deerfield Beach, FL 33441 **FT. LAUDERDALE:** 2000 W. Commercial Blvd., Ft. Lauderdale, FL 33309 **BOCA RATON:** 21301 N. Powerline Road, Boca Raton, FL 33433
*Interest fluctuates with current money market rates. **Consult your Commonwealth representative for specific details and qualifications.

FIGURE 10–1
Who's the reader of this ad? Will someone who's considering a money market account react positively to his surrogate being beat up and shot?

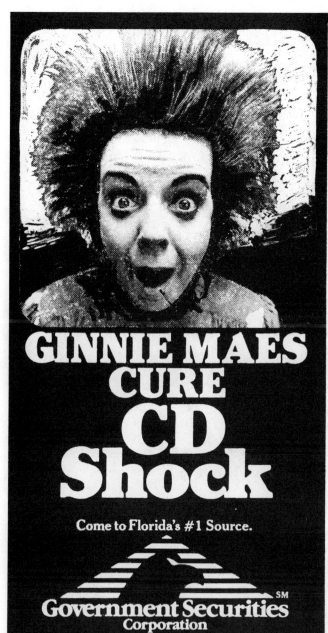
157

FIGURE 10–2
Which side of the argument is the writer on? This approach is less dangerous with a before/after picture. As it is, it's just unpleasant.

FIGURE 10–3
Clever-for-the-sake-of-cleverness illustrations don't make a coherent point; so how can
they excite the reader? If this is the "lifestyle of the future," we'd better hang on to the
old family jalopy, because the Computer-Heads are driving a bunch of 2-by-4s with
unattached wheels.

THE "PERIPHERAL PUSSYFOOTING WEAKENER"

Writing around a point drains excitement out. That's the beginning of a valuable rule, the Peripheral Pussyfooting Weakener. Let's look at the rest of the rule.

Visualize a setting: Into a sedate roomful of dinner guests bursts a breathless messenger. He gasps out:

"A short distance down the road, our bellicose opponents can't go unnoticed. Within a short period of time our defenses may be breached by hostile troops."

The message is dire but the delivery is flat. How much more dramatic, as long as he's gasping anyway, to pant an exclamation:

"The enemy is coming!"

So we form the rule to cover those thoughtless circumstances in which, dignity-driven, we forget why we're at the keyboard in the first place. The Peripheral Pussyfooting Weakener Rule can keep us from lapsing into punchless prose:

Writing around a point drains excitement out. Writing loses impact in direct ratio to the percentage of information given indirectly instead of directly.

Example? How about this line from a communication in, sadly, an advertising publication:

It hardly went unnoticed.

We all have written copy like that; but no more, not with knowledge of the Peripheral Pussyfooting Weakener haunting our brains. If you have the time right now, analyze that four-word message. It's mushy. Rewrite it, transmitting its message *directly* instead of *indirectly*.

Why go through that exercise? Because you could have a parallel piece of copy sitting on your desk right now, that's why.

Maybe if We Tell Them We're Crazy . . .

A loose deck card has this heading:

Market Test   Are we crazy?

Get a Full One-Year Subscription to These Famous $195 Financial Newsletters
for Just $19 Each . . . (as part of a daring 30-day marketing test we are doing).

Does the used car dealer approach work for newsletters? Only the publisher knows for sure. We know, though, this chap sacrificed his dignity without achieving martyrdom, because he got nothing in exchange.

"Are we crazy?" doesn't work here because nothing in the copy suggests such a state of lack of mind. It's a straight discount deal; the headline might work if the publications were free, but at $19, the "famous" newsletters may or may not be a bargain; I never heard of them, but maybe some folks who got this card did.

The word *daring* bothered me too. When an adventurer tells me he's daring, it's less effective than if he tells me something causing *me* to think he's daring. The word itself seems out of key, and because it's artificial in this context it skews the message. I'm neither excited nor challenged.

WORDS ARE OUR BULLETS

A peculiar mailing by the leading publisher of list data has a lift letter inviting me to "Take this test, to see if you've made the correct decision."

Is this supposed to excite me? A *test* puts the mailer in a superior position, which I resent; a *quiz* would have taken the brutal edge off the implication there's a qualification I might not meet; a *ballot* makes *me* superior, the most acceptable relationship of all.

Okay, what's the test?

There isn't any.

Instead, we have some testimonials, followed by this copy:

> . . . I ask you to do the most natural thing for any direct marketer: Test it.
>
> It will cost you nothing, and the returns will be far greater than you think.
>
> Remember the test is FREE! You try it in your home or office for 30 days, and if you're still convinced it's not for you, simply return it, it will have cost you nothing.

Bizarre comma use aside ("Remember the test . . ." without a comma suggests "Remember the Alamo!"; and the last two sentences are tied together with a comma), here's an enclosure whose sole purpose is to excite. Instead, it annoys me twice—first by misstating its content and second by lapsing into a tired "free trial [test]" pitch. It's aimed solely at direct marketers—he says so himself—so this mailer should have known: Most of his targets have used that same approach fifty times or more.

Words are our bullets. If we take gunpowder out, we're firing BB shots against the laser-aimed rockets our competitors might use.

Roget's Can't Help You Now

As often as not, unlimbering Roget's isn't the answer. Would a thesaurus have helped the writer who referred to his company as "among the most respected publishers" instead of the equally simple to write "one of the most respected publishers"?

The difference is fractional, I agree; but *among* makes the company one of the mob while *one of* suggests singularity. Why bother with neutral (ergo, denigrating) words?

Would a thesaurus have helped this hara-kiri line of copy glaring at us from the moment of truth, the order form of a consumer offer?

YES, please send me, right away, the referenced items I've selected.

Referenced items? Great heavens, couldn't the writer suppress his intellectual snobbery for ten more minutes, until the order form was safely processed?

Would a thesaurus have been of any value to the writer whose thin sense of reader excitement generated this deadly line of copy about art objects?

The manufacturer has told us the quantity we are to receive will be small.

Look at the mess here: *Manufacturer* (instead of, say, *producer*) for art? *Quantity* (instead of *allocation*) to suggest a limited number? *We are to receive* (instead of using *our* before *allocation*) as a bumbling comprehension delayer?

A thesaurus would have been helpful to the writer of the next example—but only as valuable as the writer's decision to *suppress* vocabulary and switch over to words paralleling what the reader accepts as a positive goad. The writer's competence isn't in question; it's the dedication to reader excitement that flagged here.

SUBSCRIBE TODAY!
Here's what your peers have said about
The Office Professional.

What is it about that word *peer* that makes us think we're either being judged by a jury or becoming part of a pre-teenage focus group?

Read It Over One More Time

Deadlines are the enemies of exquisite word selection. We all wish we had the time to polish and polish until every line shines like the hood of a Rolls-Royce. Here's a test—no, a quiz—no, cast your ballot for this suggestion: Just as you're ready to print out the words of your next piece of copy, run them back through your brain processor one last time, looking *only* for words you can goose up to the next level of excitement.

Maybe you'll be the only person consciously recognizing the difference. That's a majority, isn't it?

11

The Copywriter's Private Short Course in Grammar and Usage

The Clarity Commandment overrides some of the traditional rules of grammar we learned when we studied English in grammar school.

Some, not all. The commandment doesn't give us an excuse for illiteracy. It doesn't let us form a plural with apostrophe-s, and it doesn't let us string two sentences together separated only by a comma. But it does let us end sentences with a preposition. Why this exemption? Because contorting some sentences to force them into a purist mold impedes comprehension.

So we replace "This is the information you requested" with "This is the information you asked for." Even though we end the sentence with a preposition, we gain clarity and get a bonus besides: *requested* has a condescendingly pompous overtone; *asked for* suggests positive action.

We use *like* instead of *such as* because, mirroring speech, it's clearer and cleaner. "They kept it for people like you" reads better than "They kept it for people such as you."

162

Subject and Verb Agreement

One rule of grammar we can't violate is insistence on agreement between subject and verb. This sentence appears in a trade publication ad for a company named Arnart, selling miniature figurines based on Norman Rockwell art:

A true collector's item, Norman Rockwell is part of FIGURINE AMERICANA by Arnart . . . the most exciting and saleable collection of figurines in America today.

The statement is true only in the most ghoulish sense. The late Norman Rockwell is a collector's item if you recognize the singularity of his resting place at Stockbridge, Massachusetts. What happened here is simple misconstruction. The writer meant, "Each figurine is a true collector's item."

It's understandable that one individual, in the heat of copywriting deadlines, can make this mistake. It isn't understandable that a four-color bleed ad, which unquestionably went through many hands before immortalizing its mistake in the pages of a magazine, could escape from creative controls with the mistake intact.

A wordsmith shouldn't justify mistakes which skew the reader's comprehension. So the ad writer who referred to "Mr. Ziegler's last book" puzzles us. Does he mean Mr. Ziegler's *most recent* book? Or is Mr. Ziegler no longer among us, in which case his most recent book *is* his last book—in this life, at least?

A catalog description reads:

You'll either want red with white trim or navy with light blue trim.

Shifting the word *either* to its proper position, after the verb *want*, not only clarifies the meaning, but it enables the reader's eye to zip through the copy without having to go back for a second clarifying look.

Word Sequence

Clarity has to come first, no matter what you're writing or to whom. Throw out forever the "Throw Mama from the train a kiss" constructions—out-of-position words resulting in confusion that often is unintentionally funny. All the words are there, but sequence is helter-skelter. Here's the first line of copy from an ad for a self-help book:

As an infant, did your parents make you a partner?

Here's another, for a condominium development:

You'll live in a suite guarded by a security desk and a doorman you'll enter in complete safety.

The difference between "white man's shirt" and "man's white shirt" should have been clear to the writer of department store copy, but it wasn't.

"We offer limousine service" has at least two separate meanings:

1. "We service limousines."
2. "We'll drive you there in one of our limousines."

Why force the reader to guess? Half the time you'll lose him to someone whose word constructions are in a clearer sequence.

A magazine writer referred to the castle in which the prince of Liechtenstein lives. Said the writer, "One of its early inhabitants was Prince Joseph Wenzel, portrayed at right by Hyacinth Rigaud, known for his artillery system that was adopted all over Europe."

Whose artillery system? Prince Joseph Wenzel? Or Hyacinth Rigaud? A grammarian would insist on Rigaud, because that's the grammatical reference. Matching up the name Hyacinth and artillery, we say, "Naw, it had to be the Prince." But why make us guess?

The headline in an advertising magazine article stated, "Black marketers push power to the people." Not good. A black marketer, as a distributor of goods obtained from an illicit source, doesn't parallel a marketer whose racial background is black. We associate "Power to the people" with the latter, but this reference comes *after* the unified phrase "Black marketers," which we comprehend one way and then have to go back and re-comprehend another way.

A letter selling collectible art refers to "a time when people could walk about as fast as the cars could go." What does it mean? Are people walking about? Or are they walking as fast as automobiles can go? An easy word change saves us from having to go back over the sentence . . . or throwing out the letter.

The same letter, glorifying the artist, has this curious description of the artist:

> Acclaimed as one of the premier gallery artists of the Victorian Era, she has turned her great love of the period and her fascination with its young peddlers into a heart-warming collection to be cherished and enjoyed daily.

Yes, it's semi-pro writing. Yes, you'll find *heartwarming* on the list of no-no clichés in Chapter 3, and the word *peddlers* needs a qualifier when you're talking about art. But the major problem is calling this artist (described elsewhere as "bright-eyed," born in California, and "fast becoming recognized") as belonging to the Victorian Era. That isn't what the writer meant . . . unless the artist is a time-traveler.

EASY CLARIFIERS—HOW AND WHEN TO USE THEM

Sometimes adding clarity to a muddy sentence is as easy as pouring a bottle of clarifier into a murky spa: Before your eyes the cloudiness turns clear.

Hyphens Can Clarify

A catalog description:

Decorator Lamp Cover

Is it a "Decorator Lamp" or a "Decorator Cover"? Only the catalog writer knows for sure. If it's a decorator cover (as it was), the description clarifies itself immediately when a hyphen appears:

Decorator Lamp-Cover

When a noun becomes an adjective, the danger of confusion increases and the advisability of hyphenation is more pronounced.

Put the Qualifier Near Its Noun

A grocery store crows:

GIANT WATERMELON SALE

All right, what's the giant—the watermelon or the sale? If it's the watermelons, why not word it:

SALE! GIANT WATERMELONS

If it's a giant sale, why not word it:

WATERMELONS—GIANT SALE

(On some rare occasions you deliberately muddle your point. But the technique suggests deception, and in the Age of Skepticism deception backfires as often as it works.)

A woman's coat-and-trouser suit has this as part of the catalog writer's description:

USA-MADE AND IMPORTED

We need qualifiers. We need explanations. A suit can't be both USA-made and imported. "USA-made (silk linings from Japan) would clarify. *Writing nothing* would clarify. But this word sequence not only doesn't help; it hinders comprehension.

Puzzling copy is as inexcusable as cleverness-for-the-sake-of-cleverness copy. In my opinion the principal source of puzzling copy is desperation. A copywriter's imagination is on holiday, and out comes Roget. Rescue is temporary, like aspirin to mask the symptoms of arthritis.

THE FIRST PEOPLE.

Someone was first to reserve a hotel room with gym.

Business or pleasure, when The First People get out-of-town, they don't get out-of-shape. They're first to reserve hotels with gyms, spas, and swimming pools. First to buy workout equipment to work off all the fun new food they found first in the magazines of the Condé Nast Ltd. Every month, Vogue, Vanity Fair, House & Garden, GQ and Gourmet whet their appetite and imagination for everything new on earth. To talk to the 20 million people who do it first, telephone Neil Jacobs at 212/880-8329 for rate structure and details.

THE CONDÉ NAST LTD.

THE FIRST PEOPLE. VOGUE/VANITY FAIR/HOUSE & GARDEN/GQ/GOURMET.

FIGURE 11–1
Before you read beyond the headline: Who are "The First People"? Now read the subhead. Again: Who are "The First People"? Now read the body copy. What an obscure way to present a selling argument. Oh, and to whoever was first to reserve a hotel room with a gym—don't use my towels.

INTRODUCING THE SCANTICON-PRINCETON EXECUTIVE CONFERENCE CENTER. WHERE EXCELLENCE GENERATES PRODUCTIVITY.

With 12 years of international conference center experience, we know that businesses simply can't afford conferences that aren't 100 percent productive.

That's why Scanticon-Princeton, our $40 million Executive Conference Center is—in every sense of the word—excellent. Because excellence—in location, design, facilities and service—is your best guarantee of more productive meetings.

Consider our auditoriums and 23 conference rooms. They accommodate groups from eight to 458 and are equipped with every audio-visual aid you can imagine.

Then there's our excellent choice of restaurants offering everything from gourmet cuisine to sumptuous Danish smorgasbords and light buffets.

For relaxation, we offer you a full service, luxury facility. That means 300 spacious rooms and suites, an indoor swimming pool, lighted tennis courts and much more.

In the final analysis, however, it is our people who insure the success of your conference. From the front desk to the restaurants and conference rooms, they excel in bringing you efficient, hospitable service.

Scanticon-Princeton is *the* executive conference center where excellence generates productivity.

Call or write: **Scanticon-Princeton**
Executive Conference Center and Hotel
Princeton Forrestal Center, Princeton, New Jersey 08540 Tel (609) 452-7800
FOR INFORMATION CIRCLE 2 ON INQUIRY CARD

FIGURE 11–2
"Where excellence generates productivity" is a tortured phrase that doesn't cause any light bulbs to go on in the reader's brain. It's intellectualized puffery. Lots of grist here, but they didn't use it. The headline could have made a point of the 23 conference rooms; it could have pinpointed an exotic audio-visual aid. Instead the writer decided to obfuscate the point.

HOW TO WIN THE DANGEROUS WORD GAME

Overdependence on Roget can result in a word sequence which has color but doesn't have coherence. For example, how can we excuse the writer whose keyboard excreted this catalog copy?

Catalytic Caftan. Who says a stay-at-home caftan should be shy and retiring? This one's all glamour and gleam from shirt collar to hem . . .

What percentage of caftan-wearers know the word *catalytic*? The copywriter is sunk. If they don't know the word they either draw a conclusion ranging from *cat* to *catatonic*; if they do know the word they puzzle over what the copywriter meant.

A travel brochure has this line:

The beautiful, spectacular Japanese Alps, with their outrageous vistas and tranquil winding roads, call you to come explore.

The word *outrageous* has color; but it's a total misfit here, destroying the tranquility of *tranquil* and suggesting an effect 180 degrees skewed from the intention. Suppose the writer had clarified the deliberate misuse of the word with a qualifier: ". . . outrageously gorgeous vistas . . ." We'd have understood that *outrageous* wasn't supposed to have a pejorative overtone.

Usually a qualifier damages impact, but deliberately out-of-key qualifiers add impact—*if the reader understands what you're doing.* When you're using a word to startle or shake up the reader, be sure you don't mislead, as Fig. 11–4 does.

A Christmas catalog has this heading splashed across the first two pages:

The Season of QUINTESSENCE

Not one word of copy explains this show-off line, which is repeated, theme-like, throughout the catalog.

Merriam-Webster's isn't much help: "The fifth or last and highest essence or power in a natural body." Huh? The adjectival form, *quintessential*, means the ultimate example of something. But so what? How many people know *quintessential*? Of those, how many can squeeze any sense out of *quintessence*?

One of the "Big 3" newsmagazines changed its format. In a direct-mail letter to potential subscribers is this curious sentence, following the cliché question, "What more could you ask for?"

You'll discover the answer to *that* in our Premier Double Issue—one of the most extraordinary single issues of U.S. News we've ever published!

Why, oh, why is the word *single* in there? It suggests the issue is extraordinary, all right: It's both double and single. This isn't what the writer meant, and dropping *single* not only would clarify; it would prevent the laughter that kills subscriptions.

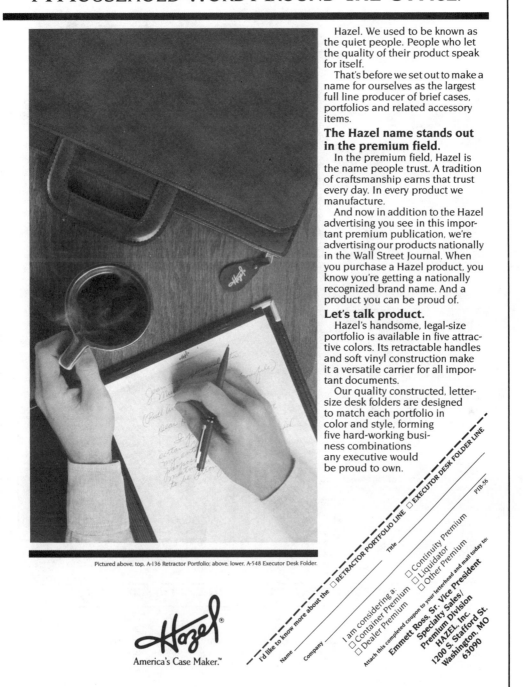
169

FIGURE 11–3

This is the kind of self-backslapping copy that has us dozing off. Is Hazel fast becoming a household word around your office? Or your household, for that matter? Are you excited to learn that Hazel used to be known as the quiet people? Any ad leaving the reader mumbling, "So what?" should be rewritten.

The latest get-rich-slow scheme.

If your investment objectives include high current income, an extra degree of safety, preservation of capital and liquidity—*consider a Government Bond Trust.*

These Trusts seek high current returns from a portfolio of U.S. Government Securities.

12.15%
CURRENT ANNUAL DISTRIBUTION RATE

These higher returns, which until recently were enjoyed exclusively by large institutions, are now available to the individual investor and retirement plans.

The magic of compounding*
*Assuming $2,000 annual contribution reinvested in an Individual Retirement Account at 12.25%.

Important features include:
- High current income.
- An extra degree of safety.
- Active management.
- Ready liquidity.
- Free checkwriting privileges.
- Low investment minimums.
- Automatic cash withdrawal.

At First Miami Securities, bonds and bond trusts are our only business.

If you need expert answers to your questions about municipal and government bonds, ask us. We know bonds best.

That's Bondsmanship.

First Miami Securities, Inc.

fms

1001 N.E. 163rd St., North Miami Beach, FL 33162
Dade: **940-6484**   Broward: **462-0084**
Palm Beach: **655-0505**   Boca Raton: **368-5284**
Out of State: **(800) 327-7097**

Call or write: First Miami Securities
1001 N.E. 163rd St.,
North Miami Beach, FL 33162

☐ Please send me more information and a free prospectus on high-yielding government trusts.

NAME _____
ADDRESS _____
CITY _____
STATE _____ ZIP _____
TELEPHONE (___) _____

*Computed by annualizing distributions from net investment income and realized short term gains of $0.40 per share paid over the preceding months and dividing maximum offering price of $13.10 on record date 4/29/86. Results for this period are not necessarily indicative of future performance at distribution rates and share price, which are not guaranteed will fluctuate.

MEMBER N.A.S.D. & S.I.P.C.

$2,000 — 1 YEAR
$14,629.34 — 5 YEARS
$41,537.34 — 10 YEARS

$91,029.71 — 15 YEARS

$182,061.92 — 20 YEARS
$349,499.09 — 25 YEARS
$657,469.28 — 30 YEARS

Bondsmanship. When you're serious about making money.

FIGURE 11–4
This writer not only loses the word game; he or she threw the game. If the intention is to show how honest this advertiser is, it doesn't work; instead it makes the advertiser seem sluggish and out-of-touch. Body copy doesn't help; it begins with equal sluggishness, "If your investment objectives include. . . ."

Underline, Capitalize, Italicize

Look at an unintentionally obscure message component you've written. What if you underlined the word you want emphasized? What if you capitalized it? What if you put it in italics?

A "Free" offer had this harmless copy:

An Extra Free Surprise for You

We don't have a major problem here. Some readers will read it as "Extra-Free," then recognize the intended message. But why put them to the test? Capitalizing or italicizing clarifies on the first reading:

An Extra FREE Surprise for You

You get an extra burst of promotional benefit—*free*.

The Rule of Copy Misdirection

The Rule of Copy Misdirection is firmly rooted in the Age of Skepticism. Its application reemphasizes the professional copywriter's insistence that substance is superior to form. The Rule:

Words which puzzle can't motivate.

EASY SUGGESTIONS FOR COPYWRITING GRAMMAR

Don't drag out your junior high school English grammar textbook for comparisons with what you read here. As I repeat a dozen times in this book, grammar is our weapon, not our god. Let's use it wisely.

Abbreviations—for states, use the two-letter code: "Chicago, IL," not "Chicago, Ill." Use *Dr.* or *St.* before a name, but spell out the words when used generically: "Dr. John Brown"; "The doctor is coming"; "St. Jude, help me"; "He's a saint." For coupons, abbreviate *St.* and *Ave.*; elsewhere, write them out—*424 Main Street; 610 Third Avenue.* Never abbreviate when the words don't refer to a specific street: "We walked down the boulevard," not "We walked down the blvd."

Active—more dynamic than passive. "We'll always remember her" has power that "She will always be remembered" can never equal.

Affect, effect—"Affect" is a verb. That's all it is. There's no such construction as "It had an affect on me." A less obvious example: "We effected the change," which means "We brought about the change"; "We affected the change," which means "We influenced the change."

Ain't—use with care. If the reader isn't sure you mean to be colloquial, don't take a chance.

Alright—no such word. The proper use is *all right*.

Among, between—Use "between" for two, "among" for three or more.

An—use only before words starting with a vowel sound. It's *an* honor, but it's *a* historic occasion and *a* humble man, Uriah Heep notwithstanding.

Anxious—suggests worry. "We're anxious to have your reaction" has a Valium-in-hand connotation. Use *eager*.

Appraise, apprise—"Appraise" means "to evaluate"; "apprise" means "to inform." The words aren't parallel, so you can't *appraise* someone of something; you can only *apprise* him.

As, like—see *like, as*.

As far as (SOMETHING) is concerned—The construction is grammatically sound, but it's a cliché. *As far as (SOMETHING)*, without "is concerned," is unacceptable.

At—one of the most misused words we have. "This is where it's at": Ugh. "Where are we at?" Ugh. If you end a sentence with *at*, reread it; can the sentence stand without it? If so, delete. (See *Where It's At*)

Bad, badly—"Bad" is an adjective. "I feel bad" is correct. "I feel badly" means the individual has lost some of the ability to find something with the hands; if you use it in place of "I feel bad," you're guilty of phony gentility. Correct use of *badly*: "We played badly."

Better, Best: Better shows superiority over one item or group. *Best* shows superiority over more than one other. "He was the better player of the two"; "He was the best player of the three."

Between—if you ever write "Between you and I," burn this book. I don't want anyone to think we ever had any kind of relationship. (Of course you know it's "Between you and me.") *Bi* refers to "every other" [period of time]. A bimonthly publication is issued every two months—every other month. (See *Semi*.)

Can, may—"Can" means "is able to"; "may" means "might" and is more conditional.

Capital letters—in advertising writing, a name gains stature by capitalizing *The*: "An official issue of The United States Historical Society."

Capitalize organizations or institutions when they're part of a name, but not when they substitute for a name: "He went to Plymouth College on American Airlines"; "He went to college on the airline."

Most grammarians suggest not capitalizing seasons (summer, winter) and directions (south, north), but for advertising writing, capital letters may add strength. It's the writer's option.

FIGURE 11–5
Just for a moment pretend we don't know who Frank B. Hall is. Now what do you do? The ad tells us Hall has "worldwide insurance market clout," but what does that have to do with the photograph? Would a distinguished assemblage of business leaders be reading newspapers uncomfortably in a spartan room, with a crumpled cloth on the floor? "International Intelligence" may typify the company but not this ad.

"It was the only thing to do when the neighbours turned to trivial pursuits."

"When people started spending their spare time in the outdoor spa, sipping Beaujolais Nouveau and asking each other trivial questions, I asked myself a fundamental question; what was I doing with my life?

What I really wanted to do was to take better pictures. Pictures that would give me personal satisfaction.

So instead of turning to trivial pastimes, I turned to photography in a big way.

It was a decision that led naturally to the Pentax 645.

It handles like a 35mm camera. It has seven exposure modes to give you incredible creative control. And for the first time ever, a medium format camera has a full program function.

I don't think that professional photography has ever been easier.

But what I like most is the larger format. 6cm by 4.5cm is considerably bigger than 35mm. The result is absolutely exceptional print quality. Of course, the brilliantly sharp Pentax lens helps as well.

As for the price, it's only about 25% more expensive than the fully fitted out 35mm cameras. The weight and handling are about the same. But the quality is more than twice as good.

The results are fantastic. Photography is becoming a bigger and bigger part of my life.

So now, while my neighbours are trying to decide how many yaks there are in the Himalayas, I'm making plans to go and shoot them."

> Please rush me full details on the extraordinary Pentax 645.
> Post to: Dept.6. C.R. Kennedy & Co. Pty. Ltd., 7 Union Street, Brunswick, Vic. 3056.
>
> NAME _____
> ADDRESS _____
> _____ POSTCODE _____

Pentax 645. Make no mistake.

FIGURE 11–6
The relationship between the headline, the illustration, and the body copy doesn't seem to exist. Why would the copywriter try to confound the reader with this notion? Turning to photography because the neighbors are a bunch of Babbitts is a little drastic, isn't it? I'd be more sold if he turned to Pentax because it's a 6-by-4.5cm camera that handles like a 35mm camera.

Collective nouns—such as group, family, people, percent—can be singular or plural. *The group is* . . . emphasizes the homogenized nature of the group, making decisions and acting as one; *the group are* . . . suggests individual actions, not in coordination.

Comma—never use one between subject and verb. This is 100 percent wrong: "It is the author's attitude, that causes us to use commas when we shouldn't."

Never use a comma to separate elements which belong together. A company advertised its computerized typesetting machine: "Introducing, a complete tabletop digital typesetting package for under $600 a month." What's the comma doing there?

For clarity, use a comma after each element in a series: "John, Mary, and I." The comma after Mary is optional from a grammatical point of view; but we're copywriters, not grammarians. Clarity is always paramount.

Separate two complete thoughts with a period, not a comma. "We pioneered home satellite systems, come to us for lowest prices." Aside from its execrable copy, this is inexcusable because it joins two sentences with a comma.

Company names—singular, not plural. Smith & Co. *is* moving to new headquarters; The Jones Corp. *is* lowering its prices.

Compared with is the construction the copywriter uses for direct comparison; you'll compare a Ford with a Toyota. Save *compared to* for comparison of unlikes: you'll compare a Ford to a cheetah.

Could of, should of, would of—illiterate constructions. Replace *of* with *have* and you're in business.

Dash—stronger, more dynamic, more exciting than a comma. It's a good copywriting tool if you don't overuse it.

A dash is also stronger than an ellipsis (three dots), and this information is helpful both ways. Sometimes you want the raw strength of a dash and sometimes you want the softer interruption of an ellipsis. Example:

"The difference between a dash—a power stop—and an ellipsis . . . a soft interrupter . . . is clear."

Use the dash when you want hair-on-the-chest copy and the ellipsis when you want to draw less attention to the effect. Shelley and Keats = ellipsis; Browning = dash.

Different than—no such construction; it's "different from."

Disinterested—not a parallel for *uninterested. Disinterested* means impartial, not having formed a prior interest or opinion; *uninterested* means without interest.

Distance—a noun, not a verb. When you read "Distance yourself . . ." find out who the writer is and call to say, "You're illiterate." (Or better: "You're fired.")

Each—a singular noun, to be followed by a singular verb. It's "Each is" or "Each was," not "Each are" or "Each were."

Each other, one another—I prefer *each other* when referring to two, *one another* for three or more; but this rule is considerably looser than it was even a few years ago.

Easy, easily—Not interchangeable. *Easy* is an adjective: "It's easy to do"; "It's an easy ride." *Easily* is an adverb: "It goes on easily"; "He finished it easily." Advertese such as "We don't give up easy" is ghastly.

Either is, either are—no such construction as *either are* or *neither are*. *Either* and *neither* always take a singular verb.

Exclamation point—never use more than one.

Farther, further—*farther* refers only to distance (I threw the javelin farther than you did); *further* refers to amount. (Let's pursue this grammatical discussion a little further.)

Finally is not a parallel for *at last*.

Good, well—"Good" is the adjective, "well" the adverb. Correct usage: "I feel good"; "I did well on this piece of copy."

Had ought—illiterate. Don't use it.

Has got, have got—no such construction. Never use *has got* or *have got*. Use *has* or *have*. This isn't parallel to *I've got* or *he's got* or *we've got*, which may be preferable to *I have* or *he has* or *we have* when you want to emphasize the one-to-one convivial nature of the relationship.

Here is—follow this only with a singular noun. "Here is several of the answers" betrays grammatical ignorance.

Historic is preceded by *a*, not *an*. It's "a historic occasion," not "an historic occasion."

Hopefully—unless you're Rebecca of Sunnybrook Farm, don't use this word. If you've been using it to mean "I hope," stop within the next ten seconds.

Hyphen—when the first of two successive adjectives is also a noun, consider linking the two words with a hyphen: "house-bound housewives"; "grammar-improving techniques"; "management-oriented writers"; "terror-stricken viewers."

I, me; he, him; she, her—"I" and "he" are subjects and predicate nominatives. "This is he" and "It was I" are correct; "This is him" and "It was me" are wrong.

We quickly see what's wrong with "Everything comes to he who waits" when we strip away the "who waits." "Everything comes to he" is just as ridiculous as "Are you calling I?" Only our phony sense of gentility changes an *object* (him, her, us) into a *subject* (he, she, we).

If you're uncertain about the case of a pronoun, take away what follows. (Purists know we can't do this with *who*, because what follows determines

FIGURE 11–7
What does the headline mean? Doesn't "Nothing gained" refer to the product? If I drink Hawaiian Punch I've taken a chance—and lost? Weird!

whether the *who* stays or gives way to the consistently overused *whom*.) If nothing follows, but a noun or pronoun precedes, eliminate what precedes and often the case will come clear: "He gave it to Jim and I" shows itself to be patently wrong when we get rid of Jim: "He gave it to I." No. It's "He gave it to Jim and me."

I could care less—corruption of "I couldn't care less." Don't use it.

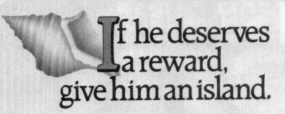

FIGURE 11–8
This ad is for The Fijian. Is it in Fiji? No way of knowing. We've seen Americana Hotels that weren't in America; we've seen New Yorker Hotels that weren't in New York; why would this advertiser assume we know where the Fijian is. The ad tells us it "occupies all 105 acres of Yanuca Island." Oh. Thanks. The ad has lots of space left. Why not tell us where it is, or at least give us a hint how to get there?

. . . ics—ending a word (politics, statistics, athletics, physics) use either a singular or a plural verb depending on the meaning: "Athletics is difficult for me"; athletics are available to all the students."

If—best writing calls for *whether* instead of *if* after verbs such as *learn, know, doubt,* or *tell.*

. . . ing—as the suffix of the first word of a sentence must refer to the person it describes. It's "Walking down the street, I saw her" if I'm the one walking down the street; otherwise it would be "I saw her walking down the street," or, for greater clarity, "I saw her as she was walking down the street."

Irregardless—no such word.

Its, it's—a good literacy test. *Its* is possessive: "The ship lost its rudder"; *it's* means *it is*: "If you're looking for the ship's rudder, it's at the bottom of the ocean."

Kind—this word is singular. *This kind of writing* is correct; *these kinds* is correct; *these kind* is wrong.

Lastly is a nonword. Don't use it.

Lay—a transitive verb. *Lie* is an intransitive verb. "Lay the book on the table" is correct, because *book* is the object of *lay*. "Lie the book on the table" is wrong because *lie*, an intransitive verb, can't take an object. What complicates the relationship between these two words is that *lay* is also the past tense of *lie*. So "Last night when I lay down to sleep I lay awake" is correct; but *lay*, meaning *lie*, shouldn't be used to describe the present: "I'll lay down and think it over"—ugh!

Less—not a synonym for *fewer*. Correct: "He has less money than I have." Correct: "He has fewer dollars than I have." Incorrect: "He has less dollars than I have." As an adjective, *less* is the comparative form of *little*. As an adverb, it means *without* ("He arrived less his luggage.").

Liable—not a synonym for *likely*. One may be liable *for* something—that is, responsible for it; but one is never liable *to* perform an act.

Like, as—since the advertising phrase, "Winston tastes good, like a cigarette should," the once-clear literacy barrier is full of holes. Good usage would have been "Winston tastes good, as a cigarette should," but today's usage often makes this distinction an artifice.

Loose, lose—*Loose* means unfastened, but it's also a verb, meaning "to let loose"; to *lose* means "to miss from one's possession."

. . . ly as the suffix on an adverb—in some cases, optional. In colloquial use we might say either "Speak loudly" or "Speak loud." Highway signs economize on character count with "Drive slow." Opinion: We aren't that colloquial yet, so use *ly*.

Masculine/feminine—in a state of flux. References to mankind in general used to have a masculine reference ("Everybody had his book"), but awk-

FIGURE 11–9
I'll give a free trip to one of the world's two or three great resorts to anyone who can find a relationship between the headline and the body copy, or any explanation of what the headline means. Sorry, you lose. So does the writer, who wastes the space with total puffery, never bothering to let us in on whatever inside information came through private channels.

wardness has hit us ("Everybody had his or her book"). Many writers have given up and use the still-jarring "Everyone took their seats." The ultimate solution will be a sexless word (*hs? h.?*) but until such a word filters into common usage the best procedure is to intersperse *his*, *hers*, and *his and hers*, or to write around the problem ("Those in the room took their seats").

In this book, as the reader will see to his or her pleasure or chagrin, I've practiced what I preach.

May be, maybe—the two words *may be* are a verb, interchangeable with *might be*. *Maybe*, as one word, means *perhaps*.

Muchly—an illiterate version of *much*. Don't use it.

Nowhere—one word. Don't write "no where."

Numbers—most stylebooks suggest spelling out numbers from one to nine, using numerals for 10 or larger. For parallels, don't intermix in a single line of numbers. Write "He owns either 3 or 13 buildings," or, "He owns either three or thirteen buildings."

In a direct quotation, spelling out the word seems to read better: "John said, 'I sent it July third.' "

Over—not a good substitute for *more than*. Starting a piece of copy with "Over 40 countries . . ." can have two different meanings; "More than 40 countries . . ." has just one.

Plurals are never formed by apostrophe-s. More than one person named Smith are "The Smiths," not "The Smith's." If the noun ends in "s" the plural is "The Joneses," not "The Jones' " or "The Jones's."

Words such as *each, no one, everybody,* and *someone* take a singular verb: "Everybody take his best hold"; "Each of us knows the rules." (See also *Singular and plural.*)

Prepositions—As an opinion, there's nothing wrong with writing the way people speak, and that means ending a sentence with a preposition. As the saying goes, "Ending a sentence with a preposition is an idea I don't approve of." The Emotion/Intellect Rule prefers "This is the information you asked for" to "This is the information you requested."

Principal, principle—*Principal* can be either an adjective or a noun, meaning "first" or "primary"; *principle* is a noun only, meaning "a rule" or "code of conduct."

Proven—a weak version of *proved.*

Possessives—for clarity, always use apostrophe-s. It's "Lewis's Laws," not "Lewis' Laws." When dignity is paramount, use the word *of* instead of an apostrophic construction: "The Laws of Lewis."

Quotation marks—American usage calls for all quotation marks to be outside commas and periods, regardless of usage; British usage calls for quotation marks to follow commas and periods in quoted statements but to precede them when quoting a title. Other punctuation falls outside unless related to the quote.

Quotes within quotes use single quotation marks. Examples: (American) I went to see "Pygmalion." (British) I went to see "Pygmalion". (American or British) I said to John, "I went to see 'Pygmalion'." (American or British) I said to John, "Did you go to see 'Pygmalion'?" Did John say, "Yes, I saw 'Pygmalion' "? Or did he say, "I didn't see 'Pygmalion' "? "Whether you've seen it or not," I told John, "we're going tonight"; John didn't seem pleased.

One other point about quotations: When a quote runs for several paragraphs, don't put a quotation mark at the end of any paragraph except the last one; but put quotation marks at the beginning of each paragraph.

Real, really—"Real" is the adjective, "really" the adverb. Correct usage: "It's the real thing"; "I was really annoyed." Illiterate: "I was real annoyed."

Receive—a passive word. Don't be afraid to use *get.*

Semi means half. A publication issued twice a week (or once each half-week) is a semiweekly. (see *Bi.*)

▼▼u.s. pencil & stationery company

SHELBYVILLE MILLS ROAD • SHELBYVILLE TN 37160

```
ZIPQUAL
HERSCHELL G LEWIS
COMMUNICOMP
BOX 15725
PLANTATION, FL  33318
```

Dear HERSCHELL G LEWIS

Because you're special, we put your name on the enclosed "Gallery Pen"!

We don't send everyone a personalized sample. It's too costly. We only mail to people like you who take an extra measure of pride in themself and their company... it's for people like you the enclosed pen was created. The COMMUNICOMP name doesn't belong on anything less.

Write with the "Gallery Pen" and compare it to any other... have you ever felt a smoother writer or seen a more attractive looking pen!

What's more, its handsome cap, rugged body and long life reservoir make this a pen you can give away proudly, knowing it will be enjoyed, displayed and treasured by your customers. Each use will be a reminder of your generosity. What better way to advertise and create goodwill!

MORE GOOD NEWS, A DISCOUNT...At retail you could easily expect to pay from $1.98 to $3.98 for this pen. Because we are direct manufacturers of this product, there are no middleman costs. So even in minimum quantities you can save money. Buy a larger quantity and pay even less.

YOUR FREE GIFTS... I'd like to show my appreciation for your order by giving you 3 Free Gifts. A CALCULATOR ALARM WATCH, MINI DESKTOP CALCULATOR AND AN AM/FM CLOCK RADIO. It's my way of telling you the same thing you'll be telling your customers when you give them the "Gallery Pen". "THANKS FOR YOUR BUSINESS, IT MEANS A LOT TO US."

SEND NO MONEY, but order now. We'll need to hear from you within 30 days.

Just use the fast and easy order form and drop it in the mail, your credit is good. We'll rush your "Gallery Pens" and Free Calculator Alarm Watch, Mini Desktop Calculator and AM/FM Radio out immediately. Then only after you've had a chance to use this great product, will we bill your company.

Sincerely,

Charles Cummins

Charles Cummins

P.S.   A Top Quality Pen, A Free Calculator Alarm Watch, Mini Desktop Calculator and an AM/FM Clock Radio plus a Discounted Price are five good reasons to act now... your satisfaction is guaranteed or you may return the merchandise within 1 year at our expense and get a full refund. This eliminates any risk or question you might have, So Act Now!

182

FIGURE 11–10

How's your grammar today? Would you write, "We only mail to people like you who take an extra measure of pride in themself"? Would you refer to your company as "direct manufacturers"? Would you connect two sentences with a comma—"Just use the fast and easy order form and drop it in the mail, your credit is good"? Would you construct the strange non sequitur, "your satisfaction is guaranteed or you may return the merchandise within 1 year"? If you think copywriters don't have to worry about grammar and usage, you ain't got nothin' to worry about from, excepting you'ns unemployment check.

Shall, will—*shall* is more formal; today's copywriter is usually safe with *will* except for emphasis ("We *shall* do it!").

Singular and plural—two or more subjects are plural: "The ship and the airplane *are* here." Two subjects linked by *or* or *nor* are singular: "Neither the ship nor the airplane *is* here." If one of the two subjects linked by *or* or *nor* is plural and the other is singular, the verb agrees with the subject nearest it: "Neither the ship nor the airplanes *are* here"; "Neither the ships nor the airplane *is* here."

None is singular or plural depending on the particular usage; collective nouns such as *council, scissors, politics, family,* or *news* are singular (in England, *council* takes a plural verb).

That—see *Who, that.*

Those kind—illiterate. It's either *this kind* or *those kinds.*

Try and—corruption of *try to:* It should be "I'll try to be there," not "I'll try and be there."

Unique—an absolute word. *Unique* is like *pregnant*—you either are or you aren't. It accepts no qualifiers. There's no such construction as "the most unique . . ." or "more unique" or "totally unique." (If Unassailable Loser Statute IV is valid, the phrase "totally unique" is a total rhetorical failure.) Instead of using weakening qualifiers, ask yourself: What makes it unique? This information is better than a nondescript, unimaginative word-label pasted onto it.

We, us—after any form of the verb *to be* (*are, were*), use *we;* avoid the awkwardness that can result from slavishly proper grammar. "The only source of these mint-condition silver dollars is we." Should be *us?* No, it shouldn't. But awkward, isn't it? You bet it is, and it isn't professional copywriting. Invert the construction: "We're the only source of these mint-condition silver dollars."

Where it's at—colloquial, too forced and cutesie-pie for writing; use "Where it is." (See *At.*)

Who, that—people are *who,* not *that.* "I'm the one that said it" is a hundred years out of date, and it wasn't an attractive construction then. No, it's "I'm the one who said it." A company can be a *which.* "We're the company which originated the flavor."

Sometimes *that* and *which* can be eliminated. Do it if you aren't sacrificing clarity: "Sometimes I think that we overuse the word *that*" isn't as crisp as "Sometimes I think we overuse the word *that.*"

Who, whom—"Whom" or "whomever" is correct only as an object; if the word is an object of one clause and subject of another, it's "who": "Whoever I called returned the call." But it's "To whom am I speaking?" Complex but accurate: "Who was that whom I saw?" Seems wrong but is right: "Who you know is what you get." (*Who* is the subject of the verb *is;* you wouldn't say *Whom is.* . . .)

Some uses aren't clear-cut. If you're uncertain, use *who* and don't worry about it.

Whose is possessive; *who's* means "who is."

See? I told you it was short. It's also painless. Best of all, it's a floor under verbalized writing and a bridge between grammarian-martinets and casual speech.

12

How to Write Direct Mail Letters That Pull

EVERYBODY WRITES LETTERS

From the day you write your first job-hunting letter to the day you write your retirement valedictory, you create letters, letters, letters.

Ads may be written in committee; various sets of hands tinker and alter, so a finished ad or brochure may be a hybridized product unrecognizable by the writer who started it.

Not so with letters. They're one person's statement.

This tends to be true not only of two-paragraph notes but of four-page and eight-page direct mail epics. Why? Because a letter is—or at least should be—a single, coherent statement. A copy chief might say, "Rewrite this section," but the writer usually is the finisher.

Are you an ongoing student of letter writing? If so, you ask yourself as you read: "What about this sentence or paragraph bothers me?" Your analysis leads to procedural rules; since you formulate them from others' mistakes, you're unlikely to make them yourself.

10 EASY RULES FOR LETTER WRITING

Here are some rules, the easiest canons for letter writing you'll ever read. I say this with confidence because they aren't abstruse philosophical notions; they're *mechanical* rules a reasonably bright 12-year-old can implement.

See for yourself:

Canon No. 1: Keep your first sentence short.

The first sentence is your indicator to the reader. From this early warning your target forms a quick impression: The letter is going to be easy to read or it's going to be hard slogging.

The short first sentence isn't an absolute, invariable law. It's just a good idea most of the time; and because it's a good idea most of the time as well as an easy idea to implement, it's on this list. (Compare the opening sentences of Figs. 12–1 and 12–2.)

Canon No. 2: No paragraphs should be longer than seven lines.

When I suggested this very tip to the assemblage of copywriters, I guess I shouldn't have been surprised to get the question, "But what if a paragraph has to be longer than seven lines?" The question brought several assenting nods.

My answer: No paragraph has to be longer than seven lines. Here's an example, from my own mailbox:

Dear Friend:

It may surprise you, as it surprised me, to learn that even
though we have high-powered, knowledgeable accountants,
we still wind up paying too much income tax . . . although
we don't know it at the time. We pay too much tax because
our accountants can only work with the figures we give
them; they can't "invent" deductions for us, they can't create
unassailable tax shelters out of thin air, and they can't find
productive uses for money that just isn't there to start with.
But, what if you could . . .

That's a double whammy, because this is the first paragraph. The writing isn't bad, but the impression is deadly.

I won't rewrite as radically as I would for pay, but here's how I'd have started this letter with the same ammunition:

Dear Friend:

Does this surprise you? It surprised me.

Like you, I have a high-powered accountant. My surprise
came when I found out that even with his hand joining mine
on the tiller, I was paying too much income tax.

I was paying too much tax, and you may be paying too much
tax because . . .

One paragraph becomes three or four, and reader fatigue vanishes.

Canon No. 3: Single-space the letter; double-space between paragraphs.

This tip is even easier to implement than the first two. It's founded on ease of readership. Manuscript and news releases traditionally are double-spaced, but

AMERICAN ASSOCIATION OF RETIRED PERSONS
1909 K Street, N.W., Washington, D.C. 20049

*Now 18 million strong speaking up for
the rights and interests of mature Americans*

Travel figures prominently in the retirement plans of a vast
majority of Americans. And for others of us 50 and over,
frequent travel is often a necessity, whether it's to visit family
or for business. So when you figure the 10%, 25%, even 50%
savings you may realize as a member of AARP, your $5
membership becomes a fantastic bargain!

Dear Reader:

Here's an interesting quote:

"On a recent trip to visit my son and his family,
I spent three nights in motels on the way. By presenting my AARP membership card at the first motel, I
received a discount of $6. The second gave me an $8.50
discount, while the third took $5.50 off my bill. Total
savings: $20. On that one trip alone I saved more than
4 times the cost of my $5 annual AARP membership!"

With savings like that, it's no wonder AARP member
David Davis of Washington, D.C. feels he's getting the
best value in years. And plenty of other folks 50 and
over must feel the same way. Because more than <u>18 million</u>
are already members.

The American Association of Retired Persons is the
largest nonprofit, nonpartisan membership organization
in the world. It's dedicated to making life more reward-
ing for mature Americans. It makes our voices heard in
Washington and in state capitols around the country. It
runs special education programs, and provides you with

-1-

FIGURE 12–1
The first sentence of this letter has four words . . . four dangerous words because of
their nonspecificity. But the next paragraph is a direct quotation, always interesting
reading; and to a prospective member of this organization, leading off with *benefit* is
an irresistible opening.

The Prudential

Ernest P. Bono, Sr., CLU
Vice President, Regional Marketing
Ordinary Agencies

The Prudential Insurance Company of America
South-Central Marketing Office
P.O. Box 4579, Jacksonville, FL 32231
904 399-2371

HERSCHELL G LEWIS
9748 CEDAR VILLAS BL
FT LAUDERDALE FL   33324

PRESTIGE...You know the meaning of the word: high standing in the
estimation of one's peers and of general opinion, superior status,
a commanding position.

At The Prudential, we, too, understand the meaning of prestige. We
maintain our superior position as the country's largest insurance
company. Investment skill and product innovation have been key
factors in our continued success and leadership. One example of this
has been the development of our "interest sensitive" plans offering
the security of permanent life insurance protection and the potential
for substantial investment earnings.

As a result of this common understanding, I believe it would be to
our mutual advantage to become better acquainted -- The Prudential
with you, and you with The Prudential.

In this regard, I've asked one of our representatives to contact you
so that you may learn more about how The Prudential can help you
reach your financial objectives. Thank you for this opportunity.

Sincerely,

Vice President, Regional Marketing

                                                        J FTLX

188

FIGURE 12-2
The first sentence is 2½ lines long, and what makes it twice as deadly is the flatness of
the opening. The first sentence was as far as I read, and that includes the second time,
when I pulled the letter out of my file for display here.

HERE'S THE MONEY/BUSINESS CAPITAL YOU NEED

We, in the Mail Order Business, have a method of raising Business Capital that really works--everytime, 100%. I am sure that you could use $50,000 to $125,000 in the next 20 to 60 days. Before you say "BULL," please study this letter carefully. This is not a chain letter, but a perfectly legal money-making opportunity; for each of us hope to generate business through this unique vehicle.

Follow my instructions EXACTLY; and, in 20 to 60 days, you will receive up to $125,000 in CASH from other business-minded Americans like yourself. I have run these promotional letters 3 times within the last 12 months. The first one brought in over $50,000: the others exceeded $75,000 each. Here's how:

IMMEDIATELY SEND $2.00 to each of the 4 names listed at the bottom of this page, and a note requesting that your name be added to their Business Mailing List. (You are requesting a service, and the $2.00 covers the cost.) Then, omit the name in the #1 position. Move the other names up one place, and type YOUR NAME in the #4 position.

NEXT, make 100 copies or more of this letter, with YOUR NAME in the #4 position. Mail them to fellow advertisers in the classified section of magazines or newspapers who ask up to $5.00 for their product or service, or you can purchase a list of names from any mailing list company. If you do not know of a list company, you may order from the following mailing list agency: MEJ Enterprises, P.O. Box 84625, Sioux Falls, SD, 57118-4625. The cost is $10 per 100. The names are newest-unused with a very strong pull. Send cash or money order ONLY and allow 5-10 days delivery. If you do not wish to change names and make 100 or more copies, you may send your letter, with your name and address to be added in the #4 position and the AGENCY will retype the corrected name slip, address envelopes, run 100 letters and mail back to you within 15 days. Send cash or money order in the amount of $25.00 for the full packet.

The 100 people whom you mail your copies to will each mail to 100 more. That's 10,000 already, and YOUR NAME will be in the #3 position at that time. Those 10,000 will each mail to 100 people, and that's 1,000,000 with YOUR NAME in the #2 position. Think of what that means by the time YOUR NAME is in the #1 position--1,000,000,000 people...

This promotional letter is initiated for the purpose of helping people in new business opportunities to acquire needed operating capital. Also, many poor, honest, hard working people are being elevated from their poverty situation to enjoy the better blessings of life. BEAR THIS IN MIND: This is not a chain letter, but it does initially cost you money. So, follow the instructions very carefully; and, in exactly 20 to 60 days, you will have all the CAPITAL you need. The participation fee is ridiculously low, when you consider what you stand to GAIN. So, please, DON'T BREAK THE SEQUENCE: consider yourself fortunate to be invited to participate, because THIS SYSTEM REALLY WORKS! Good Luck and many blessings are on the way. Have faith, be joyful, and keep in mind that your investment is a mere $10 plus postage and photocopies/envelopes--about $40.00 per 100 total. Since we are both buying and selling a service, this is completely LEGAL. Refer to Title 18, Section 1301 and 1341 of the United States Postal and Lottery Laws.

CONSIDER THE POSSIBILITIES--AND ACT NOW WHILE IT'S HOT!

1st step...Immediately sent $2.00 CASH to each of the following names below:
If you do not wish to participate, please return letter to the name in the #4 position so the invitation may be forwarded to someone else. Thank you.
...Now, plant your seed and reap the harvest!

1] Dyn[illegible] [illegible]itc[illegible]cock, P.O. Box [illegible], Co[illegible]an, OK 740[illegible]2

2] Jea[illegible] Hav[illegible], 4[illegible] Cherokee Dr., Summ[illegible]ville, SC 29483

3] Do[illegible]ld Br[illegible]t III, 27[illegible] S. Garfi[illegible]ld, Si[illegible]x Falls, SD 57105

4] Mike [illegible], 65[illegible] Ca[illegible]sbad Dr., Lincoln, NE 68506

FIGURE 12–3
Printed on tan paper in light brown ink, this letter is almost unreadable. Even if the reader stumbled through the text to the fourth paragraph, yipes! Here's a paragraph 11 lines long. That's nothing: two paragraphs down we have one 13 lines long. The combination of primitive psychology and a seemingly endless reading chore is a turnoff. The letter begins, "We, in the Mail Order Business, have a method of raising Business Capital that really works—everytime, 100%." Whatever that method is, it *isn't* writing effective letters.

SunPoint
Savings Bank
FSB

Dear Mr. Lewis:

Because people of your caliber deserve a special line of credit, we would like to invite you to apply for a SunPoint EquityCredit line--from $20,000 to $250,000.

SunPoint EquityCredit is a single, continuous personal line of credit secured by the equity you have accumulated in your home. As you make principal payments to your account, your available funds automatically build back up again.

This is the easiest, most convenient program available today. Just look at a few of the benefits SunPoint EquityCredit offers:

* <u>Easy to Get:</u> You only need to fill out a short application--no need to re-apply everytime you want money.

* <u>A Very Attractive Interest Rate:</u> Our current Annual Percentage Rate is 11%, and is a variable rate adjusted monthly. Plus you are charged interest only on the exact amount of money you use and only for the precise length of time you use it.

* <u>Best of All:</u> Your minimum monthly payment is based only on the outstanding principal balance. If you wish, you can pay your total balance, the minimum required, or any amount in between -- with no "prepayment" penalties of any kind.

To get an application or more information, just complete and return the coupon below. The sooner you reply the sooner you could begin using your SunPoint EquityCredit line.

Sincerely,

Mary Waldron
Consumer Loan Manager

SUN POINT

SunPoint
Savings Bank
FSB

SunPoint EquityCredit
Please complete this information request and return in the enclosed postage-paid envelope.

☐ I would like additional information and an application.
☐ I would like an account executive to call me.

Herschell Lewis
9748 Cedar Villas Blvd
Ft.Lauderdale FL 33324

_____
Home phone

_____
Business phone

_____
Best time to call

FIGURE 12–4
A letter's format can influence readership. I'm not interested in the proposition, but I'm tempted to read the letter because it's set up in such an inviting format. No paragraph is longer than five lines; the "bullet"-indenting helps chop the message into chewable bites.

that's because an editor needs the space between the lines to write in his blue-pencil chicken-scratch.

A letter should set itself up for easy reading; a double-spaced letter not only is harder to read, but double-spacing balloons every aspect fatly outward. A two-page letter becomes four pages, and an eight-page letter—well, don't even think about it. Worse, the page has an overall gray look because the space between paragraphs is identical to the space within paragraphs. Emphasis is harder to achieve.

A suggestion, if you disagree on grounds of tradition rather than reader attention: Set your next letter both ways. Ask 50 people which one is easier to read. If you're really scientific, ask questions based on reader comprehension.

Canon No. 4: In a multipage letter, don't end a paragraph at the bottom of any page except the last; break in the middle of a sentence.

Newspapers have known this for decades. Readers demand completeness. If you've ended a paragraph at the bottom of the page, the reader has a reason to read on only if he or she has developed a firm interest in what you're selling. If you leave the reader in mid-sentence, you're in command. That person is your captive until the end of the sentence—which is on the next page.

This is the direct marketing parallel to the movie on the Late Show. The show doesn't open with credits and titles; it opens with action. Once you've seen the first five minutes, it's too late to switch channels because you've already missed the opening of the film on the competing channel; it started with action too.

Canon No. 5: Don't sneak up on the reader.

An inverse wording of this tip might be, "Fire a big gun to start the battle." We're in the Age of Skepticism, and letter openings such as this one betray a 1930s selling attitude:

This story begins around the turn of the century, when times were peaceful and big fortunes could be made.

Way back then, someone took a look at a contraption a lot of people still called a horseless carriage, and they said, "Gee, wouldn't it be great if we could start these vehicles without cranking them by hand?" Old Silas broke his arm cranking his machine, and the danged thing never would go.

OK, it isn't dull. As this type of opening goes, it's more intriguing than most. I agree. Now read the next paragraph.

Half a century later, a guy named Al Shepard climbed into a different contraption, and a lot of smoke came out of the bottom end. Wham! Within a couple of minutes our first astronaut was not only out of sight, he'd made history.

Do you make these 5 critical mistakes when selling by Telephone?

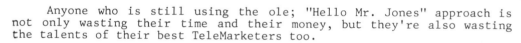

① ② ③
"Hello Mr. Jones, This is

Tom Smith with ABC Company!"
④ ⑤

You may find it hard to believe but 5 of the first nine words most telemarketers speak (when selling by telephone) are WRONG!

ALL YOU HAVE IS FOUR SECONDS!

Most TeleMarketing programs tell you that you have 30 seconds to get your prospects interest and attention. Good luck. In fact, your prospect will decide, either favorably or unfavorably, whether he will listen to you or not, within the first FOUR SECONDS!

THE OLD STUFF AIN'T WORKIN'
AND I THINK YOU KNOW IT!

Anyone who is still using the ole; "Hello Mr. Jones" approach is not only wasting their time and their money, but they're also wasting the talents of their best TeleMarketers too.

IT'S TIME FOR "PHONE POWER"!

In my new TeleMarketing Program; "PHONE POWER" I will show you how to SELL MORE of anything in LESS TIME, for LESS MONEY, and with LESS EFFORT than you have ever dreamed possible. And, whether you choose to use the "PHONE POWER" Program to improve your personal selling skills or simply use it as a "turn-key" training system for your sales reps, you will have the most effective TeleMarketing Technology that has ever been developed by anyone.

WHAT MAKES THE "PHONE POWER" PROGRAM SO DIFFERENT?

If you have ever called from a written script, you know what its like to stumble through 30 seconds of copy that sounds like Cinderella's slipper on paper, but wears like a pair of combat boots when you try it on the phone. Well, "PHONE POWER" is the first TeleMarketing Program that deals with real-life, human communications. The way people really DO Talk, Think and Act on the telephone.

192

FIGURE 12–5

Here's a powerful letter. Whoever wrote this is a professional who has my respect, even though each page of this (four-page) letter neatly ends with a paragraph at the bottom. Can you imagine a recipient reading the overline and stopping there?

FOR EXAMPLE:

With the "PHONE POWER" Program you're going to find out how the listener decides emotionally, (in less than four seconds) whether he wants to hear what you have to say or NOT. It is during those precious few seconds that your sale is either made or lost. I will teach you an incredible new technique that will show you how to successfully navigate those first few seconds, and help you instantly increase your selling ability by 200%, maybe more!

How to Double your Income in 10 Minutes!

IN THIS NEW PROGRAM YOU ARE GOING TO FIND OUT HOW TO......

1----AVOID those costly, "heart-breaking" games of "telephone-tag" i.e., call-backs on prospects you've worked on for weeks only to find out, after you've spent your time and money, that you never had a solid prospect in the first place!

2----QUALIFY every prospect on your first call and know, before you send out any printed literature, whether you have a sale or not!

3----REDUCE your Total TELEPHONE (and other) OPERATING EXPENSES by as much as 50%, and still DOUBLE or TRIPLE your SALES!

4----BE SURE that your (expensive) printed materials are not only being received, but that they are also being READ!

5----CREATE, Develop and Manage a Database of new prospects more efficiently. And the surprising answer is "eliminating" names, not just "adding" them!

6---COORDINATE all of your marketing efforts; Print, Direct Mail and Telephone, to make the most of the time and money that you do have!

7---PRODUCE powerful telephone scripts that will automatically eliminate 95% of all the objections with nothing more than your opening statement!

"PHONE POWER" STANDS ALONE!

Please do not confuse the "PHONE POWER" Program with any other TeleMarketing Package. This is not the typical 500 page, 16 cassette "Hodge-Podge" of Textbook dribble written by some college professor who never had a phone slammed in his ear. "PHONE POWER" is High Powered, Marketing Dynamite that was meant to be used every day, and not put up on some bookshelf as a corporate decoration. The "PHONE POWER" Program is direct, concise, heads-up Marketing information designed to make your entire TeleMarketing Operation more efficient, more effective and one whole "heck-of-a-lot" more profitable.

193

FIGURE 12–5
Continued

Now I'm not so pleased. It's obvious at last—we aren't talking about starters or storage batteries, and we aren't talking about outer space. We still don't know what we *are* supposed to be talking about, and we're deep into the letter.

Just for the sake of history, I'll tell you. This writer is selling acreage (land). It could have been any of 10,000 other possibilities, including aardvarks and Zoro-astrian texts.

Firing your biggest gun first is a good idea because you can't miss. As the letter opens, you're at point-blank range, and you may never have this advantage over your prospect again.

Canon No. 6: Don't open with "Dear Sir" or "Gentlemen."

Why not? Because they suggest stiff-necked, old-fashioned pomposity. Warming up the reader, establishing rapport with him, is one of the great hurdles we face. A greeting such as "Dear Sir" or "Gentlemen" adds sandbags to the obstacle when we should be shoveling sand away.

In a unisex age, I occasionally see "Dear Sir or Madame." This is the kind of opening we might expect from a bill collector but not from our friendly mail-order vendor. (If you don't believe that mailers still use this archaic greeting, take a look at Figure 12–6.)

The mail-order industry has pretty much settled on "Dear Friend" as a neutral substitute when we can't personalize the opening. Depending on the list, you can thrust your rhetorical blade closer to the heart:

"Dear Fellow Member"

"Dear Executive"

"Dear World Traveler"

"Dear Collector"

"Dear Tennis Nut" (you can see the benefit of *equivalence* in greetings when you add a word—"Dear Fellow Tennis Nut")

Do we need the "Dear" at all?

I used to attack it on the grounds it's a cliché, worn out, and the reader isn't really dear to us at all, which makes it hypocritical. I don't point a bony finger any longer because some of the substitutes I've seen are so contrived they make me long for good old Dear.

Some strong usable substitutes for the old-fashioned opening gain their strength from suggesting the communication is limited to a special-interest group:

"Good Morning!"

"To the Relative Handful of Homeowners Who Demand Pure Water:"

"This Private Notification Is Limited to Executives Earning More Than $50,000 a Year."

"Information for Experienced Collectors Only."

(In actual practice, don't let the greeting run over one line.)

• 5707 SOUTH 86TH CIRCLE • P. O. BOX 27347 • OMAHA, NEBRASKA 68127 •

EXECUTIVE OFFICE • 402/331-7245
SALES OFFICE • 402/331-7169
FAX NUMBER • 402/331-1505
TELEX NUMBER • 510-101-0855

BUSINESS LIST SPECIALIST
COMMUNICOMP
PO BOX 15725
PLANTATION, FL 33318

Dear Sir/Madam:

As a leading direct response agency, you provide your clients with **quality** in their direct mail packages....because you know the response depends on it. The creative concept, the offer, the copy, and the design must all be of the highest order. But how about the **list** ?

The simple fact is - if you're buying compiled business lists from any other source, you're **not** giving your clients the quality they deserve. American Business Lists can provide you with the most complete and accurate compiled business lists in the industry. That means you won't be missing names for small towns, or get a bunch of "Gynecologists" in a list of "Gift Shops".

Our lists can help you produce the response your clients are looking for. And you can contract for our Wholesale Volume Purchase Plan and enjoy very attractive prices. See the enclosed price sheet for details.

Why not give your clients the best? Our list catalog is enclosed for your review. Look it over, and feel free to call me if you have any questions.

I look forward to hearing from you.

Sincerely,

Jack Betts

Jack Betts
General Manager
Wholesale Accounts Division

P.S.   Not sure? You can sign up for "Level A" prices through December 31st, 1986, with **no minimum volume commitment.** Call me to set it up, or indicate "Trial - no commitment" on the agreement.

JB/jec

Enclosures

195

FIGURE 12–6
This letter is doubly ridiculous: After using computer personalization for the company name and address, whoever set this up shot personalization through the head with "Dear Sir/Madam:"

A nitpicking question: Should we put a comma or should we put a colon after the greeting?

Business letter writing classes teach colon, not comma, and I agree, conditionally. The colon suggests a respect for the reader. It's a subtle point, and it isn't absolute—especially since it's hard to stroke the reader at arm's length. But mastery of letter writing comes from exalting the reader, *then* sliding in next to him when defenses are down.

I often make the comma/colon decision based on whether or not I'll indent each paragraph. Indenting is less formal, which makes the comma more logical.

Canon No. 7: Don't close with "Yours truly."

"Yours truly" isn't as stiffly formal as the "Dear Sir" or "Gentlemen" that often begins a letter in which we see it. But it reeks of antiquity without polish.

Antiquity *with* polish is a standard and often elegant selling technique. "Your servant, sir" is an example of this writing style—which had better match in *all* components or you look foolish.

You'll find "Sincerely," (*not* "Sincerely yours") as the close on most letters; business-to-business often uses "Cordially," on the theory that "Sincerely" is more emotional a close than the text justifies.

Attacking "Sincerely" is like breaking a butterfly on the rack: Why do it? If you're doggedly determined to improve the close of your letter, try adding another pinch of salesmanship:

"Yours for more vigorous health"

"For the Board of Directors"

"Bless you, my dear friend" (fund raising only, please)

Canon No. 8: Use an overline and a P.S., if they aren't stupid.

An overline is a preletter message at the top of the page. You can type it or handwrite it. You can position it toward the right edge, or if you have a neatness complex you can center it.

What you shouldn't do is give away your message in the overline. I read this overline on the letter in a fat, heavily produced mailing:

If you've driven accident-free for the past three years, you can save 10 percent to 20 percent on your automobile insurance.

I'd have said, ". . . let me show you how to save . . ." rather than ". . . you can save . . ." My objection to this overline isn't based on this one small refinement; it's based on the notion that instead of accelerating reading, comprehension, and preacceptance, this one blunted my interest and lost me as a reader. Too much too soon.

AMERICAN EXPRESS EXPRESSLY YOURS®

KENNETH I. CHENAULT
SENIOR VICE PRESIDENT
MERCHANDISE SERVICES

When William B. Williams likes a recording,
that means a lot. When he says it's one
of his favorites, that means even more.
When he says it's one of the best ...
listen closely and you can hear the sound
of greatness.

Dear Cardmember:

This letter is about a record collection that will make you happy every time you play it.

A collection that will make you sing and dance. A collection which may remind you of blissful, romantic moments in the past, and which will suffuse the present with the delightful pleasures of nostalgia.

It's a collection that we are proud and happy to present: a collection brought to you exclusively by American Express...

The 100 Greatest Recordings from

THE MAKE-BELIEVE BALLROOM

Ever since its debut nearly fifty years ago, The Make-Believe Ballroom has played the best in popular music. William B. Williams has been the host of the Ballroom on WNEW in New York, where the program started, for more years than he cares to remember. His knowledge of popular music is vast, his taste secure, his judgment impeccable.

Now, William B. Williams has personally selected and programmed the one hundred greatest recordings ever played on The Make-Believe Ballroom. And what a marvelous collection it is!

You'll hear the great singers of past and present: Frank Sinatra, Tony Bennett, Bing Crosby, Peggy Lee, Sarah Vaughan, Billie Holiday, Rosemary Clooney, Judy Garland, Billy Eckstine and a host of others.

You'll hear the great bands: Basie and Ellington, Benny Goodman and Harry James, Artie Shaw, Glen Gray, Jimmy Lunceford and many more.

You'll hear Louis Armstrong and Gene Krupa and the Andrews Sisters, the Mills Brothers and the Ink Spots and the Beach Boys. The very greatest of the great, in their most famous and most memorable performances.

continued ...

PRODUCTS FOR GRACIOUS LIVING

FIGURE 12–7
This overline, trying to be poetic, is instead just too long. The typical reader wonders: Who is William B. Williams? The text explains his role as host of the Make-Believe Ballroom. Oh.

The purpose of the overline parallels the purpose of envelope copy. Envelope copy is like a kamikaze dive, with one purpose only: to get the reader into the letter, with more enthusiasm or anticipation than one could generate without the overline.

In my opinion, "This is a private offer" or "Do you qualify?" are stronger overlines than the "accident-free" wording. Years ago, college courses in advertising passed over outdoor advertising with a single direction: "No message longer than 11 words." We might resuscitate this suggestion today, for overlines.

Using a P.S. has easier rules. It should reinforce one of the key selling motivators or mention an extra benefit which doesn't require explanation.

Those who study such arcane matters tell us the overline is the most read part of a letter, and the P.S. is next. Automatically the format itself gives us thunderbolts to hurl. Let's not take the electricity out of them.

Canon No. 9: Experiment with marginal notes.

Marginal notes are a specialty. Not every letter benefits from them, and this suggests determining from the tone of the letter whether or not they'll be beneficial.

When you do use them . . .

The rules for marginal notes are even more stringent than they are for overlines. Two of them, in my opinion, are inviolable.

1. Handwrite everything.
2. Never use more than four words for each marginal note.

I'll explain. Marginal notes draw their power from the appearance of a spontaneous outburst of enthusiasm. The writer is so excited, so enthusiastic, that he bubbles over.

Handwritten bubbling over has verisimilitude, the appearance of truth. Typed bubbling over looks contrived. We fight like tigers to avoid a contrived look, so why take the risk?

The four-word maximum is a good idea mechanically as well as creatively. Imposing this limit means you can write big enough to grab the reader's eye the way you should. There's no handwritten marginal message that can't be transmitted in four words, *maximum*. Some examples of marginal notes:

"Here's your FREE bonus!"

"Read this *extra* carefully"

"Save 50 percent"

Don't be afraid to use hand-drawn arrows, lines, brackets, or even stars for emphasis. You're creating the impression of spontaneous enthusiasm.

Marginal notes, along with handwritten overlines, should be in a second color. What color? Don't consider any color other than the one in which you print

THE LAST OF THE SILVER COIN SERIES

1964 was the last year that silver was used in circulated coins, but for the bicentennial the government wanted to do something very special, so they issued the Ike Dollar in silver, but in proof only. This was to be the last of the Silver Ikes. Never again would a coin series be struck in silver. The Ike was issued three ways: as a regular strike, as a proof, but with no silver and with the silver proof.

THESE THREE VERSIONS SIMPLY CONFUSED THE PUBLIC

The Silver Proof was reserved as part of a special set for the bicentennial. Most people simply ordered the regular non-silver coin. They didn't realize that the silver existed. The government didn't advertise the fact either. At that time the mint didn't advertise on TV. Only 4% of all the bicentennial Ikes were ever issued as a Silver Proof coin. However, even that small number didn't sell without being advertised. When the bicentennial year was over, the mint was embarrassed. Although they struck very few, most of those were still in the mint, never released to the public. They quickly melted them down. To this day, no one knows how many were released to the public and how many were melted. The records were just never kept at the mint. I know that is hard to believe, but it is the truth. IT IS A MYSTERY.

I FIRMLY BELIEVE THE AMOUNT RELEASED WAS LESS THAN 1%
OF THE BICENTENNIAL IKES STRUCK

The supply is really thin. When I realized it had been a decade since these unused coins were struck, I started to poke around. I found quite a few dealers had one or two in stock, but no one had many. Remember, these were sold as a three piece set from the mint with a half dollar and a quarter, so the sets had to be broken up to get just the dollar. In fact, the few sets that were sold were put away as sets by Mr. and Mrs. America as a souvenir of America's birthday party. Investors never got near them, and investors rolls didn't exist. Perhaps that is why so few left the mint. Whatever the reason . . . the fact is these are scarce . . . truly hard to find. Yet . . . most people don't know this. Investors haven't started a band wagon going on these proofs. But . . . they will. Then the price will take off . . . but right now these are truly affordable.

ONLY $19.95 EACH

This is so low a price for a proof coin that it is hard to compare like values. Coins, as you know, are graded from 1 to 70, with 70 being a perfect coin. But a proof coin is in a condition ABOVE even that. It is in a category all by itself. I really can't come up with an "apple to apple" comparison. The Peace Dollar, which was the dollar before the Ike, was never struck in proof. The Morgan's were, although in tiny amounts, and today a perfect Morgan proof is worth over $6,000. I don't know if a proof Ike will ever hit that amount, but at $19.95 it has a lot of room to grow. As the Morgans and Peace Dollars get priced out of reach of most collectors, they will turn to the dollar they can afford, the Ike. Then you will see prices going up 200%, 500% . . . or even more.

NOW IS THE TIME TO ACQUIRE A ROLL OF SILVER IKE BICENTENNIALS
AND START TO BUILD YOUR FAMILY TREASURY OF SILVER

Silver right now has bottomed out which has helped to keep the price of the undiscovered Ike Bicentennial Silver Proof low. The trick, of course, is to buy low and sell high. I am sure I will never be able to offer you these coins at this low price in the future. This is a wise investment two ways; in silver and in rare coins. Either way, you win . . . and I bet you win both ways.

FIGURE 12–8
This is page 2 of a 3-page letter (the fourth panel was blank, not usually a good idea). Instead of using marginal notes, this mailer used yellow highlighting, which does not reproduce here (it is shown as a screen). Highlighting has a problem marginal notes don't: Instead of drawing attention to portions of the text, highlighting can emphasize some parts at the expense of others. It's a technique to be used carefully (see Figure 12-9). While you're looking at this letter, read the top paragraph. Hard going, isn't it?

Discover this delightful new way to get better panty-hose at better prices — from NATIONAL!

Dear Friend:

I'm sending you a $5.00 check with this letter. I hope you will use it soon.

For when you do, you will open the door to a wonderful way to save up to 50% on the panty-hose you buy -- and enjoy first quality besides.

This means you not only can save up to 50%, but you also save the $5.00 on your first order -- and what with today's high prices, that's a savings well worth taking advantage of.

Why am I willing to sell you panty-hose at below most retail prices, then take off $5.00 on your first order?

I'm sending you this check for $5.00 for two reasons:

In the first place, in today's economy, any woman who doesn't pay as little as she can is probably paying too much for just about anything she buys. The check helps you save $5.00.

But there's another reason:

You see, even though my husband, Eddie, and I have been in business for more than 34 years and have a million very well pleased customers who prefer to buy their panty-hose from us --

-- I know there are a lot more women who don't know but would appreciate knowing about our higher quality and lower prices for panty-hose.

I believe you are one of those women, and I believe we can help you save up to 50% on the panty-hose you wear from

FIGURE 12–9

This letter also uses yellow highlighting (shown as a screen) to emphasize individual lines (see Figure 12-8). Here it's used forcefully. It leads the reader through the letter with constant benefit-projection and stroking.

the signature, usually process blue. If the whole letter, including signature, is printed in one color, you have no decision to make.

For heaven's sake don't have an overline and marginal comments in beautiful writing, a showcase of fine feminine calligraphy, and then have an illegible scrawl for a signature at the end of the letter. The writing should match. (Incidentally, there *never* is an excuse for an illegible signature on a direct mail letter. It may give ego satisfaction to an executive, but it drains intimacy out of the communication.)

Canon No. 10: Use letters to test.

The letter is the most logical testing instrument in a direct-mail package. Testing one brochure against another is expensive, even if all the changes are in the black plate. Testing response devices such as order forms often gives muddy results because such tests aren't always logical; a writer, testing response device formats, often throws one to the wolves because the offer doesn't suggest a second approach.

But letters! The writer becomes a hero because his four-page letter outpulled the one-page letter—or vice versa. The letter can test the four great motivators of our era (*Fear, Exclusivity, Greed,* and *Guilt*) against one another.

The letter can test masculine wording against feminine. It can test a harrumphing executive against a hay-chawin' good ol' boy. It can test the validity of some of the tips in this chapter.

Best of all, letter tests are cheap. It costs next to nothing to print copies of two letters instead of one. (While you're at it, consider testing a tinted paper stock against white. The text has to be identical, or you destroy the purity of results. This isn't a copy test, I know, but color psychology is itself one of the creative aspects of mass communications.)

Easy rules to implement? You bet they are. What *isn't* so easy is establishing and maintaining rapport with the reader. How do you do it? Just adapt the rules from the next chapter to the rules in this chapter.

13

Direct Mail/Direct Response: 50 Profitable Rules and Tips

WRITERS ARE WRITERS? SAYS WHO?

Accumulating rules and principles is logical for direct response. More than any other medium, direct response gives us an absolute count of how we did in the competitive marketplace. Testing one writer's approach against another writer's approach is malarkey-proof, because "nth-name" sampling is the ultimate equalizer.

If you've never written direct response copy and never intend to, please, my friend, read this chapter anyway. You never know when your keyboard will be thrust into the breach by an employer or a client who thinks, "Writers are writers." More significant to you as wordsmith: Many of these tips can be valuable to the person who writes *any* form of forceful communication. The tips aren't parallel in content but they share this in common: Every one is easy to implement.

THE FIVE UNASSAILABLE LOSER STATUTES

The fifty tips are refinements of five Unassailable Loser Statutes which govern direct response writing. Keep these statutes in mind and you'll be writing your own direct mail copy tips. Want to be an unassailable loser? Nothing easier. Ignore the statutes and it'll happen.

Unassailable Loser Statute I:
When seller and buyer both are uninvolved, the seller loses.

Unassailable Loser Statute II:
> Readers are more likely to pick holes in transparent shouts of importance than in projection of benefits.

Unassailable Loser Statute III:
> Illustration should agree with what we're selling, not with headline copy.

Unassailable Loser Statute IV:
> Adding qualifying words to a statement of superiority is an admission of inability to claim superiority.

Unassailable Loser Statute V:
> Use only as much of the language as you know. Your dictionary is your verifier, not your originator.

Here's a happy little self-quiz: Dig out the last piece of direct mail copy you wrote. It might be a letter, a brochure, a catalog page, even an order form. Check it for violations of the five Unassailable Loser Statutes. Rewrite it. Then read on.

Tip No. 1: Tying two statements together with "and" adds coherent flow and subtracts impact.

Unless you believe in the super-modern "Staccato" school of writing, the word "and" is a constantly squeezed security blanket. I suggest you take your most recent piece of copy and test it for strength by cold-bloodedly taking out the "ands" when they link two complete thoughts. To retest, insert "and" somewhere else, where you didn't have it. For example: Which of these do you prefer?

1. We have our own toll-free phone number, and if you plan to charge your amplifier to your credit card, call that number—1-800-555-5555—at any hour.

2. We have our own toll-free phone number. If you plan to charge your amplifier to your credit card, call that number—1-800-555-5555—at any hour.

You can see the benefit and the detriment of each. Tying the statements together with "and" helps reading flow but saps a little strength from each side of the word; separating the statements loses their interrelationship momentarily but prevents narrative power loss.

Your choice. I offer this tiny nugget only as proof that *to a wordsmith, every word counts.*

Tip No. 2: If your mailing asks the reader to do something, such as placing Tab A into Slot B, be sure the reader recognizes a benefit in the action.

I no longer feel that "Having the reader complete the job" is a universally successful technique. Specialty print shops love tabs and stamps, because the job costs a lot more to print; some writers love tabs and stamps, because (a) they grew up with them, and (b) they can charge more for what seems to be a more complex job.

Contests and award potentials justify task performance *per se*; a straight selling job doesn't. I impose the *Workmen's Noncompensation Provisions*:

a. **The reader's pleasure from absorbing your "Do this!" message diminishes in exact ratio to the amount of work he thinks he'll have to do.**

   (An example: an unnecessary P.S. on a letter selling a calculator/memory-telephone: "When you get this remarkable electronic instrument, I suggest you find a comfortable spot and spend an evening familiarizing yourself with its features.")

b. **Excluding contests, asking the reader to perform a task which requires talent, prior knowledge, or problem-solving ability will lose that reader if he or she resents, feels inferior to, or is annoyed by the unsought challenge.**

c. **In a contest or sweepstakes whose reward is geared to apparent talent, prior knowledge, or problem-solving ability, the reward justifies the challenge.**

Reciprocity is the key to have-the-reader-do-something decisions.

Tip No. 3: Words suggesting the reader has a choice are less subliminally irritating than words suggesting you, the communicator, are issuing edicts.

Which of these is more likely to generate reader empathy?

I'm very pleased to ask you to read this reprint.

or

I'm very pleased to ask you to take a look at this reprint.

Subtle, isn't it? "Read" is (1) unemotional and (2) a demand. "Take a look at" is (1) convivial and (2) a request. In this particular instance, an even more profound difference influences the recipient's reaction: "Read" asks for completeness, a beginning-to-end scrutiny. "Take a look at" asks for a casual once-over, just enough to verify the content.

In the Age of Skepticism, I less and less dare throw an obvious gauntlet down before the person who reads my direct mail message.

Tip No. 4: Including the message recipient in a statistical recitation enhances the probability of response.

A piece of copy made this claim of exclusivity, once-removed from reader involvement because of the copy's inability to warm its own blood:

Only 1500 individuals in all the world . . .
. . . can own this splendid symbol of gallantry.

The revised version ran far hotter:

You . . .
and only 1499 others in all the world . . .
can own this splendid symbol of gallantry.

The first message is a raw statistic, apparently unrelated to the reader. Sure, she knows you want her to be one of the 1500. But since you're standing off on the sidelines, uninvolved, it's all too easy for her to stand on the other sideline, equally uninvolved. You run afoul of Unassailable Loser Statute I:

When seller and buyer both are uninvolved, the seller loses.

Tip No. 5: When you're out of ideas for envelope copy, say anything with the word "you" in it.

You'll seldom have a total flop if your envelope copy has a "you" in it and doesn't start selling too soon (see Tip No. 6). When such sure-fire old-timers as "Private Invitation Enclosed" and "Your Nomination to the Board of Advisors" don't fit, try a "you."

But be careful. "Now you can . . ." is fine for space ads, but on the envelope it suggests you're about to spill out too many of your guts. Tie the "you" to exclusivity and you're safe.

Another caution: don't put on the envelope a message that might have the recipient say, "I hope the postman didn't see this." If your envelope proclaims, in 24-point type, "Explicit sex information you asked for," expect some complaints.

Tip No. 6: The purpose of a message on the outer envelope is to get that envelope opened. Saying more, or starting your selling argument, can land your mailing in the round file.

Overselling was a nervous curse long before Shakespeare had Hamlet say, "The lady doth protest too much, methinks." If you agree that a good sales presentation builds to a logical close, then you *per se* agree you can't close on the outer envelope. If you could, why put anything inside?

This envelope message emasculates what might be a logical selling argument within its walls:

Inside!
Favorable terms on term insurance
(which experts *term* the best kind of insurance
for someone in your circumstances to buy).

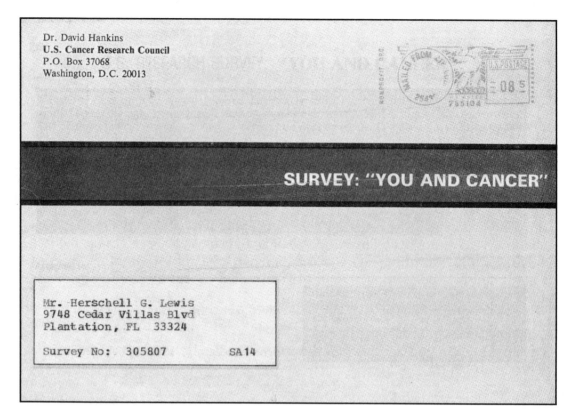

FIGURE 13–1
This envelope copy is flawed. The word "You" does appear, but consider how much stronger the copy would be if, without the softening quotation marks, the legend had been simply:

YOU AND CANCER

"You" personalizes, but being Survey No. 305807 SA14 is about as depersonalized as I ever want to be.

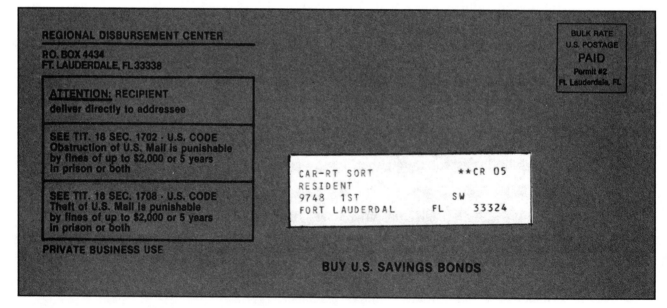

FIGURE 13–2
This official-looking envelope is addressed to "Resident," which doesn't do any damage in this instance because that's exactly the way we'd expect a government bureau to write us, telling us our property has been seized. Actually, the mailing houses a $200 certificate good for buying a Toyota or an Isuzu. Sure, we know in front the format is a phony, but can you imagine a recipient not opening it?

FIGURE 13–3

The single word CAUTION, backed up by a replication of the red Dive Flag, will impel a scuba diver to open the envelope. The mailing isn't particularly clever: As you'd expect, the caution is to avoid letting the subscription lapse. If the envelope had "Office of the Divemaster" in the upper left corner instead of the name of the magazine and its publisher, the effect might have been more dynamic.

FIGURE 13–4

This mailing is a museum piece, since it was one of the last promotional gasps of the drowning Playboy Clubs. What makes the envelope peculiar is that it's addressed to a woman. Inside, the mailing makes its sex acknowledgment, but since the postal indicia openly announces who sent this mailing, the envelope copy seems out of key.

Okay, we give the copywriter a "D" for the play on words, the inadvertently negative word "circumstances," and the betrayal word "buy." But lack of writing skill doesn't hurt this envelope copy as much as blurting out undigested sludge onto the reader. If your mail carrier brought you an envelope with this message on it plus ten other pieces of third class mail, and you could open only three of them, would this be one of the three—unless the others were equally ineptly self-serving?

Tip No. 7: Specifics have greater verisimilitude than nonspecifics.

A "full service direct mail company" sent me a mailing whose envelope had the legend "Check Enclosed." Pretty good, I thought, until I looked at the check.

The format was impeccable, with my name (mildly misspelled), the usual computer code numbers, a bank identification, and a check number. I didn't mind the words "Non-Negotiable" printed in the signature area, because I knew it couldn't be a real check. I *did* mind what was printed in the "Amount" area—"Free Service."

The sixth paragraph of the letter explained it (I'd have led off with it). I had my choice of free lettershop services, personalization, tipping of close-faced envelopes, or live wax seals, provided my mailing was 50,000 pieces or more.

The check, which usually is a powerful weapon in mailings, actually weakened this one, because "Free Service" isn't a bank-related concept. I'd have reacted more favorably if the check had been for a specific amount, payable to the company against a job I might place there. Had the check been for $500, perceived value would have been immediate and the sense of gimmickry would have been less pronounced.

Tip No. 8: Exploit the uniqueness of the direct response medium.

I have a mailing from the U.S. division of a European automobile manufacturer. The brochure is slick and colorful, obviously designed for showrooms instead of mailings. The selling job is left up to the letter, which begins:

Dear Mr. Lewis:

Car and Driver called it "a vision of the future."

They were referring to the new Audi 4000S quattro—and I'd like to invite you to come test-drive it yourself.

When you do, you will immediately discover what has the automotive world sitting up and taking notice—the quattro's revolutionary all-wheel drive, which delivers superbly refined performance, handling and steering . . .

By the time I read this far—and it was as far as I was going to read—I already had come to the conclusion that the writer was not of the direct marketing world. Read the first sentence again. Isn't it typical of *radio commercials*?

A direct response writer would have hit me in the solar plexus with his opening, using an approach something like this:

Dear Mr. Lewis:

I have the keys to a new Audi 4000S in my hand, and I want you to take them, put them in the car parked outside your local dealership, and take a 20-mile ride—on us.

What's the difference? Direct response is one-on-one, and writers who don't know how to transmit "Only you" aren't going to have much luck in this medium. A direct response letter which begins "It Happened on Wall Street!" *might* grab our attention, but head-to-head against a sales argument starting with solid reader benefit, this approach is no more likely to win than "It was a dark and stormy night."

Tip No. 9: Underlining (for letters; italics for typeset) can force the reader to emphasize the proper words and phrases.

Is there a difference between these two statements?

　　1. If only one member uses it, the program has paid for itself.

or

　　2. If only *one* member uses it, the program has paid for itself.

Words are identical. In the second example the reader has to emphasize the word *one* because the writer forces him to.

Tip No. 10: Examples should match what you're selling.

I'm looking at a mailing from a publication, reminding me to tell my clients to buy space in a particular issue. The entire message is printed on a small blue card, with this heading:

PLAY AGGRESSIVELY in MAY
with National Thrift News

The illustration? A golfer.

I'd understand this approach if the publication were *Golf Digest*, and I'd accept the cliché because typical readers would accept it. But what does a golfer have to do with National Thrift News?

I'm not so dumb that I missed the tie with "Play aggressively," but can you really defend this high school-level concept? What makes it worse is that the magazine sent the cheshire-labeled envelope carrying this nonmessage by first class mail.

So let's justify Unassailable Loser Statute III:

Illustration should agree with what we're selling, not with headline copy.

Observing this statute will help keep you out of the cleverness-for-the-sake-of-cleverness slough which gapes wide, waiting for writers who want readers to notice their wit before noticing what's being sold.

Tip No. 11: Opening a sentence with a parenthetical phrase slows down reading, impedes comprehension, and muffles impact. Use the device sparingly.

Sheldon Sachs of Simon & Schuster calls these "backward constructions." He sent me, as an example, a product mailing from a major credit card company which opened with a parenthetical phrase:

Revered and admired for its graceful flight and its powerful command of the heavens, the falcon has long been associated with majesty, lordliness, and elegance.

The opening was no accident. More than half the copy used the same device! I'll quote enough to show the pattern:

One of history's most persistent images, the winged falcon has captured the imagination of some of the world's greatest minds ...

A masterpiece of fine design and workmanship, the Winged Stemware Collection has been created in the same tradition that has produced exquisite objects for generations. Crafted of fine solid brass with silver plated bowl, each piece has been carefully cast and then, as a final touch, finished by hand to produce the finely detailed images, dramatic textures and bold shapes that make stemware objects of enduring beauty. Of high quality, the Winged Stemware is both solid and elegant ...

Especially created to appeal to both eye and hand, every aspect of these very special drinking vessels has been carefully considered to ensure that they are not only beautiful but functional as well....

The sentence beginning "One of history's ..." has enough creative problems without suffering from the oppressive weight of a backward construction; the paragraph beginning "A masterpiece ..." sets an indoor record—three backward constructions in a deadly row; the sentence beginning "Especially created to ..." is vaguely unsettling grammatically.

The biggest problem lies in the technique itself—throwaway, unexplained puffery.

Tip No. 12: Don't ask the reader to provide your sales argument.

Which would you rather have someone say to you: "I remember your name," or, "I have your mailer. Let's get together"?

Set in 24-point type, this is the total sales message in a brochure someone paid money to mail to me:

> At Sir Speedy we're always geared up to give fast service on all your printing needs. Our shelves are well-stocked . . . our gears are well-oiled and our people are always eager to help.
>
> Just give us a call or stop in and Sir Speedy will get in gear for you.

How can this printer hope to compete against the printer who sends me price lists, paper samples, and solid competitive sales arguments?

One more example of this tip. Suppose you're dissatisfied with your direct marketing lettershop and might consider a replacement. You get a brochure in the mail, and this is the copy:

> Recommend the Direct Mail Professionals
>
> At Pronto Post, we make it our business to meet your customer's mailing date. We're flexible enough to accommodate delays or other unforseen problems that might throw a schedule off course. We keep in constant communication with our clients every step of the way.
>
> At Pronto Post, you'll get the benefit of our broad range of capabilities and a total of 60 years experience. . . .

No, it isn't terrible. But I didn't call these people even though I was looking for a lettershop at the time, because as resident curmudgeon I objected to the bold misspelling of the word *unforeseen*.

But suppose I *had* called. I'd have asked questions they should have answered in the brochure. They're asking for my commitment without giving me a menu.

Tip No. 13: When you're supposedly acting as a friend, don't betray your real role as impatient vendor by lapsing into hard sell.

The evil genie is always at our elbow, prodding us to slip in just one more adjective. If we don't push the genie back into his dusty bottle, he gets loose and we wind up with copy such as this:

> Just in case you misplaced the complete, beautiful fall catalog I enclosed with [your order from the space ad], here's another gorgeous, value-packed copy.

Take out the obvious sell and the recipient doesn't feel he's being pitched:

Just in case you misplaced the fall catalog I enclosed with [your order from the space ad], here's another copy.

I don't always favor restraint. I always favor consistency of position.

Tip No. 14: In "cold list" mailings, don't assume the reader is preconditioned to know how lucky he is to be able to buy what you have to sell.

A mailer from a supplier to advertisers and their agencies has this 60-point headline on its descriptive folder:

How to track
successful advertising
for $395

These two sentences aren't the body copy; they're the subhead:

The mission of AdWatch is to provide ongoing measurement of one empirical element of advertising—awareness. Through ongoing measurement, using a strong methodology, AdWatch renders explainable this basic and critical advertising attribute—the degree that advertising can be remembered and recalled by the American consumer.

If you say, "David Ogilvy said people do read long headlines, my answer is, "Yeah, but this ain't what he meant." I submit, "AdWatch renders explainable this basic and critical advertising attribute" is *not* motivational, and if you think it is, please don't sit next to me at the next dinner party.

Think in terms of message targeting: This company sells a tracking service for $395. Who are their best prospects?

If those who don't have prior knowledge of tracking are their targets, the headline is misaimed. But if the mailer is aimed at those who already know what this company is selling, the subhead is deadly—following but not following up on the promise made in the headline.

Tip No. 15: Tell the reader what he wants to read, not what you want to sell.

A computer-personalized mailing tells me:

H.G. LEWIS'
BRAND NEW FORTUNE
ANALOG DRESS WATCH IS WAITING TO BE
DELIVERED—AND IT'S FREE WITH
YOUR FORTUNE SUBSCRIPTION

The emphasis just as easily could have been on what they want to sell. Suppose the personalized heading had read:

FREE WITH YOUR FORTUNE SUBSCRIPTION,
H.G. LEWIS—
A BRAND NEW FORTUNE ANALOG DRESS WATCH!

The folks (people? individuals?) at Fortune are astute marketers. By subordinating the subscription to the free watch, they perform delicate arthroscopic surgery inside my greed instead of hacking away with verbal hatchets from their own greed. Incidentally, a "dress watch" is infinitely more desirable than just a "watch," isn't it? "Dress" adds value without pitching—a good word.

Tip No. 16: If you have to make a choice about offending someone, choose anyone except your best buyers.

I don't think many magazine circulation departments understand this. When I'm a subscriber to a magazine, invariably a nonsubscriber gets a better deal than I do.

On my desk is a note from *Skin Diver*, telling me, "Your subscription to *Skin Diver* is about to expire. Unless you act now. . . ."

The words "act now" should be a tip-off that we're dealing with semipros, but that may be an unduly harsh criticism. I wasn't bothered by the "act now" or by the self-serving P.S.—"Renew today and avoid the risk of losing even one issue of *Skin Diver*."

What burned me was the offer: "only" $13.94 for 12 issues, "Regular newsstand $30.00." I save more than 50 percent off the regular newsstand price. What could be better?

I'll tell you what was better: a blown-in card in the current issue of *Skin Diver*, offering 12 issues for $6.97 (in 6-point type: "New subscribers only!")—a saving of exactly 50% of the amount they want from me, their loyal subscriber.

You bet I understand the logic behind pulling out all the stops to get a new subscriber. But what *they* don't understand is that they have 1001 ways to do that without penalizing existing subscribers. Oh, and did you catch the exclamation point after "New subscribers only"? That really sandpapers the wound.

Tip No. 17: If you introduce a notion foreign to the experiential background of the reader, a question may be less likely to generate rejection than a flat, imperious statement.

A direct mail service company sent me a mailing, printed in full color on 90-pound enamel. The headline:

Profitable Direct Marketing
Starts with
Profitable Fulfillment Systems

I don't agree. Until you've sold something you don't need a fulfillment system. But, sure, fulfillment is a key component of the direct marketing mix. What I don't like is the Voice of God pronouncement here.

Suppose the heading were

Just How Important Is Fulfillment
To Direct Marketing Success?

I wouldn't think I'm being pressured by an arrogant, insensitive salesman. I feel the same way about a space ad headed:

List Segmentation
Is a Myth!

In my opinion, rephrasing the same words as a question—"Is List Segmentation a Myth?"—defangs the hostility flat pronouncements breed.

A space ad for a "Wealth Seminar" seems to walk the tightrope between hurled gauntlet and provocative question and does it very well:

A Challenge:
Do You Have "The
Courage to Be Rich?"

Obviously, if someone has his druthers it would take more courage to be deliberately poor than to be deliberately rich. The reason I embrace this headline as a valid example of Tip No. 17 is that *within the experiential background* of those who might attend ("$395 Wealth Seminar for Only $39.95 for Motivated People Who Can Act Within 48 Hours"), the "challenge" is both dynamic and logical. A seminar really aimed at rich people would have thin attendance, touted with a headline such as this one.

Tip No. 18: "We" is no substitute for "You."

Are you nodding smugly with an I've-known-that-all-my-life reaction? Great! It really isn't aimed at you. It's aimed at those other guys who use the mail so seldom they're afraid the reader won't look at their offer if they don't try to cast a giant shadow.

Here's a recent example from my mailbox:

Dear Sir,
    I would like to introduce you to The Creative Network, Inc. We are an exciting new creative art company specializing in screen print art for tee shirts, hats, sportswear and illustration for fashion, logos, ad layouts and catalogs.
    Never before has a company been so direct and creative by offering our services to advertising agencies that specialize in "Ad Specialty" merchandise for their clients. . . .

Don't you grind your molars, reading all this self-love?

Tip No. 19: Get to the point.

Sometimes I enjoy the leisurely pace of a down-home letter. But I never do enjoy hunting through a high-power letter, looking for the point.

The difference is one of writing technique. In my opinion, writing a "Jes' plain folks" letter is easy; writing an *effective* "Jes' plain folks" letter is a test of the writer's talent. The infrequent letter writer is in rocky shoals there. Go with percentages, I say, and unlimber the dynamite.

But unless you're writing a down-home letter, don't you dare let half a page slip by without telling me what you're selling me. That's a *kamikaze* letter, and your text and my interest both perish in the flames.

An example is a letter which might have succeeded if, anywhere in the first three paragraphs, it had told me what they're selling:

Dear Mr. Lewis,

I'm writing to you to tell you why Computer Communications, Inc. can do a faster, more accurate and less costly job for you.

The proof is in the 300 satisfied clients we now have, more than half of whom have been with us since our company began.

Last month, for instance, we ran 498 separate jobs, ranging in size from 2,000 to over a million donor names.

There's a weak clue: "donor names." But I'm not in the mood to play detective. Suppose the letter had opened:

Dear Mr. Lewis,

I'm writing to tell you why Computer Communications, Inc., can update your master name file with greater speed and accuracy than any system you've ever used before. And we'll do it at less cost.

I'm assuming this is what the company does. The last paragraph of the letter says, "I believe we can make a difference in the quality of your file maintenance."

Tip No. 20: Assume acceptance, not antagonism.

The theory behind "lift" letters ("Open this only if you have decided not to take advantage of this offer . . .") is that an extra push, by another person and from another direction, can retrack an undecided skeptic. You'll never retrack a predecided antagonist.

That's why it amazes me when someone who wants to be a supplier comes out swinging and starts Round 1 by hitting the referee—as this mailing from a producer of personalized letters does:

Dear Mr. Lewis:

It always amazes me that less than 25 percent of the executives who receive this letter respond.

Because, we turn executives into heroes. You see, every executive has to be interested in increasing profits . . . lowering marketing costs . . . and enhancing company image. And that's what Letterex Communications can help you do. . . .

What this company *has* done is skewed 180 degrees from what they've just said they do: enhance company image. How easy it would be to have written a pleasant letter, perhaps opening with the nonaggressive question, "How'd you like to be even more of a hero than you are?" instead of pronouncing judgment on 75 percent of the executives who get this letter. They're stupid because they, the majority, don't respond and therefore have no interest in increasing corporate profits.

What can anyone with any ego of his own do but reject both the claim and the person who makes it?

Taking the position of The Last Angry Man is dangerous. It's like spray-painting your car when it's parked between two other cars.

Tip No. 21: Format can't mask dullness.

A fat woman thinks fashions from Bloomingdale's will work magic she wouldn't need if she had any willpower. An unimaginative copywriter thinks a format which labels itself "exciting" will work magic with his dull message.

Opinion: Both are wrong. Both, because they expect others to create a transformation in reader attitude they themselves can't, deserve failure.

When my office places media advertising, my wife usually supervises it. She's our media contact. I rescued this Mailgram from her wastebasket:

DEAR MARGO:

SOFTWARE MERCHANDISING CELEBRATES ITS SECOND ANNIVERSARY NEXT MONTH. WE'RE PROGRAMMING IN SOME EXCITING CHANGES THAT YOU'LL WANT TO KNOW ABOUT. THE NEW SOFTWARE MERCHANDISING IS YOUR KEY TO THE ENTIRE HOME COMPUTING AND SOFTWARE MERCHANDISING MARKETPLACE. DETAILS TO FOLLOW. . .

That's the entire message. Someone wrote this, for pay.

Suppose you, as an acknowledged expert, address a high school class. After your speech, one of the students comes up to you and asks your opinion of this piece of copy, written not for a trade publication but for the high school yearbook. Could you suppress your conscience and lie, "Use it. It's fine"?

Or would you explain, patiently or impatiently, that labeling a nonevent "exciting'' doesn't make it exciting and the Mailgram format doesn't add a thing except harder-to-read all caps?

This may not be a fair example, because I think the Mailgram format is implicitly dull (see "Speed Formats," Chapter 14). The way to overcome that dullness isn't a one-paragraph tribute to self-importance, but, rather, individual words spaced to overcome the limitations of the format, using as their foundation the solid rock of reader benefit instead of the eroding sands of self-interest.

Tip No. 22: Timeliness is second only to verisimilitude in its ability to bring dollars through the mail.

You surely remember the massive fund-raising campaign for the Statue of Liberty restoration. One of the best examples of using time as a fear motivator was a mailing two years before the 1986 completion date, from the Statue of Liberty Ellis Island Foundation, Inc., which extended its sense of urgency even to the date on the letter—"Wednesday." Clever, for a third-class nonprofit mailing which otherwise defies dating, wasn't it?

The letter started out in high gear, as a fear/time appeal should:

> The most powerful symbol of our nation's liberty is in a serious state of disrepair.

A few paragraphs beyond, another signal of timeliness crashes into our psyches. Doom isn't impending, it's here now.

> But right now the Statue of Liberty faces its most serious danger since it was officially dedicated in 1886 . . .
> . . . It is an alarming situation . . .
> . . . I've enclosed two dramatic pictures that show just what has happened and why we must preserve it now . . .
> . . . In order to continue this work we have to raise a minimum of $1.8 million of the total budget within the next 45 days. Time is crucial since there is real danger that if. . . .

Think for a moment. If you had to create a "right now" demand for a project whose fruition isn't scheduled for another two years, could you have written this any better? The letter is unrelenting; and proof of its effectiveness stands proudly renewed in New York harbor.

Tip No. 23: Be sure they know what you're talking about.

You work for a company selling fingernockles by mail. You spend your entire day saturated with fingernockles. You can assemble one blindfolded, with your toes. You're steeped in fingernockle lore.

Don't make that same assumption about the person to whom you're selling fingernockles. He doesn't spend his days in your office and he's made enough money to be considered a good prospect . . . without ever owning a fingernockle. Telling him how your fingernockle is better than anyone else's fingernockle isn't going to move him off dead-center. First you have to tell him why he needs a fingernockle.

This point came home to me a few years ago when I was trying to find a way to sell collector's plates by mail, to people who weren't collectors. The list broker was sourly unhelpful: "You can't sell collectibles to anyone but a collector."

I didn't like this Catch-22 approach. Why wouldn't lists other than lists of collectors respond on a better-than-break-even level? I staggered into a "Eureka!" discovery while reading a mailing from a company selling something to do with Dolby noise-reduction in hi-fi sets.

Like many, I had heard of Dolby for years. This mailing, *for the first time*, told me what it is.

The next opportunity I had, I tested an additional enclosure which explained in a nonpatronizing way what collector's plates are. The enclosure made little difference in the response from collector lists, but previously unresponsive lists of artbook buyers suddenly came to life.

My conclusion: Previously we had treated them as though they knew what fingernockles were; they didn't, and they not only wouldn't order, they *couldn't*, because we'd sent them "in-group" mailings and they knew they weren't members of the in-group.

Tip No. 24: Truth doesn't justify an exclamation point unless the statement excites the reader.

A savings and loan institution, referring to mortgage payments, says:

Save a big 1%!

Put this way, the reason for the exclamation point doesn't register on the reader's emotional/exclamatory computer. "Big" and "1%" just don't logically go together. The same information can lay claim to the exclamation point by dropping the obvious mismatch:

You'll save a full percent!

Better yet, if the writer can relate the one percent mortgage differential to actual dollars, he has every reason to exclaim.

If you have a 30-year mortgage, you'll save *thousands* of dollars!

Tip No. 25: Beware of words with two meanings. They can bite.

The English language has an astounding number of words with more than one meaning. Sometimes a direct marketing wordsmith *deliberately* uses a word which his lawful prey can interpret several ways. But the writer should never use a word which, misinterpreted, can generate a negative reaction.

Innocently, a writer let this construction escape:

It was handled right in our office.

A writer might get away with this in broadcast media, by instructing the announcer how to read it to achieve proper word emphasis. The direct mail writer doesn't have an intermediary; "direct" is his first name, and message interpretation is squarely in the reader's hands. Unless the reader attaches *right* to *in our office*, as a single phrase, *right* gets hooked to *handled*—*handled right*, which suggests it might *not* have been handled right on other occasions.

The sentence illustrates the reason for having a disinterested (not uninterested) party proofread the copy, which easily casts off the possibility of misinterpretation when put this way:

We handled it—right in our office.

Now the writer forces the reader to group the words as intended.

Apparently harmless constructions such as "simple child psychology" prove that the writer, who reads the words one way only, isn't the best proofreader of those words.

Tip No. 26: Test in and test out.

A kamikaze approach to direct marketing is discarding a profitable copy approach and replacing it with a new ad or mailer because "we're tired of it" or "it's worn out."

When your ads or mailings are profitable, test copy changes gingerly; but even if they're wildly profitable, keep testing. And keep records.

Replacing a good old "control" mailing or ad is a trauma for many companies. They see it dipping, dipping, but they won't initiate a quiet series of component tests to learn what might add some fresh steam. When the power finally expires, they're left marooned with no tracks to guide them back to profitability.

In direct response, refusing to test turns you into a bull elephant crashing through the veldt, with a bullet in your brain. You're dead but don't know it yet.

Tip No. 27: If you aren't sure of buyer gender, don't polarize it.

An extravagant mailing, addressed to me, has this overline beginning the letter:

You can now acquire the doll collection that every little girl has dreamed about

I don't understand the lack of punctuation at the end of the thought, but I'm bewildered by a sentence which implicitly eliminates half the readers without improving sales appeal to the other half.

By now, logical targets of collectible doll mailings have been circularized often enough to take an asexual product view. See the problem here? They can't, when the writer cuts them out of the herd.

Tip No. 28: Opening with benefit is an insurance policy. No matter how unprofessional the writing, you'll be floating in the warm sea of the reader's self-interest.

My apologies for reprinting so much of the opening of a four-page letter sent to cold list names. I want to illustrate Tip No. 28.

> YOU are personally invited
> to examine for 15 days FREE
> THE NEW "Red Books"
> and SAVE $117.00 NOW—
> if you decide to order them.
>
> These remarkable guides can save you
> many valuable hours of work and
> perhaps help you discover your most
> profitable breakthrough of the year!
>
> Please read on . . .
>
>
> Dear Executive:
>
> Imagine how much easier, more rewarding and more satisfying your job would be if you had powerful information like this at your fingertips *right now:*
>> —the names and phone numbers of those key decisionmakers *who* control the big advertising money today . . .
>> —exactly *how much* they're spending . . .
>> —the media *where* it's being spent . . .
>> —current, reliable reports on *what* is really new and important on the client *and* agency sides . . .
>> —*how to reach* the creative, production, and other people responsible for that new ad campaign everyone is raving about . . .
>> —*which* accounts your competition is likely to go after this year . . .
>
> Well, you can feel good knowing that all this exciting information—*all accurate, complete, reliable, and current*—can be yours *at a glance* when you have THE NEW RED BOOKS on your desk.
>
> And right now, because I think you're a leader who needs these essential business facts *fast* to work more effectively and more efficiently, I am making you

this RED BOOK FREE TRIAL and SPECIAL SAVINGS OFFER. More on this exciting offer in a minute.

First of all, I'm pleased and proud to announce the publication of THE NEW RED BOOKS. And *new* they are!

As you know very well, the advertising and marketing business changes rapidly and frequently. It has changed so dramatically that *up to 80% of the listings are different* than the information in last year's editions.

That's the entire first page of the letter. Let's first eliminate from consideration (relative to Tip No. 28) the grammatically incorrect "different than," the apparent lack of familiarity with the company's own statistics (". . . *up to 80% of the listings are different* . . ."), and the almost random underlining and capitalization. We're concentrating on *benefit*. Where is it?

What the writer did here was throw down a gauntlet many readers don't recognize as a gauntlet. Yes, we understand what they're selling—information. What we don't understand is the benefit. "These remarkable guides can save you many valuable hours of work and perhaps help you discover your most profitable breakthrough of the year!" isn't even tantalizing, because *every* business mailing promises to save hours of work, and we can't quite penetrate "profitable breakthrough."

How *do* we project benefit from information? I can think of two ways: (1) Specific examples of benefits RED BOOK readers have had from owning the publications; (2) A no-risk trial, which changes the reader's "I don't know what this will do for me" to "What do I have to lose while I see whether their *features* become my *benefits*?"

The no-risk trial does appear, on the fourth page of the letter. Opinion: too late for many.

Tip No. 29: The wording of information-seeking questions in a coupon or order form can have a negative effect.

Suppose you aren't a scuba diver but would like to be. From an ad for scuba gear you fill out a coupon which has a question emphasizing your second-class status:

_____ I am _____ I am not a certified scuba diver.

Someone who scraped through Child Psychology 101 would know how easy it is to avoid the negative effect:

_____ I am not _____ I am a certified scuba diver.

Reversing the two won't bother the already certified divers and makes the nondivers feel their position is the most common one.

Tip No. 30: Bullet copy forces specificity.

Bullet copy, by its very terseness, prevents those rhapsodic lapses into puffery which throw sand into the gears of a dynamic selling argument.

Which of these copy blocks transmits the most information, the most credible information, and the most action-inducing information?

Now you can have all the quality features you've wanted in a 25″ color TV and you can have it at *an outstanding value.* With this Sharp TV you have the convenience of 6-function wireless infrared remote control plus exceptional performance. There's a 105-channel cable-ready tuner, the reliable Sigma 8000 chassis with 100% solid-state circuitry and the exclusive Linytron Plus one-gun picture tube for bright, clear color.

or

The Sharp 25″ Remote Color TV

- ► Infrared wireless remote control
- ► Cable-ready to 105 channels
- ► LED channel display and 1-button picture balance control
- ► 1-year in-home parts and labor limited manufacturer's warranty

The bullets separate the selling points which, in a block of prose, sap impact from one another. To me, though, the biggest benefit of bullets is their implicit culling of puffery from the factual core.

Tip No. 31: If you're unsure of a word's use and no one in your office is qualified to judge your vocabulary, pick another word.

Writer or nonwriter, it's a good idea to learn a fresh word every day. But don't treat words like new toys you have to grab and play with until you break them.

I had bad vibes when I first spotted a space ad for one of the 320,000 collectibles "commemorating" the Statue of Liberty because the name of the poet who wrote "Give me your tired, your poor . . ." was misspelled (Lazaruz instead of Lazarus).

Yup. Body copy was overblown, always an indication of land mines. This one had to explode all over the writer:

"The Dedication Ceremony," 100 years ago, has now been faithfully documented in a work of fine art by one of our country's most famous artists, Alan D'Estrehan. Ironically, Mr. D'Estrehan was originally from France as was our Statue of Liberty.

Ironically? The dictionary shows four definitions of "irony," ranging from ignorance to incongruity. These definitions fit the writer, not the subject.

What's ironic is the image of a writer, struggling to convert a useless fact to a "Wow, look at this!" effect, using more of the language than he or she knew—and needlessly exposing this deficiency in vocabulary.

Tip No. 32: Nonsense parallels have become popular as writers' crutches. They're noncommunicative attempts at cleverness for the sake of cleverness. Don't use this device.

A laundry product called Gain used a textbook example of the nonsense parallel in its television commercial. The husband, obviously in need of psychiatric help because he becomes orgasmic over his wife's clean dress, nuzzles the dress and murmurs lovingly:

"Do you think it's so clean because it smells so good?"

His wife, carried away by the passion of the moment, responds:

"Or does it smell so good because it's clean?"

I'm not attacking the nonsense parallel because it's grade-school-easy to write or because of its format; in fact, I like parallels. My objection is to the ridiculous premise. Invariably, at least half a nonsense parallel is impenetrable. Example: "Do you think it's so clean because it smells so good?" I defy you to make sense out of that half-parallel.

Half a century ago, a Harold Lloyd movie had this line: "Clothes don't make the man. Man makes the clothes." Did this start it all? We now have nonsense parallels springing up like triffids:

"My backyard turned into the PGA-Sheraton Resort?" "No, the PGA-Sheraton Resort turned into your backyard."

Now: Are you proud because you figured this out? Or did you figure this out because you're proud?

Tip No. 33: If half a parallel is negative, the parallel itself is probably weak.

This tip isn't (pardon the term) parallel to Tip 32. A nonsense parallel is ridiculous; a negative parallel isn't. Rather, it's logical but not helpful.

A sample will clarify:

Kendall Drive used to be a road to nowhere. Now it's the road to everywhere.

Another:

> People used to say the taste wasn't exciting. They don't say that any more.

Still not convinced that a negative parallel probably isn't your best selling copy? Let's look at one more:

> Who says this computer has a poor service record? Not the users who get their Winchester hard disk drives from us.

The negative parallel plants a negative seed. Everybody in direct marketing knows negative seeds sprout at ten times the speed of positive seeds. It's because in the Age of Skepticism our readers look for negatives. Let's not feed them.

Tip No. 34: Don't assume that a mildly favorable fact is a selling weapon.

Somehow, researchers have superimposed on marketers the notion that a majority margin—51 percent or more—is ammunition. My opinion differs. I suggest the existence of a major difference between the voting majority at a stockholders' meeting and a powerful sales argument in an ad or mailer aimed at somebody who doesn't know you.

Here's an example of a fact-based copy platform:

> Fact! 93.7% of those who already have bought these self-adjusting trousers say they're satisfied.
> Fact! 72% say they plan to buy more.
> Fact! This low price can't be available forever."

My reaction to the first "Fact!" was *negative*. Aside from the weakness of the word "satisfied," I was troubled by the existence of 6.3% who *weren't* satisfied. "Planning to buy more" isn't the same as actually buying more—a common problem with attitude research. Had the copy been able to claim, "Three out of four buyers came back and bought another pair!" we'd have a *salesworthy* fact—not just a naked piece of information floating in the Dead Sea of word description.

Tip No. 35: The components of a direct mail package should reinforce one another, not parallel one another.

I say "One another," not "each other," because sometimes a letter, a brochure, a lift letter, and a third-party endorsement all will project the same message. Uh-uh.

The most common violation of this tip is writing a letter and a brochure whose sales messages are nearly identical. When copy in a sales letter and a brochure is the same (perhaps reorganized but not presenting different dimensions of thought on the subject being sold), someone has gone back 30 years and taken the old saw literally:

"Tell 'em what you're going to tell 'em. Then tell 'em. Then tell 'em what you've told 'em."

That still works, when you do it within a single component. It becomes boringly repetitious when you use a letter, a brochure, and maybe a third enclosure to restate your approach.

Instead, the letter should point out reasons to "look over the brochure I've enclosed," and the brochure might quote an excerpt from a magazine article—a reprint of which is another enclosure. When the pieces reinforce one another, the effect is synergistic: each gains power, validity, and the appearance of truth.

Tip No. 36: When you sign a letter, type your name below the signature unless you're positive the reader will recognize the signature.

This tip is mechanical rather than creative. It's based on the increasing number of idiot scrawls masquerading as signatures. Since John Hancock put his beautiful, clear John Hancock on the Declaration of Independence, we've suffered a gradual deterioration in penmanship. Some executives think it's executive-ish to have a stylishly unintelligible signature.

The reader wants to deal with a person, not a company. Clear signatures are reassuring.

Tip No. 37: Before turning a piece of copy loose, check paragraphs beginning with the word "as" and replace the word—and the phrase following it—if you spot limpness.

A paragraph starting with "As" is especially vulnerable, because the word so often begins a refer-back: "As mentioned above ..." or "As previously stated. ..."

I don't know the percentage of "As-refer-backs" which can be strengthened, but I'd guess it's at least half. We all do it; we shouldn't, since "As-refer-backs" are holding actions at best. Even in the active tense, an as-phrase probably is weaker than the same phrase without it: "As I told you, we'll ..." has far less impact than "I told you we'll. ..."

Tip No. 38: Don't suggest on the outer envelope that the reader has to do something to get a benefit.

If the purpose of the message on an envelope is to get the envelope opened, suggesting the reader has to work in order to enjoy benefits can be the reason your envelope gets the old heave-ho.

I'm looking at an envelope I never did open. This legend is on its face:

FREE REPORT!
You Can Save
Thousands of Dollars a Year
By Correcting
These Common Tax Mistakes

Heck, I think this mailer can save thousands of dollars a year by correcting his own Common Tactical Mistake. "Do You Make These 5 Tax Mistakes?" might have teased me into opening the envelope ("5" instead of "Five" for impact); the word "correcting" killed off my interest in whatever they're selling.

An envelope preaches at me:

Luck is no substitute for Knowledge.
And Knowledge doesn't come easy.

Maybe the writer was thinking of knowledge of grammar. Whatever might be inside this envelope, couldn't the writer have promised me something instead of adding more creases to my forehead?

Tip No. 39: A dash is harder and stronger than an ellipsis (three dots).

I've lifted this tip from Chapter 11, where the information refers to grammar and usage, to this position, where it refers to impact, because . . .

Careful! You may not want hardness and strength. This is a subtle tip. The difference between a dash—a power-stop—and an ellipsis . . . a soft interrupter . . . is clear. What isn't so clear is when to use which.

Generally, use the dash when you're writing dynamic copy. Use the ellipsis when you want to draw less attention to the effect. Shelley and Keats = ellipsis. Browning = dash.

Don't apply this tip to the grammatical use of the ellipsis. When you want to show an incomplete quotation, use dots, not a dash: "I was saying. . . ."

Tip No. 40: Consider perceived value when describing product use or inventing a product name.

Which one probably will sell more merchandise?

—Protects Your Lower Arms

or

—Protects Your Arms Far Above the Wrist

The typical reader doesn't regard "lower arms" as a vital area; wrists are damage-prone. I favor the second approach.

A company trying to sell children's videotapes refers to "Annie, a Pigtailed 10-Year-Old." Oh, sure, I know what they mean, and I've seen too many of these gaffes to laugh at every one I see. "Annie, a Little Girl in Pigtails" changes the emphasis from the pigtails to the girl, replacing clinical description with charm.

Use this tip to pre-test product names and descriptions, from butt steak to shoes built on U.S. Navy lasts. Example: Which is a better shoe, the *Ensign* or the *Commodore*?

What's in a name? Plenty, if you're selling by mail.

Tip No. 41: You usually can strengthen a weak headline beginning with the word "If" by changing the wording to become a question.

Donnelley List Marketing sent an enclosure with the Direct Mail List Bulletin. On both flaps was this copy:

TELEPHONE
NUMBERS?
62,861,427

Had Donnelley used standard "If" copy—"If you need telephone number appending"—the impact would have been fractional compared to this powerhouse copy.

Try it. Find an old piece of copy starting with "If" and play with it. Converting an opening "If . . ." phrase to a question, especially a terse question, can start off your message in high gear.

Tip No. 42: If you cry "Wolf!" be sure your readers can see a wolf.

Fear sometimes is too powerful a motivator. If you use it, be certain your words generate fear in the reader's heart. A fear approach which falls short is a disappointment to the message recipient; from your early warnings, he anticipates being rocked by your words.

An example is a fund-raising mailing whose key component is a note typed all caps on colored stock. Look what happens here:

URGENT   URGENT   URGENT
RECENT REPORTS FROM ETHIOPIA AND EAST AFRICA INDICATE THAT THE SITUATION CONTINUES TO BE VERY SERIOUS. THOUSANDS OF DESPERATE REFUGEES ARE STILL TRAVELING FROM ONE COUNTRY TO ANOTHER IN SEARCH OF FOOD.

ALTHOUGH RECENT SHIPMENTS HAVE PROVIDED SOME RELIEF, MUCH MORE IS NEEDED. . . .

The words *Although recent shipments have provided some relief* sap impact from the three "URGENT" headers which demand copy power. Suppose the phrase were dropped; the sentence would read, "Much more relief is needed." The sense of urgency would continue unadulterated.

If you suggest a hunter has shot out the wolf's canine teeth and trimmed its claws you make the wolf far less dangerous. It's *your* wolf. He's as fierce or as tame, as dangerous or as remote, as you make him.

Tip No. 43: Mysterious forces may terrify the reader but they won't have much luck selling him or her something.

A company which for some insane reason wants to handle my investment portfolio sent me a brochure describing their services:

Advantage #1
Your portfolio will be reviewed and analyzed, and appropriate suggestions will be made.

Big Brother is watching me! Apparently he's in the publishing business too, because his magazine starts what I guess someone thought is an effective sales pitch this way:

This NEWS
Is SIGNIFICANT
To YOU

Dear Sometime Reader:
The decision has been made. You'll be allowed to join us.

Check your own copy. If it has the giveaway passive voice—something *will be done,* not *I'll do something*—it could suffer from the Mysterious Forces Terror. "They," whoever They are, are taking over. The decisions are out of our hands.

No! By taking responsibility you build rapport. Although I hate the premise, I'd have been a reader and not an adversary had the communication begun:

I'd like to believe
this news
is significant to you.

To a Special Friend:
We've decided you're one of us. I hope you'll make the same decision.

Dispelling implicit hostility can be as easy as taking responsibility for the words you're writing.

Tip No. 44: Whenever you can add the word "you" to a benefit, you clarify it as a benefit.

A letter offering a money-back guarantee says, "There are no risks involved." The writer would have injected potency into the same information by wording it, "You take no risk whatever," or "Examine it at our risk—not yours."

Copy selling a medical reference book says, "This book supplies information about . . ."; you or I would have worded it, "This book gives you information about . . ." because our revised sales argument narrows itself to reader benefit.

Tip No. 45: The difference between "can't" and "won't" is the difference of whether or not you're able to control what you're selling.

Usually "won't" is preferable but "can't" is better when you want to emphasize that all the forces of creation are unable to influence the result.

Two examples might clear up any confusion hovering over this tip. The first is a piece of catalog copy which in my opinion grossly misstated the value of a shampoo:

A gentle shampoo that can't dry even the most delicate hair . . .

I've quoted it as it was, with the word "out" missing after "dry." But assume it reads the way the writer must have intended it to read—"can't dry out." See how the words make the product seem to fail at a job it means to do?

We replace "can't" with "won't" and *voila!*

A gentle shampoo that won't dry out even the most delicate hair . . ."

The second is copy for a ball-point pen:

Bang it. Knock it. Scrape it against a concrete wall. Rasp it with a file. You won't damage it.

The writer has given us factual accuracy, not inspiration. This situation is the reverse of the one before it, because we're supposed to think that no matter what we do this pen can take it and come up smiling. So we change one word:

Bang it. Knock it. Scrape it against a concrete wall. Rasp it with a file. You can't damage it.

In this tip we have one of the tiny keys to copy power we sometimes overlook because using one word instead of another isn't a ghastly error but only a thinning of the magic paste.

Tip No. 46: Emphasize the right point.

This means extrapolating benefit from factual information. Copy for a battery-operated typewriter crows:

Uses thermal paper (included).

As a user, I don't regard thermal paper as a benefit. In fact, the word "thermal" implies something combustible, likely to burst into flame as I stare at it. How easy it is for the copywriter to answer my "So what?" with a benefit aimed squarely at me:

Special "thermal" paper means you never have to change a ribbon.

See how the emphasis changes? Copy now focuses where it should—on what the paper does for the user, not on the structure of the paper itself.

A parenthetical point: I oppose indiscriminate use of quotation marks, but I embrace the notion of putting "thermal" in quotes here. Why? Because this device tells the reader the paper isn't really hot and fiery. The quotation marks don't help our direct comprehension but they indirectly help our acceptance of the unknown. (See the Quotation Mark Rule under "Punctuation and Grammar," Chapter 25.)

Tip No. 47: Comparative copy should specify areas of superiority. Damning the competition without giving the reader solid meat leaves your reader chewing air—and burping out your sales argument undigested.

You want me to switch from an existing supplier to you. What do you tell me?

I'll wager that an apprentice insurance salesman, armed with little more than the realities of competition, could mount a more realistic selling argument than the letter from the "District Manager" of an insurance agency, which starts off in just the wrong key:

Dear President:

I have contacted you in regard to your Pension Assets being managed by someone other than the Best. We have been ranked the #1 Manager of Pension Funds for years; and manage in excess of $50 billion dollars of assets . . .

The letter goes on to bury with unflagging success its core—the actual percentages of asset increases—in lines such as "I believe that you are a wise and successful business person" (Urp!) and words such as "utilizing," which we'd expect in a communication such as this. We aren't surprised by the "$50 billion dollars" redundancy. The writer signs his name "Edward H. Maass, EQA," as though I had even the foggiest notion what "EQA" means.

The capper is the P.S.:

WHY MANAGE WITH THE REST WHEN YOU CAN HAVE IT MANAGED BY THE BEST!!!

Tell you what, Mr. Maass. Drop your initials. Take the spats off your copy. Use only one punctuation mark at a time. Write in complete sentences. Open with benefit to me. Then we'll talk.

(You'll find a complete discussion of comparative advertising in Chapter 6.)

Tip No. 48: If you want to use testimonials but don't have any, offer a prize for the best ones. You'll get a lifetime supply.

I can't show you examples of testimonials obtained this way because in print a testimonial is a testimonial. You'll have to take my word for it. The procedure does work.

A caution, though: Don't ask for testimonials; ask for *opinions*. Results will be just as good and your ethics remain intact.

Tip No. 49: The word "needs" as a noun is never as explicit or as effective as another noun you already know.

Yellow Pages copy is shot through with headlines such as "For All Your Insurance Needs!" or "For Your Office Supply Needs." Don't use that reference as an excuse to use "Needs." Yellow Pages copy isn't a treasure-house of brilliant copywriting; your direct mail piece should be.

What set me off was a mailing from someone *within* the industry whose letter was headed:

WE CAN SERVE *YOUR* DIRECT MAIL NEEDS . . .

The heading itself wasn't peculiar. What *was* peculiar was that much of the letter which followed was bright, thoughtful, and pointed. Dullness, in the first two paragraphs, was the direct result of having to lean on the broken crutch "Needs."

If the writer of this letter had reasoned, "What *are* this guy's direct mail needs? They'll be the focus of my headline," then the letter might have resulted in an inquiry from me instead of inclusion in my "What Not to Do" file.

Try to program an automatic red flag. When the word "Needs" goes in, the red flag goes up and the writer backspaces until every evidence of this dulling malady is eradicated.

Tip No. 50: Plate your word faucets with gold.

Without getting flowery or labored, use words with magic in them. They're there, not only in your dictionary or thesaurus but in your imagination. Fertilize your imagination, nurture it, prune it, turn its face to the radiant sun of reader involvement, and it will sprout.

A writer whose imagination had some weeds in it wrote this:

> J.R.R. Tolkien's masterful epic tale of wizards, orcs, and heroic hobbits was printed as a three-volume set.

Bewildered by an attack on what seems to be a good piece of copy? Weeds choked one key word. We have *printed,* a plumber's word, instead of *published,* a wordsmith's word.

The difference between motivational copy and bulk description lies in the fraction of a degree separating the reader's almost unconscious reaction to *printed* from the reaction to *published.* It's the difference in fund raising copy between "Now we want your help" and "Today we want your help." It's the difference between the flat "This is to notify you that . . ." and the attention-grabbing "This is to alert you to . . ."

THE INEVITABLE CONCLUSION

To the copywriter, sensitivity to words is just as much a key to professionalism as the ability to put those words onto a sheet of paper. Your viewpoint is closer to the target individual than the writer's. You're the filter, the border guard, the last stop before mistakes are immortalized.

To all who write direct mail copy, the last bastion of copywriter control: Good luck. Your competitors want to drink your blood. Let them starve.

14

How to Write Speed Format Copy

"SPEED" FORMATS DON'T HAVE TO BE "HO-HUM" FORMATS

If you're old enough to remember World War II, you probably also remember the excitement a telegram could engender.

A clean-cut young man rode his bicycle to your door, and when he handed you the yellow window-envelope the surge of emotion was almost overpowering. What was in that envelope? An order? A job offer? The possibility that it might be bad news heightened the suspense even more.

I remember the telegram that came a few days after I got an advanced degree. It offered me a teaching job at a college I had no intention of considering. So powerful was the *medium* that I heeded the *message* and taught there for two years.

Where are the joys of yesteryear? Western Union drained the magic out of telegrams by phoning them to the recipient and asking, "Do you want a printed copy of this?"—an anticlimactic record, like watching an instant replay. Clean-cut young men don't ride their bikes any more; the occasional cyclist is either a ten-year-old, veering into your path on his deadly trail bike, or, if he's older than ten, chances are he isn't clean-cut. And try finding a Western Union office.

CAN BULK MAIL BE "RUSH—INSTANT!"?

One of the inevitable results of novelty is early burnout.

The Mailgram was a novelty when business mailers first started using it. In my opinion, its cool blue color damaged the emotional impact, but that's just an opinion.

Another opinion: The proliferation of speed formats has brought the whole technique close to the deadened land of ineffectiveness, where no response grows.

The original Mailgrams weren't to be bulk-mailed. They were designed for first-class postage, they had to be "handled," and they added so much expense that it was completely logical for alternative formats to appear. The ideal format would have impact stemming from the appearance of immediacy, "Open me now!" screaming from the envelope, and not too severe a letdown once trembling fingers had pried the message out of its garish womb.

Hundreds of speed message formats have appeared. Some are far more cleverly conceived than the messages they carry. All suffer from the overpopulation within their ranks.

Some Iconoclastic Notions

If you're in business, check your mail for the next few weeks. You may find, to your surprise, a dozen or more speed format mailings. The phrase "to your surprise" validates the claim I'm about to make: If these formats have become so commonplace they no longer have a singular impact, their very purpose has become self-defeating.

Only when I sorted through my files, gathering documentation for this book, did I realize that one of the samples actually *was* a genuine piece of first-class mail with an honest-to-goodness urgent message.

Hah! The joke is on the sender. I've become so jaded I treat all speed formats as third-class mail. My resistance seems to grow in direct ratio to the frenzy behind them.

From this, I've formulated The First Law of Speed Formats:

If the recipient becomes annoyed by discovering your ploy, the speed format has worked against you, not for you, because more conventional formats wouldn't have generated a negative reaction.

The Second Law implements the philosophy of the First Law:

The message must project timeliness, personalization, and possible loss of benefit, or it falls out of key with the format and violates the First Law.

Consider those first two laws before you throw them out, saying, "The speed format gives excitement to my dull message." Here's an example of how mailers misuse speed formats through their ignorance of the laws. Even as I was at the keyboard attacking speed formats, the mail carrier delivered a Federal Express Look-Alike. On the flap, in a red reverse, was this legend:

EXTREMELY URGENT LETTER ENCLOSED

Burned by my earlier ignoring of a genuine urgent letter, I opened the thing. Inside was a printed message, the urgency of which could apply only to the sender. He wanted to sell advertising space.

Nothing in the message said *You*. Nothing in the message said *You'll lose this benefit unless . . .*

My reaction: since the message was fraudulently couched, the medium was fraudulent.

THE RULE OF PSEUDO-LYING

The Rule of Pseudo-Lying is the control, the governor on what might be a disgusting runaway throttle. If enough mailers recognize this rule, matching medium to message, then "Urgent" will mean urgent and "Hurry!" will relate to reader benefit as well as sender benefit. The rule, as it appears elsewhere in this text:

When the reader thinks you aren't telling the truth about one point, he extends that opinion to include your entire sales argument. He rejects even those statements which *are* true.

Let's suppose I really could use the advertising space pitched in the "Extremely Urgent Letter." My decision on the space is still "Forget it"—not because the sender misstates the facts but because he cloaks them in duplicity.

When emotion and intellect come into conflict, emotion always wins. I reject the factual (intellectual) core of the message because I must; emotionally I'm wounded by deceit. Under the Rule of Pseudo-Lying, if fact is one percent contaminated with deceit, the whole rhetorical meal is full of maggots.

FOUR MORE LAWS OF SPEED FORMATS

To those who value form more than substance, I offer a venerable comment by David Ogilvy: "What you say is more important than how you say it."

We're in the Age of Skepticism, remember? The validity of Ogilvy's notion (published in 1963) may be blurred by a whole generation of television glitz, but for direct marketers its focus couldn't be sharper.

If you're hung up in speed formats, I beg you: Don't drive your message recipients deeper into skepticism where the rest of us copywriters won't be able to get at them. Keep the message sane and apparently true. We'll all benefit.

Four more laws can prevent the siren song of format from drowning out the victory march of message.

The Third Law of Speed Formats:

Open your message with compelling benefit.

P.O. Box 4434
Ft. Lauderdale, FL 33338

BULK RATE
U.S. POSTAGE
PAID
FT. LAUDERDALE,
FLORIDA
PERMIT NO. 191

MAIL-O-GRAM
URGENT MESSAGE — OPEN IMMEDIATELY

CAR-RT SORT
PRESIDENT
9748 1ST   ST   SW
FT LAUDERDALE   FL 33324

**CR 05

1

TELL-A-GRAM™

MR. HERB NATTER
     DIRECT MARKETING, INC.
70 MARCUS DRIVE
MELVILLE, NEW YORK   11747

2

FIGURES 14–1, 14–2, and 14–3
Here are three of the many speed formats that blossomed into popularity between 1986 and 1987. Would they fool you? Hardly. But the U.S. Postal Service, in late 1986, began militating for a ban on speed formats. The Post Office said its workers were "confused" by envelopes whose designs or outside wording suggest they should receive expedited service. A Postal Service spokesman cited section 121.42 of the Domestic Mail Manual: "Words implying expedited handling such as RUSH DO NOT DELAY shall not be used on any package except for those intended for shipment as special delivery or special handling mail." The Postal Service was unimpressed by the position of the Third Class Mailers Association, which pointed out that section 121.42 was designed for parcel post; but in 1987 the bureaucrats backed away from what may have been an unconstitutional position, resolving the issue by insisting only that the postal permit area be prominent and isolated.

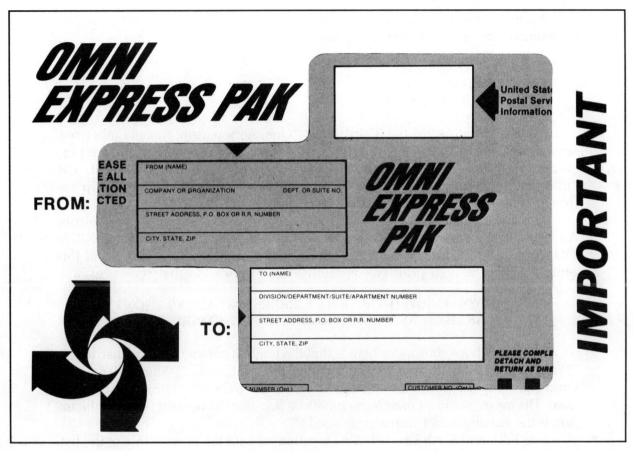

3

The Fourth Law of Speed Formats:

Don't let any distraction soften the "bulletin" copy approach.

The Fifth Law of Speed Formats:

If your message is supposed to be one-to-one, keep excitement high by keeping adjectives down; your message will match the medium if its entire structure demands *imperative action which produces benefit.*

And the Sixth Law of Speed Formats:

Slash away mercilessly at hard-selling copy. It destroys speed format verisimilitude.

Nothing difficult here, is there? Let's see how the laws work under battle conditions:

A computer-personalized yellow-and-black speed format, with the word "International" in its name, had this heading:

ONE MORE REASON TO
VISIT BOOTH 423
AT [NAME OF TRADE SHOW]

See the violations of the Third Law? "One more reason" means other reasons, more compelling than this one, exist. Visiting a conference exhibit isn't exciting *unless* benefit to me transcends the simple notion of the visit itself. The "International" band circling the envelope misinterprets the relationship between the states: The message came from Chicago.

The Fourth Law is probably the most abused of all the protective controls. An example is a speed format using the words "HIGH PRIORITY COMMUNICATION" in the standard reverse-band which girdles most of the envelopes of this genre. What's the high priority communication? Here's the first sentence:

WE HOPE YOU ENJOYED THE DIRECT MARKETING ASSOCIATION CONFERENCE AS MUCH AS WE AT [NAME OF COMPANY] DID.

What may have gone awry here is that the hapless copywriter was instructed, "Write a sales letter to those who attended the conference." The writer didn't know the company would use a speed format. If the writer *did* know, the blame is clear. His message didn't match the medium, because the opening denied the urgency the envelope and format proposed.

The Fifth and Sixth Laws are tied together and are the most subtle of the list. Even moderate attention to the discipline of force-communication would have prevented this copy from superimposing itself onto a structure that implicitly rejects it:

GET READY FOR THE BIGGEST TRUCK SELL-A-THON OF THE CENTURY! MORE THAN 2,000 FORD & GM TRUCKS "BY INVITATION ONLY", VANS TOO! AT FANTASTIC PRICES! EVERY LETTER HOLDER WILL RECEIVE A LOVELY 10 PC WOK COOKING SET, 35MM CAMERA, OR OTHER SENSATIONAL GIFT!

As purists we're jarred by the feminine adjective "lovely" in truck-selling copy, and as creative types we're annoyed by dependence on exclamation points for artificial excitement. While we're on the attack, 2,000 trucks is quite a number for an exclusive "by invitation only" sale.

After this Barnum & Bailey opening, the copy settles down but never justifies the format housing it. My question: Why use a speed format for a standard hard-sell?

A SPEEDY CONCLUSION

Like the hippies of the 1960s, speed formats try so hard to be different that they begin to look the same.

The format has logic, but logic is transgressed when the message doesn't deliver. If you mail your offer in an envelope whose face is a breathless "Here's hot news only for you!" then justify the envelope by matching the components.

You can practice by writing 15-word telegrams in the old, exciting style; before long you'll revitalize an otherwise ho-hum use of a medium that threatens to become overused. The format does work—if the writer puts on his telegram-delivery hat and envisions the young man on the bicycle, scurrying with a message the recipient knows will be hot news.

Sometimes I think American history would have been changed if Paul Revere had access to speed formats. Instead of charging through the countryside yelling, "The British are coming!" he'd have mailed an envelope, red-white-and-blue or yellow-and-black, with copy such as this:

DEAR NAME,

WE HOPE YOU ENJOYED WATCHING FOR THE BRITISH AS MUCH AS WE DID. NOW IT'S OUR PLEASURE TO TELL YOU THEIR SOLDIERS ARE AVAILABLE FOR A LIMITED TIME ONLY, IN THEIR LOVELY RED COATS.

THIS INFORMATION IS BY INVITATION ONLY. PLEASE RESPOND WITHIN THE NEXT 15 DAYS. YOU MAY INDICATE YOUR ACCEPTANCE OF THIS OFFER BY LOADING AND FIRING YOUR MUSKET. AS A PRIZE YOU WILL RECEIVE A SIGNED DECLARATION OF INDEPENDENCE.

FOR MORE DETAILS, CALL GEORGE AT 1-800-555-1212 DURING NORMAL BUSINESS HOURS EASTERN TIME.

15

How to Write Television Copy

Ask ten beginning copywriters what kind of copy they'd prefer to write. Eleven of them will answer, "Television!"

It's no surprise. Television is the glamor medium, all right. And in years past it had another advantage for the beginning writer: A charlatan could survive well in its oily waters.

Television writers who hadn't the slightest idea of how to use the most powerful and influential medium ever made available to wordsmiths filled their scripts and storyboards with spins and wipes and optical effects . . . and they got away with it, because a television commercial that called attention to itself *as a commercial* was a marvelous sample for the writer and the producer. What do you mean, did it sell? That isn't how we keep score.

Those days of golden brass are going into eclipse. Advertising agencies win awards for their television spots—then lose the account, because the award was given for artistry, not for salesmanship. When this has happened enough times, sanity will reappear in the screening room.

Until sanity returns, the journeyman writer is penalized by a harsh reality: The commercials which win awards, which are glorified, and whose key scenes appear in trade magazines are those with high visibility because of big budgets, "name" celebrities, and expensive effects. Quiet successes get their cheers in limited intra-office reports.

HOW TO STRUCTURE A TELEVISION SPOT

Video Storyboard Tests suggests you *not* mention product name in the first five seconds of a TV spot. Why? Because, they say, viewers will tune you out before you've established rapport with them; they recognize too early they're looking at a commercial.

(A qualifier, says Video Storyboard Tests: this limitation doesn't apply to brands the viewer already uses.)

I'm skeptical about this whole notion, so I'd add another qualifier: with so many commercials having a total air-time of 15 seconds or less, we can incorporate this suggestion into the First Rule of Television Impact:

If you open with a five-second episode excluding product, close with five seconds of hard visual and auditory emphasis on product.

An Explanatory Subrule helps keep the First Rule of Television Impact on the rails:

Validity of the First Rule of Television Impact increases with a decrease in spot length.

So the rule applies more profoundly to a 10-second spot than to a 60-second spot.

A 1986 survey of advertising media professionals by agency SSC&B indicated that the 15-second length (unknown as recently as 1983) by 1990 might represent 50 percent of network TV inventory—and this, said the agency's senior vice-president, is a "low estimate." Chances are the writer of television spots will have reason to consider the rule and defend its aptness.

WHAT IS THE VIEWER'S PERCEPTION?

The viewer has no sense of television timing. An advertiser will air two versions of the same commercial, one 60 seconds long and one 30 seconds long; the viewer finds them indistinguishable from each other.

With the breakdown of the traditional 30-second spot into "split-30s" in which an advertiser could air two separate 15-second commercials for each of two products in his stable, it was inevitable that networks and individual stations would begin selling 15-second spots to advertisers at large.

The argument, "Total commercial time hasn't increased," doesn't wash. If we're foot-soldiers in the army and every enemy gun is aimed at us, it's inconsequential that the total war hasn't escalated. The number of bullets fired at *us* is what matters.

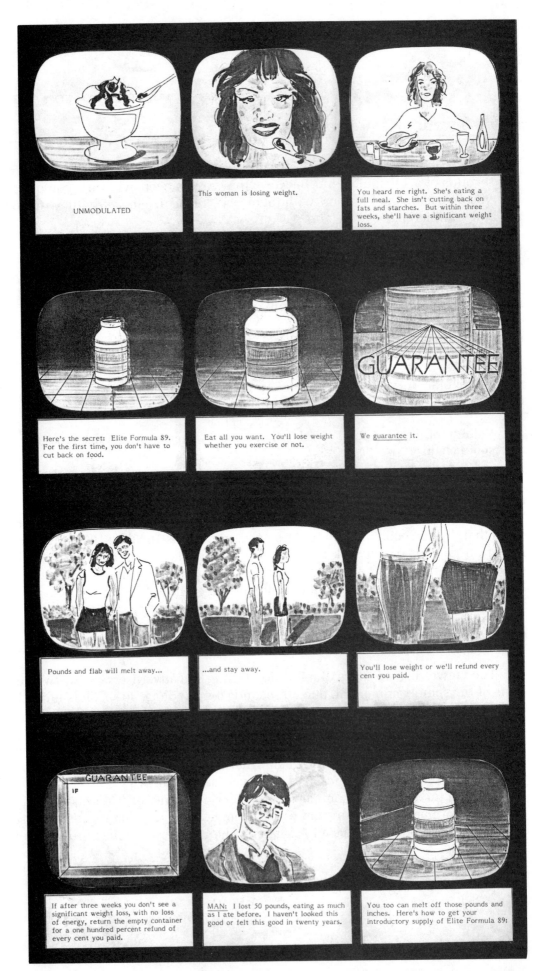

The 15-Second Flood

When networks opened the floodgates to the 15-second commercial, the challenge to television writers was a tough one, considering that the previous preferred length was exactly double—30 seconds. The typical challenge: Write a spot with the same impact . . . using half the time.

If you analyze this challenge, you'll see it's a *geometric* increase in difficulty because the commercial faces twice as many competing spots in the same commercial break.

Market research companies are enjoying the commercial glut. Peter R. Klein of the market research company McCollum/Spielman commented, "People are simply doing more testing all around. The consumer is becoming more and more desensitized to what's happening on TV. . . .

"With all this choice, there's more zapping, and this has led to more research as people attempt to break out of the crowd and gain attention for their products."*

The 15-Second Spot:
Blessing for Advertisers, Curse for Viewers

As the 15-second spot becomes "standard," television advertisers show considerable hypocrisy by coincidentally (a) saying the multiplication of spots within an allocated time period won't damage effectiveness as long as *total* commercial time isn't increased, and (b) asking stations to put their commercials in the first position within a stack of spots (called the "commercial pod" by euphemistic boosters).

Having 6 to 10 spots in a single break is an extraordinary challenge to the writer. "Think like a poster" is a good yardstick when you write short spots whose relative attention ratio will be zapped by its pod-mates.

Can you emotionalize within a 15-second spot? It's a struggle, because building rapport demands precious seconds; let's remember our ultimate goal and conclude that if the viewer loves the situation we've built but doesn't get the notion to buy something, we're dramatists, not salespeople.

A study done by the J. Walter Thompson advertising agency and the ABC network showed muddy conclusions: Informational ads by well-known brands should work well; consumer awareness of new products should increase; campaigns requiring emotion shouldn't use the shorter length; effectiveness can be as little as 30 percent of 30-second ads or as high as 80 percent.

---

*Advertising Age, Feb. 13, 1986, p.14.

FIGURE 15–1
This is a typical straight-sell television storyboard. Using unsubtle visuals, the spot makes its point by clear visuals backed by off-camera narration. (The purpose of the preliminary storyboard is to indicate how each key scene will look, helping the production team visualize the shots and avoiding mismatches that otherwise might not show up until the spot is being edited or aired.)

(The study was conducted just as 15-second spots became a major fact of life, in mid-1985. A more recent study might show deterioration of overall effectiveness because of the typical result: an increase in bulk and density.)

Some advertising giants have begun to lean on testing as a *replacement* for creative thinking. These advertisers pretest a whole group of ideas in front of a focus-group, using semifinished commercials. They then produce those with the best scores.

Better than no testing at all? Sure. Reliable? No. A self-conscious viewer looking at a semifinished commercial hardly parallels battle conditions.

For the advertiser whose 15-second spot is fifth or six in a stack of 8 to 12, life can be tough. Attention-getting devices wear out quickly; they subtract precious seconds from an already short spot; and they're a bandage at best: If every 15-second advertiser opened his spot with an attention-getting device, the whole medium would be laughable.

Commercial zapping? You ain't seen nothin' yet.

Recognizing this, reacting to the inability of viewers to sort through piles of televised messages, and anticipating clamor added to the clutter, some advertisers and agencies have begun to explore ways to enable their commercials to crash through the dull barrier of viewer apathy.

HOW TO CRASH THROUGH THE APATHY BARRIER

Take 30 seconds (lots of time, equivalent to two commercials) to think of ways for *any* advertiser to crash through the apathy barrier. Ready? Go.

Thirty seconds later. Chances are your solution (if any) involved noise or intensification of visual images. Either solution has a percentage of mechanical procedures at least as high as the percentage of creative wordsmithy.

Maybe that's as it should be. How long has it been since you saw a "stand-alone" commercial—one that wasn't preceded or followed by other commercials? It's naive to assume we can control the viewer environment or the Relative Attention Ratio our commercials inherit from their televised environment.

Startling graphics are easy when you have any mastery of computer animation. Attention-getting sounds are easy too. Ten years ago a television writer who admitted sensual dependency would have been regarded as a dilettante or a beginner. No more.

A byproduct of intensity as a television technique is the downgrading of people in spots. Traditionally, a spot showed or suggested human participation. The intensity-philosophy makes people optional—or even an intrusion into brilliantly colored abstract art.

What happens when sensory saturation cuts the Relative Attention Ratio of televised messages to a 10 percent to 15 percent minimal level? It's parallel to tasting many wines in succession without the palate-cleansing sip of water in between.

The writer might propose an experimental "limbo zone" of several seconds between spots. With a visual of clouds, trees, or the seashore, a quiet voice might say, "Take a breath." Total elapsed time: three seconds.

An impossible dream? Of course it is, unless an adventurous advertiser incorporates those three seconds into a paid commercial, and who would do that?

Zapping

Zapping is a television viewer's elimination of television spots by turning off the sound during a live broadcast, stopping the videotape when recording a show, or fast-forwarding a prerecorded tape to miss the commercials. The intention is singular: to avoid seeing commercials sponsors may have paid many hundreds of thousands of dollars to produce.

Zapping isn't a cry of outrage against any particular sponsor or any particular commercial. It's a reflection of boredom, of oversaturation, of annoyance with commercial clutter.

The natural evolution of having four 15-second commercials instead of two 30-second commercials or one 60-second commercial has been a glorious confusion of clutter. Which car is it during this break? Which toothpaste? Which detergent? Hey, there's Ford. Didn't we see a Chevvy spot 30 seconds ago?

The viewer, who doesn't time the spot but sees only a succession of tired situations—automobiles shrouded by smoke machines, too-happy waitresses lecturing customers on the virtues of paper towels and detergents, athletes thinking of their residual pay as they mumble their lines endorsing all manner of items, and orgasmic dances glorifying soft drinks or perfumes.

It's zap-time. Here's the latest electronic gadget to help the viewer escape the gnat-pack. Ahhhh!

To Avoid Zapping . . .

If you cain't lick 'em, join 'em.

Stations aren't about to retreat from the 15-second income bonanza—at least until these clustered spots reach so low a point of effectiveness that television advertisers start retrenching. So we see a counter-mini-trend. Advertisers who want to cut down zapping have begun to buy longer time periods—even old-fashioned 60-second spots—and turn them into condensed shows. The spot will open with a sports or entertainment quiz, or a news update, or a nostalgia-trivia teaser. Then, having hooked the viewer, the message pours through, like castor oil mixed into a chocolate soda.

Isn't this an expensive alternative to zapping? You bet. Obviously, only a few advertisers can use it—one per station-break—which means other alternatives have to be explored. Among the experiments are dynamic use of nonshowbiz celebrities, electronic gimmickry, and the often self-defeating technique of using up to two-thirds of the spot to stroke and entertain the viewer, limiting actual *sell* to a quick flash.

One unhappy reality of television exposure for the smaller advertiser is the relationship between name recognition and spot length: The less recognizable the name, the greater the length has to be to sell the same type of merchandise. Lower-budget advertisers, then, should look to 30-second and 60-second spots. The benefit is the greater dominance a longer spot might expect within a cluttered commercial ghetto. But look out: That word *might* puts the obligation right back onto the writer.

CAN A SPOKESPERSON BE TOO STRONG?

The creative team at Leo Burnett, the advertising agency, had an idea for their client, Pillsbury: To introduce a product called Crusty French Loaf, why not use an actor impersonating the late Peter Sellers as Inspector Clouseau (from the *Pink Panther* movies)?

Have you entered an automatic objection to the concept of impersonating an actor who himself is projecting an impersonation? Good for you.

The question is academic because the spot, as originally produced, never made it to the air. Why? Because research revealed a tragic flaw: The character was emphasized more than the product. In the words of Pillsbury's director of market research, as quoted in *Advertising Age*, "We determined that the commercial's ability to communicate and persuade were very good, but we needed to give the product more time. Also, we built in a little more exposure of the brand name."*

When you consider celebrity or fad coattail-riding, watch it! Don't fall in love with your device and don't forget the purpose of a commercial: to sell something.

Trends in commercials shouldn't affect the approach of any writer who realizes

1. Countertrends develop as quickly as trends.
2. Trends result in overuse of a technique.

Analysts who try to establish trends have to explain why, as many advertisers abandon "slice of life" advertising in favor of clinical demonstration, others begin to embrace this technique and abandon clinical demonstration. As advertisers bite the bullet and pay their impact-less celebrities for *not* appearing on camera, other advertisers seem to stand in line to sign up sports and entertainment figures to mouth on-camera messages for them. Figure 15–2 is an example. (A more complete exploration of celebrity use is in Chapter 16.)

A dangerous trend is the overproduced commercial with little impact on

---

*Advertising Age, Feb. 13, 1986, p.15.

RODNEY: I tell you, I fly a lot. That's why I look for those mileage clubs.

But it don't always pay off.

Oh there was one airline, I told the guy, "I got a lot of miles. What can you give me?" He offered me a lube job.

I told him, "Forget about it. What I'd like is a free trip. To another airline."

So now, I fly Western. I tell you, I went from no class, to First Class.

VO: No one rewards you like Western Airlines...It's the only way to fly.

FIGURE 15–2
One of Western's last celebrity-based commercials before the airline became a Delta affiliate was this one featuring comedian Rodney Dangerfield. The presenter's relationship with the advertiser has little value because nothing the comedian says gives the viewer a reason to fly this airline.

sales; after the fact, the company or its agency issues "Standard Explanation A-37": The commercial wasn't supposed to have any effect on sales; it was supposed to increase "awareness."

Many thought the trend had peaked in 1985, with a commercial for Apple's Macintosh Computer showing an endless line of people in business suits singing "Hi ho, hi ho, it's off to work we go," following one another lemming-like off the edge of a cliff.

Recall tests (an undependable method of judging, surely) showed that the public neither understood nor remembered this expensive commercial (SRI Research Center asked 300 viewers whether they recalled the spot; only 10.3 percent described the commercial correctly; 69 percent of those who said they had seen an Apple commercial said they didn't know what product was being advertised).

Apple might say: It was aimed only at that segment which is IBM-conscious. The speciousness of the argument is doubled when one reexamines the commercial in this light: It neither suggested nor demonstrated a competitive benefit, and—if it really was aimed at IBM-conscious viewers—television was a hopelessly wasteful medium for this advertising message.

But anyone who thought this would end the trend had no grasp of the psychology of major advertisers and their agencies. In 1986–87 the J. Walter Thompson Co. spent $40 million of Burger King's money on a poorly received "Herb the Nerd" campaign. *After* the campaign had flopped, the agency said its purpose hadn't been to increase sales but to increase "awareness." (The agency kept the account, for the time being, but lost it in late 1987.)

NINE EASY-TO-WRITE TV TECHNIQUES

1. The "Touchstone" Commercial

The Touchstone Commercial uses as a touchstone a monument, a person, or an event in which we have confidence. The American flag, the Rock of Gibraltar, the Statue of Liberty, and the Grand Canyon are examples.

The viewer transfers his respect, admiration, and confidence to whatever is using the touchstone.

The Great Western Savings commercial (Figure 15–3) uses a double touchstone—El Capitan, a natural "monument" in the American West, and respected actor Dennis Weaver.

2. The Lovely Payoff

We love romance, especially when a story turns out in a storybook way. The Teleflora commercial (Figure 15–4) ties the floral gift to a revived romance. The viewer's implicit hope that the story will turn out "right" turns the viewer to the item being sold.

GREAT WESTERN SAVINGS GW.

CLIENT: Great Western Savings

PRODUCT: Safe & Secure
TITLE: "Monument Valley"
LENGTH: 60 Seconds

"MONUMENT VALLEY"

**MUSIC UNDER THROUGHOUT
DENNIS WEAVER:** They call them
monuments.

And they've been around for a long, long
time.

Well, to me they're like sentinels, standing guard, watching over the West.

Kind of like Great Western Savings. You
know Great Western's been looking out
for folks and their money for nearly 100
years.

Nowadays, the Great Western family has
over $24 billion in assets. And they're
federally insured.

So you know your money is real safe
and sound.

Great Western Savings.

Standing tall.

Here to stay. Watching over the West.

For a long time to come.

249

FIGURE 15–3
Great Western Savings used quiet spokesperson Dennis Weaver for this commercial.
The "touchstone" attempt to relate the stability of monuments with the stability of the
financial institution was muddied by lack of specificity.

Call or visit your local florist today.

CLIENT: Teleflora

PRODUCT: Flowers
TITLE: "Courtship"
LENGTH: 30 Seconds

FEMALE TRAINER: Ah, I know you have a sweetheart . . .
ANNCR (VO): Recently gorillas have learned to communicate with humans.

FEMALE TRAINER: I have a friend who wants to send flowers to someone out of town. Yes, and they have to be fresh. So we want to send them by Teleflora.

No problem.

ANNCR (VO): To send fresh flowers anywhere.

Call or visit your local florist. And ask for Teleflora.

SFX: ELEPHANT SFX

SFX: GORILLA SFX

ANNCR (VO): Teleflora. The fresh way to send flowers anywhere.
SFX: GORILLA CHEWING FLOWER.

FIGURE 15–4
This Teleflora commercial typifies the "Lovely Payoff" technique of television spot copywriting.

FOLLOW THE LEADER

CLIENT: American Honda Motor Co., Inc.

PRODUCT: Motorcycles/Magna
TITLE: "Dyno Room"
LENGTH: 30 Seconds

"DYNO ROOM"

ANNCR: The Dyno Room.

Weak machines fear it.

Once harnessed to the dynamometer,

There are no secrets.

The Honda Magna.

It's V-4 power seems immeasurable.
The power of Magna. . .

SFX: REVVING

All the power you'll ever need.

251

FIGURE 15-5
In its attempt to tie benefit to technology, this commercial alienates the more sedate
viewer who objects to the old-fashioned "Wild One" image of motorcyclists.

3. Benefit Tied to Technology

The claim of benefit doesn't overcome skepticism; benefit tied to technology dissolves skepticism because of our implicit trust in technology to overcome all mechanical problems.

The Honda commercial (Figure 15–5) tries to do this, but the proof is incomplete and the commercial glorifies unharnessed power, an appeal only a fragment viewer group will appreciate.

4. Problem, Solved

Nobody wants a portable generator; but if we can show a problem-solving situation in which the generator saves the day, we can establish buyer receptivity.

The Honda Portable Generator dealer spot (prepared by the manufacturer for local dealer use) is a problem-solving demonstration (Figure 15–6), showing in only one scene the mechanical aspects of the generator; the rest is benefit.

5. Lean on Celebrities

This is the most crutchlike of techniques—the easiest to write, because the selling message is buried inside celebrity worship, but the most dubious for effectiveness because viewers remember the celebrities and not the company responsible for their appearance on screen.

A venerable Western Airlines commercial (Figure 15–7) illustrates this point. Nothing about the commercial suggests a benefit for Western Airlines passengers; the copy could as easily apply to any of the airline's competitors, an immediate betrayal of the shallowness of celebrity use.

6. Nonsense

When all competitors in a product category seem to be the same, nonsense *might* be a way to gain exposure. What claim to superiority does the Peter Pan Peanut Butter commercial (Figure 15–8) make? It's "Peanutty"; it's "made from the best peanuts in the world." Neither has substance. Without demonstrable product superiority, a nonsensical spot such as this might cause some children to militate for this brand.

7. P.O.C.B.

The Plain Ol' Country Boy approach carried Bartles & Jaymes to a strong competitive position among the various wine coolers. The fictitious Bartles & Jaymes characters (the latter character never saying anything) became folk celebrities through perfect underplaying.

"DINNER DATE"

25/05   Generator   HPTT-0753

SFX

ANNCR: Now's the time for a Honda portable generator......

Honda. Power.
Anytime. Anywhere.

MAN: Would you like some more coffee?

WOMAN: I'd love some, but don't you think it's a little bright in here.
DEALER TAG

Dealer Note: You will find the television order form at the end of the introduction section of your Dealer Ad Planner.

253

FIGURE 15–6
Honda fares better in this "Problem, Solved" spot for its portable generators. Only one scene shows the product; the rest shows what the product will do. Most consumers have no idea how a generator works, which makes this approach valid; if Honda were selling the generator to engineers, "Problem, Solved" would be too primitive to succeed.

Western Airlines
The only way to fly.®

CLIENT: Western Airlines

PRODUCT: General Passenger
TITLE: "Gene/Fred"
LENGTH: 30 Seconds

MUSIC UNDER
GENE: Hi!

Say if you could move those famous legs
a little, a fella might be able to sit down.

FRED: Well, if it isn't Mr. Kelly.

Watch your step, sonny boy.

These are new shoes.

GENE: Sonny boy,

I gotta say, you're looking pretty
turned out, kid.

FRED: Not bad for a hoofer on the road . . .
GENE: You know, Fred . . . you never
stopped traveling in style.

SFX: CLINKING OF GLASSES

ANNCR: Come see what it's like . . .

(VO PLANE FLY-AWAY)
. . . to travel in style on Western
Airlines.

FRED (VO): It's the only way to fly.

254

FIGURE 15–7
Would you fly Western Airlines because of anything in this expensive commercial?
Except for the last three panels, the spot reminisces with the two old stars and makes
no coherent selling point.

Peter Pan
PEANUT BUTTER

CLIENT: Beatrice Companies, Inc.
PRODUCT: Peter Pan Peanut Butter
TITLE: "Study Hall"
LENGTH: 30 Seconds

TEACHER: (Bell rings) Start your lunch.
I'll be right back.

SINGER: Weeeelll
I went down to school

And who did I see?

Peter Pan Peanut Butter

Peanutty!

Well, the kids
were all eatin'

That peanutty treat

Peter Pan Peanut Butter
Peanutty!
ANNCR. (Overlapped): Peter Pan
tastes so Peanutty

'cause it's made from
the best peanuts in the world.
SINGER: Eat some peanut butter.

Every time you can...

Only if it's Peter Pan!

MUSIC TAG: ...We're Beatrice.

255

FIGURE 15–8
If this approach doesn't embarrass you, you're either under age 8 or you understand
the "Nonsense" approach to television. In the absence of any claim of superiority this
advertiser recognizes that a disrupted schoolroom, a pirate, and an anthropomorphic jar
of peanut butter will appeal to children—who profoundly influence which brand of
peanut butter the household buys.

FIGURE 15–9
The Gallo Winery successfully introduced its Bartles & Jaymes Wine Cooler by introducing two fictional characters who became known as Messrs. Bartles and Jaymes. Because neither individual was known before, the two had total identity with the product.

Spots such as this (Figure 15–9) need repeated exposure to establish the characters, but sometimes an entrepreneur, in a P.O.C.B. posture, can use television effectively even with a sparse local schedule.

8. Spokesperson

A spokesperson differs from raw celebrity use in that the spokesperson doesn't self-identify; instead, he or she discusses the product or service being sold.

Effective use of spokesperson was actor Mark Harmon for Coors Beer (Figure 15–10). Credible for the product—and shown in credible circumstances—the spokesperson melds his personality with the product, adding salespower to both.

9. Empathy

Spots with empathy are hard to write; successful empathetic spots reflect high professionalism. Such a spot is the Fresh Start Detergent commercial in

FIGURE 15–10
For the late 1980s actor Mark Harmon may well be the
perfect spokesperson for Coors beer. His image: young but
not boyish, sensitive but not wimpy, athletic but not
musclebound, credible but not hyper-intellectual. The
combination of apparent traits appeals to both sexes.

which, to the rock theme "Put on Your Red Dress, Mama," a young mother looks everywhere for her red dress. She finally finds it, a mess, smeared with makeup by her little daughter playing grownup. Instead of being exasperated, she smiles and dumps the dress in the washer and it's ready to transform her into a sexy girl for the evening out. No harm done and no need to be angry, thanks to the detergent. It looks simple, but don't try to write a spot like this unless you know what you're doing, as this writer did.

Help! Where's the Year 2001?

Mightn't we, to round out the list, add a tenth technique—straightforward product sell—emphasizing why the viewer should buy?

We might, turning the clock backward as well as forward, to the antediluvian days before noncommunicators seized control of the television-writing function. As the stranglehold of term-throwers and effects-mad technicians begins to weaken, that tenth category might be a factor again.

When will this happen? I've set the year 2001 as the millennium year for a lot of changes in communication. Is the time-capsule guaranteed until then?

Good. Let's climb in.

16

How and When to Use— and When Not to Use— Celebrities

Would that more advertising agencies who lean on celebrity pitch knew this magnificent comment by Daniel J. Boorstin (in *The Image: A Guide to Pseudo-Events in America* [Atheneum, 1962]:

"A celebrity is someone who is well-known for his well-knownness."

In the Age of Skepticism even the most naive viewer knows celebrities are for sale. A young woman does well in the Olympic Games and suddenly becomes the spokesperson for products far removed from any conceivable area of her knowledge or expertise: Pay and I'll endorse your product.

Originally race-car drivers began adding patches to their garments, for Goodyear or Firestone, Autolite or Champion, Texaco or Mobilgas, STP or Wynn's, until the coveralls were themselves covered. The "sponsor" trades merchandise for a greasy byproduct appearance during TV interviews or candid shots.

Is such a trade logical? On a retentive level, perhaps, because the dollar-investment isn't extraordinary.

(A person who can afford a big advertising budget and features himself or herself in the ads becomes—voilá!—a celebrity. Figure 16–1 is an example.)

259

FIGURE 16–1
Leona Helmsley is a self-declared celebrity who became a celebrity from repeated media exposure for hotels her husband owns. The words "I," "my," and their variations appear 18 times in this self-stroking ad. In defense of the approach: The owner is a more logical spokesperson than a hired celebrity, because ownership implies responsibilty. But we can't forgive the phrase "Most importantly" or the self-importance assigned to trivialities. If you were writing a full-page ad, keeping Leona Helmsley as spokesperson, what specifics might you look for so you could project the image of a caring owner?

THE CELEBRITY WASTE FACTOR

Is hiring a celebrity, for many thousands of dollars, logical? Only if the result doesn't violate The Celebrity Waste Factor:

> **Having a celebrity move out of context is an artifice which exposes itself to the viewer or reader. A professional athlete may keep credibility endorsing athletic equipment but not alkaline batteries; an actress may keep credibility endorsing fashion or beauty aids but not machinery or automobile muffler installation.**

If your analysis of potential celebrity endorsers exposes this Waste Factor, consider scrapping the celebrity in favor of a hand-tailored personality whom you build and own—an individual whose celebrity status stems entirely from appearances in your television commercials (and in supplementary print advertising and point-of-purchase exhibits).

An unknown can't violate the Celebrity Waste Factor. But occasionally, if your budget and exposure are heavy enough, you'll become a Dr. Frankenstein. Your unknown becomes a celebrity, begins to act like one, and kills the reason you chose that person in the first place.

If You're Considering a Celebrity Presenter

The Celebrity Match-Up Principle will prevent some of the ridiculous misreadings of the Age of Skepticism some major advertisers have made lately. The principle:

> **Matching your spokesperson to what you're selling accelerates your targets' acceptance of what the celebrity is pitching.**

Here's the copy somebody put into singer Barbara Mandrell's mouth. (Figure 16–2 shows an ongoing use of this "celebrity.")

> When I first put my band the Do-Rites together we were small and our overhead seemed reasonable . . .

Okay, what is she selling? Sheet music? Uniforms? Fast food? All we see is the woman herself, no clue. Now we get the payoff:

> . . . but as we've grown our costs seem to grow even bigger. The cost of health care has skyrocketed. It's a major concern to us all. If your business wants to provide employees the best health plan, you should consider . . .

I can't believe Barbara Mandrell knows more about group insurance than I do. This parallels a space ad showing Martina Navratilova in tennis garb:

It costs you forty-five cents for a nickel candy bar,
And a dollar's worth of gas won't even start your car.
Yeah, we got problems here in the land of the free,
But there's no place I'd rather be in times like these.

Barbara Mandrell

It's Times Like These That Everyone Needs The Gold Plus Plan

Because they're doing something to help. The Gold Plus Plan is one of the leading health care plans in the country.

And it includes office visits, prescriptions, eye exams, prescription eye glasses, specialty services, hospitalization and more.

The Gold Plus Plan offers better benefits with the best quality care, while still controlling the cost for both of you. With health care costs rising three times as fast as inflation every employer and employee must seek better alternatives.

That's why the business sector is turning to the Gold Plus Plan as a desirable cost-containing alternative for their employee health care plans.

Find out more about how you can offer the Gold Plus Plan. You'll be really glad you did.

Gold Plus Plan®
FOR GROUPS
To find out more call toll-free **1-800-462-2273**

261

FIGURE 16–2
What relationship has either the music (whose notes don't match the number of syllables in the peculiar lyrics) or the photograph with the headline? Having a photograph with *any* medical overtones would have added some logic to this ad. (The company went into bankruptcy.)

FIGURE 16–3
Esther Williams is a good match for this vitamin, not only because the ad ran in a retirement magazine whose readers recognize her as their contemporary, but also because she is a symbol of ongoing good health. Unlike some celebrity-presenters, this one actually holds the product.

Trying to run my business affairs without Silver-Reed would be like trying to win Wimbledon without my tennis racket.

The body copy weakly tries to tie her to an electronic typewriter—shown separately. Can you see the tortured copywriter with an impossible assignment: "We've signed up Martina Navratilova. She doesn't type, but here's a picture of her on the tennis court. Write the ad."

This guileless reliance on a nonrelevant name is like leaning on a broken crutch: You probably have a better means of support. In no way is it parallel to the cold marketing logic of having Carl Lewis endorse Nikes or Pumas or whichever brand of sports shoe is paying him.

LOGIC IS OUT THE WINDOW . . .

Some peculiar recent celebrity uses:

- ▶ comedian Bill Cosby, already heavily exposed for Jello and Coca-Cola, for E.F. Hutton;
- ▶ austere John Housman for McDonald's;
- ▶ comedian Dom DeLuise for NCR computers;
- ▶ tennis player Chris Evert for Cirrus ATM machines;
- ▶ tennis player Martina Navratilova for Charles Jourdan watches;
- ▶ tennis player Pam Shriver for stockbroker Drexel Burnham Lambert;
- ▶ baseball player Pete Rose for SMI tanning beds;
- ▶ gymnast Mary Lou Retton for the National Bowling Council.

(Mary Lou Retton may hold the record for simultaneous product endorsements. Within two years after becoming an instant star at the 1984 Olympics, she signed endorsement agreements with companies selling at least ten products: Dobie Originals (clothing), Wheaties, McDonald's, Eveready Energizer Batteries, Vidal Sassoon, Hasbro Bradley, Pony sportswear/shoes, Ophir vitamins, the National Bowling Council, and Humana. She also gave her name to an exercise album and a ghostwritten autobiography. For most of her clients she appeared in an identical pose: arms flung wide in the "Olympic Victory Leap" and toothy smile. Ms. Retton "retired" at age 16, locked into what her agent called "long-term deals, each worth $100,000 to $200,000 a year.")

. . . And Consumers Are Beginning to Know It

Video Storyboard Tests/Campaign Monitor reported in *Adweek* the results of a survey intended to disclose why people watch TV spots—not a reliable gauge of effectiveness, but better than no survey at all.

Not surprisingly, the survey showed a decline in viewer "interest" in com-

264

FIGURE 16–4

To qualify as a celebrity, an individual needn't be in show business or the head of a hotel or automobile company. Testimonials are most logical when given by someone whose opinion has significance to the reader. This isn't a strong ad, but it's more logical than it would have been if Mr. T had glared out of the page and said, "Fool! Rent these lists and I'll let you live!"

Marilyn Harra Kaye, President

Portrait Of A Broker

PARIS, FRANCE — January, 1964: The Spring collection was being photographed for the cover of Elle Magazine and Marilyn Harra Kaye, formerly Marilyn Grano, was being photographed for the cover.

NEW YORK, N.Y. — May, 1974: After retiring at the height of her profession, followed by 4 years as a successful cooperative apartment sales broker, Marilyn Harra was named Director of the Residential Sales Department at L.B. Kaye Associates, Ltd. At that time annual sales were $8,000,000.

NEW YORK, N.Y. — January, 1983: Marilyn Harra Kaye was elected President of L.B. Kaye Associates, Ltd.

NEW YORK, N.Y.— January, 1986: Mrs. Kaye holds the position of President today, where she oversees 150 brokers whose sales in 1985 exceeded $350,000,000. Her personal emphasis has been and will continue to be in the luxury end of the residential market.

Marilyn Harra Kaye is proud of the past and present role L.B. Kaye Associates, Ltd. has played in New York City's development as the world's leading international community. She looks to the future with a defined objective—to continue serving the real estate needs of New Yorkers successfully.

LB KAYE ASSOCIATES, LTD.
477 MADISON AVENUE   NEW YORK, N.Y. 10022   (212) 415-0400

265

FIGURE 16–5
What a strange ad! This company tries to manufacture a celebrity by introducing details—some of them inconsequential—of its president. The thrust of the ad is muddy; Mrs. Kaye's background as a photographer's model isn't the strongest qualification she might present to the reader who might be interested in real estate. (The last line of this ad, "She looks to the future with a defined objective—to continue serving the real estate needs of New Yorkers successfully"—is a definite "Ugh.")

JAMES ROOSEVELT
United States Congressman (Retired)
Washington, D.C.

MR HERSCHEL LEWIS
9748 CEDAR VILLAS BV
PLANTATION, FL 33324

Enclosed find Certified Petition Number:

20291415   M4175

Please check your Petition to be certain
that your Certification Number
is correct

My father started Social Security. Now, we must act to Save Social Security and Medicare!

DEAR MR HERSCHEL LEWIS:

Will you spend 45 seconds, right now, to save Social Security and Medicare?

<u>If your answer is "Yes,"</u> then sign and return the enclosed Certified Petition. It's addressed to your U.S. Senators and Congressman:

> SENATOR LAWTON CHILES
> SENATOR PAULA HAWKINS
> CONGRESSMAN E CLAY SHAW

Never in the 50 years since my <u>father, Franklin Delano Roosevelt,</u> started the Social Security system has there been such a threat to our Social Security and Medicare benefits as the decade of the '80's.

Just consider these facts:

✓ Shortly before Christmas the government took money from our Social Security Trust Fund and used it to keep its other checks from bouncing!

✓ Last year the Senate voted to freeze Social Security benefits and cut Medicare benefits by $2,300,000,000 (2 Billion, 300 Million dollars). This action would have cost each recipient more than $1,200.00 over the next five years. The National Committee defeated these ruthless acts, but politicians are already looking for ways to cut this year's budget.

✓ Each year since 1981 Congress has debated legislation which would more than DOUBLE the premium payments for Medicare coverage. And since then, Congress has cut Medicare benefits by $56 Billion. And President Reagan has made no promise to maintain Medicare benefits so they will be a prime target of the budget cutters.

✓ Cost-of-living increases in Social Security were delayed six months in 1983, and further suspensions of badly needed cost-of-living increases are threatened in this Congress.

✓ Social Security payments are now being <u>taxed for the first time in history,</u> and there

(MR HERSCHEL LEWIS, PLEASE TURN PAGE)

FIGURE 16–6
The name Roosevelt has magic and unmatched recognition value. This letterhead maximizes use of the name; the body of the letter refers to the retired congressman's father, Franklin Delano Roosevelt. The matchup is perfect: President Roosevelt was the principal architect of social security; having James Roosevelt as spokesman for this organization (the National Committee to Preserve Social Security and Medicare) was a master stroke.

mercials, most steeply among the sought-after 35–49 age group. A parallel statistic showed that only 38.6 percent of viewers said they watch commercials "that show their favorite celebrities." The conclusion reached by the survey's sponsors: Celebrities do *not* provide a compelling reason for paying attention.

Paying attention parallels deciding to buy in only a peripheral way. If the viewer doesn't attend the pitch it's unlikely that a sale will result.

Celebrities tend to draw attention to themselves rather than what they're selling. This is the fault of the copywriter, who concludes erroneously that having the celebrity "in character" is more important than relating the celebrity to the sales argument. It ain't so.

An example: Burger King hired TV actor and sometime wrestler "Mr. T" who threatened the company for changing its "Whopper," then tasted the revised hamburger and snarled, "Fool! I'll let you live." How far we've come from gentle Ronald McDonald. (*Advertising Age* reported that the campaign was a flop.)

Another example: A campaign for Kronenbourg Beer (primarily radio) starred British comedian John Cleese, known as a member of the classic "Monty Python" sketches.

The campaign won a "Clio" award for Kronenbourg's advertising agency; but winning awards is only the alpha of advertising, not the omega. The campaign was abandoned in favor of a print campaign without Cleese because (according to a trade publication) it increased awareness as planned but failed to boost sales.

Shortly before merging with Delta Airlines in 1987, Western Airlines signed a contract with comedian Rodney Dangerfield. One of the critical comments on this alliance: "When I think of Western I think of a popeyed lecher with borderline literacy, a tight collar, and no respect." (See Figure 15–2 in the previous chapter.)

TWO-WAY CYNICISM

How much credibility do celebrities have? Those who market sports personalities claim a benefit anonymous presenters can't match: unquestioning loyalty by fans.

If this is true, danger lurks on the two-way street of fan-loyalty. An indication of sponsor cynicism is the beer commercial in which two men appear. Realizing that their names might mean little to the typical viewer, the spot superimposes their names; below their names is this additional super:

Famous Ex-Basketball Players

You can see the logical gap. If they *were* famous, the super would be unnecessary. When we've dug so deeply into the celebrity barrel that we have to tell the viewer, "These people are famous," mightn't it be time to re-evaluate?

Soon after a company named First Fidelity Financial Services was closed down by the state of Florida, leaving investors of $9.5 million without recourse, the president of the second-mortgage firm was sentenced to 25 years for organized fraud and grand theft.

But investors who decided to sue, in America's hair-trigger litigious society, said they didn't care about the president of the company. He wasn't the reason they had put their money into his pocket. Instead, they blamed former football jock Johnny Unitas, who was advertising spokesman for First Fidelity. In radio and print, Unitas had said:

"When you're standing in a huddle with ten of the youngest, roughest players and you now have a big decision, knowing that if you call the wrong play you'll be in a lot of trouble, you'd better make sure you have a lot of confidence in your game plan.

"My name is Johnny Unitas. I played football, made some key decisions, and won some important battles. I know what it's like to put your money on the line and make it count. That's where my friends at First Fidelity come in."

One of the plaintiffs commented on the ultimate irony attending so many celebrity endorsements: "He said they were his friends. He never met the people at First Fidelity until after he made the commercial."

Celebrity clutter and contagious cynicism tell the uncertain advertiser, hovering in limbo and trying to decide whether to spend money on a celebrity: *Save your money.*

AN UNCONCLUDED CONCLUSION

When television viewers remember the pitchman and not the pitch, when a spokesperson commands a fee equivalent to a huge percentage of the whole advertising budget, when the purpose of a commercial appearance seems to be to enhance the celebrity's "This is what I'm known for" image instead of what the celebrity is selling—these to me are flashing red lights: "Danger! Leave your wallet in the car!"

Ask, when considering a celebrity-for-hire: If my target-consumers were the hard-eyed jury in a court case, could I prepare evidence for this individual to recite which would convince them to find in my favor?

At the very least, don't be blinded by awe of those whom passersby ask for autographs. What will the autograph of a famous ex-basketball player be worth ten years from now, anyway?

17

How to Write
Winning Radio Copy

WHY SUBTLETY IS SECOND-BEST

Sneaking up on a target ignores the multiplicity of competing messages which causes (a) exasperation with those that aren't instantly comprehensible and (b) tuning out those messages that require effort to appreciate.

The First Rule of Radio Spot Writing explains this creative truism:

Aggressiveness leaves a stronger residue than subtlety.

Without that residue—that spoor, leading the listener back to the message source—a radio spot hasn't succeeded. You're trying to convince, or at least educate, somebody who can't see or lay hands on what you're selling.

That in itself isn't extraordinary since whenever you sell services your prospective customer doesn't have the security-blanket comfort of being able to see or feel the end product. What *is* extraordinary is the size of the Relative Attention Ratio fragment you can command.

RADIO WORDS AND TERMS

"Look into a new gas oven."

The thoughtlessness of this Auschwitz-like writing suggests to the writer of radio commercials a logical procedure: inspect each phrase for double meanings.

Watch out for word sounds too. The "sl" construction is slippery and difficult to pronounce: *Slapstick, sludge, slick, sloop.* Try Louisiana legislature on your own tongue before asking some hapless announcer to spew saliva.

Pronunciations and the Big Word Syndrome

You can't make a mistake—and better yet, the announcer can't make a mistake—if you specify the pronunciation of specific words. Unless you want to risk the embarrassment of an announcer referring to hyperbole as HYPER-BOWL, indicate the pronunciation. You do this in capital letters within a set of parentheses, immediately after the word. Here's the way it should look:

> If we told you this is the strongest rope in the world, you probably would accuse us of indulging in hyperbole (HY-PER-BUH-LEE). But . . .

I'd say you can't overuse this device. If there's any question, phoneticize the pronunciation. Resume might be REE-ZOOM or RES-YOU-MAY. Don't count on the announcer seeing the acute accent, if it still exists after multiple retypings (resumé)—or his understanding what the accent mark means.

Now, more to the point: What was *hyperbole* doing there in the first place? If you didn't ask this question about a radio commercial for rope, you probably used hyperbole to get your copywriting job.

Whenever you see the possibility of mispronunciation, ask yourself whether you've made the mistake of showing off your vocabulary. Dangerous!

I'd never let a piece of radio copy out of the printer with words like hyperbole in the text. I wouldn't use banal or insouciance. I wouldn't use words whose pronunciation differs from their parent-word, like technological or zealot. But if you have to use questionable words, create an environment in which you won't wince. This makes sense even if you have the spot recorded and you're personally on hand when it's recorded, because you'll save time.

Some local circumstances demand phoneticizing. If you were asking directions in Chicago, few would understand the question if you asked them how to get to Devon Avenue or Goethe Street, using the generally accepted pronunciations of those names. So for a radio spot aired in Chicago, you'd write:

> Two locations . . . at one-eleven East Goethe (GO-THEE) Street and two-twelve West Devon (DUH-VONN) Avenue.

Be careful when you use words with two types of spelling or two pronunciations. Examples:

complementary (might also be complimentary)

herd (might also be heard)

presence (might also be presents)

read (might be pronounced reed or red, might be interpreted as the word red)

too (might also be to or two)

From these we get The First Principle of Radio Clear Reception:

Help the announcer's pronunciation and you'll help the listener's comprehension.

So what do you write? 1001, Ten-oh-one, or a thousand and one?

Seeded into that last example is another radio copy must: Spell out numbers.

You wouldn't write on the radio copy sheet, "This is our 22nd anniversary." You'd write:

This is our twenty-second anniversary.

If you want to be in command of the way your words sound you wouldn't write "1001 Main Street." You'd write:

A-thousand-and-one Main Street

or—

A-thousand-one Main Street

or—

One-thousand-and-one Main Street

or—

One-oh-oh-one Main Street

or—

Ten-oh-one Main Street

Don't leave pronunciation decisions to a producer or an announcer. You're the creator of those word sequences.

Put hyphens between digits so the announcer can read them easier. Example:

Our savings and loan has a capitalization of more than two-billion, three-hundred-million dollars.

Don't use ampersands or abbreviations. It isn't savings & loan, it's savings and loan. It isn't Mt. Olympus, it's Mount Olympus. It isn't Ft. Lauderdale, it's Fort Lauderdale. It isn't 1111 33rd Ct., it's eleven-eleven thirty-third court. It isn't $9,256, it's nine-thousand two-hundred and fifty-six dollars.

This gives us The Second Principle of Radio Clear Reception:

Spell out numbers, symbols, and abbreviations. The words will come out the way you want them to.

Possessives are tricky, too. A good procedure is to use "of the" instead of the possessive, for plurals. Example: ". . . the boats' propellers" requires reinterpretation after the listener has heard the whole phrase. Better: ". . . the propellers of the boats." (The problem doesn't exist for singular possessive.)

It's the Way People Talk

Essay writers usually have a tough time when they try to write for radio. They're used to changing word sequence for adding artificial color to their writing. It doesn't work on radio.

An example of reversed word sequence:

Says the typical teen-ager—Cap-Cola is the soft drink I love.

Aside from teen-agers hating the term *teen-ager*, starting the thought with *Says* is an out-of-sequence beginning. The listener can't absorb it as it goes but has to wait until he has the whole phrase. Cap-Cola, too, is inside-out, because the reference just before it is *teen-ager*.

Grammar doesn't enter into it. All the writer has to remember is to write the way people talk.

Revision I, using the same phraseology restructured:

The typical teen-ager says—the soft drink I love is Cap-Cola.

Revision II, getting rid of *teen-ager* and putting *drink* where it helps message absorption:

Young people know their soft drinks—and the one they love is Cap-Cola.

Revision III eliminates the weak phrase *soft drink* and hardens the message:

ANNC.: Here's the voice of somebody who knows.
VOICE: (TEEN-AGE EFFECT) I *love* Cap-Cola.

Let's try another. This construction causes no comprehension problem in print copy:

Says John Brown, of Pinehurst, North Carolina, "I use it."

When the same message is planned for radio copy, two changes help comprehension. First, we put the noun before the verb as we did with the previous example. Second, because commas don't appear in verbalisms, we replace the word *of* with *from*, so listeners won't think John Brown is talking *about* Pinehurst. The copy now reads:

John Brown, from Pinehurst, North Carolina says, "I use it."

HOW TO MAKE AN EASY JOB DIFFICULT

The radio writer's job is technically the easiest of any form of mass communication. Usually the maximum length is one minute, or about 150 words; the writer can concentrate on only one of the senses without considering appearance.

Another benefit: The negative reaction some viewers have to a television announcer's appearance doesn't apply to radio.

The challenge: The ear has to be the surrogate for the other four senses. The writer has to create an image in the mind, without being able to demonstrate.

No question. But from a writer-technician's point of view, radio isn't a difficult medium to master. Maybe it's because radio requires less technical knowledge than print or television, so that many beginning writers either volunteer to write radio spots or are assigned to the job. The result? Humor which more often than not falls flat.

If the masters of humorous radio commercials fall flat as often as they succeed, what, then, is the batting average of the beginner?

This is why The Second Rule of Radio Spot Writing exists:

If humor isn't directly related to what you're selling, scrap it.

WHY SPECIFICS MAKE THEM REMEMBER

What's wrong with this radio copy?

ANNC.: Cars are moving at Lehmann (LAY-MAN) Motors, twenty-five-hundred Boise (BOY-ZEE) Avenue. Buicks, Oldsmobiles, Cadillacs—Lehmann has them all. Save thousands of dollars on a new Buick, Olds, or Cadillac. Isn't it time to get rid of that old clunker and move up to a beautiful new car from Lehmann Motors? There never was a better time, because Lehmann is offering top trades right now! Why? Because Lehmann needs used cars, so drive in . . . then drive out in a new Lehmann car. Lehmann Motors, twenty-five-hundred Boise Avenue—where you'll find the biggest bargains in new or used cars. Open nine A.M. to nine P.M.

What's wrong? It's the same old commercial. Ten thousand car dealers could run this commercial, changing only the name and address.

In radio, even more than in print media, *specifics sell; generalities don't motivate.* What if Lehmann Motors had run a spot like this one?

ANNC.: Are you driving a 1986 car? Hold it! Listen carefully! If your 1986 Buick Electra is in reasonable condition, Lehmann (LAY-MAN) Motors will give you at least a ten-thousand-dollar trade-in on a brand-new 1989 Buick, Oldsmobile, or Cadillac. And how about this? If you're driving a 1985 Ford or Mercury, it's time to think about a new car. Your 1985 Thunderbird or Mercury Cougar is worth at least six-thousand-dollars on a new Oldsmobile. Whatever you're driving, stop at Lehmann to find out what it's worth in trade on a Lehmann new or used car. Lehmann Motors, twenty-five-hundred Boise (BOY-ZEE) Avenue. Open nine A.M. to nine P.M.

The difference between the two commercials is the specificity of the offer, which grabs the attention of the listener. The person who drives a 1987 Chrysler will pay just as much attention, listening for his make and year; and it's easy to write a whole group of spots, each of which nails down a different *specific*.

HOW TO USE BUSINESS-TO-BUSINESS RADIO

More than the business-to-consumer advertiser, the astute business-to-business advertiser constantly asks himself three questions:

1. What group am I trying to reach?
2. Why am I trying to reach them?
3. How will this particular message influence the individuals from Question 1 to accomplish the purpose of Question 2?

For the business-to-business radio advertiser, the three questions come into sharp focus. Ads aren't running in comfortable trade publications which by their very existence support the excuse, "This is image advertising."

The radio business-to-business advertiser accepts as a given condition a tremendous amount of waste. Radio has come a long way in specializing its audience, but its reach is mass compared with any trade publication or even a mass/business publication such as Business Week.

"Why are we running this spot?" The copywriter should ask himself this question before attacking the keyboard, during every moment the creative juices flow, and after the spot is written.

Necessarily, business-to-business radio spots do have an overtone of image. Advertisers such as Executone (a manufacturer of office telephone systems), Lanier Business Products, Inc., and Automatic Data Processing Inc. (a payroll service) say radio spots are a softener, making their name both recognizable and favorable when one of their sales representatives makes a call.

No argument. What this unanimity of intention tells the writer can be codified into The Mandate of Business-to-Business Radio Spot Writing:

Break hard into the listener's usual apathy. Intrude on his easy-listening attitude. Grab attention and then shake it so the listener knows what you want to sell him.

This mandate is congruent with The First Rule of Radio Spot Writing (Aggressiveness leaves a stronger residue than subtlety), so the writer needn't worry about violating one rule in order to satisfy another.

CUTTING THROUGH THE TUNE-OUT EFFECT

A conversation can help cut through the "tune-out" effect many radio listeners develop. Drivers, especially, tune out without realizing it: Haven't you deliberately turned on the radio to hear the weather or traffic report, then realized, just as it was ending, that your ear missed it?

This spot, for Teleflora, is a light production that doesn't require a lot of concentration but might grab the listener whose self-hypnosis avoids a straight-reading commercial:

SFX: Telephone Rings

GIRL: Hello?

GUY: Hi, kid. Got any ideas about what I can get your sister for Valentine's Day?

GIRL: Sure. A bear.

GUY: What?

GIRL: The Cupid Bear Bouquet from Teleflora. It's a cuddly white teddy-bear hugging a red heart filled with fresh flowers.

GUY: Think she'd like that?

GIRL: She loves the one Tom sent her.

GUY: (ALARMED) Tom? Who's Tom?

GIRL: (CALLS) San-dee—telephone!
                                (DEALER TAG)

The spot runs 25 seconds, allowing five seconds for the dealer tag. Necessarily, the hard message is compressed into a single overcondensed line, but comprehensibility is immeasurably enhanced by the mild dramatic "frame."

WORDS TO AVOID IN RADIO COPY

Descriptive words of more than three syllables are hard for the listener to digest. As the brain chews one word, half a dozen others pour through the receptors undigested.

Other words don't form images for the listener. Perfectly acceptable in print, they cause listener block on the radio.

When an uncommon word begins with a syllable which itself is a word—such as *in, an,* or *to*—the brain has to catch up as other words are spilling out. We don't have a problem with *information* because it's a common word; we might have a problem with *anachronism* because it's an uncommon word. (A stronger reason not to use *anachronism:* At least half your listeners won't know what it means even if you tell the announcer to take five seconds to pronounce it.)

Since lots of alternatives exist, why use words such as . . .

comprehension	inconsequential
disbelieves	innovative
enervate	portfolio
envision	reciprocate
facilities	repetitive
ill-fitting suit	tabulation

Why use words that don't sound like what they are? You have a dictionary and a thesaurus to replace words such as

albeit	opt
awry	precept
bitten	ritual
carrion	seethe
equate	sequence
facile	stoic
falter	syndrome
fatigued	ware
laughably	wield
oblique	wily

Some words are homonyms. They present no problem in print advertising but have to be used in explanatory context for radio copy. Some examples:

beat (beet)

lead (led)

read (red)

suite (sweet)

tale (tail)

teem (team)

too (two, to)

Avoid literary constructions the ear has to reevaluate. A straight noun-verb sequence is always safe.

Poor: "Long have we known that. . . ."

Better: "We long have known that. . . ."

Best: "We've known for a long time that. . . ."

LET LOGIC PREVAIL

Don't make an easy job difficult. A lot of radio spots fail because of *overwriting*. The writer shoots himself in the foot.

If you write the way people talk and sincerely try to convince the listener to buy, you can't make a major mistake in radio copywriting. If you write "production" spots with complicated messages and intricate sentence construction, take off your shoe, because you've increased enormously the possibility of having a bullethole there—from your own word-gun.

18

Writing Effective Fund Raising Copy

"IT WORKED THEN, BUT IT WON'T WORK NOW"

Using the mails and media to raise funds isn't the simple, straightforward "He don't weigh much, he's my brother," celebrity endorsement, or "We need your help" that worked before the Age of Skepticism became entrenched.

The year 1990 is so far removed from the year 1970 that we might as well compare it with 1870. That friendly monster, the computer, has opened a Pandora's Box of available donors, but not just for us. Thousands of equally worthy causes compete for fund raising dollars . . . from the same people. How does one survive in this brutal marketplace?

Adherence to four rules is a strong starter-kit.

The First Rule of Fund Raising

Effective fund raising reaches the most people who might contribute and avoids those who never would or could contribute.

Simple, isn't it? A truism, isn't it? Then tell me why so many organizations mail blindly into ZIP codes, on the wild assumption that a ZIP code gives us a homogenized universe. For example, Chicago has a ZIP code, 60610, which includes a group of lakefront high-rise buildings with high-income people. It also includes the Cabrini Green housing project, a ghetto slum.

The Second Rule of Fund Raising

The second rule is the fund raising version of the "Whose Message Is It?" Rule:

Operate inside the experiential background of the person you're contacting, not inside your own background.

(This is the most useful of the four fund raising rules, because it's the core of contemporary copywriting.)

The assumption that your mailing will work because your cause is worthy, you're a good fellow, and you personally are emotionally involved with a cause is a big mistake. It's a *zero-base* motivator to someone who doesn't know you. That individual looks in the mirror, which names for him the three people each of us cares about: me, myself, and I.

As any number of current mailings exemplify, this is why a museum doesn't ask you to send a donation; it asks you to become a sustaining member of the Advisory Board.

It's why the mailing asking for money to fight kidney disease doesn't say, "Have a Heart"; it says, "Enter the Have-a-Heart Sweepstakes." The thrust of the message is as greed-oriented as a mailing from Publishers Clearing House. (See Figures 18–1 and 18–2.)

It's why the Audubon Society, asking for money to "achieve a clean, healthy planet that's safe for all living things" uses a sweepstakes featuring a Honda instead of a passenger pigeon.

It's why a local public television station does what television stations are supposed to do. It uses some showmanship. On the face of the envelope is this legend:

INSIDE:
YOUR TICKET
TO WIN!

LIMITED EDITION
COLLECTOR'S GIFT OFFER
INSIDE

Sure enough, inside is a card headed:

How would you like to have
this great TV in your home?

Fund Raising Doesn't Differ in the "Consistency Command"

If we were grading this mailing, we'd note: the word *great* isn't the greatest, but the approach is reasonably professional except for one dereliction: the writer forgot the Consistency Command, as critical to fund raising impact as it is to product/service force-communication impact. Remember it?

Components of an ad or mailing must reinforce and validate one another, or reader response to ALL components is lessened.

FIGURES 18–1 and 18–2
Are these mailings from Publishers Clearing House? No, one is from the North Shore Animal League and the other from the National Foundation for Cancer Research. The "Save-a-Pet Sweepstakes" and the "Beat Cancer Sweepstakes" join hundreds of other fund raising sweepstakes. The technique has proved itself over and over again in the late 1980s; appealing to greed in order to raise funds may be a sad commentary on our culture, but it's an apt commentary on human motivation. One problem: renewals. Getting next year's donation won't be easy, unless the organization mounts another sweepstakes.

Apparently by the time he or she came to the letter, the writer was gnashing teeth over the ignominy of having to use a TV set giveaway to get members for the station. One can almost see the writer *erroneously* concluding the communication had too much Uriah Heep in it. Result? A pompous letter out of key with the rest of the mailing.

Here, for example, is the opening of the letter, whose "we" approach ignores the Consistency Command and drenches the "you" approach with softener:

> "Excellence is a standard of measurement. It is not a title that can be won or assigned. The only way to achieve it is to earn it."

While we envision the writer emptying his basket of rhetorical frustration in this outburst, we can also see the reader, who may have been about to write a check (figuring, "What the heck, I might win a TV set"), recapping his pen with a bewildered "Huh?"

(Incidentally, the word "earn" is one of the *least* useful words in reader motivation. It doesn't matter at whom it's aimed; it suggests work.)

It may strike you as a paradox to represent a community program and have to appeal to human greed. No, it isn't a paradox at all. Greed is one of the most potent motivators of our time, regardless of subject.

The Third Rule of Fund Raising

The third rule:

Since you're operating inside the reader's experiential background, select and shape a selling argument you think will grab his or her emotional handles.

So a mailing that begins, "144 Reasons Why You Should Support the United Way" or a public service ad headed "Your Dollars Help 17 Ways" loses me before it begins. A laundry list might have some historical or archival value, but it has the impact of a wet dishrag when it's trying to pry some dollars out of someone whose mirror tells him to ignore any message that doesn't conform to Rule 2.

Figure 18–3 is a powerful example of how the Third Rule works . . . and how important *verisimilitude* is in fund raising.

The Fourth Rule of Fund Raising

The fourth rule is another adaptation of a universal communications law:

Tell the reader how much to give.

A Subrule, The Fund Raising Reminder Rule:

When writing prior donors, remind them how much they gave last time and ask for a little more.

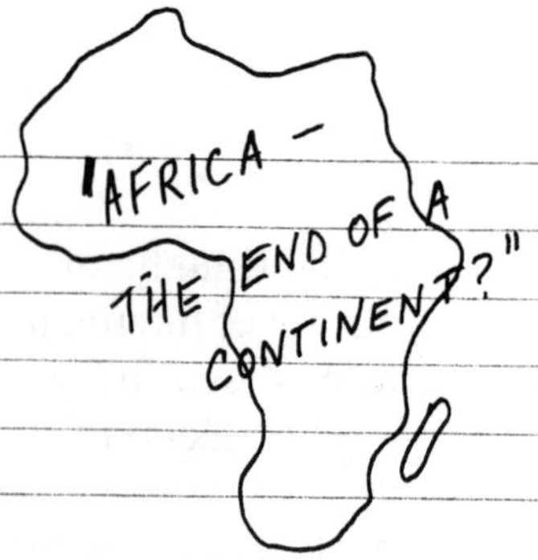

"AFRICA — THE END OF A CONTINENT?"

Wednesday, 9 PM

Dear Friend:

Today I am reminded of a quote by Father Cesar Bullo of Makale, Ethiopia, I keep on my desk. I clipped it out last November as a reminder to myself and it says...

> "What we are afraid of is that the world will forget in a few weeks, and next year we will have a million more people, dead."

As feared, yesterday's headlines and cries for help from Africa have faded, and were replaced with other headline-grabbing news.

But I cannot forget the people of Africa. As CARE's Executive Director, I have made a commitment to provide not only the short-term relief desperately needed -- but viable long-term solutions as well.

The African emergencies have prompted an outpouring of gifts to CARE from many concerned individuals. These gifts have helped us provide the immediate relief we could not possibly have given without this overwhelming show of generosity.

But as you may know, relief efforts are still relatively ad-hoc -- too little, and too late. Too late, especially, to relieve the extreme suffering and disruption drought causes.

There have been few successful attempts to link drought relief with long-term self-help. This is a challenge that is not new to CARE.

Based on CARE's years of experience in Africa, India, and other drought-prone areas, CARE has gained special insight into the problems of coping with drought.

The fact is that the drought in Africa will not

282

FIGURE 18–3

This classic mailing by CARE appears to be typed in haste on a yellow notepad. The message transmits a sense of urgency to many who don't respond to conventional mailings.

disappear -- instead, the areas in Africa affected by drought will expand.

And what about man's misuse of the environment...the high rural poverty and unemployment...and low availability of foodgrains?

These and other factors prolong and intensify the problems of a major drought.

It is impossible to eliminate the extreme changes in climate which lead to drought. But we can lessen significantly the impact of these conditions.

You see, there is evidence that if the government of a drought-prone country takes steps to allow it to respond promptly and efficiently to drought -- much suffering can be prevented.

So I am writing you today to explain in detail our plans for help to Africa, and to ask you to join a special core group of CARE supporters who have made a commitment to the people of Africa.

Because of the severity of the African situation, we have been called upon to expand our efforts with emergency relief.

Already, we have committed to many urgently needed projects in Africa, highlighted in the enclosed fact sheet.

But this is only Africa, just one of the four continents CARE serves.

Each year, CARE is able to provide more than $274 million to help the people of more than 35 of the world's poorest countries not only survive -- but work to achieve a better life.

You and I know the situation in Africa is critical. And because it is so critical I am now faced with a dilemma: I simply cannot drain funds from other projects worldwide to which we have made commitments this year.

And so, I am turning to individuals like yourself. To ask you to join our efforts.

To ask you to make a commitment to Africa this year -- a commitment to help us develop a plan for Africa -- a

283

FIGURE 18–3
Continued

commitment to Africa's future.

Today I am working with our staff to develop CARE's proposal for the DEVELOPMENT OF DROUGHT PRONE AREAS PROGRAM FOR AFRICA. The enclosed sheet describes the specifics of this THREE PHASE program.

I know that many of our supporters would like their money to go to food and emergency relief. Perhaps you feel this way as well. I assure you, crucial emergency relief to Africa will be continued in the months ahead, but it is just as important to plan against a catastrophe like this ever happening again.

Can you possibly return the enclosed card with your gift within the next week? If you are able to do so, this will help me to know just how soon and how much we will be able to commit to Africa.

The current news from Africa is shocking:

"Seven million Ethiopians and millions more in 25 other African nations face starvation because of three year drought."

If you help us make this commitment to Africa you will be part of a plan that could stop this from ever happening again.

Can I count on your support? It will mean so much.

As I close this letter I am reminded of the most horrifying headline I read this past year:

"AFRICA -- THE END OF A CONTINENT?"

This simply cannot happen......with your help we will instead create a new beginning for the people of Africa.

Thank you for caring....

Sincerely,

Philip Johnston, Ph.D.
Executive Director

FIGURE 18-3
Continued

C

CARE

Box 13186
Philadelphia, PA 19101

Dear Dr. Johnston,

I will not forget Africa. My gift to help build a new beginning for the people of these drought-stricken countries is enclosed for:

☐ $15   ☐ $25   ☐ $50   ☐ $100   ☐ $ Other _____

Please remember Africa
Be as generous as you can

4690070 58

☒

RICHARD W DOBBYS
888 W END AVE
NEW YORK, NY   10025

80006059469007058

FIGURE 18–4
CARE specifies an amount for the recipient of the mailing shown in Figure 18–3—$15 to $100, plus a box for "other." The donor who might automatically have written a check for $10 will write a check for $15 to conform with the printed amount.

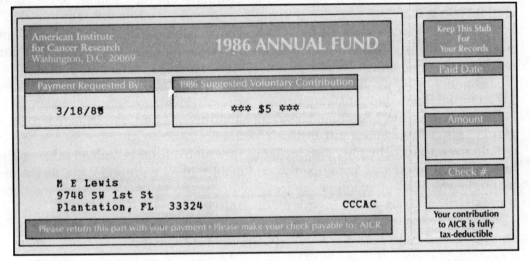

FIGURE 18–5
This mailer observes the Fourth Rule of Fund Raising too literally. By suggesting a $5 contribution and not offering higher levels, the mailing puts an artificial ceiling on donations. (If $5 was last year's contribution, the Fund Raising Reminder Rule applies: Suggest an increase this year.)

It takes a certain amount of guts to tell the reader to contribute $25 or $100 or $1000. I suggest we all develop our guts or we aren't going to maximize our dollars.

On the other hand, let's not let the fourth rule elbow all the others out of the appeal. A Muscular Dystrophy mailing comes right to a hard point, concentrating on the fourth rule while ignoring the second rule. This approach is a game of Russian Roulette, in my opinion. It doesn't say, "We need your help," or "Won't you give what you can?" Flat out, it says:

> Dear Mr. Lewis:
>
> Can you give $15 or more to support MDA's worldwide research effort and help achieve final victory over deadly muscle diseases? Thanks, Jerry

Well, he certainly told me how much to give. Yes, he followed Rule 4, but what about Rule 2? He ignores my experiential background, and the rules work only in combination.

Look at the difference between this approach and the Muscular Dystrophy Association's annual telethon. That event is about 80 percent aimed at our experiential background, because about 80 percent of it is entertainment-oriented. The demand is integrated into a palatable mixture.

Might it be that a misguided list broker said, in renting my name to the Association, "This is a list of knee-jerk donors who will give to anything. You don't have to waste pieces of paper for why-to-give arguments"? Might it be that the Association drew too broad a distinction between the mass appeal of television and the selective appeal of direct mail? Whatever the rationale, it's faulty.

Another fund raising organization includes in its mailing for a project called "Women in Development Campaign" a response device whose approach is as baldly direct as the Muscular Dystrophy mailing: "$150" is circled, with the words "Please consider a gift of this amount."

In my opinion, the only circumstance in which a fund raiser can unwrap the heavy cannons and aim them openly, asking for money without justifying the demand, is when that demand is congruent with the first rule—when the organization is writing to its own "in-group" of captive donors.

So, those are the Four Rules of Fund Raising, with ancillary subrules to grip an appeal and hold it in the center of the track.

HOW TO AVOID BEING PEDANTIC

"Emotion over Intellect" is not only just as valid for fund raising copy as it is for other types of advertising; it's critical, because showing benefit to donors isn't automatic as it might be when you're advertising an automobile or a weight-loss program or a beauty aid.

Just as a quick test, if your letters use "pass away" instead of "die," "We need your aid" instead of "You have to help us," "Combat kidney disease" instead of "Fight kidney disease," and "Did you overlook our previous mailing?" instead of "Did you let Jimmy down?"—you'd better warm up your prose, because you're firing blanks. The words make noise but they don't hit anybody.

(*Anybody*, not *anyone*, while we're on that subject. Why? Because *anybody* is a more emotion-laden word than *anyone*, and we might as well practice. The same principle applies to *somebody* and *someone*, and, yes, it's so mild a difference that about half the time *anyone* and *someone* are preferable, depending on how high up the emotional tree you're aiming.)

Why Statistics Don't Sell

The American Cancer Society sent out a mailing which said this:

The facts about cancer are startling. One cancer-related death every 78 seconds. Nearly 1100 deaths a day from cancer. As the second leading cause of death in this country, cancer will touch the lives of one person in every four.

Is this copy good or bad? My personal opinion: neither. It's terrible. Before you start throwing tomatoes, ask yourself: How much impact is there to the word "touch"? What if, instead of writing "cancer will touch the lives of one person in every four," this copy changed one word: "If yours is the average family, cancer will try to snuff out the life of one of you"?

All right, that's a minor change. We've added a little emotion to the mix. We haven't attacked the bigger problem of using statistics instead of examples.

I didn't say this was bad; I said it was terrible, and I'll justify my outrageous opinion with one clear sentence—three little words which form the Rule of Statistical Failure:

Statistics don't sell.

It's a puzzlement. You can't put together a sweepstakes, because your board would never stand for it, and you don't have the budget for it, and anyway, a sweepstakes is a genuine 100 percent headache. Now here's this chap telling you not to use statistics either, and statistics always have been a safe and true crutch. So what can you do?

I offer this option: Replace your statistics with episodes and victims, and your mailings will come to life. If you use broadcast media, the comparative impact isn't even measurable.

One easy example: instead of saying, "Nearly 1,110 deaths a day from cancer," we say something like this:

We lost Tommy today. All the love his little brother gave him, all the prayers his father said for him, all the tears his mother tried to wipe away so he wouldn't see them, and all the determination of a dedicated medical staff— none of these helped Tommy. We lost him.

But we might save Mary Lou. She's a scrapper at the age of eight, and . . .

Acres saved in
Florida:

164,036

Local Office:
The Nature Conservancy
1331 Palmetto Avenue, Suite 205
Winter Park, FL 32789

☐ I enclose $10 for one year's dues.
☐ I'd like to do more. Enclosed is an
additional contribution of $ _____

Please make check payable to The Nature Conservancy and
return it, with this card, in the postage-paid envelope to
1800 North Kent Street, Arlington, Virginia 22209. All contributions are tax-deductible.

The Nature Conservancy

1800 North Kent Street, Arlington, Virginia 22209

I'd like to help The Nature Conservancy
expand upon the 164,036 acres already
rescued in Florida where I might visit
a site like the Blowing Rocks Preserve
in Martin County and Seminole Ranch in
Orange County.
Please enroll me as a member with full
benefits, as described on the interim
membership card, and use my dues to
help protect more natural lands.

NAME	ACCOUNT NO.
Ms. Margo E. Lewis	180261
ADDRESS	
9748 Cedar Villas	
CITY STATE	ZIP
Plantation FL	33324

INTERIM MEMBERSHIP

The Nature Conservancy

The person whose name appears here:

Ms. Margo E. Lewis

is an Interim Member of The Nature Conservancy eligible to join
as a full member and enjoy all the benefits and privileges listed
on the reverse.
This registered and numbered card is valid for 45 days from date
of receipt

No. **0007**

William D. Blair, Jr., President

/86

FIGURE 18–6
The Rule of Bulk Negation suggests that the call to action "I'd like to help the Nature
Conservancy expand upon the 164,036 acres already rescued . . . " isn't the strongest
appeal this organization might mount. Some recipients might think: "164,000 acres is a
lot of land. Why do they need more for expansion?" (The objectionable word—
expand—a commercial notion, not a logical appeal for fund raising. When
organizations raise money for expansion, terminology should suggest an urgent need
for more services, not for enlargement.)

I offer for your consideration the Rule of Bulk Negation:

Bulk doesn't create an emotional reaction. Episode does.

With this rule in mind I rejected a fund raising plea which concluded, "We
have so many millions of tiny lives to save." *Millions* is too many. It's a depersonalized number, changing the challenge to a mob scene.

I rejected, too, a plea to "expand upon the 164,036 acres already rescued
. . . ." They have lots of acres, they don't need me. In my opinion the aim is misdi-
rected (see Figure 18–6).

Fact is the cornerstone, but cornerstones don't sell houses; emotional appeals do. If you still think the typical citizen is altruistic and has a genuine com-
passion for his fellow-beings, you won't agree with me that the letter which begins this way, although flawed, is better than a statistical opening:

A lady should never get this dirty, she said.

She stood there with a quiet, proud dignity. She was *incomparably* dirty—her
face and hands smeared, her clothes torn and soiled. The lady was 11.

My brothers are hungry, she said. The two little boys she hugged protectively
were 8 and 9. . . .

This letter emphasizes *victims* and *episodes*. I opine it's infinitely superior to the letter we dissected before it. Cold-bloodedly let's define "superior" as "having more pulling power," but don't you agree it has more poetry too? (I said it was flawed: The word "lady" has a patronizing, down-the-nose overtone which could infect the reader's attitude toward the seriousness of the little girl's situation.)

We see more and more dependence on *victims* rather than *statistics* in space ads. Victims are superior to statistics, if they're shown with verisimilitude and clarity. An example is an ad showing a small girl with the legend, "Marta goes to bed hungry every night."

But this is where verisimilitude has to enter the mix. The photograph of Marta shows us a winsome child—but one not particularly hungry looking. Emotion outpulls intellect, so with the pictures that have to be available, why not use one that adds visual impact to the words?

The opening sentence of the ad's copy is thin:

"When Marta goes to bed hungry, there's not much hope she can forget all the bad things that have happened to her."

The ad never does tell us what those "bad things" are. Why not have some copy with power: "What did *you* have for dinner last night? Marta had a handful of cold rice and some water."

One of our best-known fund raisers mailed me a computer-letter illustrated with a picture of a little boy. The opening of the letter:

Dear Mr. Lewis:
This little boy is lucky. Your Red Cross got there in time.

At the risk of attacking God and motherhood, I'll offer another iconoclastic opinion: this letter would have been stronger if we showed a little boy who *wasn't* lucky instead of a little boy who was. One of the great motivators is *guilt*, and I don't feel guilty over a lucky child.

I mentioned *episodes* along with *victims*. For some organizations, such as libraries, victims are hard to find. But episodes are universal and have power potential. Here's a sample, not from a library but from a U.S.O.:

It's Saturday night—late.
Normally I wouldn't sit composing a letter at this hour. I'd be watching TV, or sleeping the happy sleep of someone who knows he doesn't have to get up early Sunday morning. But tonight, I have to write this letter. I have to.

Can't you feel the sincerity? Whatever follows is true because we accept the opening—an episode—as true. You can see why a properly constructed episode works: it personalizes the communication, establishes rapport through the ring of truth, and involves the reader.

"IT'S IMPORTANT BECAUSE I SAY IT IS"

Ah, you say, but my particular venture doesn't fit that mold. I'm not lucky enough to be involved with a war or a famine or a loathsome disease or even a U.S.O. All I have to work with is a library or a museum or a college. Does this rule of reader involvement apply to me too?

You bet it does. In fact, if you're writing for an institution dedicated to education or culture it's more dangerous for you to position yourself above the reader's orbit than it is for a fund raiser who has a war or a famine or a loathsome disease as his *raison d'être*. Here's why:

No matter how poorly a fund raising campaign represents a highly emotional issue, that campaign will gather in some dollars. Some people will respond because they have a Pavlov's dog reaction to crippled or starving children. But the library or the college or the museum isn't on the emotional main line.

I needn't tell you how difficult it is to raise money from people who already have a tie to you—college alumni, those with library cards, or people who have signed the register in the museum. If getting them to respond is such a Herculean labor, what chance do you have with the outsiders?

If you approach them with ads such as this one, which ran as a full page in *Horizon* magazine, the answer is *none*. First, the headline:

Society is changing . . . and so are museums.

Suppose you're in this field. If you don't greet this nonsense with a yawn then you're as far away from contemporary society as the writer of this headline was. What about this forces the reader to stop and say, "I'd better read this"?

I'm convinced that any reader of this book can think of a better headline in 30 seconds, even if it's only a thin holding action such as "How long has it been since you've been in a museum?" or "Ben Franklin would be stunned!" You wouldn't put the reader to sleep the way this writer did—I hope.

These are the first three of the five paragraphs of copy in the ad:

Museums are no longer musty, dusty corridors filled to the brim with odd curiosities. Today, they are open, lively places attracting over 500 million visitors each year.

Museums provide a context for understanding the present and anticipating the future—an increasingly important responsibility in our world of enormous and accelerating change.

In 1982 the American Association of Museums assembled a blue-ribbon commission of distinguished museum directors, trustees and foundation and business leaders to examine the place of museums in our changing society. Over three years the Commission on Museums for a New Century engaged thousands of museum professionals, futurists, educators, businessmen, civic leaders, scientists, supporters of the arts and humanities, and members of the general public in activities that focus on the role of the museum in society.

The coupon in the ad asks for $17.95 plus $1.50 postage for a book titled *Museums for a New Century*. I want to know: *why* should I buy and read this book? Certainly I wouldn't buy it for the nonreason this group gives me:

The report is a blueprint for the future of our nation's museums—complete with recommendations, an assessment of the issues, concerns, achievements and aspirations for American museums, and examples of innovative and successful museum programs.

This "It's important because I say it is" copy—in a *consumer* magazine? It isn't the worst use of space for fund raising I've ever seen; it just happened to be one that infuriated me at the moment, and I clipped it out.

I really hope you're infuriated, too, at the decision so many fund raisers make, a decision that costs literally billions of dollars in gifts and donations that don't come in because the person who reads the mail or sees the notice in the paper or reads a slick ad in a magazine or watches a television spot is left outside the orbit.

That decision is: "This is important because I say it is. If you question my decision you don't deserve to give us money."

SOME YARDSTICKS FOR FUND RAISING COPY LENGTH

Does long copy outpull short copy?

Maybe. Results of copy tests point in both directions.

One preconceived notion we can't budge: Copy length has a specified maximum in broadcast media, a logical maximum in print media, and no maximum in direct mail.

Long copy seems to work best for religion, politics, and other areas in which prejudice can be polarized. Short copy seems to work just as well for education, health, welfare, and culture—areas in which the writer needn't build a massive head of steam. If short copy works just as well, it actually works better, because production costs go down.

Let's form the Rule of Fund Raising Copy Length:

The need for long copy is tied to the need to feed an implicit or expressed reader prejudice or belief.

A dangerous rule and a fluid one! I offer an opinion—and it's only an opinion, which is why you won't see it as a rule—If you don't know who your target is, write your message without paying attention to length. After you've trimmed the fat, if it still is long, leave it alone. Obviously this can't apply to computer letters with predetermined length or to short broadcast spots.

For fund raising mailings, do you need a descriptive brochure? The answer is tied to letter length. Results of tests seem to indicate that if you need a long letter you also need a descriptive brochure. In practice, it means if the reader knows who you are, a brochure won't justify its cost in increased contributions; if the reader doesn't know who you are, the brochure helps establish credentials, integrity of purpose, and correlation to the reader's own philosophy.

HOW TO REACH OUTSIDERS

Some fund raisers just go through the motions. They depend on a couple of big donors to keep the enterprise afloat, and everyone else is the victim of the fund raiser's overblown dignity. Why send that mail? Why pay for typesetting for an ad? Why spend money on a videotape session? The Second Rule of Fund Raising is clear and invariable. Remember it?

> **To reach an outsider, you have to communicate on his level of experience, not your own.**

Ignoring that rule or being unprepared to implement it when you contact outsiders will cost you plenty, as it has cost thousands of fund raisers billions of dollars over the past five or ten years.

I think some of the problem stems from technology. A printer calls on us. He has a novel way of computer-personalizing a communication, and we fall for it. So we become one of four thousand organizations mailing a stack of 50 address labels or a cold-blooded unjustified invoice to unwitting recipients.

We've joined the depersonalizing movement. Instead of being an oasis, in an era when so many copywriters downgrade the people they're pitching to ZIP codes and digits, we're absorbed into the ghastly trend. We say to the reader: "We don't know who you are. We don't care who you are. We don't know what you want or like. We don't care what you want or like. This is our address. Send us money." Sometimes we don't even say, "Please." Then we wonder why our mailings pull so miserably.

Ask yourself: If a store sent you a commercial mailing with no more motivation than "Can you give $15 or more" in it, would you order whatever they're selling?

Two Magic Words

Of the four great motivators, *fear, exclusivity, guilt,* and *greed,* exclusivity is the easiest to use, because we know that during the Age of Skepticism—which may last for another decade or more, or even perhaps forever—the two magic words "Only you" still work.

Remember the basis for this? I care about me, not you. If you want my money, what's in it for me? That's why a mailing from the American Film Institute starts off in a classic way. I open the envelope, and the first piece I see is a formal-looking card with an ornate border:

OFFICIAL
Membership Nomination Certificate
The Board of Trustees hereby certify that
H.G. Lewis
has been nominated to participate as a
National Member
of
The American Film Institute
entitled to all privileges and recognitions
of membership.

The card is signed by Charlton Heston, Richard Brandt, and Jean Firstenberg. I've heard of one of them, which isn't too bad. I'll even overlook the British use of words, laughable for the *American* Film Institute: "The Board *certify* instead of *certifies.*

I also have a "Dear Member-Elect" letter from Francis Ford Coppola, and the letter's third paragraph invites me to join a "very select number of people." Right on target for exclusivity.

But now we have to be careful. To combine exclusivity with heavy selling in the same document is not only an art; in most cases it's a mistake. And that's exactly what has happened here. On the last page of this letter—page 8, by the way, which in my opinion is far too long for an invitation-letter to run—I read:

> . . . but when you remember you'll also get a full year's subscription to *American Film*—10 colorful and informative issues—as well as many additional member benefits—all for *25% off* the regular member dues of $20—*a full year of AFI membership for only $15* . . .

> . . . then you have the best reason yet to accept your nomination for membership. All you need to do is send in your Membership Acceptance Form to begin enjoying *American Film* and the other benefits of membership.

See what they're doing? They're *pitching* me. They've gone over the edge. I don't believe them any more, because if this were really an exclusive invitation they wouldn't slather saliva all over the page to get my $15. They've lost verisimilitude, and it's just another fund raising letter. I no longer feel specially chosen.

THE COPYWRITER'S INSURANCE POLICY

As postal rates climb, as printing costs skyrocket, and as public apathy enshrouds us, adherence to the rules of logical force communication is our insurance policy.

If we reach the most people who might contribute and avoid those who never would or could contribute; if we operate inside the experiential background of the people we're contacting, not ourselves; if we increase impact by emphasizing one or two key arguments and subordinating the rest; if we tell the reader how much to give—we have the "accident" portion of our policy.

The "life" portion of our policy comes from adherence to the Consistency Command ("Components of a mailing must reinforce and validate one another, or reader response to ALL components is lessened") for our ads and mailings, and to the use of one of the four great motivators—*fear, exclusivity, greed,* and *guilt*—for any medium, whether mail, print, or broadcast.

One other portion of our policy: "Endowment," which we inherit because we've included the three magic ingredients in our selling mix—*verisimilitude, clarity,* and *benefit*—and we've coated them with emotional terms, not intellectual terms.

Does it bother you to codify rules and procedures for fund raising? If it does, think how bothered you'd be if the rules and procedures didn't exist and every mailing, every space ad, every broadcast appeal were a new game of Russian Roulette.

19
Writing for Special-Interest Groups

THE KEY: THE "WHOSE MESSAGE IS IT?" RULE

The key to success in writing for special-interest targets—children, senior citizens, ethnic groups—is the "Whose Message Is It?" Rule.

Remember the rule?

Your message should operate within the experiential background of the message recipient, not within your own experiential background.

You might think: If my experiential background is an exact parallel to those for whom I'm writing, I can't miss. Not so. The difference between sharing a background and using it to sell is in the communicative power you can muster.

It's common today for advertising agencies to have separate creative staffs for Hispanic and Black consumers. Some agencies specialize in just one area, and a client (such as a beer or soft drink, an automobile manufacturer, or a packaged goods processor) may split the account, assigning marketing segments to "specialists."

Buying patterns aren't profoundly different. Language use aside, ethnic differences are a smaller creative problem than the differences attending target groups whose *product choice* differs. Let's take a look.

HOW TO WRITE FOR CHILDREN

The television writer usually has a creative license not granted to writers for print media, but that license is loaded with restrictions when one writes for children.

The Writing-for-Children Rule is simple and absolute:

Don't exaggerate, either in picture or in verbiage.

Where the simplicity gets complicated is in the interpretation of the word "exaggerate." For example, the Franklin Mint ran some television spots for a coin continuity program. In the spots was the line, "Each month we'll send you two issues, each only $13.95, a price that covers it all—reference materials, mint-fresh coins, cachets, stamp, foreign postmark, and all customs charges."

No one objected until the spot ran in a children's program. Then the fan was full of flying defecation. Why?

The Children's Advertising Review Unit of the Council of Better Business Bureau's "National Advertising Division" objects to what they call "minimization." In this case, the offending word was *only*. The logic: This word blurs the cost and makes the ad an exaggeration in that it fails to convey the true cost to children.

In advertising aimed at any other group, the word *only* is an accepted bit of mild puffery, about as dangerous as *at last* or *new and improved*. But watchdog groups abound in the children's advertising arena, and effectiveness has to come from child-actors seeming to have a good time, not from puff-words.

The Franklin Mint said the ad wasn't aimed at children (although the spot did run at a time dedicated to children's programming) and agreed to avoid scheduling the spot during children's programs.

In this instance the spot could survive by changing the time period. But what about spots for toys? Hasbro's Milton Bradley division made a commercial for its WWF Wrestling Superstars Game. Interspersed with shots of the game were scenes of live wrestling—actual matches in which the contestants were "executing kicks, throws, holds, and punches." Hasbro told the Children's Advertising Review Unit the footage was a depiction of children's fantasies while they were playing the Wrestling Superstars Game. A logical explanation? The Children's Advertising Review Unit didn't think so, and Hasbro agreed to change the spot.

Disclosure Copy

You can see the challenge in writing television ads for children: Generate a fantasy without having it "pay off" visually. Or tell the media department to keep the spot out of child-dedicated viewing time. Or use media other than television.

In regulated media an advertiser usually can avoid a challenge by including "disclosure" copy. Television spots use audio or video only for this copy, which satisfies regulatory situations while de-emphasizing the point.

Cynical? Some of the rules themselves are cynical. For the writer, embarrassment comes not so much from having copy challenged but from having to reshoot a commercial. So stringent is the rein on overdemonstration that Coleco was called to task by the National Advertising Division for television spots advertising its "Sentaurs" action figures. The Children's Advertising Review Unit questioned whether the figures, manipulated by a child, could perform all the movements shown on the screen.

After testing, the Unit decided "most"—but not all—the movements could be duplicated by children. Coleco agreed to add disclosure copy to cover this suggested discrepancy and lack of information about purchase requirements.

Matchbox Toys also agreed to add disclosure copy to cover its failure to mention whether its "Robotech" figures were sold together or separately.

The Plastic Years: Ages 2 to 6

Researchers tell us that by age 6 a child has solidified many of the buying habits that will last a lifetime. Messages imprinted during the plastic period—ages 2 to 6—can be hard to overcome later. Not only do marketers have their best shot between these ages; it's when the most protection against chicanery is necessary.

If you're trying to plant a seed, don't just keep your message uncomplicated; keep your product name uncomplicated. Children have a hard time remembering product names which have three or more words. One-syllable product names are best; two syllables are fine. More than two words put you in peril, even if what you're selling is infinitely superior to the competition.

This explains the success of "Cap'n Crunch" cereal, instantly mnemonic to children. "Super Bran Crunchy Flakes" has too many words and too generic an image to compete.

It helps explain the delight children take in being able to ask for "Smurfs."

What's in a name? If it's the name of something aimed at toddlers, don't put too many words or syllables in it or you'll lose them.

EIGHT CREATIVE TECHNIQUES TO USE WHEN WRITING FOR SENIOR CITIZENS

Whatever euphemisms we use, senior citizens are the elderly. They're a huge buyer group, the fastest-growing buyer group, and if we want to sell them something, we can benefit from our knowledge of some of the common denominators of this group. Generally, they are, compared with younger age-groups:

- ► less flexible in attitude
- ► (because they're less flexible) more loyal to brands and procedures with which they've become comfortable
- ► less willing to change just because you tell them to change
- ► more skeptical and sensitive to being patronized
- ► impatient

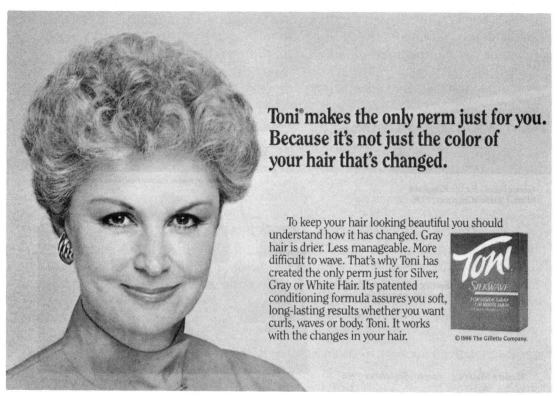

FIGURE 19–1
This ad appeared in *Modern Maturity* magazine. Targeting, illustration, and copy all match the message recipients. The copy is straightforward, benefit projecting, and credible. (Running this ad in a mass-circulation women's magazine would waste the message on many readers; running a conventional Toni ad in this magazine would have been a mismatch.)

Knowing these traits, you as writer can exploit them. Four of your procedures are mechanical:

1. No sentences longer than 20 words, and never two consecutive sentences longer than 15 words.

2. No paragraphs longer than seven lines.

3. No more than 200 syllables per 100 words.

4. If you're writing for print, no type smaller than 10-point; if you're writing for broadcast, no more than 100 words per minute.

From an argumentative point of view, eight creative procedures tend to work:

1. Instead of shouting "New!" tie newness to an established base—an improvement without discarding the security of something they recognize.

2. "Bargain!" is an exceptionally valid sales argument to those whose incomes have peaked or declined or who are on a fixed income.

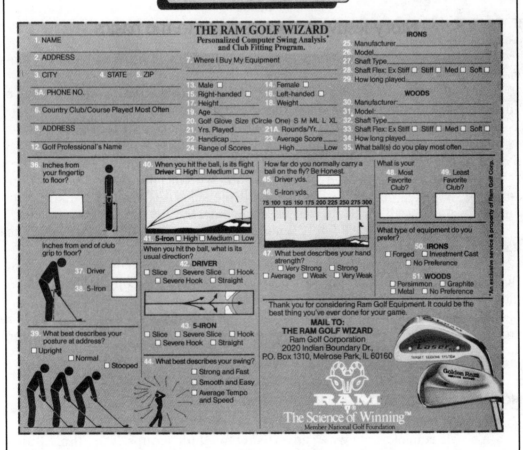

KNOCK TEN YEARS OFF YOUR GAME

You haven't grown too old to play good golf. You've outgrown your golf clubs.

Ram research clearly shows improperly fitted clubs are one of the largest contributors to a golfer's poor performance. As you get older that problem becomes even a bigger problem. But, Ram has the solution. And, it's yours free.

The Ram Golf Wizard program is a blend of computer science and real experience. For the past ten years Ram has systematically collected and classified an extensive data bank of different golfers, different golf swings and the performance of different golf equipment. Computer science allows us to draw upon these data to provide you

**It's Yours Free.
A Personalized Computer
Swing Analysis and Club
Fitting Program from
The Ram Golf Wizard™**

with an objective analysis print-out of your individual swing characteristics and what equipment best fits you.

Ram has developed advanced techniques for determining scientifically the optimum combination of shaft flex, shaft weight, swing weight and head design. Both Golden Ram® and Laser® clubs offer a broad spectrum of fitting options. Both are frequency matched and manufactured with computerized precision.

So, if you'd like to knock some years off your game, get fit to win with the Ram Golf Wizard. Complete the Personal Swing Profile below as accurately and honestly as possible. Please use a ballpoint pen. Allow 3 to 4 weeks for delivery of your print-out.

FIGURE 19–2
This ad ran in a magazine aimed at senior citizens. Copy is arrowed at this target group. Had the ad run in *Golf Digest* it would have puzzled some readers, annoyed others, and made sense to only a fraction of the readership.

299

3. Don't be overly familiar or convivial. Keep your dignity and let the readers or listeners know you respect theirs.

4. Stress ease of acquisition, ease of operation, ease of results.

5. Recapitulate your key selling argument, for clarity as well as emphasis.

6. Peer-group testimonials help dispel skepticism.

7. Refer to age in positive terms. It's "But you must be at least 60" or "60 years or over," not "60 years or older."

8. Never suggest you're compromising the individual's independence or ability to care for himself or herself unless you have a specialty product designed to enhance the ability to be self-reliant.

That's the tightrope we walk when writing for this group, which has enormous buying power and political power.

Every one of the *15 Ways to Thwart the Age of Skepticism*, listed in Chapter 25, applies to writing for senior citizens. Take a look.

If You're Writing to the Disabled . . .

Don't use the disabling word as a noun. Use it as an adjective and it seems less harsh.

So you won't write "the disabled," you'll write "people who are disabled" or "disabled people." You won't write "the deaf," you'll write "those who are deaf." You won't write "the arthritic," you'll write "People with arthritis."

Don't use words which might be misinterpreted; this group is far more sensitive than others, and copy should never have phrases such as "victim of" or "afflicted with." If you're referring to someone who has multiple sclerosis, don't be afraid to write, "a person who has multiple sclerosis." Never use "deaf and dumb" or "diseased" or "confined to a wheelchair."

(Incidentally, use "deaf" only when an individual is totally deaf. Otherwise it's "hearing impaired" or someone "with a partial hearing loss.")

And don't patronize. It's easy, so easy, to start writing "You're a hero" copy. Disabled people want reality, not fantasy. So don't write copy which reads as though you're afraid to acknowledge reality.

We're discussing writing *to* this group, not writing *about* this group. If we're creating fund-raising copy, these rules don't apply because we're after a different target group altogether. (See Chapter 18.)

HOW TO ADVERTISE TO ETHNIC GROUPS

A single rule of safety when advertising to ethnic groups: The Ethnic Rule—

Keep your dignity.

This means writing in conventional English, not argot. Even if you hire a

Simon Wiesenthal Center

9760 West Pico Boulevard · Los Angeles, California 90035

Office of the Dean

Los Angeles, Monday morning

Dear Member,

    Eventful, productive, disturbing, challenging -- that's how I can best start describing recent weeks here at the Simon Wiesenthal Center.

    It is at times like these that I most want to write and share news with you.

    I also want to ask, on behalf of all my associates, that you take a moment today to renew your personal Membership in the Simon Wiesenthal Center.

    And please review this letter carefully -- I want to share some information with you that has unfortunately gone largely unreported in the news media. You'll see at once the key areas where your renewed support will prove most timely ...

DATELINE: BAVARIA, GERMANY

    "The Jews are quick to show up when money tinkles in German cash registers."

        A leading Christian Democratic politician in
        Bavaria, Hermann Fellner, spoke these words just
        a few weeks ago. After an avalanche of protest
        -- including the Wiesenthal Center's demand that
        Premier Franz Josef Strauss publicly censure him
        -- the 35-year old Fellner finally apologized.

    What injustice, you may wonder, so inflamed this youthful Antisemite?

    <u>The successful campaign led by the Material Claims Conference -- and supported by the Simon Wiesenthal Center -- which finally forced the giant Flick Corporation to pay reparations to surviving World War II slave laborers.</u>

    An important victory. But Flick's parent corporation -- The Deutsche Bank -- has remained out of reach thus far, despite its having been the majority lender of $250 million for building a major slave labor facility at Auschwitz-Birkenau.

    The Simon Wiesenthal Center has identified the Deutsche Bank as our next target in the fight for justice.

    <u>We are investigating another disturbing trend in the area that has far-reaching implications for the future ...</u>

    Bonn is on the verge of becoming a main supplier of the most sophisticated

(over, please)

FIGURE 19–3

The narrower the group, the more dynamic copy can be. This letter begins, "Dear Member," and was mailed only to those who had contributed before. Signature on the letter is Rabbi Marvin Hier. To cold lists, unquestionably a mailing such as this would generate considerable hate mail.

never before seen, and the exhibition has been specially formatted for ease of use in schools, institutions, and communities.

Preproduction is underway on a documentary about Jews in Shanghai and Japan's treatment of "the Jewish question" during the Holocaust. We continue to regularly videotape important testimony of survivors and liberators.

We have increased the number of correspondents for our award-winning Page One radio magazine ...

And we continue to expose and defuse Louis Farrakhan's vitriolic attacks on Jews and America by accessing videotapes of this demagogue to scores of researchers, public officials, and key community members.

Who is the driving force behind all this activity? Who enables us to respond rapidly and decisively to key events?

You.

You and more than 300,000 American and Canadian families who instinctively recognize the Center's unique purpose and our unparalleled ability to work where and when we can do the most.

You, your fellow Members, and the Simon Wiesenthal Center -- together we are the worthy adversary the Fellners and Farrakhans keep wishing would quietly step out of their way.

I know you will strengthen our alliance even more by responding generously with your renewed support today. The Simon Wiesenthal Center gratefully acknowledges your actions. Rest assured, we won't let you down.

Sincerely,

Marvin Hier

Rabbi Marvin Hier
Dean

MH:rm

Add another name to the list of those who wish we'd stop working: David McCalden, who has just filed suit against the Center, claiming we violated his rights by blocking his scheduled address before the 3000-member California Library Association. McCalden was co-founder of the Institute for Historical Review, which denies the existence of the Holocaust. He was scheduled to speak on the subject of "Free Speech and the Holocaust." I'll keep you fully informed of our response to this suit.

FIGURE 19-3
(Continued, page 4)

member of the group at whom you aim your message, as test-reader or even as writer, you run the horrible risk: The reader may think you're being patronizing. The risk doesn't exist if you write as you would for any mass medium.

If the ad is to be translated into another language, you lose some control. Certainly you should have at least two outsiders read the translated copy; they never should read it together and you always should consider changing any copy they both question.

Some advertisers who make regular forays into foreign-language media use language-school teachers as their bellwethers; some use employees of foreign embassies, who are more likely to be conversant with current usage; some leave the whole job to the media, all of whom offer a translation-service from copy written in English.

If you're a careful writer, you want your translated copy examined twice: once when it's retyped, for usage; and again when it's typeset, for typos.

Most advertisers try to reshoot posed photographs, using individuals representative of their target group. The setting should be logical and not jarring, but the original Ethnic Rule applies: Keep your dignity.

A suggestion: If you have the opportunity, test your original mass-media photograph against an ethnic-slanted photograph. You just might have a surprise, because a deliberately aimed photograph can generate a "Who the hell do you think you are?" reaction.

A JOB FOR SPECIALISTS?

Should the advertising community develop a cadre of specialists to write this kind of copy? I don't think so. I'd rather work with experienced communicators, their hand on the throttle tempered by a governing device that prevents a case of foot-in-mouth disease.

What happens when a writer becomes too hung up in sensitivity to a group is a gradually evolving negative attitude: "You can't say this." "We can't write that."

The happy middle ground: a writer who's alert to what can and can't be said and who doesn't regard the logic behind the few rules as unfair restrictions.

20

Specialty Ad-Writing: Lots and Lots of Media and Techniques

A VALID TECHNIQUE FOR EACH MEDIUM

The number of advertising media seems to be growing geometrically. We have ads on taxicabs. We have ads projected onto the sides of buildings. We have ads inside fortune cookies.

If you as writer have the assignment of preparing copy for a medium for which you've never written before, this educational step is in order: Ask the representative of the medium for any information about how to write for that medium, especially samples of what others have written and found effective.

The difference between copy for a card on the outside of a bus and copy for a card on the inside of the bus isn't major; but there is a difference, and knowing what it is will result in more effective copywriting.

One more area for exploration: the news release. A news release is, generally, a public relations function, not an advertising function. But so what? You never know when you'll be pushed into the breach with the instruction: "While you're writing the ad, give us a news release too."

Let's take a quick look at some of the specialized media.

OUTDOOR ADVERTISING

Years ago, in the days of the 24-sheet poster, a standard rule was no more than 11 words on an outdoor sign.

Signs have doubled, tripled, quadrupled in size, and the rule is more pertinent than it ever was.

Some of the best signs with the highest impact have almost no text. They'll show the product and (if the name isn't on the product) its identity, plus a single descriptive line.

More dramatic and far more dangerous are signs that instead of playing up product show the *result* of product use. A huge illuminated sign will show a basketball player leaping to the hoop; in a corner of the illustration is the product name.

These "total experience" signs are much in vogue, and no one doubts their ability to win art directors' awards. More problematical is their ability to generate sales. (See Figures 20–5 and 20–6, a pair of "total experience" signs.)

Graphics Sí, Copy No

The copywriter creating a billboard has to consider total visual effect. Impact comes from the graphics, and unless graphics and copy are one—a murderously difficult achievement—the copywriter can't hit and run with a few words of copy, left to an artist's interpretation.

Color is a major factor. The Outdoor Advertising Association of America ranks these colors in order of effectiveness: black on yellow, black on white, blue on white, white on blue. Least effective: brown on yellow, yellow on brown, red on white, white on red, red on yellow, and yellow on red.

Accept these rankings with some skepticism. The black-on-yellow recommendation is decades old, because black and yellow offer greatest contrast. The other limitation to these suggestions is the assumption that your board will have only two colors. In a multichromatic mix, yellow on red might work if colors around this particular spot are filled with blacks and blues.

Technology to the Rescue?

Outdoor parallels television in that, being a visual medium, it offers the writer a host of mechanical tricks to cover a lack of ideas. Motion, dimension, and sound are becoming commonplace. Outdoor differs from television in the significance of technological help, because a mechanical trick which calls attention to a billboard can result in the viewer remembering the board he otherwise might not have noticed.

So Kodak's "Kodarama" may be one of the pillars of outdoor expansion. The backlit transparency achieves detail and visual impact a painted sign never could.

A company named Modern Graphics has produced heat-sealed PVC panels to make molded dimensional signs. A number of companies are experimenting

FIGURE 20–1
Amoco has created a perfect outdoor sign. The product name is featured, and the slogan matches the iluustration. A passing motorist can absorb the message instantly.

FIGURE 20–2
Fixed position media are an excellent way to penetrate ethnic neighborhoods within a metropolitan area. Sometimes a sign needs only word translations; this Pepsi sign came under attack by Hispanic marketing experts, who point out the lack of interest among Hispanics in "no caffeine" as a selling point.

FIGURE 20–3
Two creative factors enhance the appeal of this sign: the appealing graphic, tied to the company name; and the unique shape of the sign itself. Careful, though: Sometimes struggling to break out of the standard rectangular shape adds nothing but cost.

FIGURE 20-4
This big sign is an eye-stopper, a contemporary triumph in the classic tradition of maximizing the outdoor advertising medium. Extending the legs above the sign is an expensive addition but in this case completely logical for visual effectiveness.

FIGURES 20-5 and 20-6
These two huge signs ran as a pair. They won art directors' awards for the advertising agency that created them. Now: What are they selling? On one board (the one on the right), in the lower left corner, is the single, almost hidden word "Nike." Ultimately, as Nike's net income fell, the agency lost the account and the signs came down. The question hangs in midair: Can a visual "experience" produce results comparable to an advertising sales-message?

with highly reflective materials, multi-image eye-foolers, and signs whose images are geared to a low-power radio station (a legend on such a sign asks motorists to tune to that frequency to hear the sign's message—see Figure 20–8).

Logic tells us to write an attention-grabbing message tied to visual impact, because this medium, more than any other, is also the message.

FIGURE 20–7
This outdoor sign used light-reflecting moving discs to impart a sense of motion.

FIGURE 20–8
Synergism in media: The outdoor sign can stand alone as a reminder for Budweiser;
but the sign asks motorists to tune their car radios to the top of the AM dial, where a
low-power broadcast transforms this sign into a "talking" billboard.

RHYMES AND REVERSES

Quick: Can you remember an effective rhymed ad? I can remember a couple,
but they aren't true rhymes; they're radio jingles of a bygone era:

Pepsi-Cola hits the spot,
Twelve full ounces, that's a lot.
Twice as much for a nickel, too:
Pepsi-Cola is the drink for you!

What ever happened to jingles that deliver a hard message? They've been
swamped by tightly orchestrated and often unrhymed jingles prepared by latter-

day specialists—"jingle writers"—who pay attention to (like so much expensively mediocre advertising) form, not substance.

Rhymed copy *implicitly* calls attention to form, not substance. As a contrivance it's less noticeable when spoken than when written.

When might you take the dusty rhyming dictionary off the shelf? Rhymes are worth exploring in either of two circumstances:

1. When your company or product has an obvious rhyme with a complementary word.

2. When your message is implicitly unexciting and needs external massaging.

In print, if you rhyme copy be sure the production artist sets it up as a rhyme. Initial letters help. Capitalizing the first word of each line helps. Whatever you do, don't run the rhyme as text with a backslash indicating a new line. It doesn't work:

Roses are red / your face will be, too / if you miss the kangaroo /at the Metrozoo!

When set in type that way it's just text. Don't go halfway with a rhyme. If you use it, exploit it:

Roses are red.
Your face will be, too . . .
If you miss the kangaroo
At the Metrozoo!

COMIC STRIPS AND COMIC BOOKS

Don't laugh. Or maybe, do laugh. Comic books can solve a complex marketing-information problem if they aren't just clever for the sake of cleverness. Ever since Mickey Mouse helped train World War II bomber crews, educators have known the value of comics. Except for a handful of marketers of children's items, advertisers have been slow to test comic strips and comic books as serious message carriers.

Comics and cartoons have this advantage going in: they aren't threatening. The reader doesn't fear them. The reader doesn't have even a 1 percent feeling of inferiority or inadequacy. The immediate impression is entertainment, not instruction. What better medium to uncomplicate a complicated message?

Whether it's a comic strip in print media or a full-blown comic book for mailing or point-of-purchase distribution, copywriter and artist should work together to assure congruence of copy and art. Keep the art simple and double-check every facial expression.

If the artist says, "I need more space for word balloons," you have a danger

FIGURE 20–9
Suppose this ad, which ran in advertising trade publications, had a conventional
instead of comic-strip format. Would it have been as noticeable and as readable? To
some, the message is inscrutable, but the technique is unassailable.

signal. No more than ten words in any one balloon, please, or you get preachy.
You can add nonballoon explanatory text at the bottom of any panel.

After you've roughed out a comic-strip or comic-book approach, ask yourself: "What do I have here I wouldn't have with a conventional brochure or ad?" If
the answer doesn't hit you right in the eye, you haven't used the medium to best
advantage . . . or it's the wrong medium for this message.

Single cartoons are far more dangerous, because one cartoon probably is a
replacement for a realistic graphic. Careful! Are you being clever for the sake of
cleverness? Are you violating Unassailable Loser Statute III (illustration should
agree with what you're selling, not with headline copy)?

Consider single cartoons under these battle conditions:

1. You're selling a concept that defies illustration.
2. You fear the reader will be embarrassed if you draw too close a tie to
   what you're selling.
3. You're trying (ugh!) to establish a corporate character.
4. (Primarily in political advertising) You want to ridicule someone or
   something or create a grotesque or ugly image.

FIGURE 20–10
The cartoon technique brightens this ad, attracts readership, and projects an image of conviviality. Set in type, with more formal illustrations, the effect would be considerably more conservative.

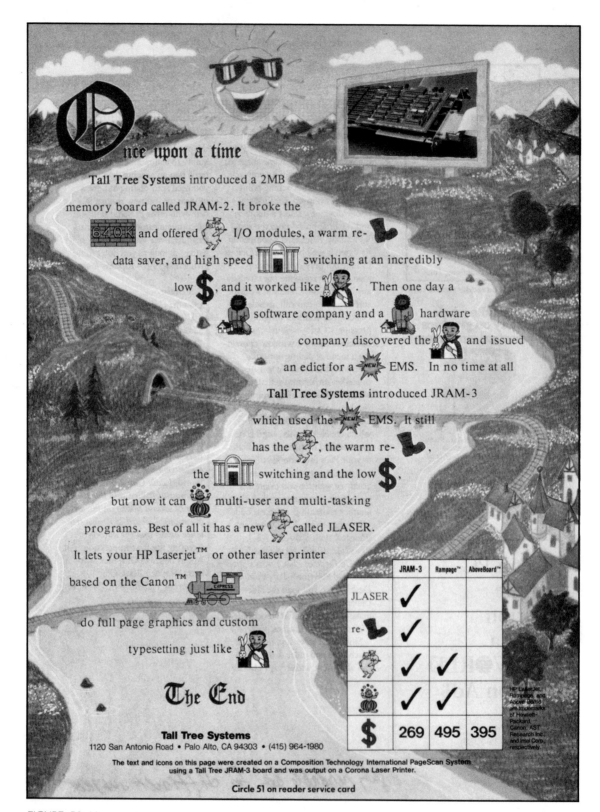

FIGURE 20–11
Tall Tree Systems solved a difficult communications problem by creating a "rebus" ad.
The one missing component is an explanation of some of the symbols. Not everyone
will understand the "piggyback" drawing. No question, though: This ad combines
visual appeal with a potent message.

FIGURE 20–12
The New York Times, breaking from standard trade advertising, ran this appealing (if puzzling) cartoon ad. Because the advertiser is *The New York Times,* the reader smiles and doesn't dare ask, "What does it mean?"

THE THREE MASTER RULES FOR WRITING NEWS RELEASES

Three master rules, or canons, cover both technique and content for news release writing.

The First Canon of News Release Writing:

> **The reader, viewer, or listener should be unaware that the message is sponsored.**

The Second Canon of News Release Writing:

> **Put puffery in quotes.**

The Third Canon of News Release Writing:

> **Replace or eliminate descriptive adjectives which suggest editorial viewpoint.**

Information, Not Raw "Exposure"

Some practitioners of "contact" publicity function on a different level. They deal in *exposure*, not *information*. The intended result of their professional activity is *mention*, not *persuasion*. Rules of writing are superfluous. This rock-'em-sock-'em variation of public relations is on the wane, not only because their outlets (gossip columnists and broadcast personalities) are fewer than they once were, but also because except for the "show-biz" personality little benefit accrues from raw "mentions."

For the rest of us, adherence to the three canons not only is an insurance policy covering our own dignity and that of our message; it also is a direct road to editorial acceptance of messages any publication has to regard as optional.

Writer-awareness should be constant to avoid backsliding into ad-copy. A news release shouldn't crow; it should have the aura of dispassionate reporting. You wouldn't write . . .

> These are the biggest bargains in fur coats Mason Fur Company has ever offered. It will be years before another furrier can equal these prices.

Instead, you'd write . . .

> "These are the biggest bargains in fur coats Mason Fur Company has ever offered," said John Mason, president of the company. "In my opinion it will be years before another furrier can equal these prices."

After you've written your news release, ask yourself the ultimate question: Does this release tell the reader how the information relates to him or her?

Keep in your forebrain the temper of the times: We're in the Age of Skepticism. The reader doesn't ask, "What is it?" The reader asks, "What will it do *for* me?"

```
RELEASED BY:  Executive Services Companies, Inc.
              901 N. International Parkway
              Suite 191
              Richardson, Texas  75081

     DATE:  September 23, 19__
```

We are very proud to announce our new Account Executive
for your region, <u>MS. MARCIE LEVINE</u>. We are very excited
to have <u>MARCIE</u> join our Consumer List Division's sales
team.

Please call <u>MARCIE</u> at 1-800-527-3933 for your direct
marketing list needs, and you will receive the professionalism and service that you require.

Sincerely,

Gene Rast
Vice President
List Marketing

FIGURE 20–13
Despite the big "NEWS" across the top, in no way is this a news release. "We are very
proud to announce . . ." is a personal statement, and the signature makes this a letter,
not a release. A true news release would have been worded something like this:
      Executive Services Company has appointed Ms. Marcie Levine
Account Executive for the Southeast Region, according to Gene Rast, Vice
President of the company.
      "We are very excited to have Marcie join our Consumer List
Division's sales team," said Mr. Rast . . .

GSC PRESS RELEASE

FOR IMMEDIATE RELEASE   CONTACT: David James
                                             Barbara Gill
                                             (301) 986-0840

GSC Appointed to Manage Government Executives from Carroll Publishing
102,000 Executives by Name and Title

Bethesda, MD (October 10, 19__) -- GSC announced today its appointment as list manager for a list never before offered to the direct marketing industry, "Government Executives from Carroll Publishing."

"We are proud to be able to offer this premier government list. It is the largest, most accurate, most current, most comprehensive government list available," said Arnold Palley, president of GSC.

Carroll Publishing markets five directories; Federal Executives, Federal Regional Executives, State Executives, County Executives, Municipal Executives. These directories are used as a major resource in corporations, TV networks, newspapers, associations, and the government. Names in every directory are telephone verified.

Direct marketers can now reach all the government decision makers listed in these directories with selections such as agency, department, function, management level, and telephone number.

Other GSC lists include Brandon Computer Professionals, IBM PC Users List, Corporate Training Professionals, National Computer Conference Attendees, Computer and Technical Professionals at Home, Main/Mini/Micro Users at Business Address, and Data Base Research Group.

For more information on these or other lists offered by GSC, please call or write GSC, 7970 Old Georgetown Road, Bethesda, MD 20814, (301) 986-0840.

316   **GARY SLAUGHTER CORPORATION,** 7970 Old Georgetown Road, Bethesda, Maryland 20814-2493 (301) 986-0840

FIGURE 20–14

Three problems with this news release: First, it isn't double-spaced, which makes editing nearly impossible. Second, what is "GSC"? At the bottom of the sheet we see the full name, but the name isn't in the release itself. Third, the final paragraph lapses into the imperative. An editor, seeing "Please call or write," may not resist the urge to pitch into the waste-basket a thinly veiled advertisement masquerading as a news release.

Don't Skimp on Information

Does your news release leave questions unanswered? Suppose, for example, you're writing about a personnel appointment. Is it a new position? Is the new appointee succeeding someone? If so, whom? What happened to the person who previously held the job?

If titles seem similar, explain the job a little: If John Jones is the new Director of Advertising, reporting to John Smith, Vice President of Advertising, what responsibilities does Jones actually have? If a Vice President is made "Senior Vice President," what's the significance of the move up?

If someone wins an award, explain the award. If you're moving to a new building, specify—you're either "streamlining" (a euphemism for cutting back) or "expanding" (in which case you emphasize the amount of space). The simple rule:

Don't leave obvious questions unanswered.

The Fact Sheet

Television interviewers, "personalities," and newspeople often regard their own on-camera position as paramount and whatever they're saying or showing as subordinate.

Many of these people prefer a fact sheet to a news release. For safety, send both to broadcast media.

The fact sheet should list in an orderly and organized way why your subject is worthy of air-time. Be sure your first point is a bell-ringer.

If someone from your organization will be on hand as spokesperson, include half a dozen questions the reporter might ask that individual. The questions should be those the station's viewership or audience regards as logical; don't lapse into questions whose answers would be transparently self-congratulatory.

Writing Cutlines and Captions

If you send out a news release without a photograph, you not only damage the possibility of your words winding up in print; you're leaving out what can be the best-read component—the cutline.

(Generally, captions are words above a picture; cutlines are words below a picture. In the news world, *cutline* is the most common term.)

Here are a few rules for writing cutlines and captions:

1. Repeat pertinent information even though it also appears in the news release. That way, a publication which runs the photograph but not the news story won't leave out something you think is important.

2. Don't be afraid to write long cutlines. The worst that can happen is the publication will edit them down.

News from PERSOFT™

FOR IMMEDIATE RELEASE   Contact: Maria Shattuck
                                          Sterling Hager, Inc.
                                          (617) 661-7220

PERSOFT INTRODUCES ANALYSIS SOFTWARE PACKAGE

FOR DIRECT MARKETING SERVICE BUREAUS

-- Sophisticated Analysis of Rental, Compiled and House Lists Now Possible --

WOBURN, Mass., June 10 -- Persoft, Inc., which successfully introduced an industry-first expert software system for direct marketers less than one year ago, today introduced MORE/2(TM), a system developed to allow direct marketers to more easily perform analysis and list segmentation at their service bureaus.

According to Persoft, MORE/2 is the only automated, service bureau system with the ability to examine large mailing lists on a name-by-name basis, segmenting and ranking prospects from most likely to respond to least likely to respond. In this way, direct marketers can determine an optimum depth at which to mail to receive the highest profit/expense ratio. By targeting those prospects and customers who represent the greatest profit potential, direct marketers can boost response, reduce overmailing and extract more profit from their direct marketing programs.

"The intent in developing MORE/2 was to make our expert system software available to those direct marketers who use service bureaus for prospect and customer mailings," said Fred Wiersema, senior vice president at Persoft.

-- more --

PERSOFT, Inc.
600 West Cummings Park
Woburn, Massachusetts 01801
(617) 935-0095

318

FIGURE 20–15

Persoft is a sophisticated user of news releases. In format and approach, this release—which runs seven pages!—shows the professional touch. A purist might regard the word *successfully* in the first sentence as a mild bit of editorializing, and the second paragraph is too long and complex; but these problems are easily edited. The key word *introduces* helps the printworthiness of this release.

3. Write complete sentences, not "bullet-style." If a publication has its own stylistic idiosyncrasies an editor will change your copy to conform, but most publications prefer full sentences.

4. Set a limit of 20 words per sentence.

5. If you include several pictures, write a separate cutline for each one, even if they're similar. Assume that only one will be used—and you don't know which one.

HOW TO HANDLE NEGATIVE NEWS

It seldom pays to write a direct answer to an accusation or a negative circumstance. Instead, have a "library" release of achievements ready. Tie it to one of these nonresponses to an accusation, built around the temporizing words *appropriate* and *inappropriate*:

—We haven't yet had an opportunity to study and discuss the matter and will have an appropriate comment once this has been accomplished.
—The matter is in litigation and it would be inappropriate for us to comment at this time.
—We have undertaken an internal investigation of the issue and are compiling information for analysis.

Using this technique, a news release or prepared statement would *never* be worded such as this:

We regard the report as biased and unfair, and we are discussing with our attorneys the possibility of strong legal action.

Instead, a reply might be worded something like this:

We haven't yet read the report, and of course we'll have a comment at the appropriate time. We do call your attention to our positive record of achievement in affirmative action hiring and civic service.

A HARD LOOK AT REMAILS

Remails—mailing a second message to someone who didn't buy from you but should have—are becoming their own medium.

Why are remails a hot media concept now?

A major advantage direct marketers have over their brethren in media advertising is the ability to pinpoint market segments. The computer, one of the two principal bases for the renaissance of direct response (the other: ZIP codes), tells us just about everything we might want to know about our buyers. We're almost able to predict who will buy what.

Tantalizing, isn't it, that word *almost*. It's the word that keeps us off-balance, not matter how big a pile of data we accumulate.

Here's Mary Jones, age 46, married, two children, exurban, ZIP code starts with 6, works part-time, household income $35,000–$40,000, husband an engineer. She bought from us three times before and she bought this offer too.

Here's Mary Smith, age 46, married, two children, exurban, ZIP code starts with 6, works part-time, household income $35,000–$40,000, husband an engineer. She bought from us three times before and she *didn't* buy this offer.

Why?

The "Random Intrusion" Factor

In my opinion, taking the time to ferret out a psychographic differential between Mary Jones and Mary Smith is for us as marketers a less-efficient use of time than remailing Mary Smith.

Why? Because if Mary Smith didn't buy, the reason might be a subtle difference between the two women; but it's just as likely that Mary Smith just didn't see the offer.

Please don't limit "see" to the standard explanations (she wasn't home that day or missed this one piece of mail or was the victim of a post office peccadillo). Include the possibility that the most uncontrollable circumstance, preventing exactly parallel situations even between Siamese twins, changed the mix. We can call that circumstance *random intrusion*.

Mary Smith may not have "seen" our mailing or ad as Mary Jones did because of her mood, buying position, family attitude, personal exhilaration or disgruntlement, or momentary aberration. These are beyond the reach of any marketer. But—happy day!—they're subject to immediate change.

So what do we do? We remail Mary Smith. We give her a second chance, because no matter how black her mood, how disgusted she is with us as vendors, how wasteful she felt after her last buying spree, or how changed her demo/psychographics might be, she still is a buying prospect of far greater value than any cold list name. We give her a second chance.

Don't Insult the Blind

We all have seen so many "You Fool!" follow-up mailings that our attitude toward this approach probably has polarized. We love it or we hate it.

The insult-lovers do have a point. Mary Smith hasn't bought. As a member of the prime target group, she should have. What's wrong with a little shock therapy?

Really, nothing. I just think it's too soon.

If Mary Smith didn't have proper exposure to our message, which of these approaches will bring in her order?

Your subscription has officially expired. Here is one last opportunity to renew your subscription at the preferred rate.

Please send us your renewal immediately, as otherwise no further issues can be sent to you.

Or

Oops!

We know our subscribers get more mail than most people. So it's possible you missed the renewal notice we sent you a few weeks ago.

Not to worry. I've enclosed a duplicate. Please send it back right away, because technically your subscription has run out.

I lean—mildly—toward the second approach not only because it's more likely to slide under the barrier the recipient may have erected (what if, yes, the first notice did get through, was considered and rejected, and went the way of all flush?), but also because it's too soon to connect the electrodes.

Sure, in a series of four follow-up letters, the fourth is loaded with explosives. Three strikes and we're out, so what do we have to lose?

What if budget or corporate philosophy dictates only one follow-up? My suggestion: Test. Test friendship against hard-boiled "You're-the-loser" copy.

We are, after all, in the Age of Skepticism. I'm increasingly antsy about a reaction I'd have regarded as strange ten years ago . . . contemptuous rejection of copy we intend as friendly. The reader concludes, "He's trying to sell me something"—and this conclusion is ground for refusal.

Subscriber turnover being what it is, it's a rare and courageous publication which gives up after only one subscription reminder. Magazine subscriptions aren't typical of our total cosmos anyway, because a subscriber may go his way and return to the fold a year or two later when the ninth follow-up offers a calculator or a camera.

We're Selling Merchandise Here

Suppose instead of a subscription offer we've mailed a merchandise offer. How do we offer the target individual a second chance? Do we just remail, with no changes? After all, the "No-See" Theory suggests we might as well, since the recipient probably didn't get a good look at what we're selling.

I don't agree, and I'll tell you why. This book is based on the four great motivators that work during the ongoing Age of Skepticism—*fear, exclusivity, guilt,* and *greed.* Here's a painless way to add *guilt* to the blend. (It can't hurt, especially since "No-See" might *not* be the reason the original mailing didn't pull a response.)

On the outer envelope, put a legend—something such as:

Did you overlook it?
Here's another copy.

Inside, add a single enclosure to the mailing. This would be a small sheet of paper, either a "From the desk of . . ." sheet or a small piece of notepaper with no heading. The message on this sheet:

I sent you this information a few weeks ago. I haven't seen a reply from you, which suggests my original message didn't reach you. So here's another copy. You still have time.

Two rules form themselves when we consider remailing. We might call them the Remail Determinants. Here's the First Remail Determinant:

If the mailing has been successful, the only content change for a single remail to someone whose characteristics match those who bought from your first mailing is the information that this *is* a remail.

The Second Remail Determinant:

Unless you're out of cold list names, send Second Chance mailings only to proved names—the "Mary Smiths." For any other prospect groups, sending additional mailings to cold lists probably will be more productive.

If you haven't tried Second Chance mailings of offers which have pulled fairly well, consider them. They can be a strong road to increased profit, and the additional creative and mechanical costs are nil.

LEARN YOUR CRAFT

Whatever you're writing—outdoor signs, comic-strip advertising, news releases, remails, or copy for an ever-changing kiosk sign in a bus station—learn your craft.

Too many writers look down on what they do: "This kind of copy is beneath me." Uh-uh.

It's impossible to know too much. And it's a lot easier to write potent copy for *any* medium if you know how that medium works.

21

A Hot New Medium: How to Write "Card Deck" Copy That Sells

What a nasty shock loose-deck cards are for the writer who usually settles in comfortably to grind out a four-page letter, eight-page brochure, or full-page ad.

The whole sales argument has to squeeze itself into one side of a 3½-by-5 ½-inch card!

That isn't the worst of it. The card is embedded in the center of a deck, with 59 competing cards elbowing it out of the way, clamoring for attention on their own.

The ambience is the contemporary equivalent of the huge classified section of *Popular Mechanics* in the 1930s—page after page of classified ads, and what hope could a little advertiser have?

Somehow that hidden classified ad did pull. And somehow that buried card does pull. But the differences between 1939 and 1989 aren't just improved technology and degraded mail delivery. They're more profound than that.

The biggest difference is in the tremendous assault of advertising messages. The 1939 reader may have subscribed to *Popular Mechanics* and no other publication; that could be why the tiny classified ads pulled. Do you know anyone who in 1989 would subscribe to just one magazine?

323

With an average of 57 weekly hours of television viewing, plus home and car radios, plus metropolitan and community newspapers, plus catalogs and mailers, plus an endless sea of signs, plus telemarketing, it isn't surprising that we become more and more desensitized to all advertising.

But we bear a nastier cross: The typical card deck is business-to-business, so we have to add to the attention-grabbing mix all the trade publications competing for attention. Question: What chance does one card have?

GRAB 'EM OR LOSE 'EM

Donald Moger, whose Los Angeles-based Donald Moger Direct Marketing specializes in card decks, offers a no-nonsense answer to the question.

The typical recipient of a 60-card deck spends 60 seconds riffling through it, says Mr. Moger. You have *one second* to grab attention, hold it, and impel the riffler to put it aside for action.

Joe Doyle, president of Federal Mailers, Fort Lauderdale, embraces the maxim of headline importance. His précis, "How to Design the Super Card," has as Point 1: Use a powerful brief headline that clearly states the benefit to the buyer.

Mr. Doyle agrees that the typical recipient will spend only one minute to look through the entire deck.

Even though some decks are printed on soft paper, he advocates full color. In the middle of a deck of four-color cards, wouldn't a dynamic two-color card stand out? "No," says this deck publisher. "If you're in the middle of the deck, color is even more important. We've tested it in split-runs, and color invariably pulls at least 20 percent better."

Folio Publishing Corp. of New Canaan, CT, whose decks reach advertising and publishing executives, has a *Basic Guide* whose opinion expands the "grab time" from one second to 3 to 10 seconds. Not surprisingly, the *Guide* says the headline represents 50 percent to 80 percent of the "value" of the entire ad; the word *new* and description of benefits are crucial; and the writer's focus should be on *you*, with copy "simple enough so it can be quickly digested."

Joseph Schachter of Top Decks, Cambridge, MA, offered advice the card deck copywriter might find practical but time-consuming:

"Find those cards you know have run repeatedly in the pack or packs you are going to use, and note the patterns among them, including type size, type style, headline length, relationship of headline content to rest of card, orientation of card (horizontal or vertical).

"What you will be able to learn from these repeated headlines is not what the *best* headlines are, but what *acceptable* headlines are . . . those good enough to run repeatedly."

Mr. Schachter also points out how ideal card decks are for testing headlines. (Many card decks offer split-runs.)

FIGURE 21–1

The heading violates the Third Great Law ("E² = 0") and misuses the loose deck card medium. This advertiser is offering a catalog, and getting the reader to write for that catalog should be the unswerving function of this copy.

FIGURE 21–2

The headline is a shade cutesy-pie, but this card proves it's possible to sell coherently on a card. This advertiser sells a drainage level, and the sales argument is complete and forceful. Nothing tricky here—just solid benefit-laden straightforward copy.

SIX PRINCIPLES FOR SUCCESSFUL CARD DECK COPY

Agreement is unanimous on one point: The recipient wastes no time dawdling over cards. I'd amend the one-second speculation a bit: A card advertiser has one second to convince the reader to spend more time on his card. Whether one second or three seconds, the time is perilously short. So let's codify some rules of our own.

The First Principle of Card Deck Copy

Your offer must be identifiable instantly.

Flash a photocopy of your card's camera-ready art at half a dozen people who don't already know what you're selling. Give them the longest estimated digestion time—three seconds. Then have them tell you, minus refinements they'd have to probe the body copy to find, what it is you want them to do.

The Second Principle of Card Deck Copy

Sell, coherently, what the headline promises, not a secondary service or product down the road.

If you're offering free details, emphasize the free details, not what you might sell later on. In my opinion this is the principal source of confusion in unsuccessful cards.

The Third Principle of Card Deck Copy

Stress benefits. You don't have room to write poetry about features and the reader has neither the patience nor the interest to read your poetry. Use a bulleted format to save space and hold attention.

The Fourth Principle of Card Deck Copy

Assume your card is buried in a deck of offers, all of which are as good as yours or better.

I suggest this principle because seldom will a direct response writer face as brutally competitive a medium as card decks.

This is doubly true if your card isn't one of the first six. Card deck publishers don't deny the fall-off rate as the reader shuffles toward the bottom of the pile. Many decks charge a premium for position within the first six.

Another penalty: Making the offer isn't good enough. You know a deck-riffler won't scribble his name on 60 cards or even 10. Why should yours be among the chosen few? Because your words burst with power and the other guy's words don't.

The Fifth Principle of Card Deck Copy

Tell the reader what to do.

You know this principle doesn't apply only to card decks. But I include it because this is the most obvious and most common deficiency in copy for cards.

Invariably the poorest-pulling cards ignore this principle. Peculiar, isn't it, since it's the easiest one to apply?

The Sixth Principle of Card Deck Copy

Force the reader to respond immediately because delay will cost money, reduce benefits, or lose business to a competitor.

Time can work for us as well as against us. The recipient is flipping through the cards, but he or she did open the deck. What went through the brain, deciding to allocate one to three minutes to turning a neatly packaged deck into a jumbled mess of discards—and a few precious cards to mail back?

Decisions are instant, and keeping this in mind can benefit the canny card advertiser. "Create urgency," says Joe Doyle. "Give them a reason to act now." That's the way to do it, all right. But it ain't that easy.

WHY SHOULD I MAIL THIS CARD?

I'm looking at a card for, of all things, a card deck. The heading on the card:

"OUR CUSTOMERS MEAN BUSINESS"

What a ghastly cliché! Sometimes, in speeches, I'll show about 40 ads for various companies, headed "[Name of Company] Means Business." I've seen this tired line so often I've quit collecting samples.

But cliché or not, where's the clarion call to action? Reading it, what am I supposed to do? Remember the First Principle—"Your offer must be identifiable instantly"? Remember the cosmic Fourth Great Law which has become the Fifth Principle—"Tell the reader what to do"?

Here's the unconvincing nonargument following "Our Customers Mean Business":

> And that means business for you when you offer your product or service to 100,000+ proven mail-order buyers with MEETING POWER CARDS.

This was the first card in the deck. I suggest a separate principle to the publishers of card decks: *Those first few cards should be barn-burners.* We look through the first few cards with boredom; then we throw the deck into the wastebasket.

What a disservice to the advertiser whose brilliantly written, perfectly produced card is number 58 in the deck!

A byproduct advantage of writing copy which doesn't violate the six principles is *clarity*. In cards, clarity and the First Principle are Siamese twins.

Here is all the display copy on a card:

> Look
> $ Trade Commodities with a Professional
> before Investing a Dime $

Okay, you have one second. Aw, make it three seconds. Tell me what they're selling.

A more leisurely inspection of the card tells us the advertiser is pitching a "unique commodity program, designed for the beginner as well as the experienced investor." Yawn. Copy ends with the suggestion we "send now for a free booklet." Why? What's in that booklet?

See the point? The card violates the First Principle, and implicitly it's unclear. What if the writer had pitched the free booklet, finding a benefit in it? Impact would be centered and clarity would justify holding the card for a few more seconds.

Compare that card with this super-clear offer:

> INTRODUCTORY ½ PRICE OFFER
> (Expires in 30 Days)
>
> 18 rolls of PCS
> SUPER-STICK
> SHIPPING TAPE
> + PLUS +
> a heavy duty
> SWEDISH STEEL
> DISPENSER
> only $29.98 (a $63.01 value)
> * SAVE $32.03 *

Not one clever word. Not one slip toward subtlety, the enemy of clarity. Sparing use of adjectives. It's an effective card, proof that yes, you can sell directly off the card.

ONE-STEP, TWO-STEP, AND MISSTEP

The shipping tape card is one of many successful one-step cards—cards making a direct offer to sell, not an offer to send information.

Remembering the postal limitations of cards (only three choices: [1] "Place Stamp Here"; [2] Business-reply "No Postage Necessary . . ."; [3] the card has to be mailed in an envelope or used for a phone call, so both sides are available for message), let's condense logic into three requirements for one-step conversion:

1. Means of ordering and billing should be simplified.
2. Product use should be known.
3. Bargain should be apparent.

FIGURE 21–3

This advertiser asks for readers to call a toll-free phone, instead of trying to sell this piece of machinery directly from the card. The two-step conversion may be a wise decision, because the buyer may want considerably more information before making a decision. (If the reader's only question is the price—and omitting the price may be a mistake—he can call the toll-free number, get the price, and order on the spot.)

The "Free Details" two-step conversion usually is less troublesome than going for the order direct from the card; but when the possibility of getting the order exists, it's a tantalizing prospect.

Examining previous issues of the deck and testing inquiry cards against go-for-the-jugular cards will start a card education which becomes increasingly worthwhile as loose deck cards become major direct response media.

22

Lots of Tips
for Writing Catalog Copy

ADDING THE RIGHT MOTIVATORS

Catalog copywriters spend their days struggling to answer the toughest question in our business: Why should I buy from you?

Raw product description depends on luck to get that target customer to lift the phone or fill out the order form. Luck won't hack it for us. Safety lies in giving the catalog reader a reason to order. Remember the magic formula?

—Only you.
—Only from us.

Sometimes one word makes the difference. A specific word can motivate. Another specific word can be a turnoff.

WORDS DO AND WORDS DON'T

What qualifies as a motivator? Headlines projecting benefit qualify. Here's one:

It's not a *copy* of the famous $125 European shoe.
It *is* the $125 shoe. Yet you pay only $79.99!

Here's another:

Exclusive Country Clothes Collection
Designed by us, made by us,
Available only from us.

A bonus is an automatic motivator, because a bonus is a pure appeal to greed, one of the great motivators.

On the inside cover of a flower catalog we find *two* bonus offers, one atop the other:

FREE BONUS
OFFER
If your order is received by September 25 . . . we will send you FREE, with your order, 6 top-size Red Riding Hood tulips. These bright red Greigii hybrids flower in early April on sturdy 12″ stems. Their foliage is a rich green with purplish stripes. Excellent for beds, borders, and background in the rock garden. A $2.95 regular value.

ADDITIONAL FREE
BONUS OFFER
12 Dwarf Daffodils Hawera
This dainty Triandus Hybrid is extremely free flowering. The flowers are usually 3 to 4 on a stem with bell-shaped cup and recurved petals. The soft creamy yellow flowers are only 8″ tall, making them ideal for borders and rockgardens. They will naturalize well and come back year after year. A $4.00 value free with orders over $40.00.

Assuming the typical reader scans the two free offers in sequence, a proof-reader should have demanded consistency—one word or two words for rock gardens. What's good here is the motivational descriptions; I might not be interested in tulips or daffodils, but the descriptions give them a universal appeal.

A minor copy note: I'd prefer the colorful word *purple* to the cardiac-arrest color *purplish*.

(Color can be a motivator. A suede skirt in another catalog gains elegance by the copywriter's touch; it might have been *red* or *vermilion*, but this writer adds value by calling it *ruby*.)

Other motivators? Even the lowly phone number can be a motivator:

24 HOURS
7 DAYS A WEEK
CALL TOLL-FREE
1-800-225-8200

(Adding the standard line "Have your VISA, MasterCard, or American Express card ready" won't hurt the motivation and will speed up the order-taking process.)

Another catalog adds the motivator of timeliness to the phone number:

Call 1-800-543-8633
For Same Day Shipping

Customizing, extraordinary wording of guarantees, direct quotation testimonials—all are motivators. Like the others, their potency depends on the copywriter's mastery of the craft of force communication.

A Sales Expert Doesn't Just Describe

What's wrong with this copy?

THE PERFECT DRESS
Wear it anywhere and enjoy being seen in this stylish and flattering timeless classic. Midnight Black or Champagne White, sizes 6–12.

No, it isn't terrible. No, it isn't professional. It hangs in that limbo separating those two universes.

It isn't terrible because it *does* describe what the catalog is selling—a dress. The photograph shows it, relieving the copywriter of some of the burden. Colors and sizes are covered.

What prevents the copy from entering the hallowed halls of professionalism is the decision—conscious or unconscious, by writer or employer—that *description* is equivalent to salesmanship.

What if, instead of the pitifully uninspired "Wear it anywhere," the writer had realized: As long as we're setting type, let's move up to descriptive sell instead of "blah" copy:

Wear it to the tennis matches.
Then go directly to your dressy banquet.
It's in perfect taste for both.

The writer now transmits a message the reader can pick up through her eyeballs. It's visual, as good catalog selling copy should be.

The Curse of "Parochial Isolation"

The curse of parochial isolation is the gradual widening of the distance between you as seller and "those people" as possible buyers.

What's parochial isolation? It's the well-intended but self-defeating practice of becoming so overknowledgeable about what you're selling, to the exclusion of outside influences, that you lose touch with the marketplace.

The friendly neighborhood grocer of pre-supermarket days never had this problem. He saturated himself in the open marketplace. He knew his demographics inside out: Who bought what, and why. He knew, within the limited sphere of his own marketing area, the survival potential of a new product. His customers kept him aware of his competition.

Early catalogers had this same advantage. They knew—whether instinctively or aggressively—that isolation stifles communication. What, after all, is a catalog if it isn't a profit-seeking maneuver in force communication?

HOW TO PREVENT COPY ANEMIA

Isolation can turn copy so anemic it becomes too weak to compete. Why? Because as the gap between seller and buyer widens, the words in the catalog mean less and less to the target prospect.

Let the writer scrabble around in the open marketplace to get those batteries recharged! Let her spend a week behind the counter at a retail store! Let him spend a week selling door-to-door or over the phone, or wandering slowly through a shopping mall making notes of comments and conversations!

The Buyer/Seller Equivalence Equation explains why inbred copy keeps seller and buyer apart:

> *The Seller's Concern* =
> **What it is.**
> *The Buyer's Concern* =
> **What it will do for me.**

Can you see the logic behind a plea for catalog writers to immerse themselves in the marketplace—to watch the television shows they reject with intellectualized disdain—to stroll through department stores and shopping malls—to listen to late-night radio call-in shows—to read one consumer magazine for each trade magazine they read?

In my opinion this makes the writer a far better keyboard gladiator than poring over a competitor's catalog ever could. In my opinion basing catalog copy on what a competitor writes is "me-tooism" which might help immortalize the competitor's mistakes. In my opinion everybody in this business should spend as much time outside the insulated corporate walls as inside them.

SIX MAGIC WORDS

Invariably, catalogers who quarantine themselves away from "those people" at whom their catalogs are aimed are unaware that what they think and like may not parallel what "those people" like and think.

Go through the catalog, item by item, and ask the logical six-word question:

What will this do for me?

You not only will overcome the "Feature Isn't Identical to Benefit" mistake, but your own attitude toward catalog copy will begin to parallel the attitude of "those people"—and they're the ones who keep you in business.

The Ultimate "Ultimate"

Falling in love with a word is like falling in love with a vampire. Every kiss drains a little more strength out of your message. Example: see Figure 22–1.

One of the better upscale catalogs has in a single issue a whole gaggle of "ultimates." A golfer can buy "the ultimate putter"; the young adventurer can buy "the ultimate remote-controlled off-road vehicle"; a dog can have "the ultimate defense against fleas" (this last shows a dog inside the house, his electronic collar probably driving the fleas deep into the carpet).

Like fine wine or good jokes, words such as *ultimate* or *supreme* or *beautiful* or *important* should be dispensed sparingly (see Chapter 11). Poured out in a glut, they sour the stomach.

Sure, a writer forgets which words he used yesterday. A catalog has two separate sets of problems: (1) More than one writer can contribute prose; (2) Copy might be written over an extended period of time, especially if some sections are picked up from previous catalogs.

The solution—as is true of all creative writing—lies in dispassionate proofreading. A person not connected to the origin of the copy reads it in a single sitting, looking for sinister duplications.

If copy comes out of a word processor, checking is a lot easier. The "search" key will pick up adjectival overuse. It's the ultimate defense against the ultimate gaffe, and ultimately it works to the ultimate benefit of the mailing.

And Just What Makes It "Ultimate"?

If we're saying what we mean, we won't use *ultimate* as the ultimate description anyway. Why? Because *ultimate* implies the end of the rainbow, the best, beyond further improvement. If in fact whatever we're selling actually *is* the ultimate, we'll sell more merchandise when our copy tells the reader just what it is that makes what we're selling "the ultimate" than we would by making an unexplained claim.

If you've been using *ultimate* and *important* as unexplained—ergo, unjustified—descriptions, a mild chiding: You're cheating the reader, whether your claim is true or not. If what you're selling really is the ultimate or if it really is important, you have more ammunition than you're using; if it isn't, you're using paper to cover a hole in the roof.

A. **My car trunk was always a mess until this unique snap-together system came along.** Installs easily in minutes and can be arranged and rearranged to fit every organizing need! Each kit includes 8 (9½″ x 9½″) interlocking plastic mats; 6 (4″ x 2¼″) movable bases and 10 (5″) stacking posts that hold packages grocery bags, boxes, etc. upright and firmly in place without spills! Great for station wagons and lift-backs, too!

#Q4760 NO-TIP TRUNK MAT $21.00

B. **Reading these days is not the simple pleasure it used to be. My arms just aren't long enough and I need help.** I found a magnifier that lights up a 10-inch area so I'm not constantly moving my hand as I read. It has a 3¾″ diameter lens with 2½ magnification power and reverses for left-handers. Two AA batteries included.

#Q4008 LIGHTED MAGNIFIER $17.50

C. **Finally, there's a garment bag designed to hold my long skirts and dresses without wrinkling the hems!** The additional 9″ length is but one of the quality features — *side hooks that keep the bag from spreading open,* heavy duty chain and hook with storage slot and strong adjustable shoulder strap. The matching carry-on tote (21″ x 9″ x 13″) fits under an airline seat. It has a main suitcase-sized compartment, a briefcase-like section that has 2 full-length dividers, plus 2 convenient outside front pockets. Made of 100% polyhide fabric that is wipeable, easy-to-keep clean and designed to keep its good looks. Quality, versatile luggage you'll love! Black only.*

#Q4738 EXPANDABLE GARMENT BAG $99.00
#Q4739 ROOMY CARRY-ON $70.00

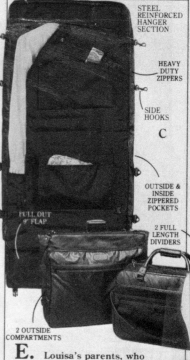

STEEL REINFORCED HANGER SECTION

HEAVY DUTY ZIPPERS

SIDE HOOKS

C

OUTSIDE & INSIDE ZIPPERED POCKETS

2 FULL LENGTH DIVIDERS

PULL OUT 9″ FLAP

2 OUTSIDE COMPARTMENTS

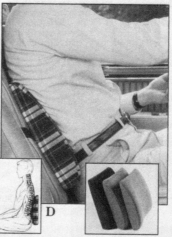

D

D. **What comfort! My son Don, who drives daily, swears by the wonderful support this posture cushion gives his back.** A quality product, it is contour molded to hold the body at the proper angle for driving, thus relieving tension and relaxing the spine. Makes contact with the lower back exactly where it's needed. It comes in beautiful patterned velours in Grey, Tan and Blue, (perfect for luxurious car interiors), and in good-looking plaids.

#Q4716 PLAID POSTURE CUSHION $22.50
#Q4758 CURVED BUCKET SEAT CUSHION, Plaid Only $22.50
#Q4759 VELOUR POSTURE CUSHION $25.00
(Please specify color)

E. **Louisa's parents, who travel to Florida by car each winter, were delighted to test these sun shields.** They know how uncomfortable it can get under a hot sun (even with air conditioning!). These shields are made of tough, perforated PVC and stop 80% of the sun's heat. They allow excellent visibility and prevent glare. Just press the suction cups to the glass. To remove, you pull the tabs on the cups and store in the glove compartment. Tested to withstand temperature extremes of +160°F to -40°F. Each shield measures 13″ x 15″. P.S. Excellent when used next to infant seats in cars and on back windows when parked.

#Q4730 SUN SHIELDS 2 for $12.50

COMFORTABLY YOURS®

*No Gift Wrap Available

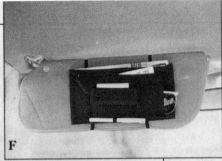

F. At last, a visor organizer with plenty of room for everything I need — all in one place! Just slip it over any car's visor, it stays secure with 2 elasticized straps. Five pockets keep maps, glasses, receipts, toll change, tissues, etc. close at hand while driving. Finely crafted of Cordura® nylon, won't crack or fade, with Velcro® and zipper closures. (USA)

#Q4765   VISOR ORGANIZER $10.00

G. "Great! At last someone has developed a steering wheel cover that keeps your steering wheel 40-80° cooler when your auto has been parked in the hot sun." Made

of newly developed reflective aerospace material and backed by ½" open cell foam, this material deflects up to 96% of the sun's rays making the steering wheel more comfortable to handle. Also doubles as a protection from a hot seat when used as a cushion.*

#Q4706   STEERING WHEEL COVER $15.00

H. This is one of the greatest mirrors we've ever seen. Once you own one, you'll want to own two: one for home, one for travel. There is a 2x magnifying side (great for make up, shaving, or contact lenses) and a regular side. The three suction cups in the base adhere to any clean *smooth* surface — a bathroom mirror, bathtub, shower wall, etc. It telescopes out 26", swivels in any direction, weighs under 5 ounces and folds flat. Comes with its own convenient travel pouch. Use this mirror once and you'll never go without it again.

#Q2000   TELESCOPING MIRROR $17.50

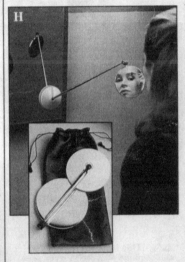

I. Finally, a lightweight container that eliminates spills, splash-back and gasoline-covered hands! The SwivelFill® is made of non-corroding, high-density polypropelene and has an extra-long spout with a 45° bend at the tip to make pouring smooth and easy, even for hard-to-fill tanks. No searching for a funnel or spout because all parts are attached to the outside of the container (not inside submerged in the gasoline). Keep an extra in your garage. 2½-gallon capacity.

#Q9646   NO-SPILL CONTAINER $13.50

J. The more I travel, the more I see people traveling in comfort — and this relaxed pant set gets you where you're going in style! Screen-printed black leaves highlighted by gold metallic drift across a comfortably oversized top with rib knit trim. Underneath, easy-going black pull-on pants have an elastic waist and tapered legs. Both pieces in machine-washable acrylic. (USA)

#Q8999   LEAF PANT SET $55.00
        Misses' 8-18.
#Q9000   LEAF PANT SET $57.00
        Women's 38-44.
        (Please specify size)

337

Telephone us for faster service (201) 368-0400   9

FIGURE 22–1
Item C on the left-hand page begins with the boldface word "Finally"; so does item I on the right-hand page. Midway between them, item F begins, "At last." Probably what happened is that some copy was picked up from a previous catalog. Judicious proofreading avoids repeats of key words.

HOW TO GIVE THEM A REASON TO DO BUSINESS WITH YOU

Visualize a selling situation in which a shopper wanders through an insane shopping center. A dozen stores have identical lines of goods. The shopper has one hour; each store gets a five-minute shot at the sale.

I can't believe, in such a circumstance, a marketer would take the position so many catalogers take: "Here's what I have to sell. Do you want it or don't you?"

Oh, no: the winner of this little battle shrewdly sizes up the prospective buyer, saying, "Aha! I know what will appeal to him/her."

"But We Can't Be Sure What They Want . . ."

Someone who sells women's shoes can't be sure all the catalogs go to women. Someone selling automobile parts can't be sure all the catalogs go to car owners.

That isn't the issue.

Except for blind prospecting, catalogs go to two groups: (1) those who have prequalified by previous purchase, cash deposit to get the catalog, or referrals; (2) those whose appearance on a particular list, residence in a particular neighborhood, or job title within a particular area of business make them logical prospects.

If we exclude ourselves from this information we wind up with bland, overgeneralized product descriptions based on the ridiculous money-losing complaint, "But we can't be sure what they want."

I suggest a conference, attended by merchandise manager, list buyer, and copywriter. The meeting should last no more than ten minutes, because the purpose is to assure congruency of viewpoint: *what are we selling, and to whom?*

Recognition of what we're selling and the individuals we expect to buy what we're selling will in one brilliant flash eliminate the gray sameness so many catalogs share.

Give 'Em a Reason to Buy

The only way you can go too far overboard in giving the reader a reason to buy is to have type running off the page.

A few sensible constraints are in order: (1) Only the most consummate master of wordsmithy can lecture or sermonize from an Olympian posture and not generate antagonism. (2) In catalogs, as in conversation, it's bad form to delve too deeply into the reader's shortcomings which we plan to correct. (3) Page after page of products for which the writer makes identical claims can kill verisimilitude.

Some catalogs implicitly answer the question, "Why should I do business with you?" by their very content. Examples:

▶ You sell dresses to women who have "fuller figures."

▶ You sell sex aids to those who have paid to get your catalog.

▶ You sell prosthetic devices.

▶ You sell cigars to men who have asked for your cigar catalog.

In such cases, recognition of the need reinforces the "who I am" recognition that prompted the original request. (For previous buyers the problem doesn't exist at all; personal products always have a high buyer-loyalty rate, because the buyer doesn't want to expose his weaknesses to outsiders any more than he must. Competitors have to find an extraordinarily compassionate approach to break the chain you've forged.)

How to Avoid Overpowering Your Own Product

In a solo mailing, product can be secondary to its emotional match with the target reader. Catalogs need a more balanced copy slant. This is because of the eclecticism of a catalog compared with a single-item mailing or an ad. Seldom do you find a customer who is wildly in need of *everything* in your catalog; and never can you prevent the various items you display from competing with one another for the buyer's favor.

So product descriptions are the floor under your selling argument, just as an uncooked, unseasoned steak is the floor under your dinner.

Which Comes First, Product or Benefit?

I propose the Rule of Catalog Attention-Grabbing:

Start the description with benefit—what the item will do for the customer. Then describe the product itself. Then recapitulate the benefit. Then list the specifics necessary to place an order.

The benefit/product/benefit/product sequence works well because benefit grabs attention better than physical product description. Inserting the product description in the middle works well because this ploy softens the enthusiasm without breaking it, so the reader doesn't feel he's being "pitched." A final few words about benefit are a logical close, just before the product specifics such as color, size, and price (which traditionally come last).

Can you do all this in one paragraph? Certainly. Some catalogers do it in 20 words.

A Catalog Cold-List Impeller

Did you ever get a catalog from a company you never bought from before, with this copy on the cover?

WE'RE SORRY, BUT . . .
Mailing costs being what they are, this is the *last* catalog we can send you unless you order *something* from these pages. We hate to lose an old friend, so won't you please look through this catalog right now, while it's in your hands? Thanks much.

The *last* catalog from a company we don't know? This copy wasn't an accident. The mailer is exercising his right to add a free shot of *guilt* to the marketing brew.

The cataloger's "Last Chance" target isn't the same as the solo mailer's "Second Chance" target. But—talking tough to those who have bought from a catalog within the past six months isn't a good idea at all. An individual who has made it to the golden plateau of your house list sees your catalog as a source, not as an impulse-buy. He's easily outraged by your expression of disaffection, unless the time-gap is a year or more.

The "Ultimate" Dressing Room

A lot of people, who should buy from us, don't. Have you ever heard this comment?

"I just don't buy anything by mail order. Well, maybe from Eddie Bauer or L.L. Bean or The Sharper Image. Oh, yeah, and occasionally from the Neiman-Marcus catalog and Spencer Gifts. But I'm not a mail-order catalog buyer."

When the cryptographers decode this message into English, here's what we get:

"I don't buy from *you*."

Some entire catalogs never devote a single line of copy to any of the gigantic advantages of buying from them by mail. They never do tell the prospective customer:

> ▶ When you order from a catalog, you get the exact size and color you want. You don't just pick over what happens to be in stock in the store.

> ▶ When you order from a catalog, you can return merchandise easily and without a hassle. You don't have to stand in line to get the department manager's signature and sour look; you send it back and you get your refund.

> ▶ When you order from a catalog, you can inspect the merchandise in your home or office and only then decide whether or not you want to keep it. You're not under pressure in a store, with someone else waiting to use the dressing room or the computer.

This boiler-plate copy is yours to use if you want it. It lists only a handful of the obvious benefits of shopping from a catalog.

FREEBIES, GIFTS, AND SWEEPSTAKES

Even now, when vigorous competition has catalogers scrambling for business, some old-timers refuse to believe excitement incentives exist. A few weeks before writing these words I sat in a meeting in which the crusty entrepreneur who for 40 years has dictated the fortunes of his company snorted, "If they want sweepstakes, let 'em go to Ireland."

I'm not militating for free gifts, and I wouldn't attempt to recommend a sweepstakes to any company that doesn't have the means to turn this whole promotion over to a specialist. My purpose is to analyze approaches to what I call "excitement incentives" and to suggest some logical rules for their use—or avoidance.

(An excitement incentive is a "booster" intended to generate orders you otherwise wouldn't have.)

The logic is obvious: Excitement incentives cost money, right? They're something of a pain to promote and implement, and they take up space you otherwise could use to sell merchandise, right?

Excitement incentives don't add image; their purpose is to add a competitive advantage by increasing dollar volume.

Then why doesn't every company use them? Even the most successful catalogers can use more business or they wouldn't be mailing their catalogs to speculative lists.

The answer lies in the First Rule of Excitement Incentives:

Adding artificial incentives to generate sales invariably lowers the quality of buyer.

I think we'd better tack on the Second Rule of Excitement Incentives, before you draw the wrong conclusion:

Lowering the quality of buyer is a detriment only if a promotion coincidentally lowers the image of the vendor with existing best buyers.

That last one means: Schlocking up your catalog a bit isn't necessarily an evil move. It may hurt you if it causes those who have been your customers to think, "We don't want to buy anything from someone who deals in freebies, gifts, and sweepstakes."

Want an opinion? With the exception of a handful of catalogs whose very existence depends on superexclusivity, it's impossible to alienate a buyer by offering him something extra. I think the extra business you'll write offsets ten times over the infrequent "How could you do this?" reaction.

Proof is the number of once staid catalogs now leaning toward excitement incentives. Proof is the adoption of freebies and gifts by business-to-business catalogers (sweepstakes are complicated and often impractical for companies with a customer base smaller than 25,000). Proof is the establishing of popular-priced, promotional adjunct-catalogs by some of the top-end merchandisers.

Where, How, and How Much

One of my clients had about a thousand inexpensive quartz watches left over from a space ad promotion. The retail price had been $29.95 to $39.95, but the markup was favorable.

We decided to give a watch with each order from the next catalog, totaling $125 or more. Why $125? This number seemed to maximize the possibility of a customer who might have ordered only one item now ordering two or more.

Using this simple, uncomplicated promotion as an example, where and how would you promote the free watches? You don't have a great many choices. Chances are you'd have followed the same path we did: We put some high-powered teaser copy on the catalog cover; we peppered the body of the catalog with drop-in reminders; we showed a picture of the watches on the order form, where we also made a big deal of the promotion ("Did your order total $125 or more? Don't forget your FREE multifunction quartz watch!"); and we added a final reminder of what became, when the order form was folded up to make a business reply envelope, the point of no return—the gummed area some old-timers call "the lickin' spot."

Sure, we used up all the watches and, in fact, had to get some more. Actually our figuring hadn't been bad because most of the extra watches we had to round up were for orders filtering in after our proclaimed expiration date.

Which just happens to bring me to my next point.

The Third Rule of Excitement Incentives is the easiest of all:

All promotions must have an expiration date.

The Fourth Rule of Excitement Incentives isn't quite as easy, but it doesn't require an Einstein for implementation:

Orders dribbling in after the expiration date should be honored as long as pre-bought supplies and computer programming make it possible; but remind the customer you're doing him a favor.

The only machinery you need is a single form letter—personalized, if you have the equipment to do it. That letter, To a Very Important Customer, says thanks for the order and expresses delight at being able to honor the request for the free gift, even though the expiration date has already passed.

I know people in this business who take the martinet position. If the expiration date was December 30, and a customer has the nerve to send in his order January 18 and still ask for the free whatever, they'll send him merchandise, but with a letter explaining he's too late to qualify for the freebie.

Oh, yeah? What happened to goodwill? Such a letter might even stimulate return of the merchandise. Instead, if the promotion is over and you're out of whatever it was, send a gift certificate good for an equivalent amount on the next order. You're dealing in paper, and the paper could bring a fast reorder instead of disappointment that degenerates into annoyance.

You can handle these situations in catalogs far better than you could in a retail store, as anyone operating both a store and a catalog operation can verify. A retailer whose specials expire on Saturday reprices his goods on Sunday or he loses both credibility and control. Catalogers don't share that problem because if your next catalog arrives with the timing and hoopla it should, your customer will order from the new catalog with its own new set of excitement incentives.

Sweepstakes are a different matter. Postal laws and some state laws prevent freewheeling use of sweepstakes promotions, which is one reason I suggest having professionals handle them. With a sweepstakes, a deadline is a deadline. The difference is, the buyer doesn't implicitly expect a bonus; it's *chance*, where freebies are a *certainty*.

Repeatedly, I get the feeling that many who use excitement incentives do so grudgingly—as though they're half-ashamed of it or want to keep it a secret.

The ancient saying, "In for a penny, in for a pound," is apt here because establishing an excitement incentive and then playing it down violates the Fifth Rule of Excitement Incentives:

If the cataloger doesn't seem excited, the customer can't get excited.

Never forget who's in charge, giving the commands. This *isn't* a meeting of equals; if you don't say to the reader, "Get excited!" the reader is unlikely to get excited.

But don't run afoul of the Sixth (and Final) Rule of Excitement Incentives:

Lack of clarity kills off excitement.

If you wonder how telling the reader you're giving something away can be unclear, take a look at some of the catalogs in your mailbox. You'll find free offers mentioned on the cover and nowhere else. You'll find an announcement of a give-away claiming "2,500 Prizes!" and no foundation for that claim *anywhere* inside the catalog.

I suggest you make a big pointed cover reference to the page number on which you list the specifics. I suggest you recapitulate the specifics on the order form. I suggest you use any vacant space on any page to remind the customer of the incentive. Each succeeding reference adds to excitement, and each one also adds to clarity.

If sales are flagging, test an excitement incentive. As in any copy test, the offer has to be clearly visible or the results are muddy.

THE BENEFIT OF THE IMPERATIVE

A business supply catalog has this descriptive copy for incentive-builders:

You can mail copies to regular customers and logical prospects.

For generations we've lionized "You can . . ." as a motivating opener. Enablement is a key to reader acceptance.

But consider: Enablement is a weak and thoughtless motivator for an action we take for granted. Of course we can mail copies. We don't have any sense of accomplishment from being able to do this. Dropping letters into the mail is neither an achievement nor a triumph. "You can . . ." adds nothing.

Removing "You can . . ." does add something—viewpoint. We transform the copy from *declarative* into *imperative*:

Mail copies to regular customers and logical prospects.

Emphasis shifts. It's where it belongs—not on the act of mailing but on use and benefit.

"If" phrases are suspect because they're conditional. You might, as you look over your catalog copy, check "If . . ." phrases. One I saw recently, selling a photoelectric light-switch, could have benefited from an "If-ectomy":

If you're out of town, leave it plugged in to discourage prowlers.

Replacing *If* with *When* makes item-use universal, not depending on forces beyond our control:

When you're out of town, leave it plugged in to discourage prowlers.

ARE YOU A WRITER OR A CLERK?

The writer who describes a cordless phone as an electronic *device* instead of electronic *instrument* parallels the store clerk who worked in men's shoes yesterday and was rushed down to ladies' hats today.

The copy chief or company head who mindlessly okays cover copy such as *Now is the time to stock up on those good things for your home* deserves to drown in the "catalog clutter" to which he has contributed so much.

The writer who puts on the order form "Please send me the referenced items" deserves to lose the orders he surely will lose from bewildered customers who just don't know what a *referenced* item is. This writer is a bookkeeper at heart, a dreadful attitude for a marketer.

The office supplies catalog writer who regurgitates *finest, the best, great, step-saver, heavy-duty, E-Z, built to give you a lifetime of service, adjusts to your needs,* and *unlimited flexibility,* for several different brands and sizes of the same generic item without explaining why these clichés are true, deserves to spend eternity in a limbo where no word from the Deity includes a single specific.

We expect the clerk, shifted unwittingly from department to department, to have only a fragmented product knowledge of what he's selling that day. We grant no such dispensation to the catalog writer.

The clerk at K-Mart aims you at the auto supply section and stands by helplessly while you try to puzzle out the comparative benefit of detergent oil, multi-viscosity oil, and synthetic oil. "The descriptions might be on the can," the clerk offers weakly.

The catalog writer whose copy stands by helplessly while you try to puzzle out those benefits has forgotten or never has learned why his medium of communication is the Ultimate Dressing Room. He, too, has descended the communications ladder to the level of clerk. His inability to transmit information is far more deadly than his fellow clerk's, who may destroy a sale to only one potential customer.

Just Answer Two Easy Questions

Effective catalog copy is less a matter of creativity than of having answered two questions the catalog recipient may ask:

1. Why should I buy this?
2. Why should I buy this from you?

Product description is a specific. Without the ability to describe, no writer qualifies to generate catalog copy. Adding the dimension of selling the buy-by-mail concept is an art. Fortunately for us all, it's a *learned* art, one catalog writers should practice until those income-earning fingers are as nimble as a concert pianist's and as strong as a wrestler's.

DON'T WRITE YOURSELF INTO A CORNER

When writing turns cute or hyper-personal, it's a violation of the First Statute of Novelty Burnout, that serviceable maxim applying to humorous radio spots, animated television spots, and mechanical production tricks in any print medium including catalogs. The statute:

The impact of repeated messages decreases in exact ratio to reliance on novelty.

Dangerous! Hung in the "cleverness for the sake of cleverness" doctrine of creative poseurs, catalog writers sit slathering, waiting for the faintest hint of encouragement to write clever copy.

I say, let them write poetry in their spare time. At the for-pay keyboard, their copy has one purpose only—selling merchandise.

Is the Reader in Your Family?

"Down home" writing is reasonably easy to do. The technique has much to recommend it, principally inducting the reader into your family. But does the reader want to be a member of your family?

I'm looking at a current catalog whose product-descriptions are related to the titular head of the company, her relatives, and her friends. I like the copywriting in this catalog, which is why I was especially sensitive to what seems to have happened when the device became too prominent.

Would you want to be in this group or be a neighbor? Let's keep score. All these references are in copy blocks selling merchandise:

▶ Pam, the salesperson, has an aching back.

▶ A favorite customer's son had the croup.

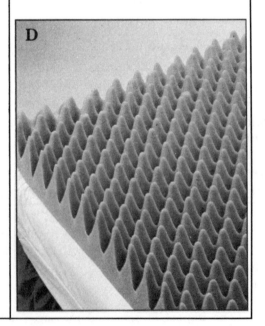

D. **My mother called one day asking my help.** Two cousins of mine, Annette who suffers from lupus, and Bob who has spurs on his spine, were unable to sleep. Because they were experiencing so much discomfort in their beds, I sent them each a convoluted foam bed pad. Moisture, friction and heat are lessened because all those spaces on the 2″ foam allow air to circulate. It adds comfort, greatly aids in preventing bedsores and converts a regular mattress into a therapeutic bed. Made of high quality medical grade foam. No Gift Wrap Available. P.S. Annette is now resting well, and Bob is off the floor and getting a good night's sleep.

#N1301	CONVOLUTED FOAM,	
	TWIN	$20.00
#N1304	CONVOLUTED FOAM,	
	DOUBLE	$42.00
#N1305	CONVOLUTED FOAM,	
	QUEEN	$48.00

FIGURE 22–2

Does this copy make you a little uncomfortable? Personalized copy can establish a personality for a catalog, but when it lapses into descriptions of diseases, the writer has made an assumption of personalization that alienates some readers for no good reason. Can you think of a more comfortable way to put this message and still stay inside the personalized framework?

▶ The writer has an aching shoulder, sore feet, a fractured wrist, has slipped while bathing, has constantly breaking nails, was late for an appointment because a hotel operator didn't wake her, had to take a pill in the middle of the night, and tripped on her mother's rug.

FIGURE 22–3
This near-perfect copy injects "you" into every description, emphasizing benefit, convenience, and the Clarity Commandment.

- ▶ The writer's husband sleeps on his side (I don't regard this as an ailment, but it seems to be one in this catalog) and has a twisted knee.
- ▶ A friend named Jerry has frostbitten toes.
- ▶ The writer's son has a cold bathroom.
- ▶ A neighbor's house caught fire.
- ▶ A neighbor named Joyce has worn-out stair treads.
- ▶ The town had a power failure.
- ▶ Friends Jackie and Fran have arthritis.
- ▶ Aunt Em had a stroke.
- ▶ Joe suffers from severe allergies.
- ▶ Aunt Sophie has arthritis.
- ▶ Marianne's mother hurt her foot.
- ▶ The writer's mother has osteoporosis, needs laxatives, and has trouble rising from the normal toilet seat height.
- ▶ The writer's friend Lil had a mastectomy.
- ▶ An unnamed friend is convalescing.
- ▶ Cousin Annette has lupus (see Figure 22–2).
- ▶ Cousin Bob has spurs on his spine.
- ▶ Friend John has insomnia.
- ▶ One of the ladies on the staff has problems with chafing.
- ▶ Pregnant Meg couldn't bend down to feed her golden retriever, and her mother-in-law has a back problem.
- ▶ The writer's daughter is sensitive to wool and linen.
- ▶ Friend Barbara flooded her bathroom and the apartment below twice last year.
- ▶ Friend Sylvia put a kettle on the stove and melted the enamel.

I'm not sure I caught them all, but every one of these episodes is in a 52-page catalog. We have enough problems here to fill a soap opera for two years.

What's my point? This: Personalizing copy for about 200 items resulted in a grotesque cataloguing of ailments and misfortunes. In my opinion the word *lupus* has no place in any catalog other than one aimed at the medical profession.

"I Care About You"

Three motivators have driven many catalogers to dip their quill-pens into the murky inks of first-person writing.

1. In solo mailings most people read the letter first. This suggests most readers accept the notion of exhortation first, product description second.

Attitude and attire,
one adorns the other

Discriminating dressing
A. Mary Ann Restivo's
well-bred pure wool crêpe
dress is a classicist's choice
for day to evening chic. The
sophisticated line, which is
slightly flared on the bias
from jewel neckline to
hem, and the long sleeves
touched with matching
soutache braid are all that's
needed to express a
restrained sensation. The
body is lined, the shoulders
softly padded. Made in
USA for 4 to 14. Fall '86
favorite chestnut
brown #406468 or
black #406469 320.00
Place Elegante Sportswear

**Calvin Klein
clarifies all**
B. Spare, chic and
powerful—that's how we
see Calvin's suede shirt, cut
along classic lines, paired
with wool flannel trousers.
Both for 4 to 12. The shirt
is soft and supple, sleekly
body-fitting. The color,
stone. Imported.
#406465 500.00
Tonal harmony—the fully
lined, pleated fly-front
trousers in sand. Belt not
included. Made in USA of
imported fabric.
#406466 210.00
Calvin Klein Sportswear

**Applause for
Julie Francis**
C. She has a very
sophisticated way with
color, design and luxurious
fabrics. Here, a tunic and
skirt, both in pure silk. The
long sleeved, button-back
top with jewel neckline in a
bewitching lace motif,
partners a softly pleated
skirt in a twin print. The
long skirt is chiffon with
Lurex® metallic threads.
Both, in teal with black,
imported by Julie Francis for
4 to 14. #406467 350.00
Place Elegante

ORDER BY PHONE
800-368-3438

6

FIGURE 22–4
The legend in the upper left corner, "Attitude and attire, one adorns the other," is
abstruse but in keeping with this high-fashion catalog. Loyal readers will suffer through
the hard-to-read type, set in black over a dark gray texture.

2. "I"-to-"You" writing is technically easier than dispassionate product description because personalization is *implicitly emotional*. Emotion outpulls intellect, a benefit in selling; "I"-to-"You" parallels the way we talk, a benefit in message-composition.

3. Some catalogs separate themselves from the milieu by becoming an extension of an individual. "I"-to-"You" writing massages two egos at once—the buyer's and the writer's.

But Does It Work?

Personalized catalog copywriting gets tricky when, after writing a dozen descriptions-plus-personalizations has exhausted the thin storehouse of facile approaches, the writer begins to emphasize "I" *over* "You."

A ghastly error: The writer believes, naively or arrogantly, that the reader will follow every word of text. Cross-references remind the reader of a personal (to the writer) episode mentioned on a previous page. Connection between writer and reader shakes loose.

You can see what generates this gradual centering of attention on who's writing and not on who's reading: Instead of "I have this for you"—implicitly exclusive, implicitly personal, and therefore implicitly powerful—copy begins to slide inward: "I did this"; "I went here to buy it or to photograph it"; "I tried this and decided it's the best for you."

"I" becomes paramount, "you" becomes subordinated . . . and yellow caution flags start to fly in the rough breeze because subliminally or directly, this is the kind of copy that makes the reader feel patronized.

How can you get the benefit of personalization without risking the detriment of reader rejection?

First, you always have the inside-the-cover message. So many catalog writers waste the space dedicated to this message! They lapse into loose puffery instead of hammering down the "I"-to-"You" link.

Adding guts to the inside-the-cover letter can build reader acceptance of almost any kind of descriptive copy—first-person, third-person, and certainly second-person.

Another technique is available, and I've never understood why more personality-based catalogs don't use it. A short personalized message appears on each page, in a format paralleling the face of God peering out of a hole in the clouds. This message, 10 to 20 words, reinforces the "I found this for you, my dear friend" concept. Specific descriptive copy for each item on the page is released from the artificial first-person constraint so it can fight its own logical battle for attention.

Writer and reader each enjoy a benefit from this procedure: The writer shakes off the shackles of artifice and can use more space to describe. The reader sees what he or she wants to see: an explanation of what's for sale unblemished by frustrating-to-read puffery.

But I Don't Mean . . .

I'm not suggesting that a catalog writer pour word-bleach over the copy to fade the copy to watery blandness. No, no. What I'm suggesting is an uncomplicated way to march around the pitfall of subordinating the message to the medium, still maintaining a facade of "personality."

Here's an easy copy test. If, instead of writing catalog copy for a pair of shoes, you were selling them in a store, how much "I" would you inject into your sales pitch? What would you say about those shoes to convince a casual shopper to buy them?

Use that same logic in catalog copy, and you're safe. The difference between retail head-to-head selling and catalog selling lies in the medium, not the message.

Why "We" Is Safer than "I"

Why is "We . . ." a safer copy block opening than "I . . ."? Suppose the copy began:

We've slashed the price on this one . . .

or, carrying through the personality approach of some catalogs, copy began:

I've slashed the price on this one . . .

A single instance may appear to be a "So what?" subtle difference. In bulk, "We" is an extension of the *company's* relationship with us, the prospective customers; in bulk, "I" is an autocratic group of fiats, unilateral decisions by a weight-throwing dictator.

So "I" becomes more dangerous than "We," which means that although first-person copy is easy to write, *effective* "I" copy isn't; it's a sales technique requiring scalpel-like delicacy.

**A Modest Proposal:
The Episode-"I," Buy-from-"We" Indication**

Here's a suggestion. Haven lies in what I call the *Episode-"I," Buy-from-"We" Indication*. It's one of the simpler and more dependable tenets of catalog copywriting:

If you're torn between "I" and "We," use "I" only when referring to personal episode; use "We" for corporate suggestions that the reader buy.

Using this Indication, will your catalog be brilliant, establishing a personality of its own? Probably not; it'll be safely in a middle-of-the road position.

If you're a bright light among catalog copywriters, ignore everything I've said here. You can carry off "I" copy with élan and effectiveness. But if you have a nagging fear that your own personality may become paramount over what you're selling, the *Indication* can dry some of the sweat off your brow.

How about "You" in catalog copy? If that glorious word is tied to *benefit*, don't you dare change it.

HOW TO BE SURE YOU'VE DESCRIBED IT

I'm looking at a photograph of a pair of cloisonné birds. This is the entire copy block:

> These lovely birds will grace any room of your home or office. Delicately designed and rendered in Oriental cloisonné, these ornate quails will add just the right touch to your decor.
> 1585-439 $149.95 Value . . . $89.95

So I read neutral copy such as ". . . will add just the right touch to your decor," and I ask the writer, "Hey, is that for one bird or two?" The photograph shows two birds. Copy says *birds*, not *bird*, but nowhere does it tell us whether we get one or two. So one of two situations will occur:

1. They'll ship two birds for $89.95, which means they've missed one of the key selling points;
2. They'll ship only one bird for $89.95, which means those readers who expected two birds won't be at all pleased.

Hifalutin' Dangers

The reason so much catalog copy loses its clarity is that literate catalog writers like to show off just how literate they are. By displaying their massive educations instead of projecting themselves inside the reader's hides, they lose contact.

The back cover ranks second only to the front cover as a determinant: Will the catalog be read or not? On the back cover of a lavishly produced catalog is a picture of a welcome mat on which instead of "Welcome" are the words "Essuyez vos pieds." Here's the copy:

> "ESSUYEZ VOS PIEDS" MAT
> A not-so-subtle command in French brings a smile to an otherwise mundane rainy-day chore. Sturdy natural fiber with non-skid rubber backing. (14″ × 13″)

In very small type, below this copy block, the words are unlocked:

9025C "Wipe Your Feet" Mat $30.00

Now, of course *we* all know "Essuyez vos pieds" doesn't mean "Fresh fish," but how about those guys down the street who didn't study French in high school? They might read the copy block, never get to the footnote, and conclude, "I don't want this mat because if someone asks me what the words mean I won't be able to answer." Clarity calls for the translation *in the copy block.*

A visually magnificent catalog, using four different kinds of paper, full-bleed, laminating, and gallery-quality photographs has this pomposity as its first copy block. Copy appears on an onionskin sheet inside the front cover (the inside cover itself is *blank!*):

> Perquisites are privileges earned by discrimination as well as by means.
> Superior design, superb engineering and exquisite taste are the perquisites of those who go beyond conventional expectations to demand excellence in everything that surrounds them.

To which I responded, "Huh?"
The first page has a single photograph of what appears to be bondage apparel, with this as the copy:

> *LIVING WELL IS THE BEST REVENGE*
> "I don't want to make myself comfortable, my dear, I want comfort to be made for me."

I guess this is profound, but I have to let the "Huh?" apply here too. I'm being led into—what? What kind of catalog is this? To us in the business, it's plain that form has become paramount to substance. I don't object to this copy; I object to the *sequencing,* because somebody is telling me he or she is superior to me without yet having given me a reason to become an admirer.

WHAT A DIFFERENCE ONE WORD MAKES

My wife is a heavy mail-order buyer. She showed me a picture of a sweater in a catalog and asked me to read the description:

> WHO CAN RESIST soft, fluffy angora teddy bears and Marisa Christina's knit know-how? In a wool cardigan style. Sizes P(4), S(6-8), M(10-12), L(14). Imported. DG5716 Teddy Sweater 98.00 (5.25).

"What color is it?" she asked me. "I thought it was black, but it sort of looks like navy. Or is that a purple-black?"
Like the person who wrote this copy, I was no help, and she sighed and closed the catalog. "I'd better not take a chance on it," she said. And a sale was lost because one word—the color of the sweater, a primitive element of clarity—wasn't there.

We don't always have the luxury of being able to pretest copy. We surely do have the professional requirement of being able to build Clarity, Benefit, and Verisimilitude into every block of copy in our catalogs.

Are You Communicating . . . or Showing Off?

On a page in a women's fashion catalog were descriptions of six items. Each picture included a stuffed bear, which obviously wasn't one of the garments but which (equally obviously) was, as the copy laboriously underscored, somebody's pet notion.

"Can You BEAR to Be Without This Bewitching Classic 'Little Black Dress'?" was the overlong heading for a relatively short copy block. A glassy-eyed model, hoisting a teddy bear the way an uncertain Statue of Liberty might hold a hot torch, was the accompanying picture.

I cringed twice: first at the emasculating effect *bear* had on *bewitching*, and second at the derailing effect the whole notion had on the "Little Black Dress," which lost position because pictorial emphasis was on the bear, not the dress.

Un-Bear-able?

Another picture on the same page had a bear peeking out of a purse, with this Trivial Pursuits heading:

Urs-Satz? You'd Never Know It!

Ursus (or if you're a girl, *ursa*) is Latin for bear, get it? So it ties to vinyl, which is ersatz leather, get it? Huh? You don't get it? Aw, that's too bad. That means you can't appreciate how this catalog copywriter labored over this nonsense.

Even before the typical reader reluctantly examines the photograph of a Lady in Red, her red-lacquered claw atop a kneeling muscleman whose only garb is a loincloth and a full bear-head mask, opinion is hardened in concrete: This writer has succumbed to the "That-Which-Is-Different = That-Which-Is-Better" cult. The heading:

Queen of the Grizzlies

I find this whole creative concept un-bear-able, and to the creative director who planned this bugbear—and to anyone else who may be succumbing to the siren song of the unholy "That-Which-Is-Different = That-Which-Is-Better" cabal—I offer the *Catalog Writing Truism*:

The purpose of catalog copy is to transmit an enthusiastic description of what's being sold, to the best prospective buyers. Unless this purpose is achieved, the copywriter has failed, regardless of the cleverness of rhetoric.

For completeness, I offer two *Catalog Writing Truism Footnotes.* Footnote 1:

The Catalog Writing Truism becomes truer when one writer has the responsibility for an entire catalog.

Footnote 2:

A catalog company can prevent its copy from becoming the extension of one person's personality by assigning eight-page sections to different writers.

To wordsmiths who may be rising up in wrath, I'll clarify and justify those footnotes.

When a writer knows his or her copy is part of a whole, that writer is unlikely to project "personality" unrelated to what's being sold. Here's a 32-page catalog. You're writing 8 pages, I'm writing 8 pages, and two other writers are writing 8 pages each. Our instructions may be loose or they may be specific; whoever will approve our copy may or may not give us style sheets. But invariably this instruction supersedes all others: Our copy has to be nondescript so the catalog won't look as though four different writers attacked it.

I'm not assailing the notion of having one writer handle a complete catalog. No, I'm trying to stick a pin through the writer who falls in love with his vocabulary and thinks his words deserve attention over what those words are supposed to describe.

Opinion: When a cataloger begins to crow about his or her copy *as copy*—"I write every word myself . . ."—hoist the danger flags. Description can give way to a rambling philosophy which can't sell as much merchandise because it's less in tune with benefits the reader wants to see.

At the very least, test "clever" copy against clearly descriptive copy. I offer the generalization that the larger the universe, the greater the edge for clear-cut; but a test is always worthwhile.

Funny and Pun-ny Won't Make You Any Money, Honey

Suppose you're a salesperson in a store. A customer asks you about some sculpted candles, shaped like unicorns. Would you grin and show off your superior sense of humor by saying, "Don't myth these sculpted candles"? If you did, you wouldn't work for that store very long.

Why, then, would a catalog writer selling those same candles think cleverness with words works better than descriptive power? Here's the total description of what appear to be attractive candles:

Don't Myth These
sculpted candles—Unicorn
and Pegasus adrift on blue
clouds. Unicorn's horn is
clear plastic. 6 × 4½ × 7″H.   Unicorn 1807107
                                  Pegasus 1807115, $15.00 ea.

If you have a spare five minutes, take a shot at this copy. What would *you* have written to sell those candles? Might you have emphasized their artistry, their novelty, their uniqueness as gifts, their translucency, their drip-free quality? What? My opinion: Any of these will outsell the weak pun.

I'll apply the same opinion to this copy for bedsheets:

Sheepy Time. 100% cotton flannel sheets for value, comfort, absorbency, to keep you warm in winter, cool in summer. Flat sheet is a perfect light summer blanket. Top quality imports. Wedgewood blue with white lambs and stars. Pre-shrunk. Machine wash/dry.

A couple of problems aren't germane to my point: (1) The spelling is *Wedgwood*, not *Wedgewood*; (2) *Sheepy* evokes the instant correlative *sheepish*, not *sheep*.

What *is* germane to my point is that the first two words, "Sheepy Time," generate a child-like image, which isn't what the writer intended. "Sleep Like a Lamb" might have satisfied the writer's desire to be clever *and* the reader's desire for information.

An Ombudsman Would Help

Some in the catalog business were surprised when an expensively produced oversize catalog went out of business; but most weren't, and if you believe the Catalog Writing Truism you weren't either.

I've saved a copy of this catalog. The heading (positioned in the center of the page):

". . . at night I play second chef to my boyfriend."

To those who applaud the cleverness of this line I ask the prosaic question: What does it mean? Nothing in the illustration suggests food. Rather, the picture is of a woman's "granny" outfit, laid out as though the model, like the witch in *The Wizard of Oz*, had melted out of them. Strange—an invisible Diane Keaton gone mad.

Most puzzling is the description of the first component of this bizarre ensemble, a cardigan sweater:

Textured stripe cardigan 75243 as shown in smoke. See On The Model for details.

That's it. After some searching I found a 6-point heading on *another* page, "On the Model." In a listing of items, also 6-point, was this copy:

Textured stripe cardigan has inky black stripes down the front and at the cuffs. Available as shown in smoke, it's made of an acrylic blend and has a zip-up front with two small pockets. Imported. See On The Figure for a closer look. *75243* Sizes S-M-L $90.00

Oh, it's a game! But how many readers, frustrated by the search for information, really want to play it to its end? Not enough, obviously, because the catalog folded.

And that's my point. An increasingly valuable tenet of effective catalog writing is one of the undeniable rules for all copywriting, *The Who's Message Is It? Rule*: Write within the experiential background of the reader, not yourself. The writer, undoubtedly under goad from above, ignored this homily, bowed to art direction which worshiped the inscrutable, and didn't sell much merchandise.

Whose Experiential Background?

Who's out there on the receiving end? I'll risk being called a fuddy-duddy by suggesting you'll sell more if you become the clone of the recipient instead of assuming, arrogantly, that he or she is *your* clone.

The difference is the *comfort level* while reading. A logical if disquieting equation:

Discomfort = Wastebasket.

That's the challenge. We compete with retailers, with solo mailings, and with what seems to be an avalanche of competing catalogs. If only the fit survive, how do we become the fittest?

The thoughtful cataloger knows the answer. Copy matches the reader's experiential background, which gives us a whopping edge over catalogs which challenge the reader to a duel of wits. In the duel, the reader has the better weapon: a tightly closed checkbook.

23

The Asterisk Exception

THE ASTERISK EXCEPTION DEFINED

The Asterisk Exception is a device which seems to have been borrowed from politicians and diplomats. Former presidential advisor David Stockman claims to have invented the "magic asterisk," a technique for nonexplanatory explanation of how the federal government would save $44 billion. He may have used the technique, but its invention predated him. Anyway, he wasn't in advertising as we understand the term.

The Asterisk Exception works like this: An ad or a brochure makes a claim—a flat statement, unblemished by an "if" or "but" clause.

Then, at the end of the statement, we see the tiny symbol of contempt for the message we just interpreted too favorably: an asterisk. We *know*, as we look down the page, what we'll find: a disclaimer. "You collect only if you're in a goat cart in Mukden," or, "Limited to the period from August 31 to September 1," or, "Optional at extra cost."

In my opinion The Asterisk Exception is a virus we have to fight; otherwise it can become another foul adjunct to the implicit skepticism we're feeding to our message recipients in increasing dosages, like saccharine to rats.

I just read a mailing from an airline, a textbook example of The Asterisk Exception.

The airline has a "Senior Class Travel Club," offering benefits to senior citizens. A $25 fee enrolls the member; for $100 the member can add this year's euphemism, a "Companion." (Very modern: The member can change companions for each flight.)

Two facets of this package puzzle me: First, although membership is open to anyone age 60 or older, a 10% fare discount applies only to those 65 or older.

Second—well, judge for yourself:

THE PRIVILEGES
OF SENIOR CLASS

> ▶ Double Frequent Flyer mileage credit for all flights.
> ▶ A 10% discount on airfares for members 65 and older.*
> ▶ Special discounts on rooms at all participating Radisson Hotels.
> ▶ Special discounts on rooms at all participating Stouffer Hotels.*
> ▶ Discounts on selected Hertz rental cars.*
> ▶ Quarterly Senior Class newsletters featuring vacation package discounts and other special offers.

*Certain restrictions apply.

I knew when I hit the first asterisk what the reference would be. As an old weasel-word artist, I'm sensitive to keys such as *participating* hotels, which tells me the ones I want aren't participants. And just who selects the *selected* Hertz rental cars? But those aren't my biggest objection to the technique of presentation.

We have six bullets. Four of them have that lethal asterisk. Nowhere in the mailer does an explanation appear. "Certain restrictions apply" is set in type about half the size of the other copy. In the Age of Skepticism, what must our logical conclusion be, even though only $25 to $100 is at stake?

Another airline, in a space ad, has this first sentence of body copy:

If you are 65 or over, you can get a 10% discount on any [NAME OF AIRLINE] airfare, even low Ultimate SuperSaver fares.*

On the way downward to find what I knew I'd find, whoops! Another asterisk:

A $25 Travel Voucher,* valid for one year, which can be used on any [NAME OF AIRLINE] flight.

No surprises here. The asterisk at the bottom of the column was more forthright than the copy it amended: "*Some restrictions may apply."

("May"? I'll bet you the $25 voucher that some restrictions *do* apply.)

Another airline, describing its similar program, doesn't disappoint the asterisk-seekers:

From our travel partners, you will receive:*

I kind of like this one, more forthright than "Some restrictions may apply." The asterisk reference says bluntly:

*Subject to Change.

The capitalization of *Change* suggests it isn't just a little change.

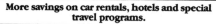
360

FIGURE 23–1
It isn't as bad as some, but this space ad is a classic example of the Asterisk Exception. In fact, the ad uses a "+" sign as well as asterisks to separate the various kinds of exceptions. At the foot of the ad the asterisk betrays the lack of candor: "Some restrictions may apply." We'll bet they do.

IS THERE A CURE?

I offer, not as antidote but as a map for exploration, this descriptive objection:

A writer uses The Asterisk Exception when he or she has no confidence in (1) personal ability to convince the reader of benefit by putting all the facts in direct context, or (2) verity of the offer itself.

Either use tells us we have to train ourselves to overcome The Asterisk Exception the way we'd lick smoking or fingernail-biting or a "You know" habit. I'm looking at a space ad for a hotel. Here's the headline:

BEST LOCATION IN
WASHINGTON, D.C.
AT A CAPITAL PRICE
$29.50*

Uh-oh. Let's sneak a look past the hard-sell bullet-copy. Yup. It's there. Yipe. It's worse than we expected, a *double* whammy:

*per person, per night double occupancy, children under 16 stay free in parents' suite. Based on availability. Rate applies to all weekends and holidays.

This writer is no beginner. Look how that last piece of negative information came out positively: "Rate applies to all weekends and holidays." A lesser scribe would have written, "Weekends and holidays only," which is what the copy really means. With this kind of talent, couldn't the writer consider options other than The Asterisk Exception?

Probably the answer is, "That's the way we write travel and leisure copy— the price is per person, not per room, and readers are trained to know most of these deals are for weekends only."

Oh, yeah? Then why did the ad run in a business publication targeted to government computer decision makers?

WHY NOT A POSITIVE ASTERISK?

Why do asterisks always have to mean bad news, like a telegram from the Defense Department at wartime?

The coupon in a mail-order ad for the Princess Diana Bride Doll has this predictable use of the asterisk:

I will be billed prior to shipment for my deposit of $37; after shipment, I will be billed for the balance in four equal monthly installments of $37 each.*

At the foot of the coupon is the troll under the bridge:

*Plus a total of $5 for shipping and handling.

What if, instead of an asterisk, we had a pair of parentheses *immediately following* the price, so the copy would read:

. . . in four equal installments of $37 each (plus a total of $5 for shipping and handling).

We aren't just ridding ourselves of the asterisk, that negative and pedantic bugaboo. We're avoiding the unnecessary negative reaction we have to an increased price after we've digested what we think is a total.

It really would shake up the system if somebody used asterisks to present *positive* addenda! Not in our lifetimes, we know, but maybe one day.

#####

IF YOU'RE 60 OR OVER, YOU'LL GO FURTHER IN THE FRIENDLY SKIES.

Right now a Lifetime Membership in Silver Wings Plus costs only $25 . . .
and you get $50 off the next time you fly roundtrip on United . . .
plus 10% off **every** time you fly on United, *if you're 65 or over.*

- Regular member's dues: $25 a year. But enroll by July 1, 1986, and pay only $25 for an individual **lifetime** membership or join for yourself and a companion, whomever you please — son, daughter, grandchild, spouse — for $100 for a lifetime membership.
- With your individual membership, you will receive a $50 Travel Discount Voucher to apply towards airfare on your next roundtrip United flight if you enroll before July 1, 1986. With a membership for yourself and a companion, you will receive $150 in Travel Discount Vouchers.

You will also receive:

- If you are 65 or older, 10% discount on airfare every time you fly on United Airlines within the 50 states and to the Bahamas — that's 10% off **any published** fare.
  If you are 60 to 64 years of age, you'll still benefit. All discounts are available to you except the 10% savings on airfares. When you reach 65, you'll automatically be eligible for the 10% airfare discount.
- Automatic enrollment in Mileage Plus, with up to 8,000 bonus miles (3,000 bonus miles if you're already a member of Mileage Plus). Mileage Plus credits you with miles flown on United and our partner airlines . . . lets you earn additional airfare discounts, or even **free** trips.

From our travel partners, you will receive: *

- Discounts on Hertz car rentals nationwide everytime you rent.
- Discounts at leading hotel and motel chains nationwide: 50% at participating Westin Hotels on a space available basis, 25% off at participating Ramadas.
- Special bargain-price vacation packages for Silver Wings Plus members only.

  * Subject to Change.

*Enroll **today** in United's Silver Wings Plus — the travel club that can save you **money on flying** — PLUS much more!*

FIGURE 23–2
Just one asterisk here, but it's a dilly: "Subject to change."

How to Help Stamp Out Asterisks

How many of these do you recognize?

* Plus sales tax, shipping, handling, insurance, and whatever.
* In pigskin only.
* Not available in colors other than white.
* Excluding purchase of sundries, beer and wine, and cigarettes.
* Not valid Dec. 15–Jan. 31.
* Subject to change without notice.

My point: It's out of hand. It's epidemic. It's the automatic choice of writers who think readers won't notice an unpleasant message appendage if it's relegated to asterisk status.

If you have a piece of copy in your word processor, hit the "search" key to see whether an asterisk has crept into the text. If it has, experiment with other ways of transmitting the same information. You may find El Dorado at the end of your search.*

---

*On the other hand, you may not. See how asterisks take the fun out of life?

24

A Tip a Day
So You Can Write
Powerhouse Copy Within
One Month

30 NUGGETS TO HELP YOU WRITE POWERHOUSE COPY

Here are 30 nuggets to store in your pocket or purse against that odd moment when you might need them. Absorb and use one each day for the next month. They're something like carrying garlic or a crucifix just in case Dracula shows up at your dinner party.

Nugget 1 (fund raising, senior citizens, nonproduct copy, copy emphasizing deadlines or expiration)

Conditional words and phrases let the prospect off the hook.

Here's the first pass at a paragraph in a contributor-seeking mailing:

We squeeze every nickel and stretch every dollar, but we're desperately close to running out of money. If we did, we'd have to cut back on programs that might have been the only act of friendship for helpless children.

Sharp-eyed editing changed a couple of words, closing the loophole the first draft had given the reader:

We squeeze every nickel and stretch every dollar, but we're desperately close to running out of money. If we do, we'll have to cut back on programs that might be the only act of friendship for helpless children.

Nugget 2 (space ads, especially for consumer electronics, high-style men's fashions, and services)

"Staccato" copy calls attention to writing as writing. Except for headlines and bullet copy, it's more likely to irritate than to inform.

Staccato copy is a repeated burst of short thoughts, unfettered by grammar. The technique applies only to print advertising; advocates say that's the way people talk. Detractors say people who talk that way aren't communicators, so why should we imitate them?

An example of staccato copy:

Move up. To a better way of life.

You have the opportunity. Now. Tomorrow? Too late. You'll love your neighborhood. Your neighbors. Not having to lock your door. Not having to keep your pup on a chain.

What do you say? Don't you deserve it? The freedom. The openness. The trees and streams. Sure you do. And you can have it. If you make your move now.

Did you, reading this short excerpt, feel off-balance? Those who embrace staccato writing say that's what you're *supposed* to feel.

My suggestion: Use staccato writing in small doses. For emphasis. Not for total message dissemination. You'll lose impact. Instead of gaining it. Because you overuse a gimmick.

Nugget 3 (business-to-business advertising, first-person "I did it and you can do it too" ads, product puffery)

Don't use an incredible premise as your principal sales argument.

A reader, listener, or viewer can identify with an episode he recognizes as probable; he rejects an episode he recognizes as improbable. That's what's wrong with the idiotic television commercial which opens with a frazzled husband railing at his wife: "The most important conference of my life and you've switched deodorant soaps!"

The newspaper consistently ranked number 1 or number 2 in circulation in the United States sent me a message I reject implicitly as romantic fiction by a Horatio Alger pretender:

On a beautiful late spring afternoon, 25 years ago, two young men graduated from the same college. They were very much alike, these two young men. Both

366

FIGURE 24–1
Does staccato copy (see Nugget 2) help this headline or hurt it? Opinion: Breaking the thought into three pieces in this instance is an artifice interfering with word flow.

had been better than average students, both were personable and both—as young college graduates are—were filled with ambitious dreams for the future.

Recently, these men returned to their college for their 25th reunion.

They were still very much alike. Both were happily married. Both had three children. And both, it turned out, had gone to work for the same Midwestern manufacturing company after graduation, and were still there.

But, there was a difference. One of the men was manager of a small department of that company. The other was its president.

What Made the Difference

Have you ever wondered, as I have, what makes this kind of difference in people's lives? It isn't always a native intelligence or talent or dedication. It isn't that one person wants success and the other doesn't.

The difference lies in what each person knows and how he or she makes use of that knowledge.

And that is why I am writing to you and to people like you about *The Wall Street Journal* . . .

What's missing here?
Credibility.
Is the story true? In the words of Rhett Butler, Frankly, my dear, I don't give a damn. It's just as possible that across the street from this "Midwestern manufacturing company" is another one twice as big. Its president is a functional illiterate and his junior clerk just celebrated 25 years of *Journal* subscriptions.
Accepting the argument that this letter has produced subscriptions, we ask, *whose* subscriptions? The caliber of subscription this letter generates simply has to be bottom-end. If the writer had used the episode as a minor indicator, leaning on a more credible rationale to get the reader to subscribe, this communication would have had far more power among prime target groups.

Nugget 4 (hard-sell)

To generate guilt, suggest a positive act, not a negative act.

The logic is unassailable: a negative act is more reprehensible than omission. So we don't say:

If you don't order something from the catalog . . .

Instead, we say:

If you decide not to order something from the catalog . . .

Nugget 5 (all advertising)

Careful with words that by their very nature will irritate some readers.

The writer whose space ad selling porcelain figurines used the phrase "hard-core collector," knows what this proposition means. A lot of readers over age 55 see those words "hard core" and reach a set-in-cement conclusion.

Instead of arguing semantics, why take this risk? When I saw a promotional piece from a syndicated creative source this nugget came into even sharper focus. A key sentence:

We make up a new ad each month and strip your name in it.

My own negative reaction to the word *strip* is a mechanical one. I don't want to be part of a creative cattle-call, and this copy emphasizes my anonymity instead of massaging my ego. And I can see that others might reach a different but equally negative subliminal conclusion about the word. Why not *print* my name in it instead of stripping it in?

(A better way of putting selling emphasis where it belongs: "Every month you'll get a new ad—with *your* name custom-printed in it.")

Nugget 6 (general advertising, business-to-business, subscription promotions)

Following "This is the best" or any other blanket claim of superiority with the self-disciplining word *because* will force you, the message originator, to structure a word-sell program designed to get those heads nodding.

The people you'll sell with hit-and-run tactics ("This is the most important [WHATEVER]" or "You'll be interested in this" without ever justifying the claim) are those who already agree with you. Don't feel triumphant, because these people reached their conclusion before your message arrived.

A publisher mailed me a well-produced offering for a one-year subscription to a market guide. The subscription costs $1,950, and in that stratospheric region I need a heavy injection of benefit to get me to open my checkbook.

The two-page letter begins rationally enough, if a little on the slow-moving and patronizing side:

Dear Mr. Lewis:

As the president of a direct marketing agency, we believe you will be especially interested in information on the size, characteristics and geography of the consumer market—basic structural data—that will provide you with important guidelines for designing sales strategy, developing new products and the planning of almost all your marketing activities.

The Conference Board's Consumer Research Center is designed to improve decision making: (1) by keeping you abreast of current consumer trends and sentiment; and (2) by placing at your fingertips the marketing data you require daily—at a price far below any alternative service you may now use.

Yawn. The letter goes on and on, always logical and always in a "Who We Are, What We Do" vein. What it *doesn't* tell me is why I need it. Instead of building, the letter winds down as it dips instead of peaks on the second page:

The Center's income service and expenditure series makes accessible to you the detailed facts and figures of continuous and extensive surveys conducted by the federal government—in a form designed to meet your decision-making needs in the most cost-effective fashion.

The communication misses the target not because it sells something I can't use but because the thrust is analytical rather than inspirational. Copy which leans on phrases such as "basic structural data," "important guidelines," "the planning of almost all your marketing activities," "abreast of current consumer trends and sentiment," "make accessible to you," and the ghastly "in a form designed to meet your decision-making needs," is the work of a textbook writer, not a commercial writer.

Nugget 7 (all copy, especially spoken words)

When potency-draining "if . . ." follows the main clause, it twists the interpretation the reader—or, especially, the listener—already has reached, forcing a negative change. So an "if" clause is a better beginning clause than a follow-up clause.

Here's a primitive example:

You can lose as much as five pounds the very first week, if you follow this simple weight-loss system.

We change nothing but the sequence:

If you follow this simple weight-loss system, you can lose as much as five pounds the very first week.

Can you see the difference? The residual image of the first piece of copy is the condition, because that's the last part of the message. The residual image of the second piece of copy is the benefit, because that's the last part of the message.

The "if . . ." clause unwittingly feeds skepticism when it follows a positive thought. Your listener thought she understood the benefit, then is forced to re-evaluate because of a condition introduced after the benefit has been promised.

Nugget 8 (collateral literature, high-tech ads, introducing product at new lower user-level)

If you have to exclude the reader, explain why.

The difference between having a buddy and having an antagonist is obvious.

The ease with which you can couch the message should be equally obvious. A vendor of business software crows:

> We have a special, private 800 number for dealers.

What's wrong with this supposed benefit is this: the company makes the statement in a mailing to *users*, not dealers. How easy it would be to include the user instead of treating him like an outsider:

> Have a question? Ask your dealer. He can call a special 800 number and get the answer for you.

Nugget 9 (self-improvement products, p.o.c.b. copy)
(p.o.c.b. = plain ol' country boy)

When your claim is weak or hard to prove, enlist the reader as an ally.

An ad for a weight-reducing tea, whose claims might be hammered by the FDA if they were too strong, does a neat job of enlisting the reader as an ally with this headline:

> If You Drink This Delicious Tea
> You Just Might Lose Weight.
> We're Not Sure Why.

Body copy reinforces the nonclaim:

> READ THIS CAREFULLY
>
> We make no specific claims for Oriental Slimtea, not only because it's against the law to do so but also because we ourselves aren't sure how or why this wonderful-tasting tea has the power to help you get rid of excess fat.
>
> All we can do is offer you a *100% Absolute Money-Back Guarantee.* If it doesn't . . .

See how it works? No ammunition for the skeptic who wants to say, "I don't believe your claim"—and now can't say it.

Nugget 10 (consumer advertising)

Don't risk the reader's wrath by using words with multiple meanings.

A mailing from a financial institution has this headline copy on its brochure:

> Put the Cash Hidden in Your Home to Work for You.

What's wrong here? The word *hidden*. If I did have cash hidden in my home I'd wonder how this savings & loan knew about it. *Hidden* has so many negative connotations it's best used when telling someone what *not* to do.

All the writer had to do was hold the homeowner harmless:

> Did You Know There's CASH Hidden in Your Home, Waiting to Go to Work for You?

Nugget 11 (all copy)

When you project an assumption, base it on a psychological truth or a known psychographic fact, not on a self-serving fantasy.

Measure this next example—an argumentative presumption whose self-serving fantasy isn't even masked—against that nugget.

> Dear Gold Card Member:
> Like you, the Japanese love nature.

Of all the "So what?" statements we've read this year, this one ranks way at the top. Maybe I'm a nature lover, maybe not. Even if I am, loving nature isn't among the 8,000 leading motivators of our time.

Nugget 12 (all copy)

If inconsequential fact doesn't enhance the possibility of response, don't introduce it. If you include copy which lowers the competitive position of what you're selling, use it to prove your integrity.

You aren't an investigative reporter. Your job is to present a *selection* of facts, not an "If the truth hurts, so be it" confession.

A trade ad for a magazine which boasts about its superiority offers this statistical evidence:

> A Solid SECOND
> In Reader AND Advertiser Preference!

If I were a space-buyer, this copy would motivate me, all right—to head for Standard Rate & Data, looking for the magazine that's a solid FIRST. You don't have to be a copywriter to blurt out copy like this. Think: How would a good copywriter have used this same information to generate a positive image? Did Avis say, relative to Hertz, "A Solid SECOND"? Nope. They built a campaign out of their second position: "We Try Harder."

This isn't an exposé; it isn't a learned treatise. It's forceful communication. What's forceful about this headline for a computer magazine?

Seven good reasons why you should
subscribe to *Creative Computing*

The first reason:

Creative Computing
gives you things to
actually do with a
computer.

This is the top reason? What this does is make mashed potatoes out of the other six reasons. We can't accept this copy as projecting anything other than useless, comparatively benefitless fact. (Proof: The magazine went out of business.)

A copywriter asks me to buy art by a painter, but nonenhancing fact does the writer in:

Ms. Kuck is an exceptionally gifted painter. She has devoted her considerable talents to child-subject art for the past decade, and as a result has sold more than 1,200 original paintings—and a number of her paintings have sold for over $1,000 each!

Count your objections. I find two.

First, if this artist has sold more than 1,200 paintings over the past decade, she's sold 120 a year, or about one every two working days. That's about as exclusive as a caricaturist at a party.

Second, $1,000 each is a barely respectable price for a painter of any consequence at all.

Think of the ways the writer might have made the point of desirability and value if the desire to introduce all the facts, negative as well as positive, hadn't interfered.

Nugget 13 (all copy except fashion and entertainment, and, conditionally, those too)

Kick out extra words. Good copy is lean.

The most common writing weakener is the easiest to correct. A writer fills his paper edge to edge with words. Some of those words are as useful as extra water in an overflowing bathtub, because they add neither description nor selling power.

What do these typical lines of copy have in common?

The finest in sporting goods . . .
The best in electronic wonders . . .
Designed for the use of the novice and the experienced user alike . . .
Ours is a business of which it might be said that . . .

Right. Each has weakener words, just as this sentence would be weaker if I wrote, "Each *of them* has weakener words." Good writing is lean.

So, accepting the useless word *finest* as a descriptive word, which it isn't, the phrase unplugs its clogged artery when changed to: *The finest sporting goods.* Accepting the outrageous arrogance of *best*, an unproved superlative, we still help drag the phrase back a foot or two from the abyss of somnolence when we drop a word: *The best electronic wonders.* Exorcising the redundancy, we add at least 15 miles per hour as we claim: *Designed for novice and experienced user alike.*

How about that fourth example? My suggestion: Drop the whole wordpile. As an exercise, you might complete that sentence, then eliminate the opening and see how much higher octane your words have.

Nugget 14 (all copy except textbook promotion)

For the wordsmith, communication is more professional than grammatical correctness.

A forceful communicator who puts grammar ahead of results parallels the senator who puts Roberts' Rules of Order ahead of legislation. It's a dedication to form instead of substance, means instead of end—a tribute to fogeyism.

If in the pursuit of grammatical excellence we let form be paramount to substance, we can cripple reader rapport. As an example, not long ago I used this sentence in a piece of selling copy:

Every man, woman, and child on this planet needs something to write with.

Try writing this without ending the sentence with a preposition. You'd have "... something with which to write," a weak way of putting a strong idea, and awkward as well.

So "It's a book you'll never grow tired of" is superior to "It's a book of which you'll never grow tired." I write *formulas* even though I know the plural of *formula* is *formulae*, because I'm writing to communicate, not to impress the English Department. If I have to use *graffiti* I always stay in the plural, because to most readers and all listeners the singular *graffito* seems odd.

Now for the big BUT—

Nugget 15 (same targets as Nugget 14)

Don't lapse into illiteracy.

If you hire writers, you have applicants who hand you a test piece crawling with wormy misspelled and misused words and who become annoyed when you chide them mildly about *to* instead of *too* and *it's* instead of *its*.

Don't let them give you the dumb argument that someone can write professional copy and not know there's no apostrophe in the possessive *its*. Don't let them tell you it's inconsequential that they haven't learned that the contraction for *you are* is *you're*, not *your*.

Apply, with as much vigor as the argumentative circumstance warrants, The Illiteracy Rejection:

Communication in the Age of Skepticism is informal, but it isn't casual.

You know the next line of the specious argument defending casual use of wrong words: "Anyway, a proofreader will catch those little word changes."

I submit: If a proofreader can learn the English language, so can the writer whose words are being proofread.

Nugget 16 (all advertising)

Don't use unexplained and unbacked comparatives and superlatives.

Take a look at your last ad or mailer. Read through it, circling adjectives ending in *er* and *est*.

Have you crowed, "Compare!" without offering a specific comparison? Have you shouted at the reader or viewer, "I make this claim!" without validating that claim?

With the backing of solid information, comparatives and superlatives are potent selling words.

Information + comparative/superlative = product or service superiority.

Without that backing, look out! You're making a lot of noise but firing blanks. (For silver bullets: Chapter 6.)

Nugget 17 (all print advertising and direct mail)

When a sentence has too many commas, consider using parentheses instead of one pair of commas. You can speed up both reading and comprehension.

A sentence read—

We think the combination of a successful history, going back to 1866, and such dynamic new trading techniques as *Commodex*, are unbeatable in today's pressure-laden economic environment.

The sentence seems sluggish. Comprehension isn't easy because all the elements set off by commas aren't parallel. A five-second revision had the copy reading this way:

We think the combination of a successful history (going back to 1866) and such dynamic new trading techniques as *Commodex* are unbeatable in today's markets.

The words flow past the eye faster, and changing the explanation of the company's history to a parenthetical phrase makes the third comma unnecessary altogether.

Nugget 18 (on-camera testimonials; first-person ads)

Get rid of qualifiers.

Flab can attack fingers as well as hips and thighs, when those fingers are writing copy. Can you spot the flabby qualifiers in these constructions?

You may be a bit surprised to learn . . .
We were rather pleased when . . .
I would like to take this opportunity to tell you that . . .

Why should I be *a bit* surprised when by dropping those two words the writer can have me flat-out surprised? The second copywriter is better off being pleased than being *rather* pleased.

What was your conclusion about the third example? If it's anything other than throwing out the phrase altogether, go to the foot of the class and sit next to whoever wrote it.

Words such as *practically, largely, somewhat*—these are giveaways of a syndrome I call Expository Uncertainty. Hedging stems from the writer's lack of assurance; the result is lack of message strength.

Nugget 19 (for copy intended to generate a positive attitude)

Don't make the reader write your copy for you.

If you say, "For many reasons," name some of those reasons. If you say, "Among other things," name some of those things. If you use the word "Important" justify your claim, or it becomes dull arrogance. While you're at it, be sure it's important to the reader, not just to you.

Information important to you but unimportant to the reader is a signal of "Mirror Strategy"—pleasing the mirror instead of whoever is outside the window.

One word which always tips off the reader that you're out of gas and want to siphon some from his imagination tank is *etc.*

Whenever I see this nonword, I draw two assumptions:

1. The writer is lazy.
2. The writer thinks whatever he's selling may have additional features, but he doesn't know what they are.

Never use *etc.* again, except in satire, parody, or a production of "The King and I."

Nugget 20 (financial, insurance, computers)

Don't use nouns as verbs.

Careful, now: Some words *are* both nouns and verbs—*fish, cash, slip, pick, watch*—thousands of words qualify. But not *input, access, impact, network, reference,* and *window.* These are computer-talk.

Leave computer-talk to the in-group. It isn't terrible, and unquestionably it's going to wind up in the dictionary one day, but it isn't yet the use of language a professional should emulate.

Take a look at some computer magazines and verify for yourself: the superior ads don't use in-talk.

Nugget 21 (print media)

Keep copy references in character. Decide what state of mind you want to generate, then stay inside it.

Your copy style might be grim. It might be funny. It might be Olympian. It might be documentary. It might be p.o.c.b. It might be frantic.

Whatever it is, keep it consistent.

A piece of copy, selling recordings of vintage radio comedy shows, read this way:

> These timeless masters of wit and humor never had to depend on sight gags.
> Their exquisite timing and detailed observance of the human condition were
> their hilarious weapons to make us chuckle at ourselves.

What would *you* do with this piece of copy? You might be vaguely dissatisfied, but unless you can pinpoint *why* you're dissatisfied you can't fire it back at the writer or rewrite it yourself.

Which words are out of key? Right! "... detailed observance of the human condition ..." reads like something out of a military medical manual. While we're at it, "timeless" doesn't help build a word image for us, so let's replace it too:

> These are the giants of laughter, the masters of wit and humor. They never had
> to depend on sight gags. Their exquisite timing and sense of the ridiculous
> were their hilarious weapons to make us chuckle at ourselves.

Getting rid of "detailed observance" keeps the copy in character. Our word choice no longer confuses the reader.

Nugget 22 (business-to-business, occasional consumer)

Amputate your arrogance before you start to write.

To whom can you say, "You're lucky to do business with me," without generating antagonism?

I can think of two groups: (1) someone who owes you money and whose payment is long overdue; (2) someone who depends on you for livelihood or peace of mind.

The neighborhood pusher can say this to the addicts he controls, but the world of normal commerce blesses us with two kinds of choices: the choice between "yes" and "no," and the choice between you and a competitor.

How easy the choice becomes when we get a brochure with this copy:

EVERYONE
ELSE
IS A
PRETENDER
We Hate to Say It, But . . .
If You Pass Up
Our "Sense Off" Sale
You Deserve What You Get . . .
Having to Buy from
One of Those Other Guys.

Sure, "Sense Off" doesn't make sense, but we might forgive this sin if the advertiser hadn't jutted out his jaw and played General Patton with us.

The trickiness of this nugget is being able to amputate arrogance without cutting off muscle.

Nugget 23 (all advertising)

Look for ways to inject "you" into the word mix.

An insurance company had this piece of copy:

We value your trust and confidence, and that is why we have worked so hard to make this unique coverage possible.

We have a not-dreadful, not-strong string of words. If the writer had considered Nugget 23, we might have had:

We value your trust and confidence, and that is why we have worked so hard to make this unique coverage possible for you.

The final two words tie the benefit to the target individual, just as the opening tied the premise to the target individual.

Nugget 24 (consumer advertising)

Coattail-riding isn't terrible, because it has a built-in identification factor; but it probably isn't the best you can do.

Bemused readers, listeners, and viewers are deluged with "clever" imitations whenever a catchy campaign takes hold.

One sample: Wendy's had a short-lived but popular campaign, "Where's the beef?" As the campaign burned out, we heard and read:

- ▶ for a paging system, "Where's the beep?"
- ▶ for a scuba diving cruise, "Where's the reef?"
- ▶ for a grass-catching attachment to a lawn-mower, "Where's the leaf?"
- ▶ for a security system, "Where's the thief?"
- ▶ for a time-sharing condominium, "Where's the beach?"

Where was the coattail-riding funeral director to advertise, "Where's the grief?"

Purists may mount arguments of piracy. One campaign fastens itself, leechlike, on the neck of another better-known campaign. I say, what's wrong with that? We use Cadillac and Rolls-Royce every day as touchstones. Why not a current ad-fad?

The question is when to get off the communications train in which you're riding the caboose. All these coattail-riding campaigns *begin* when the coat-wearing campaign *has already peaked.*

No writer can become a communications guru scrabbling around for scraps in the wastebaskets of successful campaigns. Coattail-riding is serviceable, but seldom is it the best approach you might have used, because you're at the mercy of another advertiser for recognition value and you can't use the campaign for long; it has a self-destruct timer built in and clicking away even as it starts.

Nugget 25 (all advertising)

If the reader feels proud to do business with you, you have a competitive edge.

A less theoretical way of putting this nugget: You can shock to get attention, but a lapse into bad taste will cost you.

If we never get their attention we're 100 percent losers. This alone is justification for writing what we must to get them to open the envelope or keep reading the page or to keep their finger off the "zap" button. But doesn't this ad, from the *Wall Street Computer Review*, make you feel the Treasury agents will come after you if you do business with the company?

If Al Capone
had our file-scrambler,
he might never have
done hard time.

PRIVILEGED
INFORMATION

Protects your files by enciphering them . . .

This next example, from a catalog, is actually funny:

Let's face it. There's nothing more disabling than a sinus attack.

Oh, yeah? I'll match my Colt .45 against your sinus attack any day. (Why, oh, why are the words "Let's face it" in there? Those three words are supposed to enlist the reader as an ally; instead, they start an argument with her.)

Nugget 26 (all copy)

Hyphens are an underused clarification-tool.

Sometimes, reading a piece of copy, we aren't sure what it is that bothers us. It just doesn't read right.

If the bothersome sentence has an adjective followed by an adjectival noun, you have the tip-off—a clarifying hyphen can eliminate the bother. An example:

Your attractive counter display . . .

What's wrong here is the word *counter*, an adjectival noun. The rules of grammar work against us, because *attractive* could modify either *counter* or *display*. We seize firm control of the reader's interpretive potential by adding a hyphen:

Your attractive counter-display . . .

Nugget 27 (subscriptions; lead-generating)

As you make it easier for people to respond, the quality of responses goes down.

Those who toil on the treadmills in the murderous world of magazine subscriptions know the trap: Without incentives you can't get enough subscribers, but as you add incentives you drive down the buying level and subscription renewal rate of those you recruit.

Adding "free gifts," shipping before payment, giving two for one—these venerable motivators bring bulk, which, regrettably, is the way we so often have to keep score. Our difficult job is even tougher than it first appears, because only by tracking the renewals or purchases over a year or more can we tell whether or not we've gone too far in order to get early action.

(My own viewpoint may not coincide with that of a theoretician who would take the high road. I side with those who pull out all the stops to get a name. We can't milk the goat unless she's in our own barnyard.)

The value of Nugget 27 may be its role as governor on our copywriting throttle. If we begin to assume automatically that salvation lies *only* in freebies, ultimately we force downward the image and value of what we're selling. But I'd be more afraid of the "expert" who damns all incentives as undignified.

Nugget 28 (all advertising)

A claim of superiority is in no way as convincing as ostensible evidence of superiority, and a feature is in no way as convincing as a benefit.

We as writers too often face this dilemma: Someone for whom we're writing an ad or a mailing piece says to us, "What I want you to do is make it clear this is the best on the market. And it is, it is!" We're given some background information which fails to prove that theory. No matter; our obligation is to regurgitate corporate philosophy. We come up with something like this copy for a cosmetic:

A Beauty Care Breakthrough!

Now there's a new and better way to help your skin look soft, supple, and inviting.

It's the ICE-BORN™ way. Our skin care products contain only *totally natural* ingredients which are deep-frozen for purity.

With ICE-BORN you can have beautiful skin—without any chemical additives.

What have we written? We've claimed superiority without offering evidence. "Totally natural ingredients" aren't benefits in themselves; it's *what they do* (if anything) that's the benefit. Does freezing something give it purity? If so, how? What does it do for the user?

Transforming features into benefits is what we're supposed to do, or we aren't going to sell much.

Nugget 29 (all copy)

When logic says you can, make the buying decision for the message recipient.

Phrases such as "You can . . ." or "If you . . ." suffer in a head-to-head battle for business against a direct statement. So instead of "You can make money . . ." we drop the first two words and add vigor: "Make money. . . ." Usually a nonconditional statement will come to mind once the writer asks the mirror, "Could I write a stronger piece of copy?"

Nugget 30 (all copy, for the rest of your life plus six months)

Practice using words effectively. Don't let your copy run on tracks.

How many of us actually *practice*? Somebody needs a piece of copy by tomorrow noon; we do a workmanlike job, always with the hollow excuse, "I could have done it better if I'd had more time."

Is that really so? We work with words. If we had more time, would we find more exciting words, more motivational words, words our readers/ listeners/viewers will find more credible and stimulating? Or would we just spend more time looking over the background materials and then write the same tired, trite descriptions marbled a little with puffery?

For those with true grit, I have a suggestion to help practice the noble art of wordsmithy. Pretend, as you write every word and phrase, you have only two inches of space in which to transmit the message.

That pretense will result in your optimizing the impact. As a wordsmith, you'll have entered a new level of consciousness.

Welcome, friend!

25

Some Valuable Rules for Effective Copywriting

Rules always are controversial, because an antagonistic practitioner usually can find an exception to any rule. This list of usable rules for the copywriter is no exception to exceptions.

Here we begin an endless process, not only of unearthing and codifying rules but of refining exceptions. Future listmakers may regard this beginning tabulation as primitive. To them, this author sends greetings and the request that the project continue full speed until at least a thousand rules are in inventory. Meanwhile, we have a beginning.

THE "UMBRELLA" RULE

The Umbrella Rule is the most foolproof, universal rule in all copywriting. Copywriters who know and follow this master rule are at the top of the marketing mountain.

Your copy must succeed if it has these three ingredients:

1. Clarity
2. Benefit
3. Verisimilitude

THE FOUR GREAT LAWS

The Four Great Laws override all other rules for force communication. They're congruent and noncompetitive with the Umbrella Rule.

The laws are the key to copywriter survival during the Age of Skepticism, an age spawned by television, self-aware politicians, and universal backlash against unproved claims of superiority by a multitude of competitors.

The First Great Law:
Effective force-communication reaches and influences, at the lowest possible cost, the most people who can and will buy what you have to sell.

The Second Great Law:
In this Age of Skepticism, cleverness for the sake of cleverness may well be a liability rather than an asset.

The Third Great Law:
$E^2 = 0$. (When you emphasize everything, you emphasize nothing.)

The Fourth Great Law:
Tell your message recipient what to do.

Don't overlook the qualified relationship within the First Law of two elements, "reaches" and "lowest possible cost": a hopelessly underproduced advertising message may not "reach" its target.

The Fourth Great Law is mandatory for direct response copy but becomes optional if the message has a purpose other than message-recipient action (not usually a good idea).

Adaptation of the First Great Law for Fund Raising and Political Campaigns. (See complete list under *FUND RAISING*, this section.)

Effective fund raising copy reaches the most people who might contribute and avoids those who never would contribute.

BENEFIT

The John F. Kennedy Buyer Attitude Truism

In this Age of Skepticism, the prospective buyer's first question isn't "What will it do?" but "What will it do for me?"

The Benefit/Benefit Principle

First announce the benefit. Then tell the reader how the benefit benefits him.

The Benefit/Benefit/Benefit Principle

This is the "can't-miss" approach to copy that sells—a three-step procedure:

1. State a claim of superiority over others.

2. Relate superiority to the reader.
3. Tell the reader how your superiority will bring specific improvements to his life. (See *SPECIFICS, The Specifics Superiority Principle.*)

The Benefit/Feature Bloodline Comparative

Features are cold-blooded and benefits are warm-blooded, so benefits are more emotional than features. It follows directly that benefits outsell features.

The Rhetorical Benefit Error

Telling the reader a product or service is beneficial is in no way parallel to *convincing* the reader a product or service is beneficial.
(See *SUBTLETY, The Second Rule of Negative Subtlety.*)

The Credible Benefit Proposition

Maximize benefits within the limits of credibility.

The First Nonargument = No Benefit Rule

Copy depending on a nonargument invariably omits reader benefit.

The Second Nonargument = No Benefit Rule

Details unrelated to the buyer's appetites become nonarguments which because of their irrelevance skew the reaction.

The Rule of Partial Disclosure

Tell the target individual as much as you can about what your product or service can do for him or her. If you have space or time left over, don't move down to the next information level (facts unrelated to benefit); instead, restate or illustrate some of the benefits. (See *IMPORTANCE,* this section.)

The Profit-Killer Equation

Inability to specify benefit equals lower response.

The Puffery-Defeat Inevitability

No amount of puffery or self-applause can sell as effectively as a listing of specific benefits.

BRAGGADOCIO

The Braggadocio Avoidance Procedure

For space ads, write headlines, and for letters, write first paragraphs as though you have only two inches of space for your entire selling argument. For broadcast commercials, write the first two sentences as though the spot were half its actual length.

BUYER ATTITUDE

The Artificial Loyalty Rule

Personal products have a high buyer-loyalty rate, because the buyer doesn't want to expose his weaknesses to outsiders more than he or she must. To break the chain forged by this rule, a competing advertiser of such products has to use an extraordinarily compassionate approach.

The Buyer/Seller Equivalence Equation

The Seller's Concern = What it is.
The Buyer's Concern = What it will do for me.

The "Whose Message Is It?" Rule

Your message should operate within the experiential background of the message recipient, not within your own experiential background. (See *BENE-FITS, The John F. Kennedy Buyer Attitude Truism.*)

CARD DECKS

The First Principle for Card Deck Copy

Your offer must be identifiable instantly.

The Second Principle of Card Deck Copy

Sell, coherently, what the headline promises, not a secondary service or product down the road.

The Third Principle of Card Deck Copy

Stress benefits. You don't have room to write poetry about features and the reader has neither the patience nor the interest to read your poetry. Use a bulleted format, to save space and hold attention.

The Fourth Principle of Card Deck Copy

Assume your card is buried in a deck of offers, all of which are as good as yours or better.

The Fifth Principle of Card Deck Copy

Tell the reader what to do (a direct application of the *Fourth Great Law*).

The Sixth Principle of Card Deck Copy

Force the reader to respond immediately because delay will cost money, reduce benefits, or lose business to a competitor.

CATALOG WRITING

The Rule of Catalog Attention-Grabbing

Start the description with benefit—what the item will do for the customer. Then describe the product itself. Then recapitulate the benefit. Then list the specifics necessary to place an order.

The Catalog Writing Truism

The purpose of catalog copy is to transmit an enthusiastic description of what's being sold to the best prospective buyers. Unless this purpose is achieved, the copywriter has failed, regardless of the cleverness of rhetoric.

The Catalog Writing Truism Footnotes

Footnote 1: The Catalog Writing Truism becomes truer when one writer has the responsibility for an entire catalog.

Footnote 2: A catalog company can prevent its copy from becoming the extension of one person's personality by assigning eight-page sections to different writers.

The Episode-"I,""Buy-from-"We" Indication

If you're torn between "I" and "We," use "I" only when referring to personal episode; use "We" for corporate suggestions that the reader buy.

CELEBRITY USE

The Celebrity Match-Up Principle

Matching your spokesperson to what you're selling accelerates your target individual's acceptance of what the celebrity is pitching.

The Celebrity Waste Factor

Having a celebrity move out of context is an artifice which exposes itself to the viewer or reader. A professional athlete may keep credibility endorsing athletic equipment or beer but not alkaline batteries; an actress may keep credibility endorsing fashion or beauty aids but not machinery or automobile muffler installations.

CLARITY

The Clarity Commandment

When choosing words and phrases for force communication, clarity is paramount. Let no other component of the message-mix interfere with it.

The Say What You Mean Mandate

The reader invariably will apply a negative interpretation to statements which violate the Clarity Commandment.

The Concept of Reader Dominance

The writer's knowledge of the colorful words in a piece of copy is inconsequential. What matters is whether or not the reader knows them. (See SPECIFICS, *The Specifics Superiority Principle*.)

The Tightness Rule

Keep copy tight enough so it fits the reader's skimming without forcing a comprehension-stop.

COMPARATIVE ADVERTISING

The Comparative Imperative

Good marketing strategy calls for Brand No. 2 to shout superiority over Brand No. 1; good marketing strategy calls for Brand No. 1 to shout superiority over all others without singling out any one of them.

CONDITIONAL WORDS AND PHRASES

See also *QUESTIONS.*

The First Rule of "If"

Let *if* relate to your buyer, not to you, because *if* seems to take objectionable high pressure out of your sales argument without actually doing it.

The First Rule of "If" Subdecree

Logic stands behind the writer who makes an action conditional for the buyer, since buyer-control is proper stroking; but to give this control to the seller through an "If" reference suggests seller superiority, which can provoke buyer antagonism.

The Second Rule of "If"

Don't use *should* instead of *if.* The pomposity not only is less straightforward but also puts greater distance between seller and buyer.

The Third Rule of "If"

Don't use the phrase "if you can," which suggests difficulty or problems. Linking *ability* ("can") to "if" is a *double* condition.

The Principle of "If" Control

An "If" condition should imply a "then" promise.

The Conditional Declension Syndrome

The more conditional the statement, the weaker it is.

The Comparative Conditional Declension Syndrome

The conditional isn't as impelling as the imminent.

The Subjunctive Avoidance Commandment

(See next rule also.)
Avoid the subjunctive. It denies actuality.

The First Rule of Positivism

(See previous rule; see also PSYCHOLOGY.)
Stay out of the subjunctive and replace *can* with *will*.

The Second Rule of Positivism

After telling the reader you've presented a logical argument, take acceptance for granted.

CONFUSION

The First Confusion Factor

Don't let any piece of copy off your desk until you can say without crossed fingers, "My mother would understand it."

The Second Confusion Factor

A message matched to the recipient can't be confusing. (See the *Whose Message Is It? Rule* under *BUYER ATTITUDE*, this section.)

The Third Confusion Factor

A sales message which violates the Second Great Law inevitably adds confusion and lowers sales. (See *The Rule of Copy Misdirection* under MOTIVATORS, this section.)

CONSISTENCY

The Consistency Command

Components of a mailing must reinforce and validate one another, or reader/viewer/listener response to *all* components will be lessened.

The Precept of Factual Agreement

When facts within a message are in disagreement, the reader disbelieves all of them, even though one of them probably is true.

The Rule of Word Matching

Use words that match the image you're trying to build. An out-of-key word changes the image.

DIRECT MARKETING (DIRECT MAIL, DIRECT RESPONSE)

Unassailable Loser Statute I

When seller and buyer both are uninvolved, the seller loses.

Unassailable Loser Statute II

Readers are more likely to pick holes in transparent shouts of importance than in projection of benefits.

Unassailable Loser Statute III

Illustration should agree with what we're selling, not with headline copy.

Unassailable Loser Statute IV

Adding qualifying words to a statement of superiority is an admission of inability to claim superiority.

Unassailable Loser Statute V

Use only as much of the language as you know. Your dictionary is your verifier, not your originator.

Workmen's Noncompensation Rationale

Reciprocity is the key to have-the-reader-do-something decisions.

Workmen's Noncompensation Provision 1

The reader's pleasure from absorbing your message diminishes in exact ratio to the amount of work he thinks he'll have to do.

Workmen's Noncompensation Provision 2

Excluding contests, asking the reader to perform a task which requires talent, prior knowledge, or problem-solving ability will lose that reader if he or she resents, feels inferior to, or is annoyed by the unsought challenge.

Workmen's Noncompensation Provision 3

In a contest or sweepstakes that has reward geared to apparent talent, prior knowledge, or problem-solving ability, the reward justifies the challenge.

EMOTION VS. INTELLECT

Emotion vs. Intellect Rule I

When emotion and intellect come into conflict, emotion always wins.

Emotion vs. Intellect Rule II

Emotion outpulls intellect.

The Rule of Emotional Mandate

Unless you specifically want to avoid reader involvement in your message, always write in the active voice, regardless of the type of communication.

ENVELOPES

The Outer Envelope Function

The only purpose of graphic treatment on a direct-mail envelope is to impel the recipient to open that envelope.

FUND RAISING

The First Rule of Fund Raising

Effective direct-mail fund raising reaches the most people who might contribute and avoids those who never would or could contribute.

The Second Rule of Fund Raising

This is a version of the *"Whose Message Is It?" Rule* listed under *BUYER AT-TITUDE.* Operate inside the experiential background of the person you're contacting, not inside your own background.

The Third Rule of Fund Raising

Since you're operating inside the reader's experiential background, select and shape a selling argument you think will grab his or her emotional handles.

The Fourth Rule of Fund Raising

Tell the reader how much to give.

The Rule of Fund Raising Copy Length

The need for long copy is tied to the need to feed an implicit or expressed reader prejudice or belief.

The Fund Raising Reminder Rule

When writing prior donors, remind them how much they gave last time and ask for a little more.

The Rule of Bulk Negation

Bulk doesn't create an emotional reaction. Episode does.

GENERAL RULES FOR WRITING

The Rule of Chromatic Imagery

Write in color, not black and white. Superimpose your imagination atop your reader/viewer/listener's imagination, to enhance receptivity.

The Rule of Concealed Ballooning

If you're trying to make something big out of something little, don't let the buyer know it.

The Dullard's Lament

The more a copywriter depends on mechanical tricks, the more that writer exposes an imaginative sterility.

The Factual Edge

Teaser mailings and space ads, which don't tell the reader what the mailer has for sale, are almost always less effective and less productive than mailings which include facts on which the target individual can formulate a buying decision. (See IMPORTANCE, rules of, this section.)

The Peripheral Pussyfooting Weakener Rule

Writing around a point drains excitement out. Copy loses impact in direct ratio to the percentage of information given indirectly instead of directly. (See also CONDITIONAL WORDS AND PHRASES.)

The Power-Filter Effect

Surplus words are power-filters, reducing impact.

The Reader-Fatigue Effect

Drama in writing is implicit, or it doesn't exist at all. Labeling isn't parallel to colorful writing. Claiming "drama" or "excitement" is an uninspired and punchless substitute for using words to prove that claim.

The Stupidity Equation

Stupid questions and statements equal lower response.

The "You First" Rule

Tell the reader, listener, or viewer what's in it for him, not for you.

GRAMMAR

See *PUNCTUATION and GRAMMAR*.

GUARANTEES

The First Rule of Guarantees

Unless a guarantee specifically offers a refund, it probably is a cynically inspired sales gimmick, not a true guarantee.

The Second Rule of Guarantees

When the buyer feels he is in total command, the offer becomes true regardless of its incredible nature.

The Third Rule of Guarantees

Deliver what you promise.

HUMOR

The Pagliacci Syndrome

Beginning writers want to write funny copy. Don't let them, and don't do it yourself.

The Humor-Avoidance Rationale

When writing to people who don't know you, humor is never the best possible approach and often is the worst. When writing to people who do know you, almost always humor is at best no better than straightforward exposition; at less-than-best humor can kill any impression of sincerity, verisimilitude, and credibility.

The Comic Exception

The "almost always" assertion in *The Humor-Avoidance Rationale* is tempered by this exception: When you apologize for a mistake, quiet humor, carefully handled, can defang a venomous buyer. You benefit from this paradox: admitting you're a fool makes you less of a fool.

The Clown Nonequivalence Rule

The onlooker always feels superior to a clown.

IF

See *CONDITIONAL WORDS AND PHRASES; QUESTIONS.*

IMPACT

The First Statute of Novelty Burnout

The impact of repeated messages decreases in exact ratio to reliance on novelty.

The Redundancy Control Rule

Use redundancies only when you want the reader to know you've repeated or doubled words to show emphasis.

The Principle of Expository Uncertainty

Words such as *practically, largely,* and *somewhat* are hedges betraying the writer's lack of assurance. The betrayal results in a weaker message. (See *GENERAL RULES FOR WRITING,* this section.)

The Shock vs. Dignity Decision

If you exchange your dignity for shock value, be certain the shock is positive for your best buyers. (See also sections on *PSYCHOLOGY* and *SUBTLETY*, this section.)

IMPORTANCE

The Rule of Importance Determination

If you claim importance, prove it.

The First Rule of Implied Importance

Everything we do is important to us. Almost nothing someone else does is important to us, unless what he does directly affects us.

(See the *"Whose Message Is It"* Rule, this section, under *BUYER ATTITUDE.*)

The Second Rule of Implied Importance

Importance should relate to the state of mind of the reader, not the writer.

The Third Rule of Implied Importance

If the copy message following the word "Important" is a letdown to the reader, the copy is more likely to breed rejection or contempt than to initiate a buying urge.

The Automatic Importance Technique

Capitalizing a word makes it important.

The Nonimportance Fault

Calling something "important" when your best readers will know it isn't important will cost you some business you otherwise might have had. (See *LOGIC, The Phony Claim Mistake.*)

The First Rule of So-What Turnoff Control

Select as your key selling arguments those facts and suggested benefits which

SOME VALUABLE RULES FOR EFFECTIVE COPYWRITING

satisfy the intended buyer's probable psychological motivators. (See *MOTIVATORS*, this section.)

Using a so-what statement as a major selling point adds confusion in direct ratio to the reader/viewer/listener's own product/service interest/knowledge. (See *MOTIVATORS*, this section.)

The Third Rule of So-What Turnoff Control

"So what?" becomes "Here's why I want it" if benefit is added to the rhetorical mix. (See *BENEFIT*, this section.)

The First Rule of Excitement Incentives

Adding artificial incentives to generate sales invariably lowers the quality of buyer.

The Second Rule of Excitement Incentives

Lowering the quality of buyer is a detriment only if a promotion coincidentally lowers the image of the vendor with existing best buyers.

The Third Rule of Excitement Incentives

All promotions must have an expiration date.

The Fourth Rule of Excitement Incentives

Orders dribbling in after the expiration date should be honored as long as prebought supplies and computer programming make it possible; but remind the customer that you're doing him a favor.

The Fifth Rule of Excitement Incentives

If the seller doesn't seem excited, the customer can't get excited.

The Sixth Rule of Excitement Incentives

Lack of clarity kills off excitement.

LOGIC

The Bluster Mistake

The suggestion "You must ..." unbacked by a reason the reader/viewer/listener doesn't regard as logical is bluster rather than logical sales argument because it has no factual core. Beginning the sentence with "This is why" forces the writer to add that core.

The Phony Claim Mistake

Those whom you most want as buyers are the same individuals who are most likely to see through phony claims. (See IMPORTANCE, *The Nonimportance Fault.*)

MOTIVATORS

The four great motivators of our time:

1. Fear
2. Exclusivity
3. Guilt
4. Greed

A fifth "possible," Envy, is actually an amalgam of all four.

The Motivating Word-Choice Proposal

When choosing words, use terms and phrases your target buyer regards favorably unless you're using *fear* as a motivator.

The Rule of Contemporaneous Transmission

Unless the writer has a knowledge of his target prospect, copy can be a horrible psychological mismatch.

The "Diarrhea of the Keyboard" Syndrome

Details unrelated to the buyer's motivators slow down or kill off the sale.

The First Rule of Fear

The reader must always know that you have the answer to the problem you expose.

The Second Rule of Fear

Unless your own fear of overkill suggests a weaker message, write a direct challenge, not a "What if . . ." subjunctive. (See the *Subjunctive Avoidance Commandment* under *CONDITIONAL WORDS AND PHRASES*, this section.)

The Third Rule of Fear

Don't lose your nerve halfway through and begin polluting your fear approach with light-heartedness.

The Truth-as-Motivator Noneffect

Apparent truth is insignificant in a selling argument unless that truth is built around the target individual's motivators. (See rules of *VERISIMILITUDE*, this section.)

The Rule of Copy Misdirection

Words that puzzle can't motivate. (See factors of *CONFUSION*, this section.)

The Rule of Statistical Deficiency

Readers respond less to cold-blooded statistics than they do to warm-blooded examples.

NEWS RELEASES

The First Canon of News Release Writing

The reader, viewer, or listener should be unaware that the message is sponsored.

The Second Canon of News Release Writing

Put puffery in quotes.

The Third Canon of News Release Writing

Replace or eliminate descriptive adjectives which suggest editorial viewpoint.

The Five Rules of Cutline Writing

1. Repeat pertinent information even though it also appears in the release.
2. Don't be afraid to write long cutlines.
3. Write complete sentences, not "bullet-style."
4. Set a maximum of 20 words per sentence.
5. If you include several pictures, write a separate cutline for each one, even if they're similar.

PERSONALIZING

The De-Icer Rule

Personalizing helps melt the ice of skepticism and apathy.

The Capitalization-Loss Rule

Setting copy in all caps depersonalizes a message.

PREDICAMENT USE

The Predicament Method Principle

Establishing a predicament as a sales argument has these five sequential components:

1. Create a predicament the reader, viewer, or listener finds logical.
2. Put your target individual into that predicament, either by unmistakable association or by hard use of the word *you*.
3. Demonstrate whatever you're selling as the solution to the predicament.
4. Restate the circumstance with a happy conclusion.
5. Have the central character in the predicament state satisfaction.

PRODUCT IMAGE

The Rule of Buyer Defense

A product is what it is, plus what the buyer thinks it is.

PRODUCTION

The First Rule of Production Reduction

Poor production won't destroy a good message.

The Second Rule of Production Reduction

Lavish production that tries to mask an inferior message usually doesn't pay for itself.

PROFESSIONALISM

The Form Worship Maxim

The writer who puts *form* ahead of *substance* implicitly admits a creative deficiency. Communications with this deficiency call attention to format rather than to what they say. Invariably the writer has a more effective way to transmit the message. (See *GENERAL RULES FOR WRITING*, this section.)

Roget's Complaint

With all the specific descriptive words available, the writer who regards neutral, nonimpact words such as *needs, quality, features,* and *value* as creative should agree to work for no pay.

The Professional/Amateur Differential

The amateur says: "Most people will get the idea, no matter how poorly I say it."

The professional says: "Every word is our weapon, and anyone who thinks otherwise is an amateur."

The Fat Copy Procedure

Good writing is lean. Slice weak, forceless words out of your copy the way you'd trim fat from a steak.

The First Nonprofessional Revelation

The worst, most pompous, least imaginative, and most unprofessional advertising line of this decade is, "If you can find a better (WHATEVER), buy it."

The Second Nonprofessional Revelation

Forbidding words lock your target individual out. Familiar words and verbalisms, short of losing your dignity, invite this person in.

The Third Nonprofessional Revelation

If you have to show off your erudition or use a foreign phrase, explain the phrase and also explain why you had to use it in the first place.

The Fourth Nonprofessional Revelation

Write on a level of mutual interest, rather than instructor-to-student. At the very least, preface your verbal strutting and preening with the words "As you know."

The Fifth Nonprofessional Revelation

Eliminate adjectives which do nothing to further comprehension.

The Sixth Nonprofessional Revelation

The professional writer of force communication has three areas of knowledge: basic psychology, vocabulary suppression, and salesmanship roughly equivalent to that of a vacuum cleaner salesperson.

PSYCHOLOGY

(See also QUESTIONS.)

The Challenge Response Principle

People respond to challenges that don't suggest incapability.

The Connotation Rule

Substitute words with a positive connotation for words with a neutral or negative connotation.

The Generic Determination Rule

The generic determines reaction more than the number.

Generic Determination Subrule "A"

When the experiential background of your primary targets includes a date within the adult experience, numbers of years, months, or days are apparently longer ago than the date itself.

The Rule of Negative Transmission

Unless you want the reader or viewer to think you're the generator of the reason for negative information, don't put this information aggressively.

The "I'm Not Responsible" Stipulation

Second and third person writing, which begins "There is" or "There are"; "You have been selected"; "It was determined that"; and passive voice verbs are implicitly weaker than statements in which the message-sender assumes responsibility for the action.

The "Only You" Blessing

You can search for a hundred years and not find a sales argument more powerful than "Only you . . . and only from us."

The Chosen People Effect

If what you're selling has any aura of rarity or scarceness, this three-step sales argument is an easy winner:

1. Everybody wants it.
2. Nobody can get it.
3. Except you.

(See The "Only You" Blessing, above.)

The Renunciation Proposition

It's easier to renounce the obvious than to renounce the traditional. This human characteristic is grist for the sales promotion mill, but it can be a deadly attitude if the writer is caught up in an unrenounceable tradition of his own.

The Shock-Therapy Negation

If you exchange your dignity for shock value, be certain the shock is positive for your best buyers. (See *GENERAL RULES FOR WRITING* and *PROFESSIONALISM*, this section.)

The Psychological Truth Injunction

When you project an assumption, base it on a psychological truth or a known psychographic fact, not on a self-serving fantasy. If the person you're trying to convince might regard your argumentative presumption as incredible, *acknowledge* the presumption as incredible. Then explain, with logic comprehensible to the reader, why it isn't incredible at all.

PUBLIC RELATIONS

See *NEWS RELEASES*.

PUNCTUATION AND GRAMMAR

The Illiteracy Rejection

Communication in the Age of Skepticism is informal, but it isn't casual.

The Decimal Cheapener

Decimal-zero-zero after a dollar number has a cheapening effect without the accompanying effect of seeming less expensive. $500.00 has less class than $500. The effect is psychological, and some readers may be more comfortable with the cheapener; choice depends on the context.

The Quotation Mark Rule

Putting quotation marks around a word or a phrase the reader may not recognize tells the reader we share the novelty of the idea . . . and helps him or her accept the unknown. Without the quotation marks, we say to the reader, "We know something you don't."

QUESTIONS

See also *CONDITIONAL WORDS AND PHRASES; PSYCHOLOGY.*

The First Rule of Question Asking

Don't ask a question that risks rejection by your best potential buyers.

The Second Rule of Question Asking

Don't be afraid to shake up borderline buyer-prospects by challenging them to make up their minds.

RADIO

The First Rule of Radio Spot Writing

Aggressiveness leaves a stronger residue than subtlety.

The Second Rule of Radio Spot Writing

If humor isn't directly related to what you're selling, scrap it.

The First Principle of Radio Clear Reception

Help the announcer's pronunciation and you'll help the listener's comprehension.

The Second Principle of Radio Clear Reception

Spell out numbers, symbols, and abbreviations. The words will come out the way you want them to.

The Mandate of Business-to-Business Radio Spot Writing

Break hard into the listener's usual apathy. Intrude on his easy-listening attitude. Grab attention and then shake it so the listener knows what you want to sell him.

REMAIL

The First Remail Determinant

If a mailing has been successful, the only content change for a Second-Chance remail to someone whose characteristics match your buyers is the information that this *is* a remail.

The Second Remail Determinant

Unless you're out of cold-list names, send Second-Chance mailings only to proved names. For any other prospect groups, sending additional mailings to cold lists probably will be more productive.

SALESMANSHIP

The First Canon of Salesmanship

When the prospect says yes, quit selling.

The First Rule of Upscale Selling

Reverence for what you're selling, not overblown descriptions, suggests exclusivity. (See *Rules for Exclusivity*.)

The Second Rule of Upscale Selling

Put yourself, as vendor, on a par with your buyers, not above or below them.

The Third Rule of Upscale Selling

For the upscale buyer, a credible benefit needn't be a product's usefulness; it can be the product's origin. "Only you" works when coupled with "Only from us."

The Fourth Rule of Upscale Selling

Because the words "classless society" are in quotation marks, the assumption that a single motivator works for all potential buyers is as specious as the assumption that all media or mailing lists pull with equal strength.

The Fifth Rule of Upscale Selling

Since "upscale" is a state of mind, not a homogenized group with parallel interests and knowledge, appeal to the state of mind and your sales argument is safe; appeal to an assumed common-base of knowledge and a significant percent of target individuals won't have the information core to decode the benefits.

The Sixth Rule of Upscale Selling

The Fifth Rule being true—that "upscale" is a state of mind—individuals move in and out of any particular group, motivated by factors the marketer can't control. Copy should include this reminder: You're indeed a member of our group.

The Seller/Buyer Differential

The seller's concern: What it is. The buyer's concern: What it will do for him. (See *BENEFITS*, this section.)

SKEPTICISM

15 Ways to Thwart the Age of Skepticism

(See *THE SECOND GREAT LAW*; *BENEFIT*; and *VERISIMILITUDE*, this section.)

1. If you make a claim, prove it.
2. Don't lie.
3. Draw attention to what's being sold, not to a celebrity who's selling it.
4. Don't clown.
5. Imply bulk or community acceptance.
6. Personalize—"Only you . . . only from us."
7. Be positive and specific.
8. Cut down the puffery.
9. Don't assume the public knows your "in" terminology.
10. Showing innocence or artlessness can prove your sincerity.
11. Tie newness to an established base.
12. Don't make something big out of something little.
13. Tell the reader, early, something he already knows.

14. If you talk down to the reader, be gracious and benevolent; and observe this next point (No. 15).

15. Don't be omnipotent; admit an Achilles' heel.

SPECIFICS

The Specifics Superiority Principle

Specifics outsell generalities. (See BENEFIT, *The Benefit/Benefit/Benefit Principle*; TESTIMONIALS, *The Second Testimonial Rule*; CLARITY, *The Concept of Reader Dominance.*)

The "Whoever You Are, Hello!" Principle

Since specifics outsell generalizations (The Specifics Superiority Principle, above), if you don't know who will read your message you can't be as specific as if you do know. The writer who doesn't have target data at hand can't sell as much as the writer who does.

SPEED FORMATS (MAILGRAMS, JET EXPRESS, ET AL.)

The First Law of Speed Formats

If the recipient becomes annoyed by discovering your ploy, the speed format has worked against you, not for you, because more conventional formats wouldn't have generated a negative reaction.

The Second Law of Speed Formats

The message must project timeliness, personalization, and possible loss of benefit, or it falls out of key with the format and violates the First Law.

The Third Law of Speed Formats

Open the message with compelling benefit.

The Fourth Law of Speed Formats

Don't let any distraction soften the "bulletin" copy approach.

The Fifth Law of Speed Formats

If your message is supposed to be one-to-one, keep excitement high by keeping adjectives down; your message will match the medium if its entire structure demands imperative action that produces benefit.

The Sixth Law of Speed Formats

Slash away mercilessly at hard-selling copy. It destroys speed-format verisimilitude.

STATISTICS

The Rule of Statistical Failure

Statistics don't sell.

The Victim-Statistic Rule

In fund-raising copy, individual stories of victims are superior to statistics even though statistics represent bulk numbers.

SUBTLETY

These rules are aimed at violators of the Second Great Law.

The First Rule of Negative Subtlety

The effectiveness of your message decreases in direct ratio to an increase in subtlety.

The Second Rule of Negative Subtlety

Don't mask benefit with subtlety. Benefit is why the recipient pays attention to what you've written, so state it clearly and directly.

The Teaser Complaint

Teaser mailings and advertising, which don't tell the reader what the mailer has for sale, are almost always less effective and less productive than mailings which include facts on which the target individual can formulate a buying decision.

SYLLABLES

The First Theorem of Word Construction

When naming or describing product or company, matching word sounds to the intended effect will heighten that effect until repetition blurs it.

The Second Theorem of Word Construction

One-syllable words are harder, tougher, and stronger than their softer, more reasonable multisyllabic equivalents.

The Third Theorem of Word Construction

Flat vowels are crisper and are spoken faster than long vowels, so the words they represent seem crisper and faster.

TELEVISION

The First Rule of Television Impact

If you open with a five-second episode excluding product, close with five seconds of hard visual and auditory emphasis on product.

Explanatory Subrule to the First Rule of Television Impact

Validity of the First Rule of Television Impact increases with a decrease in spot length.

TESTIMONIALS

The First Testimonial Rule

The relative value of a testimonial by an authority or expert, compared with a celebrity, is in direct ratio to the message-recipient's knowledge of the product or service being sold.

The Second Testimonial Rule

In testimonials, as in all force communication, specifics outpull puffery.

VERISIMILITUDE

The First Verisimilitude Commandment

Regurgitating all the facts, undigested, invariably results in a poorer selling argument than selecting facts the message recipient perceives to be (1) true and (2) beneficial.

The Second Verisimilitude Commandment

The most effective sales argument is not clinical truth but, rather, what the reader, viewer, or listener perceives to be true.

The Third Verisimilitude Commandment

Consistency prevents the buildup of skepticism, which erodes verisimilitude. (See rule under CONSISTENCY, this section.)

The Fourth Verisimilitude Commandment

Evidence is more credible than an unexplained statement of position.

The Fifth Verisimilitude Commandment

Use fact to make a point, not just for the sake of using fact. (See the *First Law of Turnoff Control* under IMPORTANCE, this section.)

The Specificity Principle

Specific details build verisimilitude.

The First Rule of Cheating

To be acceptable from any viewpoint, an ad that cheats must be unassailable factually.

The Second Rule of Cheating

To be competitively preferable, an ad that cheats must boost the product or service beyond the ability of a conventional sales argument to do so.

The Third Rule of Cheating

Surrounding a thoughtful cheating-argument with weak and thoughtless cheating-arguments saps strength by thinning the base of reader credulity. (See the *Second Verisimilitude Commandment*, this section.)

The Fourth Rule of Cheating

As cheating moves toward lying and betrays a lack of integrity, effectiveness among the best buyers vanishes in direct ratio.

The First Rule of Lie-Avoidance

A lie visible to the target individual is a symbol of a weak imagination.

The Second Rule of Lie-Avoidance

Lying is never necessary nor preferable in a sales promotion message.

The Third Rule of Lie-Avoidance

When the reader thinks you are not telling the truth about one point, he extends that opinion to include your entire sales argument. He rejects even those statements which *are* true.

WEASEL WORDS

The First Rule of Weaseling

An effective weaseled claim is written so the reader slides past the weasel without realizing it.

The Second Rule of Weaseling

The main purpose of writing weasel words should be credibility.

The Third Rule of Weaseling

"Parity" advertising—a statement of "We're as good as they are," worded to appear to be "We're better than they are"—is an effective weasel whose impact is gradually weakening through competitive overuse.

The Fourth Rule of Weaseling

"Can" and "may" as substitutes for "will" usually are successful and acceptable weasel words. An unidentified accolade such as "One art authority says . . ." or "Consumers choose . . ." is a weak and unacceptable weasel.

A Glossary
of Communications Terms

AFTRA: American Federation of Television and Radio Artists, the union for television and radio actors and announcers.

agate line: A measurement of the depth of print ads—1/14 inch (14 lines = 1 inch). This measurement is almost obsolete but some publications still use it.

bait-and-switch: The unsavory technique of advertising a big bargain and then, when the customer comes to the store, switching to a similar but more expensive item.

bangtail: An extra detachable flap on the backside of an envelope, on which an additional offer has been printed.

b.f.: Bold face, referring to the weight of a typeface.

bingo card: Reply card inserted in a publication; reader circles the code numbers of those items for which he wants information.

bleed: Printing to the edge of the page, with no uninked border.

body copy: The copy block of a print ad, excluding headlines, coupons, or signatures.

bounce back: An enclosure with merchandise, offering additional merchandise for sale.

box: An insert into a piece of copy, usually bordered by a thin rule.

b.r.c., b.r.e.: Business reply card, business reply envelope.

broadsheet: Standard newspaper advertising page, 21 inches deep and 13 inches wide (see *SAU*).

broadside: A big single sheet of paper, folded to mailing size; the most standard size is 17″ × 22″.

camera-ready: A finished ad ready for reproduction (see *paste-up*).

caps: All capital letters.

caps and l.c.: Capitalized first letters, "lower case" for other letters.

caption: Descriptive words above a photograph (see *cutline*).

column inch: Advertising depth measurement, one column wide by one inch deep.

comprehensive, "comp": An artist's layout, closely resembling the way the finished ad or literature will look.

computer personalization: Insertion of individual's name and other personal information in a letter or mailing piece.

continuity: Radio copy.

continuity program: A direct mail term for a series of items (for example, collectibles or books) shipped in sequence over a period of time.

copy test: Testing one copy approach against another.

counter card: A point-of-purchase sign, usually set up as an easel.

c.p.m.: Cost per thousand.

CU: (television term) Close up.

cut: A printed illustration or halftone.

cutline: Descriptive words under a photograph (see *caption*).

dealer imprint: An area on a manufacturer-prepared brochure in which the dealer prints its name, address, and phone number.

demographics: Characteristics of a target-market group—for example, age, sex, education. Often tied to ZIP codes.

display ad: A print ad other than classified.

dissolve: In television, the gradual cross-fading of one scene into another.

double truck: A two-page spread (facing pages).

ECU: (television term) Extreme close up.

force communication: Delivery of an imperative message through mass media—print, broadcast, direct mail, or (on a campaign level) telemarketing. (See *mass communication*.)

four-color process: Full color printing, a blend of the four "standard" colors—red, blue, yellow, and black—in hairline registration to give the photographic effect of many colors.

free-standing insert: A preprinted promotional piece inserted into a newspaper or magazine.

gimmick: A technique unrelated to the message, designed to grab reader/listener/viewer interest to the message.

go to black: (television term) Fade out the scene.

gutter: The inside margins of two facing pages.

hairline:

    (a) Perfect registration of colors in printing.

    (b) A thin rule used as a border.

halftone: A dot pattern which simulates a continuous-tone photograph. Reproduced in print, the picture is actually a group of individual fine dots, usually ranging from a coarse 65-line "screen" (newsprint) to a very fine 200-line screen (enamel paper). Number of halftone screen lines is per inch. (See *cut*.)

hitchhiker: A commercial at the end of a program, selling one of the sponsor's products not associated with program-identification.

ID: "Identification"—a short commercial delivered at a station-break between programs, just before or after the station's identification of its call letters.

impulse buy: Purchase of something the buyer hadn't intended to get when entering the store or picking up the mailer.

insert: See *free standing insert*.

insertion order: The formal and specific written notice by an advertiser or advertising agency to a medium, requesting the insertion of a specific ad.

institutional advertising: Advertising designed to build image or good will rather than to sell something.

island:

(a) A store display unattached to any other display.

(b) An ad completely surrounded by editorial matter.

jingle: A musical composition integrated into a broadcast commercial to give sound-identity to what's being sold.

justified: Type set so the right margin lines up evenly. (See *ragged right*.)

key: A code enabling the advertiser to determine the source of sales or inquiries (i.e., Department A).

leading: (pronounced "ledding") Spacing between lines of type to separate the lines from one another. (See *set solid*.)

lift letter: An extra exhorting enclosure in a mailing package; sometimes called a "publisher's letter."

line: See *agate line*.

line shot, line drawing: A graphic element without halftone dots; solid areas are reproduced but shaded areas become either solid (black) or nonexistent (white).

lip sync: (television term) Synchronized lip movements. If the mouth movements don't match the words, the two are *out of sync*.

lower case (l.c.): No capital letters.

LS: (television term) Long shot.

magalog: Half-magazine, half-catalog—a sponsored magazine whose editorial content reinforces the items advertised.

mass communication: Delivery of a message to large numbers of people through mass media. (See *force communication*.)

matte shot: (television term) Combining two elements, shot at different places, into a single shot (i.e., putting a studio announcer into a Parisian street scene).

MCU: (television term) Medium close up.

medium: An individual mass communications outlet, such as a radio station or a newspaper. Plural = *media*.

merchandising: Any technique for selling goods or services.

monitor:

(a) To watch TV or listen to radio for the purpose of checking a particular segment or commercial.

(b) A television set in the control room or studio.

montage: An illustration in which a number of images are laid over one another.

mortise: A hole cut in a reverse or illustration.

m.o.s.: (television term) Without sound; literally, "Mitout sound."

MS: (television term) Medium shot.

negative option: A direct mail continuity program in which the seller continues to ship and bill for merchandise until the customer asks for discontinuation.

newsprint: The soft, coarse paper used for most newspapers. Newsprint usually takes a 65-line to 85-line screen (see *halftones*).

news release: A self-serving statement whose format and writing style mirror that of a news story.

optical: (television term) A special video effect.

outline: A halftone in which all elements other than the main image have been cut away.

oxymoron: A phrase combining two contradicting words, such as "Icy Hot" or "Giant Midget."

package insert: A promotional or sales piece enclosed with product shipment. Unlike a *bounce back*, it usually is supplied by a different company which pays for each enclosure.

pan: (television term) Left/right movement of the camera.

paste-up: The original camera-ready art, in which elements are pasted onto a cardboard backing.

photostat: A copying process used for art and type.

pica: A lateral measurement, $\frac{1}{6}$": six picas = one inch wide.

p.i. deal: Per-inquiry advertising, in which the advertiser pays the medium a fixed amount per inquiry or sale.

p.o.c.b.: "Plain ol' country boy"—a technique of writing which uses "ain't" and "he don't" and other country-style verbalisms.

point: A vertical measurement of type— $\frac{1}{72}$" high. 72 points = one inch.

p.o.p.: Point of purchase—a display at a store.

press release: Obsolete term for *news release*. (Broadcast media made it obsolete by requiring a more generic phrase.)

psychographics: Attitudinal characteristics of specific groups of buyers, prospects, or nonbuyers—lifestyle, interests, and degree of sophistication.

public relations: Organized sponsored activity or dissemination of selected information designed to improve the issuer's image and build good will.

ragged right: Type set so the right margin is uneven; spaces fall where they will.

reading notice, reader ad: An ad structured to resemble the editorial content of the publication in which it appears. Some publications insist on the word "Advertisement" set in small type at the top of the ad.

recall: A questionable but common way to measure the effectiveness of ads. Individuals who had the opportunity to see the ad are given clues about ads, then asked to recall specifics related to those clues.

relative attention ratio (r.a.r.): The percentage of attention the reader, listener, or viewer focuses on the message. Under hypnosis the r.a.r. might be 100 percent, with every external demand for attention excluded; but for a typical television commercial within a group of spots it could be 20 percent or lower.

release: A standard form authorizing an advertiser to use a person's statement or likeness.

reverse: White-on-black or white-on-color—the reverse of standard typesetting, in which type appears in black or a color on the white paper.

Roman typeface: Type which has "serifs" (see *serifs*). Readership surveys indicate that Roman faces are easier and more pleasing to read than sans-serif faces.

rough layout: A sketch showing position of elements in an ad but few details (see *comprehensive*).

S.A.G.: Screen Actors Guild, the talent union for film actors and announcers.

sans serif typeface: Type without serifs (see *Roman typefaces, serif*).

SAU: Standard Advertising Unit, a system introduced by the American Newspaper Publishers Association which makes it possible to run 57 "standard" ad sizes in all full-size newspapers and 33 in tabloids. One column width = $2\frac{1}{16}$" two-column width = $4\frac{1}{4}$". A full type page = 13" wide, 21" deep (six columns).

script: Radio, television, and film continuity for program or ad.

self-mailer: A direct mail piece that needs no envelope.

serif: A decorative cross-stroke at the top and bottom of Roman typeface letters.

set solid: Type set at a height equal to the type size with no leading between the lines. Eight lines of 9-point type, set solid, would be 72 points high, exactly one inch. Eight lines of 9-point type leaded to 11 points would have exactly as many characters on each line, but the type-block would be 88 points deep—almost $1\frac{1}{4}$".

share of audience: In broadcast, the percentage of sets-in-use tuned to a particular program.

spectacular: A big, illustrated outdoor sign, often with motion or effects.

split-run: Testing two ads against each other in the same issue of the same publication. A perfect "A/B" split prints each of two same-size ads on alternate copies.

spot announcement: A broadcast commercial.

spread: Two facing pages (see *double truck*).

SRDS: Standard Rate and Data Service, publisher of information on advertising rates and production requirements.

stat: See *photostat*.

stet: Literally, "Let it stand": a proofreader's instruction to ignore a change marked on a proof.

statement stuffers: A printed piece enclosed with a customer's bill; the stuffer need not be from the company sending the bill.

storyboard: A series of sketches indicating how a television spot will look. Usually, the words are printed or typed below each sketch. A typical one-minute storyboard will have 8 to 20 panels.

super: (television term) Superimposition of lettering over a scene.

supplement: A special extra section in a publication.

tabloid: A newspaper whose size is about half the standard size. Most standard tabloid advertising pages are 14 inches deep and $10\frac{13}{16}$" inches wide; some, called "N"-size tabloids, are $9\frac{3}{8}$" wide. (See *broadsheet*.)

tag: An addition to a commercial, usually information of where to buy what is advertised. The tag may be live or separately taped or filmed.

tear sheet: The page on which an ad appears, taken from an actual copy of the publication.

teaser: An ad or envelope copy that transmits just enough information to "tease" the message-recipient into looking or waiting for more.

thumbnail: A rough layout in miniature size.

tilt: (television term) Up/down movement of the camera.

trade publication: A magazine aimed at wholesalers or retailers.

trim size: Actual physical dimensions of a sheet of paper after trimming.

truck: (television term) Lateral movement of the camera relative to the subject being televised.

type page: The area within a nonbleed page actually occupied by type or illustration (see *bleed*).

type weight: The degree of blackness of type, from lightface to extra bold.

typo: Typographical error.

unaided recall: A method of determining advertising effectiveness in which individuals who saw or heard an ad are asked to answer questions about the ad without having another look at it (see *recall*).

upper case (u.c.): All capital letters (see *lower case*).

velox: A paper copy of a complete ad with halftones in position, usually made up to send to publications for reproduction.

VO: (television term) Voice over—narration by an unseen announcer.

VTR: Videotape recorder.

widow: A single word or short line ending a paragraph.

window envelope: A mailing envelope with a die-cut opening in the front, through which the name and address of the recipient (usually on a response form) are visible.

wipe: (television term) Replacement of one scene by another which "wipes" out the first scene vertically, horizontally, or diagonally.

Zip pan: (television term) A blurringly fast pan (see *pan*).

zoom: (television term) A lens which enables the camera operator to change the apparent distance from the subject without actually moving the camera.

Index

419